Edited by

E. Melanie DuPuis and Peter Vandergeest

Creating the Countryside

The Politics of Rural and Environmental Discourse

Temple University Press

Philadelphia

Temple University Press, Philadelphia 19122

Published 1996
Printed in the United States of America

♾ The paper used in this book meets the requirements of the American National Standard for Information Sciences—Permanence of Paper for Printed Library Materials, ANSI Z39.48-1984

Text design by William Boehm

LIBRARY OF CONGRESS CATALOGING-IN-PUBLICATION DATA

Creating the countryside : the politics of rural and environmental discourse / edited by E. Melanie DuPuis and Peter Vandergeest.
p. cm. — (Conflicts in urban and regional development)
Includes bibliographical references and index.
ISBN 1-56639-359-0. — ISBN 1-56639-360-4 (pbk.)
1. Rural development—Environmental aspects. 2. Rural conditions. 3. Environmental policy. I. DuPuis, E. Melanie (Erna Melanie), 1957– . II. Vandergeest, Peter. III. Series
HN49.C6C725 1996
307.1′412—dc20 95-5167

Creating the Countryside

Conflicts in
Urban and Regional
Development,
a series edited by
John R. Logan
and
Todd Swanstrom

Contents

Tables, Figures, and Illustrations

Acknowledgments

Compiling a book on nature as both country and wilderness—blending the disciplines of environmental and rural sociology as well as anthropology—has been a challenging undertaking. Our willingness to approach such a project is due in no small part to the help and enthusiastic encouragement we received from many people, particularly Series Editor Todd Swanstrom, who first got us thinking about the common threads of thought between the diverse group of authors in this book. As editors, we have to thank first of all the contributors, who patiently endured a long wait and stuck it out through many revisions. Many of the contributors were also important in initiating the discussions leading to the sessions for which some of us first prepared the papers in this book.

In addition to the series editors, Todd Swanstrom and John Logan, we would like to thank Temple University Press Editor-in-Chief Michael Ames and an anonymous reviewer who provided the critical input necessary for the creation of a quality product. Mike Ames always kept our eye on the goal of producing a book for a broader audience than just academics, and we appreciate his direction.

We also acknowledge the various institutions that have supported us while we have thought through the issues and produced this book. The Program in Agrarian Studies at Yale University gave Peter Vandergeest the time and support necessary to initiate his work on the book. At Yale, Kay Mansfield and James C. Scott made life and work both pleasurable and easy for a year. Melanie DuPuis first began to explore research on social discourse concerning nature while an Aspen Institute/Woodrow Wilson rural policy fellow. She began work on this book while a visiting fellow in the Department of Science and Technology Studies at Rensselaer Polytechnic Institute, where Linda Layne and David Hess introduced her to new frameworks for thinking about rural and environmental issues.

Finally, we thank all of our mentors and teachers who have encouraged us to pursue the intellectual and activist projects central to this book and who, through their enthusiasm, helped us stick with it. In particular, we thank Frederick Buttel and Tom Lyson, whose guidance and support will continue to help us for a long time to come.

Creating the Countryside

1

Introduction

Peter Vandergeest and E. Melanie DuPuis

Environmental themes have come to pervade our everyday lives. T-shirts, bumper-stickers, and TV spots constantly exhort us to save this species of animal or that patch of nature. An equally persistent, though less pervasive, "ruralist" movement has called for saving the countryside, family farms, and rural life. Rurality, moreover, is often linked to nature, so that the recent surge in interest in saving nature means interest in rurality is also on the rise.

As attention becomes more focused on rurality and nature, the once accepted meanings of words like "environment," "country," "family farms," and "wilderness" are becoming less and less clear. What does it mean to save nature and rural life? Do people know what they are trying to save? Do they know why? What do people mean by "save"? These are difficult questions to answer.

Governments, for their part, create environmental conservation and rural development policies with the stated goals of saving nature, farm families, and rural communities. Yet these policies neither deal with the ambiguous meanings of the words used to describe the goals nor explicitly recognize the political and economic ways in which words take on meanings. The meanings of these concepts are more than just points of view because people act on their understanding of key concepts like rural, nature, and wilderness. In many cases they do so by trying to create, in the landscape, the concepts they imagine, talk about, and write about.

The contributors to this book have therefore begun to look closely at the concepts people use to describe rurality and nature. Each of the chapters in this volume takes up an example of how government administrators, writers, academics, movement activists, or people in their everyday lives create and implement these concepts. In doing so, the authors go beyond abstract statements characterizing nature and rural people to look at the historical evidence and the experiences of people in particular places and situations.

The essays show how separation—of country from city, improved land from wilderness, and human activity from natural processes—remains the basis for most development programs, for most environmentalist and ruralist thought, and for actions that aim to save rurality and nature. The construction of boundaries between these categories may contradict the "real" histories and lives of rural people whose everyday lives may not be governed by these boundaries or who may understand these categories in a way very different from those at the centers of power. Participants in environmental debates often understand and describe the countryside in ways that gloss over the diverse and complex lives of rural people. Even the phrase "rural people" simplifies many of the situations described in this book.

Because the real world is often much more ambiguous and varied than the abstract categories formulated by land use planners or proponents of environmental and rural preservation, governments often need to resort to coercion to implement policies based on these categories. This coercion may be overt or hidden. Governments may use army and police forces to patrol the boundaries of nature parks or conservation zones, or they may simply discourage agriculture in areas they classify as wild.

Unfortunately, as many of the chapters in this book show, the critics of these policies frequently work within the same basic categories, and this results in concepts of resistance that often limit the political options of rural people. Supporters of environmental or ruralist movements tend to understand nature as sacred and timeless, and somehow outside of human society. For example, when environmentalists identify rural people with nature (that is, as if they had no social history), these people are less able to fight for social justice. At its worst, the fight to save nature assumes the air of a religious mission in which almost any means is justified, since the goal is greater than mere human interests. As a consequence, many proponents of environmental and rural conservation may eventually find themselves condoning the coercive actions of government agencies.

Many participants in these social movements are beginning to feel uncomfortable about much of what is going on under the rubric of saving nature or rurality. Through this set of essays, we hope to contribute to current debate on these problems, by emphasizing the importance of observing how planners and movement activists construct theoretical frameworks that divide landscapes and rural people and the effects of programs that are based on these divisions. Our aim is also to highlight the differences between these theoretical frameworks and local understandings of landscapes and nature. We do not argue that urban policy-makers, movement activists, and intellectuals must adopt these local meanings; however, groups working on behalf of nature and the countryside should, at the very least, recognize that their views often differ from those of people who live in these areas. This awareness would foster real dialogue between activists, policy-makers, and rural people about the policies and programs that affect them.

Approach and Themes

It is useful to separate the questions considered in this book into three themes: first, the chapters describe and explain the cultural frameworks that people use to make sense of particular situations or to justify policies and programs. Second, many chapters show how these categories frame environmental and rural "problems" and how people act on these problems. Third, many chapters question the congruity between these frameworks and the histories and lives of people in rural areas.

All chapters explore how dominant groups can exercise control over the production of meaning. Although these dominant groups are sometimes classes and states, in other contexts they include such varied groups as environmental organizations, cooperative managers, nongovernment organizations (NGOs), and migrant men. But the essays also show that the construction of meaning cannot be reduced to political and economic interests alone. People make meaning in part by re-creating cultural traditions. The authors show how dominant understandings of rural landscapes and the people who inhabit them might be thought of as expressions of old and new Euro-American stories and assumptions about the Garden of Eden, rural communities, the American Frontier, the efficiency of the market, nature without people, and national progress.

In particular, the essays show how the meaning of rurality is often construed as if in opposition to urban life, while visions of nature are often opposed to human life. Rurality and nature are typically linked: urban people, for example, think that rural people live close to nature, although they sometimes exclude from their vision of nature all humans, including rural inhabitants. People also place rural–urban and nature–culture in temporal and spatial sequences. Thus urban people think of rurality and nature as both the past and that which is peripheral, far away, or strange. In contrast, urban life and culture are the present and future and that which is nearby and familiar. Opponents of development, by virtue of their opposition, not only adopt the same key concepts but characterize them in a similar fashion: nature is rural, sacred, timeless, and located in the past and the periphery.

The second major set of themes consists of an account of how modern categories are actively imposed on the landscape and the people who live there. Many of these categories are dualistic. Modern states attempt to create unambiguous spatial boundaries between city and country, private and public property, parks and agriculture, or residential and industrial land. They also categorize people and their activities, for example, into urban and rural residents, indigenous and nonindigenous, or small-scale mixed farming and large-scale specialized farming. Finally, they create and implement policies that conform to these categories, so that people will be treated differently according to their classification.

Dualistic categories are not limited to modern or Euro-American traditions, and not all modern categories are necessarily dualistic. What distinguishes the modern approach is first, the attempt to draw strict boundaries between multiple categories of people and space, and second, an unprecedented technical and coercive capacity for reconstructing the landscape to conform to these bounded and exclusionary categories. Modern states and other organizations have employed a number of technical, bureaucratic, and coercive measures to control people and to transform the landscape. They do so by setting boundaries in ways that fit their own understanding of the landscape, and by specifying which kinds of activities will be permitted in the resultant land use zone.

The result is the marginalization of many rural people who do not fit into the categories, who are deemed inefficient in their use of rural resources or destructive toward nature. Rural people frequently attempt to undermine these efforts, because the policies often fail to come to terms with the real complexities of rural life. Nonetheless, policies that reorganize rural activity on the land have also transformed rural life with a rapidity that would have been unimaginable just a few centuries ago.

Many rural and environmental activists participate in this categorization process. They do this by framing their goals in terms of resistance to modernity or attempts to "save" species, family farms, or rural communities from unchecked progress. This often becomes tantamount to removing the city from the country—culture from nature—and setting sharp boundaries between them. At best, this resistance ignores the wishes of those rural people who may not want to be saved from all aspects of "progress." At worst, it places some rural people on the wrong side of these boundaries, converting them into human encroachers from whom nature should be protected.

The third set of themes is thus the disjuncture between cultural frameworks adopted by various dominant groups (classes, states, genders) on one hand, and the histories and lives of rural people on the other hand. Governments and other groups, as well as the writers and social movements that resist these groups, are caught between their exclusionary accounts of nature and rurality and the actual histories and lived experience of rural residents. The acceptance of a limited set of meanings may block both inquiry into the social histories of marginalized peoples and alternative courses of action.

Local people may construct alternative meanings that exist outside of these development-based categories and that challenge boundaries and exclusive dualisms. For example, rural life may be far from an idyllic harmony with nature, while urban life may present opportunities for cultivating nature. Rather than completely accepting or rejecting development, rural people may reject some aspects of the development agenda and yet enthusiastically embrace others.

The disjuncture between ruralist and environmentalist thought and actual histories in rural areas can also result from the spatial separation between people who want to save nature and rurality, and people who live in contested areas. In noting this, we do not intend to dismiss movement activists, policy-makers, or academic intellectuals. As Amita Baviskar argues in Chapter 7, intellectuals and activists are important to rural and environmental movements because they have influence in powerful institutions that are reconstructing rural landscapes, they are often committed to social justice, and they are able to add a global perspective to particular issues. We also do not intend to simplify the many debates among writers and activists, debates that echo many of the issues raised in this book. We do think, however, that these debates must give more attention to the ambiguity and variety in the actual lives of people who live in contested areas, and recognize that the perspective of those who reside in an area is in all probability different from the perspective of those who do not. That is, state planners, intellectuals, and movement activists should recognize that they cannot "represent" all local people in all ways; instead, they must enter into a dialogue that recognizes and respects differences as well as commonalities.

The Construction of Meaning

Although this book is intended to demonstrate the value of paying attention to the construction of meaning, the chapters also situate their work in the tradition of political economy. It is not possible to understand the construction of meaning without attention to the means by which local and nonlocal groups (colonizers, wealthy urban classes, and so forth) can exercise widespread political and economic control over the countryside. Political and economic control allows these groups to impose modern concepts on the countryside—such as dividing private land from nature or separating wilderness from the garden—in ways that serve their political and economic interests.

In the 1970s, world systems and dependency theorists successfully challenged the modernization approach and its ahistorical assumption that rural or peripheral peoples are *outside* of modernity and therefore need to be modernized or saved. They specified the ways that the periphery and rural hinterland are made and remade by institutions located in the core and in cities, including multinational corporations and state agencies. This observation is also applicable to rural areas in wealthy countries that are often characterized as outside of modernity in popular and academic writing.[1] Thus the essays in this book draw on dependency and world systems ideas to make explicit the ways that political and economic forces centered in cities have shaped not only the country but also the way that people think, speak, and write about the country.

For example, Bill Fisher describes how both development and environmental interests have constructed the Amazon as undeveloped wilderness. The successful contemporary portrayal of the Amazon as undeveloped, despite a long social and economic history, justifies both contemporary exploitation of the region from one point of view and salvation of the region as pristine nature from another. Because the labor of the native Amazonians is no longer needed by the dominant economic interests, the Amazonians' history of economic participation and exploitation is forgotten, and they become redefined as guardians of the undeveloped rainforest—out of society and into nature. Melanie DuPuis shows how urban food interests, allied with industrial agriculture, shaped an ecological rhetoric to legitimize the restructuring of the New York State countryside during the early twentieth century in ways that marginalized small mixed farmers. Nancy Lee Peluso links the environmental valuation of wilderness as areas that should be out of bounds to human activities to the state's interests in taking the control of resources away from local people. Other chapters link particular representations of rurality and farming to the division of labor (Goldring), the need for cheap labor, the selling of rurality (Hinrichs), managerial control (Taylor), and East Coast industrial interests (Bell, DuPuis).

This book, however, is much more than a demonstration of the utility of a political-economic approach in explaining the construction of the countryside. The authors step outside of the orthodox political economy approach by emphasizing the role of culture and nonclass social movements.[2] Nonclass organizations such as environmental groups and NGOs often construct accounts that oppose state and dominant class interests but that are not necessarily in accord with the perspectives held by inhabitants of the area being contested. We return to this issue in the final section.

The chapters in this book also investigate the importance of culture to the reorganization of physical space and rural life. In the past, most political economists assumed that the economic basis of society functioned as the final arbitrator of how people created meanings. Thus, they explicitly rejected culture as an important influence in creating the hinterland. This rejection of culture was heightened during the 1970s, when critical scholars rejected culturalist approaches to development and modernization programs that attempted to eliminate "backward" rurality (Vandergeest 1988).[3] The essays in this book show how both modernizers and many of their critics often think within the basic framework of modernization. Our intention is therefore to provoke increased critical reflection on the categories used in both political economy and cultural critiques of development.

All of the chapters in this book show how people draw on opposing principles inherent in modern or Euro-American thought to label and divide rural people.[4] Cooperative managers in Spain labeled farmers as either progressive or backward by seemingly neutral criteria derived from market standards of efficiency (Taylor). Policy-makers and planners in the United States designated farmers as either marginal or permanent according to their scientific analysis of the productive potential of land (Bell, DuPuis). Government officials either define all rural residents as traditional and backward in opposition to urban modernity (Vandergeest), or, in what amounts to the same thing, see them as representatives of a marketable rural authenticity (Hinrichs). Environmental groups pass over the social history of selected peoples, favoring accounts that idealize them as living with nature, apart from a polluting social world (Fisher, Baviskar). Perhaps most disturbing are cases where conservation programs define people out of nature altogether (DuPuis, Peluso), opening the way for their removal from the landscape through policies that may be more or less openly coercive.

The cases in this book show how dualistic categories such as nature–culture or city–country are invoked and applied in concrete instances in ways that affect people's lives. It is thus important to know something about the history of these categories in modern or Euro-American thought.[5]

City and Country

The city–country dualism has been fundamental both to the popular imagination and to the formation of basic social science categories. Nineteenth- and twentieth-century intellectuals like Émile Durkheim, Karl Marx, Ferdinand Tonnies, Max Weber, and Robert Redfield focused their lifework on explaining the growth of urban-industrial capitalist societies and their effects on social life. These writers characterized rural life as more bound by the past, by tradition, by community ties, and by nature. In contrast, they characterized urban life as future-oriented, breaking with tradition, lacking close community ties, secular, and more cultured. Modern life was life in the industrial city, which was also the site of progress, scientific rationality, and the specialized efficiency of industrial production.

For most people, rurality invokes the past. The idea that the trip from the country to the city is a journey forward in time appears in both social science writing and in popular culture. In highly urbanized areas, the farm is a place from the past, where grandparents once lived. Travel agencies advertise the Third World as a place where urban tourists can go to see truly primitive people while trekking in natural surroundings.

In the academic world, the distinction between modern and traditional was institutionalized as disciplinary boundaries were drawn up between those who primarily studied traditions in the agrarian colonies (anthropologists) and those who primarily studied modernity in industrial Europe and North America (sociologists). Rural sociology took up the interstice: the study of country life in Europe and North America. Since the object of their study was the traditional countryside in "advanced" societies, rural sociologists retained an interest in the tradition–modernity continuum, expressed as a rural–urban continuum (Sorokin and Zimmerman 1929; Buttel, Larson, and Gillespie 1990, Bell 1993).

Romantic authors' criticisms of rapid urbanization and industrialization did not challenge these dichotomous conceptions. On the contrary, Romantic writers (for example, Henry David Thoreau, Thomas Hardy, J.R.R. Tolkien) reaffirmed these images, not only by extolling the simple life of the country and decrying the dislocation inherent in modern city life but also by associating the country with the past—sometimes the immediate past to which an urban dweller could return, and sometimes a more timeless or fanciful past. For many environmentalists, rural people living near forests and on the peripheries of modern society are contemporary representatives of a past where rural people lived harmoniously with each other and with nature (Baviskar and Vandergeest, this volume). NGO critics of state policies often agree with state promoters that rural villages represent the past, and are therefore critical of state policies because they believe that more of this past should be preserved. Ironically, the high value placed on preservation can lead to a commodification of preserved rurality. In Vermont, for example, state promoters and local companies such as Ben and Jerry's have taken advantage of the notion that past farming methods and products were more natural and authentic than present methods (Hinrichs, this volume).

These descriptions of the continuity and community orientation of rural life all too often ignore a parallel and concurrent history of class exploitation and drudgery, as Raymond Williams (1973) has argued in his classic analysis of depictions of the English countryside. Many of the chapters in this volume (Fisher, Baviskar, Lynch, Hinrichs, Vandergeest, Goldring) similarly question the idealization of rural community and depictions of rurality and wilderness that omit the social history of residents—a history that is often replete with exploitation, marginalization, division, and feuding. For example, Luin Goldring shows how in the United States, women migrants from Mexican villages are much less likely than men to idealize the village as a place of rest since for women, rural life means hard work and a lack of modern amenities. For these women, progress and urban life are not all bad. Amita Baviskar describes how her attempts to understand Adivasi reverence for nature were confused by evidence of intergroup feuding.

The basic divisions associated with the city and country have often been rethought as divisions within the countryside: between improved, agro-industrial forms of agriculture on one hand and traditional, subsistence agriculture on the other; between productive land on one hand and wilderness on the other (DuPuis and Peluso, this volume). Policy-makers, academics, and environmental organizations construct these oppositions in the context of programs to modernize rural people, or to save some aspect of rurality or nature. In the United States, rural sociologists divided farmers according to their willingness to innovate and modernize—meaning willingness to adopt commercial technologies. These divisions were incorporated into policy in diverse contexts, as DuPuis shows for New York State during the 1930s, and as Taylor shows for an agrarian cooperative in northern Spain. The result has been the neglect and marginalization of large numbers of people—

pushed off land considered inappropriate for agriculture, pushed out of cooperatives for being inefficient. Policies based on dividing people into modern and traditional were incorporated into Third World development programs initiated by the United States from the 1950s onward, with similar results.

People and Nature

As country is often opposed to city in modern perspectives on rurality, nature is often opposed to society. The notion that social life is opposed to nature is unconsciously reinforced in countless ways in academic and popular modes of speaking and writing. Even ecologists who criticize this separation are apt to draw on it. For example, in their important book on land degradation, Blaikie and Brookfield (1987) write about human "interference" in natural processes, implying that natural processes do not include human activities. Although humans also have a "nature," it is generally understood as that which is biological rather than social and those activities that are not based on conscious control or planning.

As we noted above, rurality and nature are often linked. Both popular representations of rurality and the academic literature on rural development describe rural life as being close to nature. Although the wilderness is believed to be antithetical to country landscapes transformed by farming, the two are linked in that both are often vulnerable to modernization. For example, in many countries, NGOs argue that Green Revolution technology threatens the "traditional" methods of peasant cultivators, while governments and some environmental groups believe that these same peasant cultivators threaten the wilderness.

Nature is also associated with a specific temporality: if rurality represents the past, then nature is out of time altogether. They are often linked, however, in a kind of timeless past, opposed to what seems like the incredibly rapid pace of change in modern society. As with rurality, we often project our impressions of nature onto places outside of our direct experience: unpopulated wilderness, the sea, the atmosphere. Most of us think that more distant places are those that do not change; according to Tuan (1978, 122) the past recedes, like the horizon or a rural landscape, into the distance. Both the past and faraway places are seen rather than experienced, for example, on television or on vacation.

The association of timelessness with both nature and faraway places has often led Europeans to juxtapose European progress with the timelessness of the rest of the world. Thus, early social theorists in Europe identified faraway places in the non-Western world with an unchanging nature and tradition, and anthropologists represented native societies as people without time and history (Wolf 1982).

Within this broad notion of nature as separate from secular human activity, three very different views of the morality of nature are relevant to this book (although they are not by any means exhaustive): first, nature as dangerous, wild, and in need of being tamed; second, nature as a set of morally neutral processes within which society operates and that affect society; and third, nature as pure and idyllic, the antipode of everything bad about progress and civilization. These three views of nature justify and shape what people do, and therefore become incorporated into our social and physical landscapes.

Hardin's (1968) well-known argument describing the tragedy of the commons provides an example of the first view of nature—in this case, of the effects of uncontrolled human nature. According to Hardin, the human proclivity to breed is a natural process, which, if left unchecked, allows families to take advantage of a global resource pool. The only way to control this and avoid a tragedy of the global commons is for society to control breeding by an act of intervention. Birth control policies must include sanctions to be effective; thus, coercion to prevent uncontrolled population increase is justified. Hardin's approach associates nature with unchecked individual self-interest, which must be controlled by societal institutions.[6]

For writers like Hardin, nature is dangerous unless humans act to control it. This view of nature remains important for many people. In popular Euro-American culture, images of wilderness and nature continue to be strongly associated with fertile dark tropical jungles, fierce tribal peoples, African famines, Bangladeshi floods, and population explosions of dark people that seem to mimic the fertility of anarchic jungle growth and threaten to overwhelm cities and Western societies. Much of the current sense of crisis about the global environment can be traced to a fear of uncontrolled human nature in the peripheries. For colonial and postcolonial states, mobile rural people living "in nature" were similarly wild and uncontrollable, and states continue to devote great efforts to taming such people by forcing them to settle down.

People whose livelihood is centered on farming may perceive the wilderness as a threat or an area that is best tamed and controlled through settlement. This attitude toward the forest has been dominant among American farmers, but it is by no means limited to the modern or Euro-American traditions. For example, among wet rice cultivators in Thailand the word that is closest to the English "wilderness" (*pa*) connotes that which is wild or untamed, not yet cultivated or civilized (Stott 1991). In China, the agrarian state has long emphasized settlement of wildlands as a means of bringing it under control (Menzies 1992, 723).

In many places, people try to control or tame dangerous nature by offering gifts to its spirits. In the modern tradition, however, people think that nature is best controlled by understanding it. The founders of modern science, such as Francis Bacon and Sir Isaac Newton, linked the aims of modernization to the scientific understanding of and informed intervention in natural processes. For them, knowledge of nature gave humans a power to improve their lives. Modernization thus implies substituting scientific knowledge for superstition and fatalism among rural peasants (Vandergeest, this volume). From this perspective, modern people have the cultural and technological capability to take control of their own destiny, thereby making their own history, while traditional people remain controlled by the forces of nature. Modernization is thus the process of taking control of nature, in Hardin's case, by forced contraception of fertile women. It also implies specializing and professionalizing farming practices so that farming is less susceptible to natural processes (Taylor, this volume), or even separating nature into that which is modernizable and that which should be preserved as wilderness (DuPuis, this volume) in clearly demarcated territories (Peluso, this volume).

Because people frequently understand nature as that which is not self-consciously controlled by humans, nature can also be characterized as a set of morally neutral processes, the second view of nature. Dangerous nature can be neutralized by understanding its dynamics through scientific inquiry. Neutral nature can be made into a nonhuman scapegoat, allowing people to avoid taking responsibility for the suffering caused by their actions. For example, Peter Taylor (Chapter 3) shows how cooperative managers labeled market processes as "natural" and then blamed their abandonment of small farmers on this natural process. Michael Bell (Chapter 2) similarly argues that by blaming New England's rocky soils for the decline in New England agriculture, we can absolve ourselves from finding societal causes for this decline. In New York, the decline of extensive mixed farming has been presented by agricultural economists as the result of poor soils, not state policies (DuPuis, this volume).

In many contexts, the separation of nature from society allows us to idealize it as free from the moral failings of humankind (Bell 1994) and, therefore, as an alternative basis of morality—the third view of nature. This view of nature emerged in Europe during the eighteenth century (Tuan 1990). The shift is typified by the European attitude toward mountains, an aspect of nature that seems to defy taming through human control. Prior to this, Europeans were unsympathetic toward mountains (nature as dangerous), but beginning in the eighteenth century Romantic poets began to praise the splendor of mountains. Also during this period Europeans began to regard mountains as a good environment for revitalizing the human body, a belief that eventually led to reconstructing parts of Switzerland as Magic Mountains for the sick and tired and as vacation playgrounds.

These attitudes crossed the Atlantic to the United States, and Americans began to build resorts in mountainous areas, while activists launched campaigns to preserve mountains and forests in a natural state (Nash 1982; Tuan 1990, 111). The nineteenth-century Eastern establishment in the United States, influenced by the Romantic view of nature, disliked farmers and was offended by the unkempt farms of upstate New York and New England (Tuan 1990, 63–5). This attitude is illustrated by Thoreau's disdain for farmers near Waldon Pond. Bell and DuPuis (Chapters 2 and 4 in this volume) show how this disdain was turned into policies to marginalize and remove these unkempt farms from the landscape.

For the Romantic movement in Europe, anything that was remote or relatively inaccessible could become the object of a nature mythology. Traveling explorers, naturalists, missionaries, anthropologists, and painters helped to produce images of timeless nature in faraway places as they traveled to the corners of the globe in search of resources, exotic species, and native societies (Haraway 1989, 7; Savage 1984). The search for the Garden of Eden was important in the initial phase of European expansion (Grove 1990, 17–18). Among the early romantic and conservative critics of modern industrial societies, the myth of faraway Edens easily turned into the idea that tribal life was in itself an intrinsic critique of modern capitalism. Comaroff and Comaroff (1991, 110) write that for nineteenth-century Romantic naturalists, "[the savage] took his place—along with children, yeoman, and the virgin landscape—as an indictment of the 'jarring and dissonant thing' that civilization had made of man."

The third view of nature, nature as good, has evolved as a critique of modernization.[7] Contemporary critics of progress invoke these myths in arguments based on the idea of a peasant "natural economy" destroyed by capitalism. Many of the chapters in this volume also give examples of the use of nature myths to criticize the environmental degradation and marginalization caused by development. Ideal landscapes and nature myths are not monopolized by European Romantics; for example, Lynch (Chapter 8) shows how people of the Caribbean appropriated the writings of European conquerors to construct myths of ideal landscape destroyed by the conquest. These myths have now been carried into urban environmental movements by Caribbean immigrants seeking to reshape the landscape of New York City.

The three views of nature frequently have more in common than critics realize. In particular, all start from the assumption that nature is separate from society. The idea of nature as opposed to society can result in a vision that saves and purifies nature by eliminating the social, including local histories of human activities.

Media depictions of nature often reinforce this separation. Movies such as *Gorillas in the Mist, At Play in the Fields of the Lord,* and *Fern Gully* describe seminaturalized heroes and heroines bravely using whatever means necessary to defend innocent savages or befriended animals against civilization. These sorts of movies, together with nature programs on television, tend to present humans as either destroyers of nature or as its saviors but seldom as participants in nature (Wilson, 1992, 135). Today's most prevalent image of endangered nature remains the dripping rainforest, the Amazon as "nature's preserve" (Hecht and Cockburn 1989a, 11). This vision "excludes man altogether and proposes a world whose lineaments reflect only the purity of natural forces, freed entirely from man's despoiling hands" (Hecht and Cockburn 1989a, 14).

For romantic writers, nature is also sacred, opposed to the secular and everyday world of human beings. Like other sacred places (heaven, Eden) nature is timeless and for the most part outside of lived experience. This view of nature has entered into popular culture as a place of renewal (Marx 1964); the foray into nature is a modern equivalent of Christian rebirth. People get in touch with themselves by stripping away all but the physical essentials—sometimes through physical action, and sometimes by trips to areas demarcated as "natural." Renewals through trips to nature have been institutionalized in the form of the annual vacation in mountains and forests, or by trips to the seashore or just to the country. For many modern people, in other words, nature is regarded as much more than a set of mechanical processes; it has become part of the sacred—that which is timeless, flawless, and provides for short periods of personal renewal.

When nature is understood in this way, it becomes extremely important to save it, and almost any means can be justified. Moreover, because nature is not dynamic and changing, but a timeless heritage, it must be preserved without change for future generations, often in strictly delimited territories. In the hands of government, this vision has produced the national park: land claimed by the government with the justification that it is defending nature against human encroachment. International environmental organizations support these policies, while the ecologically sensitive media call on governments to devote greater efforts to defending nature against people. Television viewers, for their part, send checks to international environmental organizations to assure themselves that the natural world that they see on their television screens will continue to exist exactly this way.

In Chapter 5, Nancy Lee Peluso shows how the high priority placed on preservation of such sacred places leads some people to take drastic coercive action in their attempts to save them. Other chapters indicate the ubiquity of the concept of nature as an escape from complex and self-interested urban life (especially DuPuis, Lynch, Hinrichs, and Goldring). If the preservation of nature is linked to saving it as an escape for nonresidents, then the priorities of actual residents who rely on local resources for a living, and who may have a different sense of nature aesthetics, are likely to be marginalized in arguments over disputed areas.

Disjunctures

The essays in this volume show how exclusionary categories often limit the range of policy options we can imagine. It restricts our ability to formulate policies and programs that accept people as part of the dynamism of nature and that bring nature and activities associated with the countryside back into the lives of urban or suburban peoples.

The contributions to this collection show that cultural categories are not just ways by which people understand the world; they also control how they act in it. The attitudes of different agencies about the village (either as backward or as a site of authenticity) shape development projects (Vandergeest). Mexican men initiate projects that reconstruct the village as a site of fun and relaxation (Goldring). In Vermont, state authorities promote the construction of rural landscapes that conform to urban tourists' ideas of an idyllic rural vacation (Hinrichs). Land users deemed inefficient have been marginalized, excluded from government support, or expelled through the enclosure of land and nature (Bell, Taylor, DuPuis), while elsewhere, resource users who found themselves in areas demarcated as nature preserves were evicted (Peluso). The characterization of Amazonian Indians as part of nature has demarcated their opportunities for exerting political influence (Fisher). These processes have continued to the present through the ongoing proliferation of boundaries, the increasing enforcement of boundaries, and the development of more policies relating to these boundaries (Vandergeest).

It is no accident that a theme running through many of these essays involves the spatial dimension of planning.[8] We can see the effects of spatial zoning when we cross the boundaries set up between, for example, city and country, "improved" property" and "wilderness reserve," or "industrial zones" and "green spaces." All of these environments exist because of the establishment of borders and boundaries, based on maps, laws, plans, and administrative rules. We live in a landscape shaped by land use zones and political territorial categories. Our lives continue to be shaped by the increasingly detailed implementation of these categories.

One of the central spatial boundaries in the modern nation-state is between privately owned land and public land. In a capitalist economy, land is divided into "private" and improved land on one hand and nonprivate, nonimproved "nature" on the other. In legal definitions of property, "nature" is at the frontier; it refers to land not yet enclosed and appropriated as private property. It also refers to land not yet "improved" by human activities. Other types of property relations have been marginalized in the modern imagination (MacPherson 1978, Cronon 1983).

It is only a small step from the modern conflation of all types of property into private property to the conflation of all property not legally private into the category of nature. According to this view, nature must be free of property rights and undisturbed by human livelihood activities. Preserving nature means keeping it free of property claims. The exception is the nation-state's claim that it must control nature in order to preserve it for the nation as a whole (DuPuis, this volume). The division of land into private property and nature produces the assumption that people who truly exist in a state of nature have no notion of property at all. The denial of alternative legal definitions of ownership results in social dislocation in nature's name as these ambiguous places become redefined as natural—and national—places or parks. Consequently, places owned by the nation-state, rather than the individual, become space that can be visited and viewed, but not lived in and used.

Yet these ideas and policies nearly always contradict claims that local people have on resources in these areas, as well as their social histories of exploitation and marginalization. Even in urban areas, pressures to reclaim public spaces for habitation by homeless people compete with the established definition of a "park" as a space in which working families might spend a small portion of their leisure hours.

The essays by Peluso, Fisher, and Baviskar in this volume document the threat that people face when local resource rights do not fit the definition of private property. From the view of state bureaucrats, land used in common or noncontinuously falls into the unimproved category, making it open to enclosure, appropriation, or "preservation." Enclosures have not only demarcated improved land but also distinguished land legally defined as wilderness and "owned" by the state—off bounds to residents (Peluso). State agencies justify state claims on wilderness land by arguing that the state represents the public interest, or the interests of humankind. This bounding and categorizing of land according to strict legal definitions developed in tandem with the rise of national and regional planning capacities (DuPuis).

The problems that we have identified—and that appear throughout the chapters in this volume—are the result not only of powerful institutions such as states and corporations, but also of many groups who are trying to resist these powerful forces and save nature or rural areas. Both tend to separate out what they believe should be improved or saved, dividing it from opposing land use categories. This has produced divisions within the environmental movement between those who take a more "biocentric" point of view, and who would save nature by eliminating people, and those who believe that saving nature is compatible with human livelihood activities (Guha 1992).

In many cases the key players in struggles over rural land use do not live in the contested areas. The views of local residents are often surveyed and invoked, but these views are seldom investigated in all their complexities and contradictions. And residents do not have much direct political clout, compared to elite groups in urban areas; their influence derives from what they do on the land, more than from what they say or write. The separation of the major political players from residents in contested areas raises difficult questions about accountability and about the general relationship between residents and nonresidents in these struggles. Even the distinction between "local resident" and "nonresident" is ambigious, as people situate themselves and others within and outside of boundaries.

Beyond Culture Versus Nature

People who live in or near forests, or in rural areas, often do not think of nature as being either benign or sacred. Neither do all rural people have similar views about rural life and nature. People's views on rural life and nature vary greatly, following local cultural traditions, livelihood practices, gender, class, and so on.

It is possible, however, to make some tentative generalizations about how local people who actually live in a place experience it differently from visitors. Tuan (1990, 64), for example, notes how "a visitor's evaluation of the environment is primarily aesthetic. It is an outsider's view. The outsider judges by appearance, by some formal canon of beauty. A special effort is required to empathize with the lives and values of the inhabitants." Development tourists driving through a rural area in the Third World will react to what they see primarily on the basis of their aesthetic evaluation of the landscape—as will tourists everywhere. Visitors usually have simple viewpoints about a place, which are easily expressed. Natives have complex attitudes derived from their immersion in the environment. Visitors' viewpoints are easily stated, while natives express their complex attitudes either with difficulty or indirectly (Tuan 1990, 63). The visitor's evaluation of a given environment can vary tremendously, depending on his or her own cultural background. For example, European attitudes toward wilderness shifted dramatically during the eighteenth century, from wilderness as threat to wilderness as sublime (see above). Nevertheless, this reaction remained primarily aesthetic.

There is no doubt that these observations on differences in environmental perceptions carry over to current environmental and land use debates. Many urban people sympathetic to environmental conservation react to scenes of environmental change such as deforestation with aesthetic revulsion, and their viewpoints are simple, compared to the complex attitudes of those who have lived all their lives in a rural place. There is also no doubt that some environmental groups encourage aesthetic dismay through campaigns that draw attention to the negative aesthetics of environmental change.

The recognition that the ideas, interests, and agendas of rural environmental planners and activists are often different from those who reside in contested areas is now the basis of vigorous debate among movement activists and intellectuals. Participants in these debates have raised many of the same issues as those identified by contributors to this volume. For example, Hecht and Cockburn (1989b) presented arguments similar to those of Fisher (Chapter 6) when they accused American environmental organizations of failing to report the union and leftist associations of Amazonian rubber tappers while presenting them to the world as saviors of the rainforest. Invoking these sorts of incidents, Larry Lohmann, writing for *The Ecologist,* has pointed out that dissident groups often recast other people's movements to suit their own purposes, forcing subordinate people to act out parts assigned to them—a form of "green orientalism" (Lohmann 1993; Said 1979). Environmentalist writers like R. Guha (1992) have staked out a "Third World" perspective in criticizing radical American environmentalists and organizations such as the World Wildlife Fund (WWF) for their inattention to livelihood issues. Guha also points to environmentalists' highly selective and orientalist interpretation of diverse "Eastern" traditions, which in effect recasts them to express a monolithic American ecological ideal.

Publications such as *The Ecologist* and *Third World Resurgence* have vigorously argued that rural people should not be separated from nature, and that only rural people are equipped to understand and preserve biological diversity. Writers who take this position criticize organizations like the WWF for supporting governments whose policies are based on the separation of nature from people. In a similar vein, many academic writers (such as Cronon 1983) have shown how even environments that are often represented as pristine have been shaped by human activities.

The dualistic approach to nature and culture, North and South, indigenous and nonindigenous, simplifies the contrast between aesthetic and livelihood interests (Lynch, Chapter 8), implying that local or rural Third World people have no aesthetic interest in the landscape. Current rural environmental debates should not involve only aesthetics versus livelihoods. They should also involve an appropriate set of principles or morals by which we should plan for the future. But different groups look to very different kinds of principles. In particular, nonresidents sympathetic to environmental concerns often evaluate a local situation based on abstract or globalizing principles such as effects on biodiversity, while local residents may evaluate the same situation based on a complex set of principles derived from intricate attachments to features of a particular landscape and from the need to make a living.

Although we believe that it is important to point out the separation between the everyday lives of many environmental writers and activists and the places about which they write and argue, in no way do we intend to dismiss their importance. International organizations located in global centers contribute important knowledge about the global effects of local activities. Nevertheless, it is important to be aware that this knowledge is not usually based on local meanings; such meanings seldom fit the abstract dichotomies presented in many modern critiques of development.

At the risk of oversimplification, we might say that nonresidents may take one of two political positions vis-à-vis rural residents in contested areas. The first position is that of technocratic authority, as exemplified by state agencies that try to control the spatial activities of rural residents through land use planning activities. This approach may lead to policies that attempt to save nature by eliminating people. The second position is that of representation, a position taken by both nation-states and by NGOs that claim to represent the interests of rural residents. These groups try to promote policies that save nature by turning its management over to local people.

However, the distance between residents and nonresidents always raises the question of whether externally based organizations really represent rural people, or whether they merely project their own principles onto rural people. The latter situation is all too common, although there are many exceptions, including small local groups whose members live in the contested areas. By virtue of their immersion in the local environment, they frequently do represent some (but generally not all) local people and are often more aware of local diversity in their perceptions of a given issue. Larger organizations based in capital cities and in the United States and Europe are more likely to project their own interests onto rural people. Many of the essays in this volume tell the disconcertingly similar story of how the definition of various people as either in or out of a demarcated natural environment provides a very selective account of their history. In the worst cases, such accounts eliminate elements of a people's real history, because that history is as much social as it is natural.

If we keep in mind the fact that our categories are social products, we are more likely to question them and thus open up alternative ways of thinking. Instead of a wilderness without people, we can imagine a "wilderness" that includes people with a social history. Instead of envisioning modern or traditional farming, planners and rural activists could recognize a series of different farming and land use strategies, all of which have their place. Instead of extolling the moral superiority of one land use practice over another, we might admit that many practices have a legitimate role.

We can also incorporate alternative ways of thinking by paying attention to the categories of people living in contested areas and to diverse cultural traditions of environmental discourse that do not fit easy categorization (Lynch, Chapter 8). Understanding the social history of people in rural or wilderness areas serves to draw our attention to the importance of issues of exploitation and marginalization, typically endured by most rural people, even those in places remote from the "centers" of the world system.

Greater attention to local history might also engender a recognition of important divisions within rural society, along lines of class and gender, for example. Past political economy approaches to understanding rural society tended to emphasize this,[9] but the recognition of differences among people living in contested areas has often been forgotten in the new agenda to save traditional rural life or nature. Recognition of marginalization and of difference might encourage us to pause before leaping into generalizations about "other" people's relation with a timeless nature.

Our final point is that we need to acknowledge the spatial and social gulf dividing state planners, intellectuals, and activists in environmental and ruralist movements on one hand and the people living in contested areas on the other. This acknowledgment does not mean that we should dismiss the ideas of nonresidents, since they add an important global perspective to local issues. Although it is important that those participating in current debates over environment and resource use pay close attention to the stories and perspectives of rural people, these perspectives should not be sanctified as the only authentic voice. That would constitute the sort of entrapment that we have already described: it would dichotomize the debate and give one particular voice the moral high ground. The activities of nonresidents would be reduced to merely seeking out and representing the authentic rural voice, or to acting as mediators between rural people and other powerful groups, masking their role in selecting and constructing rural voices. In such a scenario, there is a very real danger of overlooking any rural voices that do not agree with the viewpoints of their external representatives.

Another possible approach would recognize the differences in points of view between different rural residents and movement activists, planners and such. If activists and state agencies recognized that they had interests and perspectives that differed from those of many local residents, they might give more thought to whether they can "represent" residents. An appropriate path would replace representation with dialogue, and mediation with alliance or solidarity (Lohmann 1993). Doing so might induce activists, academics, and planners to listen to and be sympathetic to diverse local perspectives that are different from their own.

NOTES

Acknowledgments: This introduction has gone through many stages, in part because of the helpful comments of many readers. We would especially like to acknowledge input from Todd Swanstrom, Michael Ames, Barbara Lynch, Luin Goldring, Michael Bell, Clare Hinrichs, Peter Taylor, Michael Bodden, Nancy Peluso, and an anonymous reviewer for Temple University Press.

1. The Sociology of Agriculture School, pioneered by Buttel and Newby (1980), first applied these observations to rural society in rich countries. Other early writers in the sociology of agriculture included Mann and Dickinson (1978), Friedmann (1978a, b), and Friedland, Barton, and Thomas (1981). See also Buttel, Larson, and Gillespie 1990.

2. Earlier political economy approaches emphasized structure and class/state forces. They thus tended to neglect agency and exclude culture. A few scholars, notably Mooney (1983, 1987) and Newby (1977), have reintroduced the cultural orientations of farmers as important causal factors in the structuring of American and English agriculture. Writers like Kloppenberg (1991), Mormont (1990), and Marsden et al. (1990) have also proposed approaches similar to the one taken in this volume.

3. Although Howard Newby and Frederick Buttel did not reject culture in setting the agenda for the sociology of agriculture, writers like Mann and Dickinson (1978, 1987) dismissed culture with the label "subjectivist." Dependency and World System theorists like Wallerstein and Frank at best allowed that "ideology" helped to sustain people's acquiescence to exploitative relationships between the center and periphery, or city and country.

4. We should note that although European thought is certainly pervaded by dualisms, so are the categories of people in other times and places. Many people have organized their lives around paired concepts such as "hot" and "cold" (food), tame and wild (see, for example, Tuan 1990). Leo Marx traces European pastoralist critiques of urban sophistication to Virgil and the Roman Empire.

5. Writers who have described how people perceive and write about rural landscapes and the countryside include Leo Marx (1964), Williams (1973), Cronon (1983), Jackson (1980, 1984), and Wilson (1992). Writers who have explored changing perceptions of wilderness and nature include Nash (1982), Merchant (1980), Haraway (1989), Shiva (1989), Worster (1977), Hecht and Cockburn (1989a), Wilson (1992), Guha (1989, 1992), and Tuan (1990).

6. This invokes a long intellectual tradition in European social science, often called the Hobbesian Problem of Order.

7. Examples include Shiva (1989) and Sachs (1992).

8. Despite its obvious importance in understanding the construction of both rural and urban landscapes, space has been relatively neglected in academic and popular writing on the subject until recently (outside of the discipline of geography). The recent concern with space has been stimulated by the post-Modern emphasis on built environments and spatial relations (see especially Soja 1989 and Harvey 1989). A book edited by Derek Gregory and John Urry (1985) was probably the first in recent decades to try to develop a political economy approach to spatiality, though the contributors had different views on how this should be accomplished. The first writ-

ers in the sociology of agriculture also called for more attention to space (Buttel and Newby 1980, 4–5), although there was no response to this call until relatively recently. Examples of recent authors who give explicit attention to space in describing the construction of rural landscapes include Marsden et al. (1993), Cronon (1983), and Wilson (1992).

9. Political economy approaches had drawn on a Leninist understanding of rural differentiation to document class-based inequality among peasants and farmers. Another literature on gender or "women in development" has documented the many forms of gender inequality in rural societies.

REFERENCES

Bell, Michael. 1993. "The Fruit of Difference: The Rural–Urban Continuum as a System of Identity." *Rural Sociology* 57 (1): 65–82.

———. 1994. *Childerley: Nature and Morality in a Country Village.* Chicago: University of Chicago Press.

Blaikie, Piers M., and Harold Brookfield. 1987. *Land Degradation and Society.* London: Methuen.

Buttel, Frederick, Olaf Larson, and Gilbert W. Gillespie Jr. 1990. *The Sociology of Agriculture.* New York: Greenwood Press.

Buttel, Frederick H., and Howard Newby. 1980. *The Rural Sociology of the Advanced Societies.* Montclair, N.J.: Allanheld, Osmun.

Comaroff, Jean, and John Comaroff. 1991. *Of Revelation and Revolution.* Chicago: University of Chicago Press.

Cronon, William. 1983. *Changes in the Land: Indians, Colonists, and the Ecology of New England.* New York: Hill and Wang.

Friedland, William H., Amy Barton, and Robert J. Thomas. 1981. *Manufacturing Green Gold.* New York: Cambridge University Press.

Friedmann, Harriet. 1978a. "World Market, State, and Family Farm: Social Bases of Household Production in an Era of Wage Labor." *Comparative Studies in Society and History* 20: 545–86.

———. 1978b. "Simple Commodity Production and Wage Labour in the American Plains." *Journal of Peasant Studies* 6 (1): 71–99.

Giddens, Anthony. 1985. "Time, Space, and Regionalization." In *Social Relations and Spatial Structures,* ed. Derek Gregory and John Urry, 265–95. London: Macmillan.

Gregory, Derek, and John Urry, eds. 1985. *Social Relations and Spatial Structures.* London: Macmillan.

Grove, Richard. 1990. "Threatened Islands, Threatened Earth." In *Sustaining Earth,* ed. D.J.R. Angell, J. D. Comer, and M.S.N. Wilkinson, 15–32. New York: St. Martin's Press.

Guha, Ramachandra. 1989. "Radical American Environmentalism and Wilderness Preservation." *Environmental Ethics* 11 (Spring): 71–83.

———. 1992. "Prehistory of Indian Environmentalism: Intellectual Traditions." *Economic and Political Weekly* 27 (1,2): 57–64.

Haraway, Donna. 1989. *Primate Visions.* New York: Routledge.

Hardin, Garrett. 1968. "The Tragedy of the Commons." *Science* 162: 1243–48.

Harvey, David. 1989. *The Condition of Postmodernity.* Cambridge, England: Blackwell.

Hecht, Susannah, and Alexander Cockburn. 1989a. *The Fate of the Forest: Developers, Destroyers, and Defenders of the Amazon.* London: Verso.

———. 1989b. "Defenders of the Amazon." *The Nation* (22 May).

Jackson, J. B. 1980. *The Necessity for Ruins and Other Topics.* Amherst: University of Massachusetts Press.

———. 1984. *Discovering the Vernacular Landscape.* New Haven, Conn.: Yale University Press.

Kloppenberg, Jack Ralph Jr. 1991. "Social Theory and De/Reconstruction of Agricultural Science: Local Knowledge for an Alternative Agriculture." *Rural Sociology* 56 (4): 519–48.

Lohmann, Larry. 1993. "Green Orientalism." *The Ecologist* 23 (6): 202–4.

MacPherson, C.B., ed. 1978. *Property: Mainstream and Critical Positions.* Toronto: University of Toronto Press.

Mann, Susan, and James A. Dickinson. 1978. "Obstacles to the Development of a Capitalist Agriculture." *Journal of Peasant Studies* 5 (4): 466–81.

———. 1987. "One Furrow Forward, Two Furrows Back: A Marx-Weber Synthesis for Rural Sociology?" *Rural Sociology* 52: 264–85.

Marsden, Terry, Jonathan Murdoch, Philip Lowe, Richard Munton, and Andrew Flynn. 1993. *Constructing the Countryside.* Boulder, Colo.: Westview Press.

Marx, Leo. [1964] 1977. *The Machine in the Garden.* London: Oxford University Press.

Menzies, Nicholas K. 1992. "Strategic Space: Exclusion and Inclusion in Wildland Policies in Late Imperial China." *Modern Asian Studies* 26 (4): 719–33.

Merchant, Carolyn. 1980. *The Death of Nature.* San Francisco: Harper and Row.

Mooney, Patrick H. 1983. "Towards a Class Analysis of Midwestern Agriculture." *Rural Sociology* 48: 563–84.

———. 1987. "Desparately Seeking: One Dimensional Mann and Dickinson." *Rural Sociology* 52: 286–95.

Mormont, Marc. 1990. "Who Is Rural? Or, How to Be Rural." In *Rural Re-*

structuring: Global Processes and Their Responses, ed. Terry Marsden, Phillip Lowe, and Sarah Whatmore, 21–45. London: David Fulton.

Nash, Roderick. [1967] 1982. *Wilderness and the American Mind.* New Haven, Conn.: Yale University Press.

Newby, Howard. 1977. *The Deferential Worker.* London: Allen Lane.

Sachs, Wolfgang, ed. 1992. *The Development Dictionary.* London: Zed Books.

Said, Edward. 1979. *Orientalism.* New York: Vintage.

Savage, Victor. 1984. *Western Impressions of Nature and Landscape in Southeast Asia.* Singapore: Singapore University Press.

Shiva, Vandana. 1989. *Staying Alive.* London: Zed Books.

Soja, Edward W. 1989. *Postmodern Geographies: The Reassertation of Space in Critical Social Theory.* London: Verso.

Sorokin, Pitiram A., and Carle C. Zimmerman. 1929. *Principles of Rural–Urban Sociology.* New York: Henry-Holt.

Stott, Philip. 1991. "Mu'ang and Pa: Elite Views of Nature." In *Thai Constructions of Knowledge,* ed. Manas Chitakasem and Andrew Turton, 142–54. London: School of Oriental and African Studies, University of London.

Tuan, Yi-Fu. 1978. *Space and Place.* Minneapolis: University of Minnesota Press.

———. 1990. *Topophilia.* New York: Columbia University Press.

Vandergeest, Peter. 1988. "Commercialization and Commoditization: A Dialogue between Perspectives." *Sociologia Ruralis* 27 (1): 7–29.

Williams, Raymond. 1973. *The Country and the City.* New York: Oxford University Press.

Wilson, Alexander. 1992. *The Culture of Nature.* Cambridge, England: Blackwell.

Wolf, Eric R. 1982. *Europe and the People without History.* Berkeley: University of California Press.

Worster, Donald. 1977. *Nature's Economy.* Cambridge, England: Cambridge University Press.

Part I

Modernization and Marginalization

2

Stone Age New England: A Geology of Morals

Michael M. Bell

New England, as virtually everyone knows, is a lousy place for farming. Too hilly, too infertile, but most especially too rocky, the New England landscape has seldom been considered providential. This widely proclaimed fact of nature has become, in various ways, a part of the region's popular identity. As a few old chestnuts that purport to describe New England have it,

> Nature, out of her boundless store,
> Threw rocks together, and did no more.

> Maine's number two-crop is potatoes. It's [*sic*] number one crop is stones.

> When you buy meat, you buy bones.
> When you buy land, you buy stones.

> Passer-by: You've got a lot of rocks in your field, haven't you?
> Farmer: Yup, most two rocks for each dirt.

Or, as this one-liner goes,

> A native Californian on his first visit to the East casually remarked that if the United States had been settled from the Pacific coast New England would not yet have been discovered.[1]

Consequently, according to this traditional view, New England's meager farm economy did not stand a prayer after the opening of the Erie Canal in 1825. In the face of competition from what the rich topsoil of the West and Midwest could produce, New England's hardscrabble farmland was doomed to abandonment. Already bent over from building countless stone walls to dispose of the region's number one crop, the collective back of New

England farming was soon broken. The region's farmers lit out for the Prairies, and even further West, leaving behind little else but their accursed stone walls. Thousands of miles of stone walls continue to criss-cross much of the forest land that grew up afterwards. And that's why there is so little farming in the region today.

Or so it is often said. But there is another plausible—I think more plausible—interpretation of what went on than this received history of the early decline of a Stone Age past. New England was not as inhospitable to agriculture as it has appeared, and continues to appear, to most. And understanding why New England's nature did, and does, appear that way has much to hold our interest. For, as I hope this chapter shows, the traditional history of New England agriculture's early decline retains its appeal in part through its resonance with the social imagination of those who have told this tale of nature.[2]

"The idea of nature," wrote Raymond Williams ([1972] 1980, 67), "contains, though often unnoticed, an extraordinary amount of human history." In other words, how we see ourselves—our history, our future, our social relations—has a considerable influence on how we see that realm we often call nature. Moreover, such visions vary. It is, therefore, really a matter not of *one* idea of nature and of history, but of *ideas* of nature and of history. In sum, nature is a relative matter.

This is an unsettling observation. Nature—that realm of settled truths, itself unsettled—is not supposed to be like that. According to the first sentence of the *Declaration of Independence,* "the Laws of Nature and of Nature's God entitle," *us,* and not the reverse.[3] But this paradigmatically modern hope is fast becoming untenable in the face of recent critical scholarship, such as that contained in this book.[4]

Yet how big should our post-Modern appetite be for social and cultural "constructionism," as this perspective has come to be called, lest we consume constructionism itself in the process? For if all is relative, so too is relativism.

My aim in this chapter is to demonstrate the significance of looking at nature as something we construct, we entitle—but also to discover some way to limit this all-consuming appetite. I try to do so through a historical and moral chewing-over of the famous, but rocky, story of New England's agricultural decline. I also chew over why I am telling a different tale (and why a few others over the years have too). I conclude by suggesting an unsurprising, but I think strong, antacid for the relativist heartburn of post-Modern overeating.

To put it another way, the point of this essay is to conduct a field trip, as it were, through the conceptual scenery of New England nature and agriculture. The contours of New England's landscape history vary markedly, depending on the vantage points from which the land is viewed. As we cross this varied terrain, I stop the van at a series of overlooks, from which we may sample the prospects of the land. I hope thereby to provide an occasion for us to consider, as a kind of moral geology, the social ideas that continue to shape these stony hills.[5]

Scenic Overlook One: The Traditional View

I do not exaggerate how New England's agricultural past has been, and still usually is, portrayed. The subject has long served to inspire lively prose, even in the normally restrained writings of scholars. Take this summary of conditions in New England from two agricultural historians:

> In an agricultural sense it is customary to speak of New England as "rock-ribbed," thin-soiled, hilly, unfriendly, hard-scrabbly, and other uncomplimentary terms. Yet, when one travels over the area with an eye to farming rather than history, culture, or industry, even a native of the region must admit that the unenthusiastic terms, for the most part, approach the truth. (Haystead and Fite 1955, 29)

Or here's an economist repeating the Californian visitor's joke, albeit with more measured language: "Thus, New England has few unique locational advantages and many significant disadvantages. It is a historical accident that the region is an important population and manufacturing center" (Eisenmenger 1967, 112).

In the similar writings of other economists, New England has been portrayed as "a region not even moderately endowed with natural soil resources" (Black 1950, 180). Decent productivity, said another, was possible "only by rather heavy fertilization." The region's farms "could remain prosperous only as long as they had no serious competition" from "the incomparably rich farmlands of our Middle West" (Raup 1967, 6).

Many authors based their conclusions on detailed case studies of specific New England towns—Lyme, New Hampshire and Petersham, Massachusetts being the most carefully studied. But the interest a case study holds is always, in part, what it might suggest about the wider world. Thus, when Walter Goldthwait (1927) put the peak of agriculture at 1830 in Lyme, and Hugh Raup (1967, 6) put it at 1850 in the Petersham region, adding that a rapid decline ensued and "probably half the open land, and perhaps more, went out of farming within 20 years after 1850," most readers took these dates as representative of conditions in New England as a whole. These writers wrote nothing to discourage this interpretation.

This vision of the New England landscape is perhaps best exemplified in the Harvard Forest Models, a series of beautiful dioramas showing two hundred years of landscape change in central Massachusetts, starting about 1700. Specifically, they show the sequence of change on the land John Sanderson and his family used to farm in Petersham, Massachusetts, land that later became the Harvard Forest. The dioramas were built in the 1930s, and are on permanent display at the Harvard Forest's Fisher Museum of Forestry.[6]

Like the writers cited above, the dioramas stress two aspects of New England's agricultural history. First, they emphasize (by implication, at least) the hardscrabble stoniness and infertility of the soil. Second, the course of agricultural decline they chart begins immediately after the Erie Canal opens in 1825, and proceeds rapidly thereafter.

Note the first diorama I have reproduced, the one for 1740, whose museum label reads "an early settler clears a homestead" (Photo 2–1). Here we see a farmer who has built stone walls as a part of the initial act of clearing. The implication is that the land is so stony the rocks must be cleared out before cropping can begin. By 1830, the land is at what the second diorama's caption calls "the height of cultivation for farm crops" (Photo 2–2). More stone walls have appeared, and only a single short segment of wood fencing (in the left foreground) can be seen. By 1850, in a diorama entitled "farm abandonment," agricultural decline is already pretty far along (Photo 2–3).

Like other case studies of agricultural decline in New England, the Harvard Forest Models have frequently been taken to be representative of the whole region and have been reproduced in books a number of times for this reason, most recently in Carolyn Merchant's 1989 work, *Ecological Revolutions*. This is the sole source Merchant uses for the timing and scale of agricultural decline in New England, noting that "in Petersham, the height of cultivation occurred by 1830 with 77 percent of the land cleared for agriculture" (Merchant 1989, 195).

Photo 2-1.
Harvard Forest Models diorama for 1740, entitled "An Early Settler Clears a Homestead." Note the diorama's implication that building stone fences was a necessary part of clearing rocky ground for cultivation. (The Harvard Forest Models, Fisher Museum, Harvard Forest, Harvard University, Petersham, Massachusetts.)

Photo 2-2.
Harvard Forest Models diorama for 1830, entitled "The Height of Cultivation for Farm Crops." Note the almost exclusive dominance of stone walls. (The Harvard Forest Models, Fisher Museum, Harvard Forest, Harvard University, Petersham, Massachusetts.)

Photo 2-3.
Harvard Forest Models diorama for 1850, entitled "Farm Abandonment." Note that agricultural decline is already shown as well advanced by this date. (The Harvard Forest Models, Fisher Museum, Harvard Forest, Harvard University, Petersham, Massachusetts.)

Merchant, though, was careful to note that her figures come from a single location, Petersham. Other writers, mainly (but not always) of popular histories of New England, have written in more sweeping terms. Thus in Susan Allport's 1990 book, *Sermons in Stone,* we read how New England's stone walls "seem endless. They speak, of course, of how extensively New England was once cultivated, that 150 years ago, seventy-five to eighty percent of the area was cleared and farmed" (Allport 1990, 16).

The implication is that the peak of farming was roughly 1840, and that cleared land then dominated the landscape. Similar figures are often cited in the popular press.[7]

It's a compelling story. The endless stone walls evoke the mystery of ruins. They are New England's own Tintern Abbey, Chichén Itzá, and Great Wall of China.[8] (This is far from the only reason behind their popularity, though, as I'll come to eventually.) But as compelling a story as it may be, it's wrong.

Scenic Overlook Two: There Is Less to Stone Walls Than Meets the Eye

I too was once captivated by the traditional view of New England's agricultural history. Back in the early eighties, while writing a book on the landscape of Connecticut, I went looking for a visual image of the stone-walled past I had accepted from my reading, from the Harvard Forest Models, and from climbing over so many walls in New England's woods. But instead of using photographs of the dioramas as had many other books, I thought it might be more interesting to use a contemporary picture of the nineteenth-century landscape. A historian friend of mine suggested that I look at John Warner Barber's 1838 *Connecticut Historical Collections,* a gazetteer of Connecticut describing each town in detail and including 165 engravings of the landscape across the state, "executed from drawings taken on the spot," as Barber ([1838] 1856, iv) explains.[9] Written at the supposed peak of New England agriculture, it seemed an excellent source.

Flipping through the volume, I soon grew impatient and annoyed as I passed over view after view showing remarkably few stone fences. There were plenty of fences, but they were mainly wood (Photos 2–4 and 2–5 are examples of these). I eventually found a few views that showed the dominantly stone-walled landscape that I desired, one of which (Photo 2–6) I used. If you ever happen upon my 1985 book, *The Face of Connecticut: Peo-*

Photo 2-4.
John Warner Barber's 1838 view of Farmington, Connecticut. In contrast to The Harvard Forest Models, Barber shows only wood fences. (Barber [1838] 1856).

Photo 2-5.
John Warner Barber's 1838 view of Litchfield, Connecticut, a hilltop town in what is conventionally regarded as the rocky Western Uplands of southern New England (Barber [1838] 1856).

Photo 2-6.
John Warner Barber's 1838 view of the countryside near Groton, Connecticut. This is one of the few engravings in which Barber shows the dominantly walled landscape thought typical of nineteenth-century New England (Barber [1838] 1856).

ple, Geology, and the Land, you'll find it there, right on page eight. (It wasn't until several years after the book was published that I noticed—or perhaps *could* notice, as I will explain—the little wood fence on the lower left hand side of even this most stony of views.)

But I remained puzzled. A few years later, I picked up Barber's *Historical Collections* again, and went through it with some care, measuring the lengths of walls of various types which Barber shows. What I found is that, overall, wood fences outnumber stone by two-to-one. Moreover, there is considerable regional variation, with a ratio of four-to-one for the soft, level lands of the Central Valley of New England. Along the coastal slope, the rocky topographic apron of southern Connecticut, Barber does show twice as much stone as wood fencing. Yet in the Uplands, the region the traditional view of New England sees as most characteristically rocky and walled, Barber's engravings actually show more than twice as much wood fencing as stone.[10]

Was Barber especially attracted to landscapes with wood fencing? Perhaps areas with more wood fencing were the best lands for farming, something a regional booster, like he was, would have wanted to emphasize. But a national statistical survey of fencing included in the 1871 annual *Report to the Commissioner of Agriculture* found the same ratio.[11] One-third of Connecticut's fencing was stone, with the rest various forms of wood: "worm" fencing, board fencing, and post and rail. Even less of the fencing in Vermont and Maine was stone—one-fourth and one-fifth, respectively. To be sure, the survey reported a higher rate in Massachusetts, where county returns indicated that "nearly half of the fences are of stone, or stone and wood combined." The proportion was even higher in Rhode Island, which "is mainly fenced with stone" (USDA 1872, 500). (The survey does not give a separate overall figure for New Hampshire, although from one table it is clear stone fencing could have been no more than 51 percent of the total.)

Considering the emblematic status of stone walls as the primary commonsense evidence of New England's supposedly tragic agricultural conditions, Barber's engravings and the Commissioner of Agriculture's 1871 report are worth pondering. The conclusion we should draw first of all, it seems to me, is that the majority of fencing in New England during the nineteenth century was wood, not stone. If we apply the above figures to the total length of fencing the survey gave for each state, the total proportion of fencing in New England that was stone in 1871 was 35.9 percent.[12] Second, we need to recognize the wide variability in the stoniness of New England's farmland from region to region. To be sure, there are many areas densely packed with stone walls. If a photographer looking for scenes for next year's local calendar wants to go out and find an area with lots of stone walls, that is not hard to do. Yet there are also many areas of New England with few walls, and some with no walls at all.

That still adds up to a lot of walls, some might say. Indeed, one estimate suggests that the effort required to build the walls for Petersham equaled that of building a pyramid one-quarter the size of Giza's largest, and that was only in one small town.[13] Allport (1990, 18) calculates that "it would have taken 1,000 men working 365 days a year about 59 years to build all the stone walls of Connecticut." To be sure, building stone walls did take a lot of physical work, but so too did washing clothes, plowing, cutting and hauling fuelwood, feeding livestock, and a host of other domestic and farming chores.

And so too did building wood fencing. In fact, nineteenth-century observers saw stone walls in a much more positive light than we typically do today, often praising stone walls for how much work they saved. And when you think about it, in the days before the wide availability of barbed wire and wood preservatives, that must have been so. As the U.S. Commissioner of Agriculture's 1871 report put it, "the best fences are made of stone, and they are also the cheapest, repairs costing little, though their first cost exceeds that of any other kind" (USDA 1872, 509). The 1867 *Young Farmer's Manual* explained that "stone fence or stone wall is about the best and most durable and efficient fence that can be erected, when it is properly built" (Todd 1867, 145). There are even records of farmers in regions which had little stone who imported rock from miles away to build these long-lasting fences—fences whose quality needs no better testament than the fact that most of them are still standing.[14]

Scenic Overlook Three: The High Productivity of New England Cropland

But even if New England soils are not as uniformly rocky as they are often portrayed, what of their infertility, especially in comparison to the Midwest and Far West?

In fact, New England is, farm acre for farm acre, one of the most productive agricultural regions in the country—and this has long been the case. Even in the eighteenth century, the supposedly "marginal, largely self-subsistent farmers of New England," as Allport (1990, 149) describes them, were capable of producing a hefty surplus. For example, Destler (1973) has

Table 2-1
Per Acre Yields of Cereals in New England, 1879 (in bushels)

Region	*Corn*	*Oats*	*Wheat*	*Barley*	*Buckwheat*
Connecticut	33.7	27.5	17.6	21.4	12.3
Maine	31.0	28.8	15.9	21.8	19.0
Massachusetts	34.2	31.0	15.2	25.3	11.9
New Hampshire	36.8	34.5	16.4	22.5	20.7
Rhode Island	31.4	28.6	15.1	24.9	11.9
Vermont	36.5	37.6	16.3	25.4	20.2
New England	34.5	32.6	15.5	23.6	17.5
U.S.A.	28.1	25.3	13.0	22.0	13.9

Source: United States Bureau of the Census 1880.

shown that Connecticut was so capable of producing above the subsistence needs of its people that during the Revolutionary War it was the main supplier of food for both the American and French forces. Eighteenth-century farm families not only produced the majority of their own subsistence needs, many of them also produced for the market, gaining the capital that would later support the urban-industrial transformation of the nineteenth century.[15]

The productivity of New England agriculture continued into the nineteenth century, as the comparative statistics on cereal yields in Table 2-1 demonstrate. In 1879, the first year for which there are data for the whole country, per acre yields of corn, oats, and wheat exceeded the national average in every New England state, in some cases by as much as 25 percent. Yields of buckwheat were high as well—33 percent above average in New Hampshire, and 20 percent above in the region as a whole. Barley yields were also above average, although only slightly.

New England was also an important horticultural region in the late nineteenth century, producing vegetables and fruits for the nearby expanding urban markets. "Truck farms" (the phrase refers to a commercial orientation, not internal combustion engines) in the Boston Basin shipped far beyond the New England region. In a reverse of the present state of affairs, a late nineteenth-century source maintained that the only vegetables available one winter in Florida were shipped down from Boston![16] Potato yields in Maine led the nation, with New Hampshire and Massachusetts ranking third and fifth. The Hartford region was famed for its onions and seed production. In Vermont, farmers supported the largest corn-canning factory in the country (Wilson 1931).

Yields remain high today. Agriculture is more specialized than in the nineteenth century, and there are fewer farm products on which national comparisons can be made, but New England ranks well in most of them. Between 1981 and 1983, New England farmers produced 30 percent higher yields of corn for silage, per acre, than the national average—higher than the famed corn states of Kansas, Ohio, Illinois, Iowa, and Wisconsin. Wheat is grown only in small amounts in the region, but three of the four New England states that grow significant crops still exceed the national yield. Maine's oat fields rank fourth in the nation in productivity. New England's cows yield well above the national average and lead the country in yield of milk per unit of feed, an important measure of dairy productivity. Hay yields are below average, largely because New England's shorter growing season usually prevents third and fourth cuttings as is routine in some other regions.[17]

Moreover, per acre of farmland, New England agriculture yields a lot of money. Table 2-2 shows the numbers for 1890, with comparisons for 1880, the first census for which these figures are available (and when, admittedly, New England's productivity was not quite as stellar as it was in 1890). In 1890, Massachusetts, Rhode Island, and Connecticut ranked second, third, and fourth in the country in value of farm products per farm acre, while Vermont, New Hampshire, and Maine placed fifteenth, nineteenth, and twenty-third. Table 2-3 shows that, a century later, the situation has not changed. Although New England farms are generally small, the value of agricultural products per farm acre in Connecticut, Rhode Island, and Massachusetts ranked first, third, and fifth in the nation in 1987.

Well, maybe farmers just work the land intensively in New England, since the region's farms are so close to urban markets. This is true. But even taking labor into account, New England farms are apparently highly productive—at least according to the only source I have uncovered on this point, a 1950 U.S. Department of Agriculture study. Based on data from the 1930s, this study found that New England led the country in the average value of agricultural production per hour of labor, exceeding the national average by 40 percent (Hecht and Barton 1950, 38).

And maybe New England farmers manage such high yields only by dumping a lot of fertilizer on their fields. That turns out not to be true, as

Table 2-2
Value of Farm Products per Farm Acre, 1890 Census

Region	*Value ($)*	*Rank*
Nation	3.95(4.13)	———
New England	5.39(4.81)	———
New Jersey	10.89	1
*Massachusetts	9.36	2(4)
*Rhode Island	8.99	3(5)
*Connecticut	7.96	4(3)
New York	7.36	5
Pennsylvania	6.61	6
Delaware	6.14	7
Illinois	6.06	8
Louisiana	5.69	9
Michigan	5.66	10
*Vermont	4.63	15(21)
*New Hampshire	3.94	19(28)
*Maine	3.57	23(30)

Note: Figures in parentheses show rank or value for 1880. The asterisk denotes New England states.
Source: United States Bureau of the Census 1890.

Table 2-4 shows. With the exception of Rhode Island, which only amounts today to 18,500 acres of cropland, New England rates of fertilizer application are actually low by East Coast standards. In fact, the region as a whole had the lowest rate of fertilizer application on the East Coast in 1889, and the second lowest in 1879. Compared with the West and Midwest, New England did use a lot of fertilizer in the nineteenth century. Initially, there assuredly was a Western advantage in fertilizer costs. But there was never a specifically New England agricultural disadvantage in this regard; all East Coast states faced the same situation. And today, rates of fertilizer application in the West and Midwest are comparable with those in New England.

Furthermore, New England farmers achieve their productivity with comparatively little in the way of direct government subsidies for their farm products. For example, in 1991 the average U.S. farm received $3,865 in di-

Table 2-3
Value of Agricultural Products per Farm Acre, 1987 Census

Region	*Value ($)*	*Rank*
Nation	141.06	——
New England	382.23	——
*Connecticut	879.85	1
Delaware	729.27	2
*Rhode Island	643.88	3
New Jersey	554.55	4
*Massachusetts	553.43	5
California	455.00	6
Maryland	412.69	7
Pennsylvania	391.23	8
Florida	388.72	9
North Carolina	374.84	10
*Maine	302.02	12
*Vermont	266.74	16
*New Hampshire	251.54	19

Note: The asterisk denotes New England states.
Source: United States Bureau of the Census 1987.

rect farm program payments. But the average dairy and poultry operation—two of New England's biggest farm industries—received only $1,707 and $308, respectively. The lion's share went to grain farms, which received $9,905, on average. Moreover, the bulk of this money goes to the biggest farms, with farms in the $87,275 to $218,187 annual revenue class bringing in $8,392 in direct payments, and farms in the $43,638 to $87,274 annual revenue class bringing in $4,075. The smallest farms in revenues, those with less than $43,638 annually, took in just $1,110. With its generally smaller farms, New England largely does without here again.[18]

Consequently, as Table 2-5 indicates, direct government subsidies accounted for 5 to 15 percent of gross farm income (as opposed to off-farm income) in the Midwest and High Plains states, from 1989 to 1991. The highest figure was 17.8 percent for North Dakota. It was 7.4 percent for

Table 2-4

Commercial Fertilizer Application in New England and Selected States

Region	*1879 (cents/acre[a])*	*1889 (cents/acre[a])*	*1981–83 (tons/acre[b])*
New England states			
Connecticut	30.3	44.2	0.29
Maine	6.1	15.0	0.20
Massachusetts	30.7	54.1	0.31
New Hampshire	7.2	14.3	0.20
Rhode Island	47.0	63.0	0.68
Vermont	3.9	8.2	0.09
New England	13.7	15.8	0.19
Other East Coast states			
Delaware	62.6	60.4	0.26
Florida	7.7	74.8	0.75
Georgia	53.0	59.7	0.39
Maryland	84.9	70.9	0.26
New Jersey	76.4	91.9	0.32
New York	15.3	22.1	0.14
North Carolina	32.5	36.8	0.38
Pennsylvania	26.2	29.2	0.13
South Carolina	64.4	73.6	0.30
Virginia	25.1	25.4	0.27
Selected Nineteenth-century Frontier states			
Arizona	—	—	0.35
California	1.0	1.2	0.41
Illinois	0.7	0.5	0.17
Indiana	2.4	5.1	0.21
Ohio	3.0	8.7	0.21
Wisconsin	1.9	1.1	0.30
United States	10.0	10.8	0.15

[a]Per acre of improved farmland.

[b]Per acre of harvested cropland.

Sources: United States Bureau of the Census, various years, and United States Department of Agriculture 1984.

Table 2-5

Proportion of Economic Returns to Farming due to Direct Government Payments: New England and Selected States, 1989–1991 Averages

Region	*Percent*	*Rank*
Nation	6.5	—
New England	0.9	—
North Dakota	17.8	1
Montana	16.1	2
Louisiana	9.7	3
Kansas	9.5	4
South Dakota	9.1	5
Mississippi	8.8	6
Arkansas	8.0	7
Texas	7.9	8
Iowa	7.4	9
Missouri	7.3	10
Maine	1.5	40
New Hampshire	1.3	42
Vermont	1.2	44
Massachusetts	0.6	46
Connecticut	0.4	48
Rhode Island	0.2	49

Sources: United States Department of Agriculture 1990 (table 578), 1991 (table 573), and 1992 (table 571).

Iowa, and 6.8 percent for Illinois. But in New England, it was only 0.9 percent for those three years. Maine had the highest New England rate, 1.5 percent, and Rhode Island the lowest at 0.2 percent. To look at it another way, in the Plains and Prairie states the government pays farmers a dollar of subsidy for every ten dollars or so of agricultural production. In New England, the government pays farmers a dollar of subsidy for every hundred dollars or so of production.

These figures are mainly based on crop subsidies and other direct payments. Imagine what the figures would be like if we included the vast sums of federal money that have gone into irrigation projects or disaster relief for Plains and Prairie farmers devastated by drought and, more recently, flood. Lack of water, nor its surfeit, has never been a serious problem in New England's stable, rainy climate, and that's one important reason why the region has such comparatively high crop yields. But it also means that a lot less federal money has flowed the way of New England farmers. (Similar arguments could be made about road-building and rural electrification for Midwestern and Western farms, which are typically more remote from urban areas, as well as the allocation of federal support for the land grant university system—not to mention the kind of research and extension these institutions have concentrated on.)

The Federal Government does, of course, provide some support to New England agriculture, and perhaps the most important ways are the maintenance of a national system of regional markets for milk, as well as a price support program for dairy products. But dairy remains one of the few major agricultural industries with producers and processors in all fifty states; however, milk "market orders," as they are called, divide most of the country into marketing and pricing regions (Fallert, Blayney, and Miller 1990). These programs, therefore, provide support to agriculture across the whole country, not just New England. Dairy farmers in New England do receive a somewhat above average "blend price" for their milk.[19] The region's price ranked, on average, twelvth highest among the, on average, 39 market orders which were in operation from 1986 to 1991.[20] Nevertheless, the support that comes from this differential (which is paid for by local consumers, and not the Federal Government, which only oversees the program) is dwarfed by the real giants: direct crop subsidies, price support programs for other agricultural commodities not produced in New England (most notably corn for grain, sorghum, sugar cane, cotton, and soybeans), irrigation and drainage projects, disaster relief, and institutional buttresses for Western and Midwestern farmers.

Scenic Overlook Four:
The Mainly Post–World War II Decline of New England Agriculture

If New England agriculture is, per acre of farmland, so productive, why did it decline in the early and mid-nineteenth century? The simple answer is, it didn't.

The most basic measure of the prominence of agriculture on the New England landscape is a category the national agricultural census has been keeping track of since 1850: land in farms. Figure 2-1 plots this category for New England through 1987. As this chart indicates, New England agriculture remained strong throughout the nineteenth century, even con-

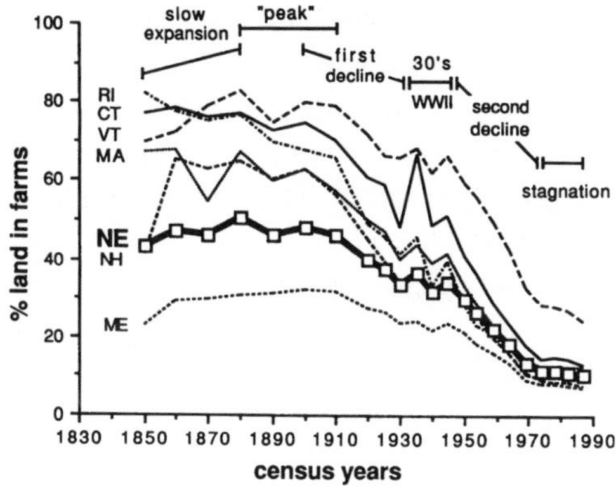

Figure 2-1

Schematic history of New England agriculture, 1850–1987.
Source: United States Bureau of the Census (various years).

tinuing to expand in Maine and Vermont. For 1860, the census does give slightly higher figures for Connecticut and Massachusetts than in 1880 and 1900, registering a drop of less than 5 percent over these forty years. Land in farms in Rhode Island dropped 5 percent between 1850 and 1880, and nearly another 10 percent between 1880 and 1900. In New England as a whole, however, land in farms did not begin to decline until after 1880—and even then, decline was initially just 2.2 percent through to 1900. There was no major region-wide decline until after the century's end, and after 1910 in Maine and Vermont.[21]

When widespread decline did occur, it was neither as severe as has often been suggested nor confined to New England. Using land in farms as a measure, New England agriculture declined 34 percent between 1880 and 1930. This was a substantial loss, but less than the 50 percent in twenty years (between 1850 and 1870) described by Raup for the Petersham region, and which many have taken as indicative of all of New England. Over the same period (1880–1930), Pennsylvania declined by 23 percent, New York by 24 percent, and New Jersey by 40 percent. Even Ohio declined as farmers gave up 12 percent of their land.[22]

In fact, the majority of agricultural decline in New England, if we are to use land in farms as our guide, has taken place *since World War II*. Between 1945 and 1972, the amount of land in farms declined by 67 percent. These 27 years account for 58 percent of all loss since 1880.

Not surprisingly, I suppose, most traditional histories of New England agriculture do not emphasize the land-in-farms figures, and usually make only selective use of them when they do. Instead, the emphasis has usually been on population data.[23] And, to be sure, population began declining precipitously in much of rural New England beginning about the time of the 1830 population census. But, as Hal Barron has pointed out, population decrease usually had no necessary impact on land use in New England, for improvements in technology allowed fewer people to farm more. Barron (1984) even suggests that technological improvements actually may have driven many New England people out and westward, as fewer people were needed to maintain New England's farm economy.

Moreover, when traditional histories have made use of census data on land use, they have often gotten it wrong. The most common mistake has been reading the land in farms figures as a measure of the amount of cleared and open land. For example, a recent article in the *Christian Science Monitor* (Mouat 1990) described Vermont and New Hampshire as having "three times as much farmland as forest a century ago." Likely the author did not realize that the census category "land in farms" includes woodland owned by farmers. This amounted to a third or more of the land in farms in most nineteenth-century New England states, according to the census. Subtracting out woodland gives a figure of 57 percent cleared land in Vermont and 42 percent cleared land in New Hampshire in 1880.

In fact, at the 1880 high point of land in farms, only 33.2 percent of New England as a whole consisted of cleared land. If we exclude the comparatively large and little farmed state of Maine from this figure, the total rises to just 48.9 percent. Again, far higher figures are often cited, or extensively cleared areas are taken as indicative of the whole region, increasing the drama of New England's Stone Age past.

Pointing Fingers

Who, then, is to blame for the decline of agriculture in New England? "Much responsibility," says Allport (1990, 146–47), should go "to the land itself." Consequently, decline was "inevitable; the hilly, rocky, exhausted soil of [New Englanders'] farms would never have been a match against those of the western states." As another writer (Kittredge 1993) recently put it, "The wet stony fields of our part of the globe have always had a hard time outproducing the deep topsoils of the Midwest."

Much of New England is indeed very rocky and unsuitable for farming. New England farmers recognized this, and at the peak of agriculture, 1880 to

1900, only a third of the land was cleared. But most of the land that was farmed, and the land that is still in farms, was evidently quite good land. Moreover, New England agriculture did not decline in response to Midwestern competition. The timing of agricultural decline simply does not support the notion that the Erie Canal pulled out the plug on New England. Some farmland, such as the rocky fields John Sanderson used to ply in Petersham, may well have been abandoned as early as 1830. But in the region as a whole, farmland continued to expand through to 1880 at least, albeit slowly.[24]

True, Western and Midwestern farms did begin flooding Eastern markets with grain in the mid-nineteenth century, but only at tremendous premarket cost. Drought, locusts, sod-busting, drainage (in some places), irrigation (in others), road-building, social and economic isolation—these factors laid a tremendous burden on those who left their (more likely their parents' and grandparents') stone walls behind. As the disenchanted settlers on the High Plains sang, with the dry humor appropriate to the climate they contended with:

> Hurrah for Greer County, where blizzards arise,
> Where the sun never sinks, where the flea never dies.
> I'll sing of its praises and tell of its fame
> While starving to death on my government claim.
>
> My clothes they are ragged, my language is rough.
> My bread is corn dodgers, both solid and tough.
> And yet I am happy and live at my ease
> On sorghum, molasses, and bacon and cheese.
>
> My house it is built of the national soil.
> Its walls are erected according to Hoyle.
> Its roof has no pitch, but is level and plain;
> I always get wet if it happens to rain.[25]

In contrast to the trials of sod-busting an isolated government claim in Greer County, Oklahoma, or even plowing up and draining the gentle but swampy loess of north-central Iowa, New England farmers had a burgeoning urban market close at hand. Consequently, they had plenty of options for adjusting their operations to the effect of Midwestern grain on East Coast markets, and many did so successfully. For example, in New Hampshire, milk production between 1870 and 1900 grew from 2 million gallons to 29 million gallons; poultry production increased by 73 percent (Munyon 1978, 78–85). In these and other ways, New England's farm economy adjusted and, in most areas, retained its overall productivity until the century's end.

The fact that decline is almost exclusively a twentieth century, and predominantly a post-1945, phenomenon points elsewhere than what Reverend A. W. Jackson (1890, 694) called New England's "rigorous and parsimonious nature." It points instead to the effects of urban competition right at home in New England: urban competition for land in a time of explosive suburban growth, and urban competition for labor, where better-paying jobs could be had. The very same cities that gave New England farmers an advantage in perishable commodities like dairy, poultry, fruit, and vegetables also gave them competition for land and labor. New England's farms were not so much abandoned as expropriated of these two most essential means of production—and not by Western and Midwestern farms, but by urban capital.[26]

There was probably a cultural side to this urban competition as well. As nearby cities grew, the Jeffersonian ideal of the independent yeoman farmer began to lose its hold on rural New Englanders. In place of the image of the sturdy yeoman arose the stereotype of the "rube" and the "dumb aggie," encouraging rural labor to head for the higher incomes and brighter lights they expected to find in the cities.

Actually, Western and Midwestern competition has been crucially important in one regard—competition for federal dollars for agriculture. Instead of government money being spent on protecting New England farmland from suburban development, government money flowed westward in the form of direct and indirect subsidies for crops grown out on the prairies and plains, for cattle and sheep grazing at low fees on government-owned range land, and for protection of the precarious water-supply of many Western and Midwestern farms and drainage of the overabundant water-supply of many others. (In fact, the practice of federal subsidization of Western and Midwestern agricultural development dates back to the time of Greer County's government claims, at least.) Consequently, New England was left at a fiscal disadvantage with the increasing industrialization of agriculture following World War II, as U.S. farms switched more and more to the mass production of regionally protected commodities.[27]

This was made possible in large measure by the logic of congressional coalition building. That is to say, when congressional delegations have gone to Washington to divvy out the federal pie, representatives and senators from the Northeast have counted up where their votes came from, and have usually sought places on industrial and military subcommittees. They have hardly ever taken seats on agriculturally related ones (Hansen 1991, table 7). But the Northeast delegation has looked across the chamber at those who were sitting with the Farm Bloc, and they have caught each other's eyes. The agreement, sometimes tacit, sometimes explicit, has long been along the following lines: You vote for our military contracts and urban welfare programs, and we'll vote for your Western and Midwestern farm subsidies.[28]

Landscapes of the Mind

I have offered evidence that has long been available to those who have pondered New England's agricultural history—and I am not the first to offer it. As early as 1911, George French complained that "we have been obsessed with the stale idea that New England was a sucked orange," and went on to raise some of the same evidence that I have of the region's continuing high agricultural productivity (French 1911, 35). Edward Higbee, a geographer from Clark University, argued in 1958 that "Poor and stony soils have often been cited as the cause of the agricultural decline in New England, but examination of much of the land does not confirm this opinion." He pointed instead to lack of investment in the region's agriculture, and the effects of what he termed "human glaciation"—the spread of urban and suburban development (Higbee 1958, 267, 282).

The question I want to turn to now is, why has this been the quieter voice? Why has this evidence usually been ignored? Or, when it has not been, why has it been interpreted so differently? For example, the very same fencing statistics from the 1871 *Report to the Commissioner of Agriculture* that I used to show how little stone fencing New England actually had, Allport cites as well. But Allport (1990, 17–18) cites these figures as evidence for the "astounding" amount of stone walls that New England farmers, in desperation, threw up alongside their rocky fields. Why?

Let me begin by suggesting, with no particular evidence, a few things about the traditional New England story. First, there is a clear Whiggish ring to it. For many, stone walls have likely served to represent a vision of a nasty and brutish past, where the back-breaking labor required to wrest a living from a stern land weighed down the lives of all. Looking at an old wall, we are comforted by the present—a present which, in contrast with this Stone Age past, we would be ungrateful to complain about.

There are also, I think, the hallmarks of that deepest of American tales—a Westward-looking, Manifest Destiny sense about the inevitable movement of European America. The traditional New England story helps explain why we had to move West. Thus, it is easy to imagine a nineteenth century railroad baron with some real estate to sell telling the joke about the Californian visitor, implying that New England might as well revert to wilderness, or at least that its potential bears little comparison with the Gold Rush opportunity of the West. (And it is easy to imagine someone steeped in Western or Midwestern regional pride telling that joke again.)

It also seems fairly clear that the traditional view of New England helps support the big-is-more-efficient credo of conventional agriculture by pointing out a negative example. The concept of efficiency, so central to the economic thought of conventional agriculture, virtually requires the existence of marginal regions and marginal farms to make the argument. New England, with its rocky and hilly land, with its small farms and small fields, fits the bill, for many observers.

And for this I have some evidence, particular evidence. New England is a place a supporter of conventional agriculture like John Fraser Hart could point to in his 1991 book, *The Land That Feeds Us,* which won the prestigious John Brinkerhoff Jackson Award of the Association of American Geographers. For Hart, the truth about the agricultural economy is that "small-scale operations are just as outmoded on the land as they have become in the city." For Hart, the truth about the Northeast is that it is an area "where much of the farmland is marginal and will continue to be abandoned" (Hart 1991, 371, 374). The gospel of efficiency, in other words, requires losers, and New England serves that purpose.

But for even the hardest-hearted free-marketeer, there is a disquieting side to this gospel—a side to which the traditional New England story offers some solace. For behind the land-in-farms figures, behind the beauty of the Harvard dioramas, there was a lot of human suffering. Few familiar with the New England story, I think, could honestly deny this. Although many rural New England families gladly chose to give up their farms for what they hoped was a more prosperous life in the region's burgeoning cities, and although many gladly sold their farms for suburban subdivisions, others did not so gladly choose. Moreover, these choices were made in the face of great constraints. Unable to hire sufficient labor, unable to bring goods to market as the region's institutional and economic structures of agricultural support slowly dissipated, unable to compete for the federal dollars so vital for supporting most U.S. farms, New England farmers had to leave the land. And those who stayed behind watched as their communities withered on the vine. Moreover, life in the new cities and the new factories was, in fact, often harder and meaner than it had been on New England's little hilltop farms.

Such is the case with probably all major changes in economic structure: many people suffer. And this is very disquieting, even to those who praise the dynamism of what they regard as the economic efficiency of the free market. My suspicion is that most people, to the extent that they support this economic principle, must also look for moral reassurance about the plight of those who become marginalized by changes said to stem from the workings of the market. Are we right, we ask, to do this to ourselves and to others? The traditional story of New England provides this reassurance by finding the roots of economic change not in us, but in Nature—in the hardscrabble, rocky hills which she, out of her boundless store, threw together.[29]

New England in the Ecological Eye

But the traditional New England story is also popular among many who reject the market credo; many ecologists have found solace it in as well. For ecology builds its moral house in part with the following thought: that humans are a part of nature, not apart from it, and that therefore nature acts on us even as we act on it. As Merchant (1989, 7) puts it, "an ecological approach to history reasserts the idea of nature as historical actor." This, Merchant suggests, is something that conventional patriarchal, capitalist, and scientific wisdom ignores, seeing nature instead as a machine, "passive and manipulable." And like any other perspective on the world, ecology needs examples on which to ground its point of view.

Central to Merchant's account of New England's ecological history is the notion that European development of the region was in constant tension with ecological constraints. For New England farmers, Merchant argues, "The more their market orientation increased, the greater were the ecological repercussions." The land's fertility declined, leading to the abandonment of the farms of Petersham and elsewhere—farms with "marginal soils" whose organic matter was "quickly depleted." These and other "ecological side effects appeared as externalities hidden from economic calculation" (Merchant 1989, 153, 155, 188, 232). The lesson is plain: We need to listen to nature, lest we repeat these nineteenth-century errors.

Now, I build my moral house in much the same way as Merchant and other radical ecologists. I am no fan of free markets. (In fact, given what I know of New England's agricultural history, I am not even sure that such things exist.) I think that many of the factors we have considered external to that peculiarly modern vision of ecology, economics, are not so separate from us. I too worry about the way agriculture in the United States, including New England, has developed with little regard for ecological limits and constraints. It makes me angry, as it does Merchant, that we have allowed the undermining of agricultural sustainability. (However, I see no specifically *New England* problem in this regard.)[30] I'm also inclined to connect ecological impoverishment with the forces of power and domination within human society, noting how this connection usually leads to the human impoverishment of the many in favor of the few.

Why then is my story of New England's nature so different from Carolyn Merchant's? For good ideological reasons. My moral ecological house (and Merchant's as well, I suspect) is built on a few other home truths too—like the importance of local production for maintaining a sense of connection and intimacy both between people and their physical environment, and between people and people. Local production also fits with my own small-is-more-efficient credo. I worry about the energy used in shipping food long distances. I worry about the long-term sustainability of growing food in places where rainfall is erratic. I worry too about the social and even spiritual effects of concentrating capital and control in the hands of a privileged class of large industrial farmers and big international food merchants. And I find great comfort in the main moral lesson I draw from the alternative New England story I have told: that it is ecologically possible to have in New England a more locally based food system, as well as the kind of society I believe that would encourage. While I don't believe New England could (or even should) grow all of its own food, I'm pleased by the thought that spending more money on protecting New England farmland from urban and suburban development might be an ecologically, and economically, plausible use of federal subsidies for agriculture.[31]

Nature, Truth, and Consequences

And so, we now need to raise the issue that inevitably surfaces after any social constructionist account of how we view the world and build our sense of its reality: the all-consuming, post-Modern, social relativity of it all. I would like to conclude with a few thoughts about why there is no social constructionist specter to fear here, or perhaps anywhere.[32]

It has been my main purpose to argue that the traditional story of New England agriculture is surely wrong, and that, moreover, its inaccuracy is of a piece with a host of Modernist ideological presuppositions—presuppositions with which I do not agree. And I have also pointed out that, somewhat ironically, stories of New England's agricultural marginality have been told from vantage points as disparate as Merchant's ecology (an ideology with which I agree) and Hart's economics (an ideology with which I do not agree). The same ideological irony can be found in the alternative version of New England's agricultural decline that I have offered. George French was not advocating an ecological vision with his rejection of the "sucked orange" image of New England; his concerns were strictly about encouraging the growth of capital in New England, as a quick glance through his book, *New England: What It Is and What It Is to Be,* readily shows. (I don't know enough to say about the ideological motives of Edward Higbee, the Clark University geographer who also rejected the traditional New England story.)

So do we only tell the stories we want to tell? Do we only see the landscape we want to see? No. There is more to the many visions of New England agriculture than the simple, or even ironic, lens of ideology. The various perspectives on New England (including my own, I imagine) do pick and choose, certainly. But there is real evidence to pick and choose between, I feel sure, and this places real limits on our images of the land.

Furthermore, any particular moral position may, in the face of new evidence, lead to a new vision of the landscape. Why does Carolyn Merchant tell a different story about New England agriculture than I do, despite the similarity of our moral outlooks? The main reason, I suspect, is simply that she has not read John Warner Barber; she has not seen the engravings from his 1838 *Connecticut Historical Collections,* which present such a different image of 1830s New England than the Harvard Forest Models do. Neither has she seen the regional comparisons of agricultural productivity and fertilizer use that I have seen, nor has she had occasion to study the agricultural census with the same attention that I have given to it. (At least her book does not mention Barber, these regional comparisons, nor the census's land-in-farms figures.) And indeed in my 1985 book, before I had encountered this contrary evidence, I too retold the traditional story of New England's agricultural decline as a cautionary tale about environmental constraints and the dangers of ignoring them. If Carolyn Merchant ever has this same opportunity, I think it seems reasonable to expect that her vision of New England would also change, unless she has reason—evidence—that *I* have not seen or unless there are in fact some moral differences between us.

In other words, there are indeed ideologies of landscape. These do influence what we see and what we overlook when we stand before a scene, as well as where we choose to stand when we gaze upon it. But there is also real evidence, if not true facts of the matter. There really is a landscape out there to look at and to envision in our minds. We may even hope that the two, evidence and ideology, are not unconnected—that an ideology might be forced to shift, at least a small bit, in its effort to take account of what others have pointed out in the scene. I can thus take some small hope that if John Fraser Hart and kindred spirits happen upon this work of mine, they will be compelled to shift their moral and political outlook at least somewhat closer to my own.[33]

But of this I cannot be sure. In the end, my claim can only be this: if you look at New England from where I do—and I think you should—my story makes the most sense. And if you don't agree, then I think you've got some explaining to do. We can expect from New England's stony land, from nature itself, truth no firmer. Indeed, this may be nature's hardest truth of all.

NOTES

Acknowledgments: Many kind and thoughtful people gave me valuable critical feedback on this chapter: Brian Donahue, Melanie DuPuis, Gail Evans, Will Goudy, Diane Mayerfeld, Barry Smith, Don Worster, and Peter Vandergeest. A collective thank you to all of you!

1. These and other old-time New England jokes, and variants, can be found in many sources. I have culled these, verbatim, from Smith (1946, 235), Allport (1990, 59), Hubbell and Edy (1989, 141), and Wilson ([1936] 1967, vii).

2. For a theoretical justification of the metaphor of resonance, see Bell (1994).

3. That sentence from the *Declaration of Independence,* of course, is "When in the Course of human Events, it becomes necessary for one People to dissolve the Political Bands which have connected them with another, and to assume among the Powers of the Earth, the separate and equal Station to which the Laws of Nature and of Nature's God entitle them, a decent Respect to the Opinions of Mankind requires that they should declare the causes which impel them to the Separation."

4. This idea can be found both in and out of explicitly "post-Modern" works. For explicitly post-Modern examples, see Bell (1994), Evernden (1992), Foucault (1970), Griedor and Garkovich (1994), Harding (1986), Hubbard (1982), Martin (1991), and Strathern (1992). For examples from other traditions, see Berry (1977, 124), Kolodny (1984), Novak (1980), Shkilnyk (1985, 232–38), Smith (1984), Thomas (1983, 61–67), and Winner (1986, 135–36). Actually, this observation is an old one in sociological writing, for example Durkheim and Mauss ([1903] 1963, 82–85), and Engels ([circa 1890] 1940, 208).

5. I should remark that much of the evidence discussed herein I have presented elsewhere, in a less sociological form (Bell 1989). My thoughts on the sociological significance of that evidence have greatly developed since then. However, I need to repeat much of the evidence in order to make the points I would like to make here, and I ask readers who know that other work to indulge me in this.

6. There is also a similar series of dioramas at the American Museum of Natural History in New York.

7. For some recent examples, see Allen (1988), Mouat (1990), and Schneider (1991).

8. For the past seventy years at least, New England authors have often capitalized on this allure. I'm thinking in particular of the many books by Wallace Nutting (see for example Nutting 1922, 1923), which often mixed photos of stone walls with a good helping of rural nostalgia, and also William Robinson's 1976 book, *Abandoned New England.*

9. It's important to note that Barber's engravings are quite realistic. Historical preservationists sometimes even use them as the basis for reconstructing the original appearance of extant historical buildings.

10. I have found the same dominance of wood fencing in the work of a number of New England landscape painters (Bell 1989).

11. U.S. Department of Agriculture (1872). Conceivably, of course, in the 34 years since Barber's work was originally published, a lot of stone fences might have been removed. But although many stone walls were removed in the twentieth century in order to enlarge fields, there is no evidence that this was a widespread practice in the nineteenth century. In fact, until the introduction of barbed wire, the likely pattern was just the reverse—wood fences being progressively replaced with stone as a part of continuing farm improvement. Barbed wire did not become widely available until the 1874 founding of the first large-scale producer, the Barb Fence Company of De Kalb, Illinois, although the first patent for barbed wire was issued in 1867 and there was some earlier experimenting (McCallum 1965). It is unlikely that many new stone fences were built after the 1870s.

12. I arrived at this figure by assuming the proportion of stone fencing to be 33, 25, 20, 50, 75, and 51 percent in Connecticut, Vermont, Maine, Massachusetts, Rhode Island, and New Hampshire, respectively.

13. This estimate is from a permanent display on stone walls located on the second floor of the Fisher Museum of Forestry.

14. This is reported somewhat incredulously by Russell (1976, 189) who, given his traditional view of New England's agricultural potential, perhaps couldn't quite believe it. It is also common to encounter stone walls in stone-free suburban regions of New England, built by residents who desired the traditional New England look of their imagination. I have personally heard of a couple of instances of suburban residents who *purchased* stone walls from rocky regions and transported the walls to their own stone-free property.

15. Merchant (1989, 150 n. 3), contains an excellent discussion of the debate over the subsistence versus market orientation of eighteenth-century New England agriculture.

16. This is another report given, incredulously, by Russell (1976, 452).

17. All of the above figures are from Bell (1989).

18. All figures are from Barnard (1993).

19. The "blend price" is what dairy farmers within a market order receive for their product. It is based on a pooled and weighted average of all the prices farmers in an order receive for all the end uses of their Grade A milk, such as yogurt, ice cream, cheese, butter, and fluid milk.

20. Derived from Table 482 of USDA (1988), Table 483 of USDA (1990), and Table 483 of USDA (1992). Market orders have been consolidating recently, and the number dropped from 42 in 1986 to 37 in 1991.

21. Land in farms essentially is a measure of property owned by farmers, and might disguise abandonment of land still held, though not farmed. This possibility can be taken into account by using another land use measure: the percentage of "improved land," which the census defined as land in farms exclusive of woodland and "old fields." There is virtually no change in the proportion of improved land between 1850 and 1880, holding steady at 61 percent (Bell 1989).

22. All of the above figures are from Bell (1989).

23. For example, see Goldthwait (1927) and Wilson ([1936] 1967).

24. Merchant (1989, 158) offers the interesting suggestion that some nineteenth-century farmers may have used a scheme similar to shifting cultivation—what Merchant terms a "long-fallow system." Thus, some land that may have appeared abandoned was in fact still part of a low-input production process. Moreover, when farms did eventually go out of production, some fields would have already been in fallow for ten to fifteen years. The regrowth of forests, then, may well have proceeded the cessation of production in some areas, perhaps accounting for the "white pine" phase of forest succession discussed in Raup (1967) and the Harvard Forest Models.

25. I quote here the pioneer song, "Greer County Bachelor," which was sung to the A-part of the well-known fiddle tune "The Irish Washerwoman."

26. Some studies have argued, incredibly, that development pressures have little role in the continuing general demise of farming in suburbanizing and exurbanizing areas of the Northeast. For example, Hirschl and Long (1993) argue, based on a survey which compared dairy farm "survivors" versus dairy farm "exiters" in New York's Dutchess County, that family troubles and the age of farm operator are "the most important factors" behind farm "exits"—*not* development pressures. But this individualistic account completely neglects the question of why the next owners of these farms are typically developers, not other farmers.

27. Actually, some of New England's post–World War II farmland loss can be directly attributed to the greater industrialization of agriculture. At this time, dairy

farming across the country increasingly switched away from pasturing cows in hayfields—bringing the cows to the food—to the tractor-based intensive raising and harvesting of corn, alfalfa, and hay—bringing the food to the cows, who were increasingly kept in and near the barn. Consequently, the more distant and marginal land, which earlier suited well as pasture, was given up as attention switched to close-by cropland. But had New England farmers received the same grazing subsidies that many Western ranchers do, far more of this land would still be in production today. A similar process was responsible for the abandonment of New England's high sheep pastures, beginning in the 1880s.

28. It is also important to note that, without the (expensive) development of Western and Midwestern agriculture and the politico-economic structures which helped make that development possible, New Englanders would not have been so foolish as to let their farmlands go.

29. For more on the use of nature as a source of moral reassurance in the face of potential social guilt, see the concept of the "natural conscience" in Bell (1994), as well as the chapters by Taylor and DuPuis in this volume.

30. In fact, neither does Merchant, I suspect. She sees New England as a "window on the world," as she puts it in the beginning of her book. She does, however, apparently see New England as an especially good example of the consequences of exceeding ecological constraints. I do not.

31. My argument, in other words, should not be read as an attack on the use of subsidies to structure agricultural markets. Rather, my argument concerns the naturalization of the structure of agriculture that results.

32. Before making this argument, I would like to express my thanks for the clarifying experience of reading a wondrous observer of the relativism of the New England scene, Jane Tompkins (1985).

33. They, of course, may have the same small hope for me and their own works. But, alas, I have read many of their works already and remain both empirically and morally unpersuaded.

REFERENCES

Allen, Henry. 1988. "New Hampshire: Look behind the White Steeples." *International Herald Tribune,* 2 December, 4.

Allport, Susan. 1990. *Sermons in Stone: The Stone Walls of New England and New York.* New York and London: Norton.

Barber, John Warner. 1856 [1838]. *Connecticut Historical Collections,* improved edition. New Haven, Conn.: Durrie, Peck, and Barber.

Barnard, Charles H. 1993. "Financial Characteristics of U.S. and Canadian Farms, 1991." *Agricultural Income and Finance* 50 (September): 28–33.

Barron, Hal S. 1984. *Those Who Stayed Behind.* Cambridge, England: Cambridge University Press.

Bell, Michael. 1985. *The Face of Connecticut: People, Geology, and the Land.* Hartford, Conn.: State Geological and Natural History Survey of Connecticut.

———. 1989. "Did New England Go Downhill?" *Geographical Review* 79 (4): 450–66.

———. 1994. *Childerley: Nature and Morality in a Country Village.* Chicago, Ill.: University of Chicago Press.

Berry, Wendell. 1977. *The Unsettling of America.* San Francisco: Sierra Club.

Black, John D. 1950. *The Rural Economy of New England.* Cambridge, Mass.: Harvard University Press.

Destler, Chester M. 1973. *Connecticut: The Provisions State.* Chester, Conn.: Pequot Press.

Durkheim, Emile, and Marcel Mauss. [1903] 1963. *Primitive Classification.* trans. Rodney Needham. Chicago: University of Chicago Press.

Eisenmenger, Robert. 1967. *The Dynamics of Growth in New England's Economy, 1870–1964.* Middletown, Conn.: Wesleyan University Press.

Engels, Friedrich. [circa 1890] 1940. *The Dialectics of Nature.* trans. Clemens Dutt. New York: International Publishers.

Evernden, Neil. 1992. *The Social Creation of Nature.* Baltimore: Johns Hopkins University Press.

Fallert, Richard F., Don P. Blayney, and James J. Miller. 1990. *Dairy: Background for 1990 Farm Legislation.* Washington, D.C.: United States Department of Agriculture, Economic Research Service.

Foucault, Michel. 1970. *The Order of Things: An Archeology of the Human Sciences.* New York: Random House.

French, George. 1911. *New England: What It Is and What It Is to Be.* Boston: Boston Chamber of Commerce.

Goldthwait, James Walter. 1927. "A Town That Has Gone Downhill." *Geographical Review* 17:527–52.

Greider, Thomas, and Garkovich, Lorraine. 1994. "Landscapes: The Social Construction of Nature and the Environment." *Rural Sociology* 59 (1): 1–24.

Hansen, John M. 1991. *Gaining Access: Congress and the Farm Lobby, 1919–1981.* Chicago: University of Chicago Press.

Harding, Sandra. 1986. *The Science Question in Feminism.* Ithaca, N.Y.: Cornell University Press.

Hart, John Fraser. 1991. *The Land That Feeds Us.* New York: W. W. Norton.

Haystead, Ladd, and Gilbert C. Fite. 1955. *The Agricultural Regions of the United States.* Norman: University of Oklahoma Press.

Hecht, Ruben W., and Glen T. Barton. 1950. *Gains in Productivity of Farm Labor.* Washington, D.C.: U.S. Government Printing Office.

Higbee, Edward. 1958. *American Agriculture: Geography, Resources, and Conservation.* New York: John Wiley and Sons.

Hirschl, Thomas A., and Christine R. Long. 1993. "Dairy Farm Survival in a Metropolitan Area: Dutchess County, New York." *Rural Sociology* 58 (3): 461–74.

Hubbard, Ruth. 1982. "Have Only Men Evolved?" In *Biological Woman: The Convenient Myth,* 17–45, ed. Ruth Hubbard, Mary Sue Henifin, and Barbara Fried. Cambridge, Mass.: Schenkman.

Hubbell, William, and Roger Eddy. 1989. *Connecticut.* Portland, Ore.: Graphic Arts Center.

Jackson, Reverend A. W. 1890. "New England and California." *New England Magazine,* n.s., 1 (6):691–96.

Kittredge, Jack. 1993. "On Farming in the Northeast." *Natural Farmer* 2 (16): 2.

Kolodny, Annette. 1984. *The Land Before Her: Fantasy and Experience of the American Frontiers, 1630–1860.* Chapel Hill: University of North Carolina.

Martin, Emily. 1991. "The Egg and the Sperm: How Science Has Constructed a Romance Based on Stereotypical Male–Female Roles." *Signs* 16 (3).

McCallum, Henry D., and Frances T. McCallum. 1965. *The Wire that Fenced the West.* Norman: University of Oklahoma Press.

Merchant, Carolyn. 1989. *Ecological Revolutions: Nature, Gender, and Science in New England.* Chapel Hill and London: University of North Carolina Press.

Mouat, Lucia. 1990. "Boom in Forests Is Turning to Bust." *Christian Science Monitor,* 22 May, 6.

Munyon, Paul Glenn. 1978. *A Reassessment of New England Agriculture in the Last Thirty Years of the Nineteenth Century.* New York: Arno Press.

Novak, Barbara. 1980. *Nature and Culture: American Landscape and Painting, 1825–1875.* New York: Oxford University Press.

Nutting, Wallace. 1922. *Vermont Beautiful.* Framingham, Mass.: Old America Company.

———. 1923. *Connecticut Beautiful.* Framingham, Mass.: Old America Company.

Raup, Hugh M. 1967. "The View from John Sanderson's Farm: A Perspective for the Use of the Land." *Forest History* 10:1–11.

Robinson, William F. 1976. *Abandoned New England.* Boston: New York Graphic Society.

Russell, Howard S. 1976. *A Long Deep Furrow: Three Centuries of Farming in New England.* Hanover, N.H.: University Press of New England.

Schneider, Keith. 1991. "Scholar Looks at Quaint Stone Walls and Sees Pioneers' Garbage Heaps." *New York Times,* 17 November, 14.

Shkilnyk, Anastasia. 1985. *A Poison Stronger Than Love*. New Haven, Conn.: Yale University Press.

Smith, Chard Powers. 1946. *The Housatonic: Puritan River*. New York: Rinehart.

Smith, Neil. 1984. *Uneven Development*. Oxford: Blackwell.

Strathern, Marilyn. 1992. *After Nature: English Kinship in the Late Twentieth Century*. Cambridge, England: Cambridge University Press.

Thomas, Keith. 1983. *Man and the Natural World: Changing Attitudes in England, 1500–1800*. London: Allen Lane.

Todd, S. Edwards. 1867. *The Young Farmer's Manual*. New York: F. W. Woodward.

Tompkins, Jane. 1985. " 'Indians': Textualism, Morality, and the Problem of History." In *"Race," Writing, and Difference*, ed. Henry Louis Gates, Jr., 59–77. Chicago and London: University of Chicago Press.

United States Bureau of the Census. Various years. *Census of Agriculture*. Washington, D.C.: U.S. Government Printing Office.

United States Department of Agriculture. 1872. *Report to the Commissioner of Agriculture for the Year 1871*. Washington, D.C.: U.S. Government Printing Office.

———. 1984. *Agricultural Statistics 1984*. Washington, D.C.: U.S. Government Printing Office.

———. 1988. *Agricultural Statistics 1988*. Washington, D.C.: U.S. Government Printing Office.

———. 1990. *Agricultural Statistics 1990*. Washington, D.C.: U.S. Government Printing Office.

———. 1991. *Agricultural Statistics 1991*. Washington, D.C.: U.S. Government Printing Office.

———. 1992. *Agricultural Statistics 1992*. Washington, D.C.: U.S. Government Printing Office.

Williams, Raymond. [1972] 1980. "Ideas of Nature." In *Problems in Materialism and Culture*. London: Verso.

Wilson, Harold Fisher. 1931. "The Roads of Windsor." *Geographical Review* 21:377–97.

———. [1936] 1967. *The Hill Country of Northern New England*. New York: AMS Press.

Winner, Langdon. 1986. *The Whale and the Reactor*. Chicago and London: University of Chicago Press.

3

The Farm as Firm: Rhetoric and the Remanufacturing of Basque Agrarian Production

Peter Leigh Taylor

In the field of development sociology, recent discussions of contemporary global economic processes have focused on the "impasse" to which economistic and essentialist theories have led (Booth 1985; Corbridge 1990; Vandergeest and Buttel 1988). This chapter uses the case of a Basque agrarian cooperative to examine how such metatheoretical impasses may confront not only critical and mainstream scholars but practitioners charged with combining theory and practice in order to actually "produce" development. The restructuring of agrarian society in much of the industrialized West has been inadequately theorized as a more or less inevitable, if not automatic response to market pressures. "New economic sociology" approaches (Granovetter 1990; Swedberg, Himmelstrand, and Brulin 1990) argue persuasively that economic action is more appropriately viewed as being embedded in a framework of social institutions and relations. This chapter argues that the specific trajectory of structural change in a given case is shaped by social actors involved in often highly political processes of interpretation and persuasion. The paper focuses on public rhetoric as a means of pursuing the link between the negotiation of meaning and political and economic processes of change. Language use not only signals the ideologies and material interests of various social actors, but constitutes a crucial part of the political and cultural processes which help direct structural change.

Other chapters in this volume explore how the nature of development intervention is shaped by how actors define and redefine rural places and processes. The creation of conceptual dualisms, as the editors point out in this book's introduction, are more than rhetorical flourishes after the fact. They represent acts of power which reorganize rural peoples' lives and often produce exclusions. The task of helping to "save" a crisis-ridden Basque agrarian sector given to the agrarian cooperative LANA by its powerful sponsors rested on a particular way of defining the rural area. Saving the

Basque family farm, from this perspective, meant rescuing it from its chaotic, irrational traditional character and remaking it from above, according to an ideal of factory-like manufacturing and efficiency.

In LANA, policy responses to changing market conditions were guided by idealized, contrasting images of the agrarian industrial firm and of the small-scale, diversified family farmer. The cooperative's more powerful participants employed a rhetoric in which the agrarian industrial firm represented a development ideal of the future: professional, flexible, rational, and, above all, efficient. The family farmer represented the "traditional" past: unprofessional, rigid, irrational, and inefficient. The rhetorical strategy of these powerful actors was intimately linked to restructuring policies that ultimately carried the cooperative far from its original commitment to the Basque family farm, as they led to the exclusion of many of the members whom the firm had been established to serve.

This scenario is not new; for decades, small-scale farmers worldwide have been marginalized as rural areas undergo massive losses of population and as market pressures militate in favor of highly capitalized, specialized farming. LANA's case, however, is unusual because its formally democratic policy-making process facilitates the exploration of the political, social, and cultural processes through which this marginalization occurs. The cooperative's experience illustrates how structural change and ideology may shape each other. Although structural constraints on development are real, their impact is mediated by interpretation according to the conceptual model of the observer. The analysis of public rhetoric in LANA shows how a particular group of participants pursued its ideal of development by successfully shaping the agenda and terms of debate and deflecting internal opposition. But more than being a tool of persuasion, rhetoric in LANA had a constitutive dimension, by helping open up and close off particular structural opportunities for change. LANA's experience brings to mind Fred Block's observation that politics today are dominated by "claims of 'false necessity'—arguments that market realities radically constrain our range of political and social choices" (Block 1990, 4). The cooperative's virtual abandonment of the small-scale, diversified farmer, in an important sense, was a self-fulfilling prophecy made inevitable by a development ideal that provided both the goal of efficiency and particular standards by which efficiency would be judged. But paradoxically, as will be discussed below, this redefinition of agrarian production may actually have been "inefficient" to the extent that it failed to sustain the social relations upon which the firm's effective operation depended.

Why did LANA's arrival at this juncture appear to be so logical and inevitable? Why, for most of the history of an organization established to serve small farmers, did a perspective steadily gain ground that saw their interests as diametrically opposed to those of the organization as a firm? Below, I will look at the language of public discussion in LANA to show how influential images were created of the firm and of the rural world that left little space to search for ways to reconcile the small-scale farmers' interests with the cooperative's interests as a firm.

LANA

Based in Oñate, a small town near Mondragón, Spain, LANA is a cooperative which processes and markets dairy and timber products supplied by small-scale diversified Basque farmers. In 1988, it had 214 worker and farmer members. As one of nine agrarian cooperatives in the Mondragón cooperative complex, LANA forms part of what is internationally known as one of the most successful experiments in industrial democracy and "the most impressive refutation of the widely held belief that worker cooperatives have little capacity for economic growth and long term survival" (Whyte and Whyte 1991, 3). The Mondragón system began in 1956 under the guidance of a Basque Catholic priest, José María Arizmendiarrieta. By 1989, the complex had grown to comprise a group of 198 worker-owned and democratically managed firms linked to each other through several common institutions, including a powerful cooperative bank, an autonomous social security system, a vocational school and a research facility. The complex in 1989 had almost 20,000 worker members, about 7 percent of the industrial workers of the Basque region (Greenwood and González-Santos 1991, 16). Ninety-four of the associated firms were industrial cooperatives; nine were agrarian cooperatives. Most of the member firms are organized into sectoral or geographic groups. LANA is the core firm in the agrarian group, EREIN.

From the outset, LANA was plagued with internal tensions arising from conflicting perspectives on the cooperative's purpose. LANA was originally founded in 1960 at the behest of Father Arizmendiarrieta, by the cooperative bank Caja Laboral Popular (CLP) and by thirteen farmers. For small-scale, diversified farmers, LANA would provide a secure outlet for farm products and a source of technical services. For the CLP, LANA would be the vehicle for remaking the crisis-ridden Basque agrarian sector into a modern, viable economic sector. The CLP's approach to restructuring rural production was shaped by Mondragón's remarkably successful experience in the industrial manufacturing sector. The bank's model of rural structural reform drew heavily on an ideal of a modern factory, characterized by centralized planning and control, professionalism and discipline, and a close articulation with the demands of the market. As will be discussed below, this model of development did not easily fit with the autonomous, diversified, small-scale character of LANA's farmer members' production operations.

Research Methodology

This chapter is based on data from archival research, participant observation and semi-structured interviews in LANA in the spring of 1988. I examined a range of internal documents, including minutes of meetings of administrative bodies and general assemblies, internal reports and publications prepared for the public. Interviews were conducted with white collar and blue collar workers in LANA and in its agrarian group, EREIN, and with a limited number of farmer members.

LANA's management was generous in providing me with access to a wide range of internal information and documents. Its top executives devoted a great deal of their time to explaining, with justifiable pride of accomplishment, the history and current operation of their cooperative. However, access to farmer members for interviews was limited, with the consequence that the voices of those participants in this essay are muted. This should not suggest that there necessarily existed in LANA a consensus perspective on policy issues. Indeed, the desire of the management to attempt to select my informants and to limit my presence at potentially conflictual meetings suggested that lively debate was at least considered a possibility.

This chapter necessarily focuses to a great extent on the written record of LANA's situation. The fact that so little overt disagreement emerges from these documents is significant, given the penchant for preserving an elaborate "paper trail" of policy-making elsewhere in the Mondragón complex. Internal archives in the cooperatives generally describe exhaustively the participation and diverse perspectives of specialized representative bodies (Greenwood and González-Santos 1991; Taylor 1991). While the written record obviously cannot fully represent the social reality of LANA, it does yield insight into the process by which change can be managed and channeled by a limited group of participants. The cooperative's development has been closely managed by an influential group of CLP advisors and LANA management staff. These actors have successfully employed a rhetorical strategy emphasizing centralized control, professionalism, the synthetic interest of the firm and the identification of the market with rationality in order to facilitate their control of the cooperative's development trajectory.

Rhetoric, Culture, and Structural Change

> Increasingly, public debate has come to hinge, not on what kind of society we are or want to be, but on what the needs of the economy are. Hence, a broad range of social policies are now debated almost entirely in terms of how they fit in with the imperatives of the market. (Block 1990, 3)

The "new rationalization" (Altmann et al. 1991) of an increasingly competitive international economy is said to drive firms either toward ever greater efficiencies or toward oblivion. Some optimistic writers argue that "a new generation of participation" will be made possible by "the new cardinal virtues of the enterprise: flexibility, rapidity of reaction, fluidity, quality, integration and openness" (Gaudier 1988, 313, 319). Both of these perspectives tend to understate the social costs of restructuring, such as falling real wages, deteriorating working conditions and higher unemployment. They also tend to leave untheorized the mechanism by which these scenarios will supposedly emerge, assuming instead that market signals, if correctly understood, will produce adaptation by successful economic actors.

This chapter builds on two directions sociology has recently taken in trying to theorize economic action. A "new economic sociology" (Granovetter 1990; see also Swedberg, Himmelstrand, and Brulin 1990) tries to account for how economic actors' responses to market signals are shaped within a framework of social institutions and social relations. A second, related approach tries to account for the cultural influences on economic action (Biggart 1991; DiMaggio 1990). This chapter builds on these approaches by examining how the openings and limits to structural change in LANA have been shaped by groups of social actors involved in an often political process of interpretation and persuasion. As Daly observes, "The economy, like all other spheres, is the terrain of political struggle, and is governed not by a single logic, but by a proliferation of discourse/language games" (Daly 1991, 100).

Following the lead of Gusfield (1981) and others, this chapter pursues empirically the link between political and economic processes and the negotiation of social and cultural meaning by focusing on the use of language. The chapter examines "rhetorical practices," a category of phenomena that includes the use of language to persuade, but more broadly encompasses those human behaviors and communication that are aimed at influencing others (Burke 1969; Gusfield 1989). Rhetorical practices yield insights into the cultures, ideologies and relative influence of participants in debate as well as into the diverse goals they pursue.

Culture, for the purposes of this paper, influences action in LANA by helping shape the practical interpretation of the firm's situation and by providing authoritative guidelines for action. Swidler (1986) rightly argues that culture provides a "tool kit" of habits, skills and styles from which strategies for action are constructed. Yet hers is a utilitarian conception of culture (Robertson 1988, 13), influenced by her concern to avoid the excesses of a theoretical preoccupation with static, overarching "ultimate values" (Swidler 1986, 273). This essay, by contrast, analyzes the often conflictual process of creating and re-creating organizational culture, seen as historically structured "patterns, values, attitudes and sentiments" (Friedrich 1989, 99).

This essay shows how LANA's organizational culture has emerged and been re-created as distinct internal social groups have competed to influence structural change in the cooperative. Consistent with the theoretical linking of language use to a broader range of persuasive action, this chapter will look at language use and the political and economic dimension of LANA's experience together. Rhetorical practices in LANA have helped constitute the culture and social relations of the firm by influencing what can be said in public about its situation and the range of action deemed possible. In LANA, the prerogative the management and its CLP advisors have been able to assume in creating and putting into practice particular ideals of agrarian industry and of the small farmer, has facilitated their control of the cooperative's development trajectory.

Rhetorical Practices and Structural Change in LANA

A large part of the success of LANA's management in implementing its policies resided in its ability to manage the cooperative's democratic procedures by successfully defining both the agenda of issues and the terms of debate over policy issues. Below, I show how the management and its CLP advisors constructed an ideal world in which no other policy perspective but their own could be considered to be conceivable or even to be rational. This is not to argue that LANA's farmers internalized a "dominant ideology" (Abercrombie, Hill, and Turner 1980). Rather, the farmer members had little legitimate entry into the realm of public discussion to openly pose alternatives to the management's policies. Instead, they passively thwarted management's efforts to increase its influence over their production activities and occasionally resisted actively by exercising a negative vote in general assembly. This essay argues that in LANA, the exclusion of points of view that differed from that of the management hindered the possible development of alternative development strategies, making the expectation of a complete conflict of interests between the small-scale farmers and the cooperative a self-fulfilling prophecy.

From a Service to an Agrarian Industrial Orientation

LANA was established toward the end of Spanish autarky and at the beginning of the restructuring of the Spanish agrarian sector and the crisis of the family farm (Etxezarreta 1977; Etxezarreta and Viladomiu 1989). In the Basque region of Spain, much of agrarian production historically has taken place on small, diversified family farms (*caseríos*). Beyond their economic importance, these family farms have been a prominent symbol of Basque rural culture (Etxezarreta 1977, 392), which itself has been vested with great significance in public discourse on Basque identity in recent years.

Father Arizmendiarrieta's vision of a response to the Basque agrarian problem was to develop a rural industry with workers, both in the factory and on the farm, all serving the collective. The CLP's ongoing commitment to the ailing Basque rural sector emerged from an appreciation of its symbolic value but also from an evaluation of its business potential for the bank. Investing in the agrarian sector has helped the CLP to compete for savings in rural areas where people are aware that their capital has generally flowed outward to develop other economic sectors (Caja Laboral Popular 1985). In putting Arizmendiarrieta's vision into practice, LANA's management and its CLP advisors pursued an ideal of rural production based on an equally ideal model of industrial manufacturing believed to underlay Mondragón's successful industrial cooperatives. LANA's agrarian industrial ideal had several principal elements: a focus on centralized control; an emphasis on professionalism; a view of the firm's interest as synthetic, and an association of the market with rationality. Over time, this way of conceptualizing agrarian production would gradually carry the cooperative further and further away from its original commitment to the Basque family farm.

In its early years, LANA's principal aim was to provide its farmer members with technical assistance, and fruit, vegetable, and raw milk marketing services. It soon became clear, though, that taking responsibility for processing members' products could generate greater economic returns for the firm. LANA soon built a pasteurization plant to begin its own milk processing. LANA later added marketing services for its members' pine timber and in similar fashion acquired a sawmill in 1964.

During this early period, much attention was given to promoting structural change among LANA's farmer members' operations. The CLP supplied technical advisors who sat on the cooperative's management council. Bank staff carried out technical and economic studies of member and nonmember *caseríos*. A monthly bulletin was edited to disseminate information among farmer members, and agricultural and forestry extension agents visited farms regularly.

The efforts of the CLP and LANA's management to directly restructure farmer members' operations reflected their the view that agrarian cooperatives, "in addition to being profitable by themselves, should constitute an example of business-like structuring and of the application of technology" (Caja Laboral Popular 1987, 1). An early statement by LANA's management in 1971 expressed hope that the Basque family farm could be made such an example: "We have dedicated our best efforts to agricultural and livestock development out of the desire to create an efficient and viable plan for the benefit of the *caserío*" (LANA, Plan de Gestión 1971, 1).

LANA's extension agents' mandate, to advise on "precise solutions aimed at better agricultural practice: grouping, crop changes and techniques" (Van der Broek and Van der Schoot 1983, 12), reflected the bank's tendency to see agrarian problems primarily as technical problems. Critics of neo-classical approaches to economic decision-making argue that they are "under-socialized," unduly isolating problems from their social and cultural context (Etzioni 1988; Granovetter 1992).

Yet the CLP's technocratic approach did devolve from a distinct analysis of rural Basque society and culture. It assumed that "an unproductive agrarian sector [is] the product of socioeconomic disequilibrium . . . [It] is a reflection of deeper socioeconomic problems" (Caja Laboral Popular 1985). According to the Bank's technical advisors, the *caserío*'s problems emerged from social and cultural roots in an unscientific, unprofessional past. Their description of those few farmers able to pull themselves away from the past describes eloquently their vision of that "tradition."

> We are thinking about the group who have lost their fear of the pen and who carry out an exhaustive management of the farm. Of those who cannot conceive of a pasture without a rational formula of fertilizer. Of those who request studies and advice in order to respond to the exigencies of progress. Of those who have broken with antiquated systems and who raise their cattle with the most modern management techniques. Of those who cannot conceive of a stable without rigorous sanitation control. Of those who do not overlook a single available means to develop themselves into authentic businessmen. Of those who have reached a state high enough to be able to talk and act with their own criteria, defending their ideas with solid arguments. (LANA May 1973)

From this perspective, because of their embeddedness in a "traditional" social context, LANA's diversified farmers not only are not authentic businesspeople, but also lack the ability to reason systematically.

LANA's management and its CLP advisors in the seventies became increasingly disillusioned with the failure of farmer members to restructure their operations as advised. To what extent it was this disillusionment that fueled LANA's growing tendency toward a greater industrial orientation or the other way around is not clear. The instability of LANA's production sectors seemed to make restructuring all the more urgent for the cooperative as a firm. The "green gold" boom era of the Basque forestry sector ended around 1970. The volume of the pine offered to LANA, however, increased as its members' stands reached maturity, creating difficulties for the cooperative, whose by-laws required it to purchase its members' products. Competition among sawmills, furthermore, was fierce and many were eliminated (Van der Broek and Van der Schoot 1983, 21). LANA's response was to begin manufacturing more profitable timber products with greater value added. With the construction of a new sawmill and of new offices near Oñate in 1974 , LANA began an ambitious expansion program. This development, which included the incorporation of a number of new worker members, began to alter the balance between farmer and worker members, and with it, the balance between farming and manufacturing operations.

LANA's management and their CLP advisors became increasingly convinced that the restructuring trends in the firm's sectors required more market-oriented, specialized and professional organization at all levels. By 1975, the CLP's "guiding hypothesis" had become that it was necessary to "industrialize the rural area" (Caja Laboral Popular 1975, 4). "If . . . we want to industrialize the Deva's[1] agriculture through the creation of agro-industries, the difficulties we foresee are the very ones that create the choice of converting the existing *caserío* or creating new firms that integrate or modify the *caserío* according to modern industrial patterns" (Caja Laboral Popular 1975, 116). Advisors were soon engaged in research and planning which aimed "not to search for solutions for a *caserío* but to create profitable agricultural firms with a future, of optimal size and with technical management" (Caja Laboral Popular 1975, 4). With time, the bank despaired completely of being able to make over the small farmers' operations and turned elsewhere. "Today we want to experiment with other, more business-like forms. The cooperative (possessor or renter of lands and agricultural machinery) takes responsibility, through its executive team, for programming worker members (with schedules that must be regular), for productivity in all its aspects, for marketing and other areas, the same as in all firms and in any industrial cooperative" (Caja Laboral Popular 1977, 11).

The immediate result of this new resolution was to begin to circumvent LANA's dependence on the raw milk of its small-scale member suppliers. An internal milk production division incorporating its own dairy herd was developed in LANA in 1977, which, organized according to the agrarian industrial ideal, would better conform to the management's expectations of rational business behavior. This division eventually would be spun off as the independent cooperative, Behi-Alde, but would continue to supply LANA.

Global restructuring trends in the 1980s reinforced the development trajectory that LANA was pursuing. A new era began for the agrarian sector after Spain's recovery from its worst economic crisis since the post–Civil War period. Spain's agrarian enterprises faced increased competition in restructured markets, rapid technological change, and the concentration of firms. Foreign investment in the agro-food sector, which had been increasing since the seventies, began to escalate in the early eighties (Cadenas and Fernández 1988, 37). After Spain's long-anticipated entry into the European Economic Community in 1986, its borders were progressively opened to foreign competition. From the perspective of LANA's management and the CLP, these restructuring trends were further evidence that LANA needed to conform more strictly to their agrarian industrial ideal.

Control

> Caja Laboral Popular never leaves its associated cooperatives without financial support at any moment. But it does require that abnormal situations be corrected. (LANA General Assembly 1976, 27)

Control and the Production Process

In Chapter 4 of this volume Melanie DuPuis's analysis of the development of an ecological rhetoric in land use planning in New York State shows the influence of what has been called a managerial approach to natural resources. In similar fashion, LANA's agrarian industrial ideal encouraged the maximization of management control over all relevant production factors from farm level production to marketing. The CLP's support for agrarian activities, as with Mondragón's industrial cooperatives, was ultimately limited by "the efficiency of the endeavor being realized and the profitability of the firms created, since business solidity is the fundamental basis for any balanced and coherent process of development" (Caja Laboral Popular 1987, 1). According to one CLP policy paper, the decision to risk capital layouts for agrarian ventures that were greater than those customary for industrial ventures would be vindicated if, once an agrarian investment reached profitability, returns could be maintained with the proper control of production. Fluctuations in sales could be compensated for by adjusting the prices paid for raw materials (Caja Laboral Popular 1987, 7).

LANA had difficulty, however, in controlling raw material costs. In its dairy division, the cooperative struggled to maintain a stable milk supply. Members dissatisfied with LANA's prices often sold their milk to other intermediaries. LANA also faced problems of competition from blackmarket milk vendors and of seasonal fluctuations in supply and demand stemming from bovine biological cycles and consumer preferences. At one point in the early seventies, the cooperative seriously considered closing its dairy operations. Instead, LANA turned to nonmember milk supplies (Van der Broek and Van der Schoot 1983, 12), sold surplus milk to competitors and marketed less-perishable milk products to control supply fluctuations. In addition, LANA's internal milk operation was established with CLP urging and over the objections of many of its farmer members. This internal milk production division grew to encompass milk production, beef cattle-raising and calf-raising activities (Van der Broek and Van der Schoot 1983, 25), each of which was eventually spun off as an autonomous cooperative. LANA also began using price incentives to encourage larger scale, higher quality milk and timber production. Although the bonuses were formally available to all, in practice only the larger-scale members with more highly capitalized operations benefited from these incentives. LANA's business activities, in effect, came to be conceptualized as beginning at the farm gate with the purchase of raw milk or timber. Therefore, in contrast to experiences with agrarian cooperatives elsewhere in Spain (Taylor 1989), technical and social services to farmer members were not considered a cost of production and as such, service to the firm itself. Rather, they came to be considered as "social" costs that drained resources better reinvested in the firm.

The pursuit of greater centralized control, however, has been difficult to reconcile with the fact that the associated farms are autonomous business enterprises. By 1978, LANA, by its management's own account, had arrived near the top of its sector in its region. But LANA's leaders had also abandoned most of the technical services aimed at small-scale farmer members. Since farmer members resisted efforts to restructure their operations more "rationally," LANA had sought to minimize its dependence on these suppliers by creating internal supplies that could be managed directly. For their part, many farmer members became increasingly dissatisfied with what they saw as LANA's turn away from a "service response to an entrepreneurial response" (LANA 1981a, 4).

The bypassing of dependence on small-scale supplier members represented by LANA's internal milk division had become CLP general policy by the time the bank's 1980–85 agrarian portfolio plan was published. The plan made no mention of the family farm, but spoke instead of optimizing the natural resources of the Basque region, capitalizing the sector through human, technical and financial investment and improving the living conditions of the workers of the sector (Caja Laboral Popular 1984).

Control and Policy-Making

Given LANA's formally democratic organization, it would seem that the cooperative's policy-making process would militate against the highly centralized control of the production processes inherent in the agrarian industrial ideal. Yet LANA's internal political configuration actually facilitated greater management control. The organizational diagram represented in Figure 3-1 shows the formal workings of LANA's administrative, executive

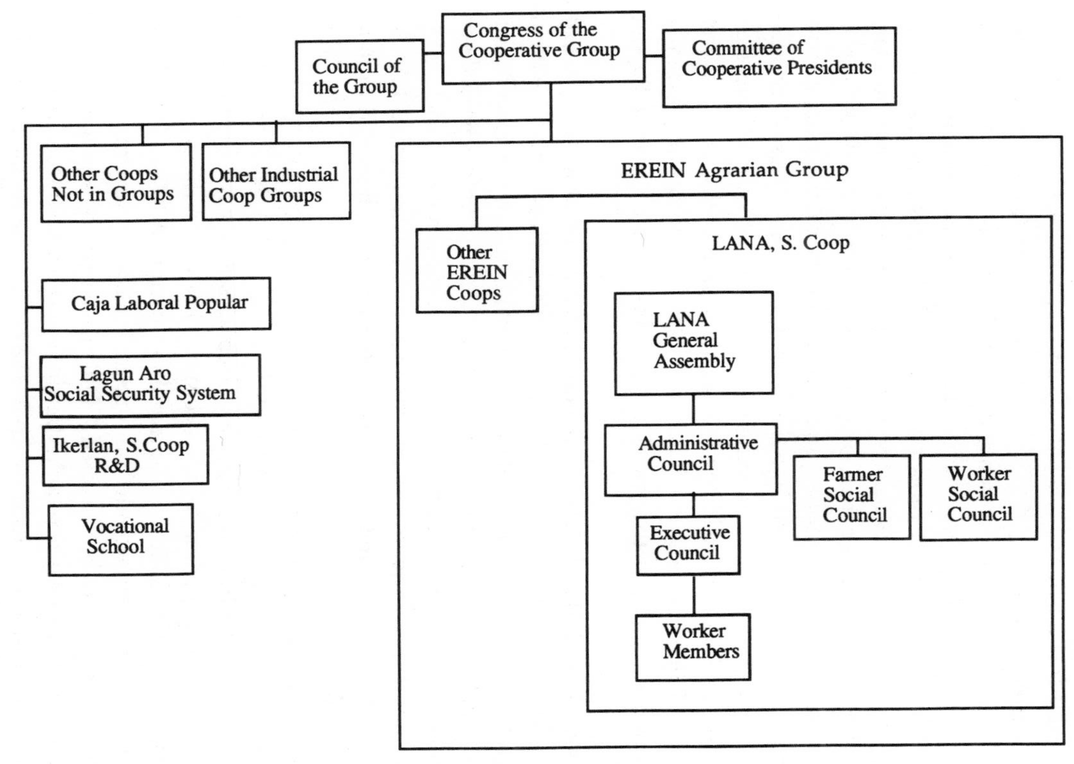

Figure 3-1.
LANA and the Mondragón Cooperative Complex.

and social councils, all theoretically under the direction of the general assembly of members.

The formal Mondragón cooperative model provides for representative administrative and social councils to balance the decision-making power of the executive (management) council. Yet in practice in LANA, the rectors' (elected representatives on the administrative council) lack of technical knowledge and technical experience hampered their ability to debate policies with management. As one rector put it: "The executive [management] council is the body with the most power in LANA. That is logical because they have knowledge that the rectors do not, because they prepare the plans, etc. . . . Only in this body are there people on top of the demands of the market, who know the weaknesses and strong points of the competition" (quoted in Van der Broek and Van der Schoot 1983, 60). This observation implicitly accepts the CLP's assumption that control over management should not necessarily coincide with legal ownership of the land, but rests with "those who demonstrate a business and technical capacity that guarantees continuity, productivity and profitability" (Caja Laboral Popular 1975, 113).

The founders of Mondragón's cooperatives realized that in order to provide an effective counterbalance to "the pragmatism that is coherent with all that is involved in management and the pursuit of immediate efficiency" (Caja Laboral Popular 1983, 88), the administrative council members needed special training. Yet in contrast to other cooperatives in Mondragón such as Copreci (Taylor 1991), little investment has been made in improving LANA's member representatives' ability to make independent analyses and to influence policy-making.

As one executive told researchers in 1983, "Management knows what a rector has to know" (quoted in Van der Broek and Van der Schoot 1983, 67). According to LANA's manager, this implies seeing participation in the cooperative as participation "not in decisions, but yes, in the process of information." (SUSTRAI, 60). An internal evaluation in 1981, indeed, observed that the manager attended administrative council meetings and provided the information to be discussed. "Only decisions appropriate for it are given to the administrative council, decisions that are well studied and disseminated by the management" (LANA 1981b, 3). The social council, for its part, though quite active in other Mondragón cooperatives, had little influence on management decision-making in LANA. "The social council does not make decisions, although it is consulted when it can have a social impact" (LANA 1981b, 3).

Table 3-1

LANA Members by Production Activity, 1988

Activity	*Number*	*Percent*
Farmers	102	48
Workers	97	46
Mixed	9	4
Institutional	4	2
Total	212[a]	100

[a]missing data: 2

Whatever effective counterweight to management decision-making that existed in LANA originated in the general assembly of members. Because of the stipulations of its contract of association with the Caja Laboral Popular (and the Mondragón system), both LANA's farmers and workers were voting members, an unusual arrangement for agrarian cooperatives. This organizational structure conformed to Arizmendiarrieta's vision of unifying the interests of rural farmers and urban workers through the collective endeavor of the cooperative. Both groups would be workers for the cooperative—one on the shopfloor, the other on the farm. Yet in practice, the general assembly was deeply divided by conflicting interests.

In absolute numbers, farmer and worker members in 1988 were evenly matched (see Table 3-1). Worker members and larger-scale farmer members were said to be the most closely identified with LANA's interests as a firm, at least as those interests were envisioned by the management. Under the terms of the contract of association with the CLP, worker members enjoyed job security, though wages were set with reference to the labor market. Larger-scale farmer members relied on transactions with LANA for a large part of their income. By contrast, as a management report put it in 1980, "a large number of farmer members have not developed (for diverse reasons) at the rhythm that the cooperative laid out for them, so they have become disconnected from [the firm] and either do not identify with it or are discontented with its policies" (LANA 1980, 8).

Despite the discontent of its smaller-scale farmer members, a voting coalition of management, workers, and larger-scale dairy farmers in the cooperative's general assembly prevented serious challenge to LANA's overall development strategy. One senior farmer member of the administrative council remarked in 1983: "Before the management had less weight. But since the industrial activities have over time expanded, more and more people from all professions entered executive positions, generally well-educated people. And now, with the cheese factory, there will be another well-educated person and there will be less possibility for the administrative council to oppose things, because it has to confront more and better educated people" (quoted in Van der Broek and Van der Schoot 1983, 163).

Most of the small-scale, diversified farmers, by contrast, were by the late seventies effectively marginalized and being encouraged, directly or indirectly, to leave the cooperative. But up to 1984, disaffected members had occasionally succeeded in blocking unpopular management initiatives requiring a two-thirds majority to pass. For example, in order to correct financial imbalances stemming from heavy borrowing from the CLP to finance LANA's restructuring programs, the management had begun to ask for individual capital contributions from members. After two consecutive failures to persuade members to approve an obligatory contribution, in 1984 a general assembly resolution was passed by a coalition of management, worker, and larger-scale farmer members to require a contribution. To the protest of small-scale farmer members that they could not afford the lump sum payment, LANA's management replied that the cooperative could no longer afford to do business with those whose operations could not support the contribution. Seventy-five of the smaller-scale dairy and timber farmers left the cooperative. The management directly attributed this "self-selection" to the "evolution" of the agrarian sector (LANA 1986a).

The management's subsequent comments on the incident reflected its view of who enjoyed the right to participate in policy-making. "Without a doubt, the business development achieved and the decisions to which it has carried us will mean a self-selection of members, above all farmers, in the next few years. For those who are left and who incorporate themselves, we will embark on a policy of reconciliation and integration into the cooperative, so that feeling ourselves owners will be a reality in all activities and decisions where we are supposed to participate" (LANA, Plan de Gestión 1984, 4). Statements such as this cast doubt on whether the departed members' legal status as owners of the cooperative actually entitled them to participate in decision-making. Indeed, the management, along with many worker and larger-scale farmer members, had often objected to the influence Mondragón's one person–one vote system gave to farmer members whose material contribution to the cooperative was small.[2] LANA's 1986–1990 Plan stated that the "self-selection" of members would lead to a new equilibrium, "that will lead us to give greater relevance to worker members in the cooperatives' decisions" (LANA 1986a, 4). The cooperative would continue to support those farmer members who adapt to "the new situation" (LANA 1986a). Internal by-law changes passed in 1986 to permit approval of major policies with a simple majority further consolidated the discretionary power of LANA's management and its agrarian industrial orientation.

Specialization and Professionalism

LANA's agrarian industrial ideal viewed agricultural production as a specialized profession with a discrete body of knowledge and techniques requiring a full-time commitment. Far from being "professional," dairy and timber operations were not considered serious business activities if they formed part of a diversified family economic strategy. On the contrary, one policy paper dismissed nonspecialized production as a weekend "hobby" for the industrial worker, a complement to family income. "It seems apparent to all that the future *caserío* must be specialized and must forget the system of producing "a little of everything" that was part of a subsistence or autarkic regime of the past" (Caja Laboral Popular 1975, 104).

This view of professionalism not only shaped the distribution of decision-making power in LANA but also informed the management's notion of those obligations that farmer members owed to the cooperative and the cooperative, in turn, to the farmers. The member's responsibility should be to "fulfill his professionalism. This response should, neither in individual nor collective form, harm the sectoral vocation nor the continuity and survival of the cooperative as a firm and economic unit" (LANA 1986a, 4). For its part, the cooperative "should offer the member the opportunity to satisfy his professional needs and ambitions as long as they do not distort [the sectoral vocation and business continuity of the firm]. . . . Toward this end, it will continue to create jobs for those who choose the profession and it will support and join whatever initiatives emerge that are professionally interrelated with the cooperative and possess a clear business viability" (LANA General Assembly 1981).

Unfortunately, most of LANA's diversified farmer members, from this perspective, were living hand-to-mouth on nonspecialized, undercapitalized farms using unprofessional methods. The bulk of LANA's farmer members in 1988 were still small-scale diversified farmers without highly capitalized production facilities. LANA in 1988 lacked a detailed census of the size of its members' dairy and timber farms. Its management estimated, however, that 25 percent of the dairy members operated with only 4–6 milk cows in 1988, well below the 1989 Basque average of 17.7 head (Mauleón Gómez 1989, 99). A minority of dairy farmer members had larger-scale, more highly capitalized and specialized production. According to delivery records, 20 percent of LANA's suppliers, including the internal milk operation LANA set up in the late seventies, provided over 80 percent of the firm's milk supply in 1988. LANA's timber producers were in 1988 almost all small-scale producers. Although overall, the farmers had an average of 15 hectares of forest, 75 percent owned only 1–2 hectares of pine trees (LANA manager, personal communication).

Adopting the full-time, specialized dairy and timber production implied by LANA's agrarian industrial ideal was not a realistic option for most of the cooperative's small-scale farmers. For most, advanced age, lack of heirs, or lack of access to capital precluded developing the long-term professional orientation that LANA promoted. As a result, LANA's policies began quite early to bypass these members who failed to signal their professionalism by adopting full-time, specialized production. In 1971, for example, LANA's annual management plan proposed a controversial system of differential prices for milk deliveries that would reward production in higher quantity. To members' complaints that these incentives discriminated against small, diversified farmers, LANA's president replied that the policy did not run counter to the cooperative spirit "since it applied to all members, and it tried to guarantee a living to those who were working full-time in dairy production" (LANA Plan de Gestión 1971, 17).

A complaint by a member ten years later that "certain actions harm the small *casero* [*caserío* operator], stepping on him and oppressing him excessively," was answered in similar fashion. The President replied that "the small [farmers] of course participate in the advantages of membership to a lesser degree than the larger [farmers] but this is because of their volume of activities, not because the Cooperative does it in a premeditated way" (LANA General Assembly 1981). This statement, interestingly, clearly links the distribution of benefits to the volume of transactions with the cooperative. Yet the obligatory capital contribution that in 1984 precipitated the departure of most of LANA's farmer members was required as a single lump sum payment rather than as a payment linked to the volume of transactions.

In addition to its advantages on the farm, greater business-like professionalism, according to the agrarian industrial ideal, encourages involvement with a firm. In contrast to farmers in Europe, a CLP policy paper observed, Basque farmers were insufficiently integrated into processing or service firms. "This lack of entrepreneurial tradition constitutes a great 'handicap' in the face of the need to compete with European organizations that are perfectly capitalized and well endowed with technical and human resources" (Caja Laboral Popular 1984).

From the perspective of the agrarian industrial ideal, the familial character of the Basque *caserío* hindered such cooperation by encouraging excessively personal and individualistic economic behavior.

> The marked individualism of the *casero,* educated in an environment of independence created by his being the owner and master of his lands, is known by all. The family farm, with no clear division of functions, has created a favorable context for the development of the *casero*'s individualism. [The] primary obstacle that must be overcome in order to develop a viable agrarian unit will be to break the family–business–individual structure that weighs over the *caserío,* making possible advance toward other forms of association such as the cooperative or private firm. (Caja Laboral Popular 1975, 112)

This identification of professionalism, and even business-like behavior, with the renunciation of individualism relative to the firm underlies a third major principle of LANA's agrarian industrial ideal.

Synthetic Interests: The Firm as Collective or the Collective as Firm?

> No one should feel martyred for the rest, because the effort is from all and for all. (LANA General Assembly 1980, 34)

> Each category [of member] tries to defend its particular interests, and various conflicts result: between small and large farmers, between farmers and workers and between these groups and management. (LANA staff member, cited in Van der Broek and Van der Schoot 1983, 66)

Despite Arizmendiarrieta's vision of farmers and workers together serving the collective, LANA's farmer and worker members often viewed each other's interests as a zero sum situation. Farmer members tended to favor charging as high a price as possible for their raw materials and reducing processing costs (wages) to allow the firm competitive final product prices. Worker members tended to favor acquiring raw material at the lowest possible price to retain a profit despite greater processing costs (wages). Furthermore, farmers often expressed resentment of "special" benefits accruing to worker members: fixed hours, a five-day work week, paid vacations each year and pension benefits. Workers, for their part, complained that small-scale farmers with little capital invested could make decisions about the factory (Van der Broek and Van der Schoot 1983, 51).

In Chapter 4 of this volume, DuPuis discusses the political competition, often dominated by urban-based business and consumer groups, that underlay the environmental rhetoric of New York State policy discussions. This case differs because the resources in contention within LANA were explicitly represented as being for collective, rather than private benefit. LANA's leaders dealt with conflicts of interest between farmer and worker members by proposing that their participation in the cooperative embodied a higher-level, synthetic interest: "Only with a wider vision, with a longer-range perspective can one arrive at a congruence of interest. In other words, although [workers' and farmers'] interests are counterposed, by exercising social and economic rights, one should identify with the primordial and higher-level objective, which is to obtain the maximum economic and social yields in the joint activity" (LANA, untitled, undated internal document). Nevertheless, LANA's synthetic interest was ordinarily interpreted in a relatively narrow, economic fashion. Maximizing economic and social yields were seen as virtually identical because to achieve the social objective, economic profitability was said to come first: "We cannot forget that the fundamental requirement for attaining our social objective is that the firm must consolidate itself, economically and financially and it must reach a sufficient size so that it can modify the productive structure of the members' farms and ultimately, the productivity of the land. That is where the possibility of improvement lies" (LANA, untitled, undated internal document, 2).

Furthermore, according to LANA's agrarian industrial ideal, the collective interest becomes subsumed into the interest of the firm. As LANA's general manager put it: "The cooperative must not condition its development and business stability by the short-term interests of a section of its members. Here is where with the greatest force we must employ the argument that we members leave and can disappear, but what we must guarantee to the maximum is that the cooperative continue so that it can continue to fulfill its social objective" (LANA General Assembly, 1985). In the 1977 General Assembly, members publicly criticized a management plan to legally change the cooperative's name from a "rural" to an "industrial" cooperative. To the president's reply that the proposed name change posed no significant implications for the farmers, one member responded that in an industrial cooperative there would no longer be "farmer" members, but merely "worker" members. The president "made him see that in reality it was just so, since because its farmers supplied the Cooperative, they in their private lives, worked for the Cooperative" (LANA General Assembly 1977, 2).

The management's ability to collapse collective interests into those of the firm yet draw selectively upon the concepts of "collective" and "firm," facilitated the deflection of opposition to its development policies. For example, when in 1981 a worker member objected in general assembly to the management's request for an obligatory capital contribution, the manager expressed surprise, saying that "given the ownership structure of this business, when someone adopts such a position, in opposition to his own function, he is doing it against the rest of the members" (LANA General Assembly 1981). This rhetoric serves to remind the worker both of his proper place within the firm's hierarchy and of his obligations to the collective.

In the 1977 assembly, one member protested that "once [LANA's] name is changed from rural to industrial, the farmer cannot be industrial. What is being attempted once more is to squeeze the one who is weak." Another member read a statement that observed that the small farmer felt oppressed and that in a cooperative this should not be permitted. The president "let him know that he did not agree that the Cooperative had oppressed the small farmer and what we should do is forget about large and small, rich and poor and try harder to unite ourselves to form a strong firm" (LANA General Assembly 1977, 12).

Because it saw itself as promoting the collective interest as embodied in the firm, LANA's management perceived itself as the most "neutral" group of participants in the cooperative. Rather than acting as a neutral arbiter of conflicting internal interests, nevertheless, by the 1980s LANA's management came to require a choice between the cooperative's own interests as a firm and those of a majority of its farmer members. Given the competitive state of LANA's markets and the characterization of a firm as having "two basic aspects, profitability and permanence in time" (LANA 1981b), the link seen between competitive production bases and the firm's survival led LANA to write off most of the cooperative's farmer members. As its manager explained in general assembly, "a deficient technical and business evolution of part of the membership has provoked a sharp divergence of interest that threatens the functioning of the cooperative" (LANA 1980, 124, 125). After the departure of the small-scale farmer members, a management spokesman articulated the general principle at stake: "to fulfill the basic premises of survival and development, it is clear that we must follow a policy of quality in members, since quantity in members without quality will lead the cooperative to the same sad end: disappearance." (LANA General Assembly 1985).

Rationality and the Market

For LANA's management, Spain's incorporation into the EEC in 1986 underlined the structural inadequacies of most of the farmer members' operations. Until then, pasteurized milk prices had been set officially and urban processing plants enjoyed monopoly concessions. The deregulation of the dairy market after 1986 resulted in both a greater variety of milk products in the market and lower prices. Yet, though European competition now entered Spain freely, Basque dairy firms were not prepared to enter outside markets. The result, according to a LANA executive, was "an authentic commercial chaos" (LANA General Assembly 1987). Furthermore, LANA's timber sector entered a slump after 1986 as the cost of uncut pine rose sharply at the same time that the number of sawmills competing in the local market had greatly increased. LANA abandoned its sawmill activities and began, with Basque government subsidies, a major investment program aimed at specializing in carpentry products.

For LANA's management, its legitimacy as a neutral arbiter between farmer and work interests (Van der Broek and Van der Schoot 1983, 66) rested on its reliance on the market as an objective reference for making policy decisions. Social considerations, from this viewpoint, distort an objective reading of the market's dictates: "For those in charge, a new firm should be designed with the maximum focus on and orientation toward the market. In principle, social factors should be forgotten which might derail dramatic decisions which must, without doubt, be made, if one really wishes to develop a business-like, long-term solution to the situation" (LANA General Assembly 1988, 27).

LANA's agrarian industrial ideal encouraged the cooperative's management to associate the operation of the market with rationality itself. In 1971, for example, the management wrote: "[Planning] requires knowledge of the situation, a profound analysis that indicates the causes and possibilities that encircle the [agrarian] sector in the general economic framework. [This allows] programming the adaptation of production means to the needs of the market in a rational manner, within the possibilities that are presented" (LANA, Plan de Gestión 1971, 2.) Decision-making, from this perspective, is an entirely rational process that draws upon specialized analysis and the appreciation of objective market limits. The purpose of this exercise of rationality is to adapt production to the needs of the market.

Yet from the perspective of LANA's management, most farmer members operated in an irrational fashion and hence had an unbusiness-like character. "The choice of specialization [by the small farmer] is not decided by criteria of economic rationality, of better or less profitability. . . . Ultimately, the structure of production of the *caserío* reveals the absence of an entrepreneurial character, the lack of an orientation toward the market" (Caja Laboral Popular 1975, 94). And, if the farmers themselves were unbusiness-like, they could not properly understand the character of the cooperative. They "are not capable of understanding the entrepreneurial character of the cooperative because on their own farms, they function in a totally intuitive and anarchic way" (LANA 1981a, 22). From this perspective, only a strict orientation to the market can supply a rational dimension to the farmer's activities and a business-like dimension to his character.

According to LANA's agrarian industrial ideal, the farmers' irrationality and lack of business-like character were closely related to their individualism. When staff members in the CLP and in LANA complained that farmer members lacked interest in developing themselves because of their traditional, conservative mentality, they not only remarked that the farmers lacked "sufficient motivation" (LANA, Plan de Gestión 1973, 4), but by implication, that their irrational operations were associated with a marked individualism. A rational, business-like perspective would lead the farmer to recognize the advantages of integration with a manufacturing industry like LANA. But in the Basque primary sector, by contrast, LANA's management declared "people prefer to live day by day, with short-term demands and without integrating themselves into activities that, in the medium and long term, will guarantee economic returns, [that] come as a function of the benefits of integrating production and manufacturing" (LANA General Assembly 1988).

The eighties brought greater strains on LANA's always shaky coalition of diverse farmer, worker, and management interests. In its dairy division, LANA had by 1980 virtually eliminated its milk supply fluctuations through its internal milk production section. Nevertheless, it now had chronic surpluses and depended on other processors to buy its extra milk. LANA introduced price incentives for producers to alter their cows' biological rhythms to produce more in the winter. It entered new markets in nearby Vitoria and established a plan to develop milk derivative products with Eroski, Mondragón's consumer cooperative. LANA also planned new investments to increase processing capacity and, in 1984, built a cheese factory. Although LANA's timber activities were still relatively profitable during the early eighties, its pine products had reached maturity. The cooperative's vulnerability became clear as its principal customer, the Mondragón cooperative Ulgor, began after 1983 to turn to synthetic packing materials. LANA began developing a product line with greater technological content, such as carpentry supplies and intermediate products for the furniture industry. Many of these restructuring measures were unpopular with farmer and worker members alike. Farmers complained of being marginalized by the cooperative's policies; workers objected to additional obligatory capital contributions requested to finance the changes.

An Exclusive Claim to Rationality

Claiming that its own analysis alone was rational, LANA's management dismissed the credibility of its internal opposition and maintained that its diagnosis and prescription for the cooperative were the only ones possible. In 1983, for example, LANA's management responded to internal criticism of a pricing plan for raw milk based on quality and quantity. "The decision that was made is practically irreversible. It should be considered a great advance for all to adapt ourselves to more rational production systems that contemplate the possibilities of the market" (LANA General Assembly 1983). This invocation of rationality diverts attention from the advantages and disadvantages of specific policies. In the above case, for example, it does not leave space for considering other possible ways of organizing a pricing plan that might potentially be both rational and responsive to the market. Instead, discussion is limited to whether or not to be rational and whether or not to operate in a market economy.

Its association of rationality with the market led LANA's management to greet the 1984 departure of most of the small-scale farmer members with satisfaction. "We must keep in mind that this has been an event that reflects the advance of technology and order and business logic, [that] will determine in general the agrarian sector of our [Basque] country" (LANA, Plan de Gestión 1984, 4). Not only was this event inevitable, according to this view, it was rational that it occurred. The management's association of rationality with the unrestrained operation of the market, nevertheless, had historically been inconsistent. The windfall doubling of pine timber prices in the early seventies, for example, helped pay for LANA's new central offices in Oñate (Amunarriz 1975). Yet the management would later decry pine timber price increases as "irrational," once LANA found itself more dependent on activities with greater value added and unable to easily transfer raw material cost increases to sales prices (LANA General Assembly 1988, 26).

Conclusion

The efforts of LANA's management and its CLP advisors to reconceptualize Basque agrarian production steadily transformed the original service organization, which had sought to provide secure, fair market access to farmers and secure jobs with good conditions to workers. The preoccupation with control, seen as the basis of efficient, industrial-style processing, led the cooperative's management to see member farms as but one more link in a business chain from production to marketing, a link to be dealt with mainly through price mechanisms. The emphasis on full-time, specialized professionalism encouraged the rejection of diversified, noncapital intensive dairy and timber production, and by extension, precluded the continued participation of the majority of farmer members of the cooperative. The emphasis on the firm's interest as the synthesis of conflicting internal interests encouraged the perception of LANA as a firm to which raw material and labor inputs were supplied rather than as a cooperative serving the needs of members. The agrarian industrial ideal's association of rationality with the operation of the market assumed that the management's policies represented the only possible means for LANA to survive. Yet ironically, these policies may have actually undermined the firm's resilience. The premature closure on debate helped deny an effective public voice to internal dissent that would have encouraged serious discussion of LANA's development trajectory and the exploration of alternatives that might have been profitable and acceptable to a wider range of participants.

By the mid-eighties, LANA's purpose as an organization had been formally changed to reflect what had become its practice. The cooperative's original by-laws had called for an increase in agricultural and animal production in the rural Basque region. This original statement of purpose, in the view of LANA's management, reflected the time in which it was written but failed to consider the importance of the firm's profitability and permanence (LANA 1981b). The new bylaws after 1986 called for an increase "in *profitability* [emphasis added] and of agricultural, animal and timber production" (LANA 1986b). One LANA executive summed up the management's judgment of LANA's past and its expectations for the future: "The small *casero,* normally an old *casero* whose children work in industry, has no future. There is no one there with the desire to modernize and develop. It is very clear that the cooperative will not, either now or in the future, support this type of agricultural member–because there is no future. The small farmer is going to disappear. A firm like ours cannot base itself on so fragile a base. Supporting the small farmer–that is not efficient" (quoted in Van der Broek and Van der Schoot 1983, 44).

The persuasive power of the management's use of terms like rationality and efficiency rested on its assumption that only one authoritative reading of the market's dictates was possible. Leaving aside the thorny issue of whether the market itself operates in a rational matter (see Friedland and Robertson 1990; Granovetter 1992; M. Taylor 1989), this essay has argued that the management's analysis was embedded in a particular set of objectives and means provided by its agrarian industrial ideal. This ideal gave greatest priority to the pursuit of the firm's interests as a goal, albeit one believed to be in the interests of participants perceived to be legitimate. It assumed that proper means included a particular kind of professionalism and centralized control.

The issue of whether this was the only possible interpretation of LANA's structural situation needs to be addressed on two fronts. First, was the management's approach actually unambiguously rational and efficient, even on its own terms? LANA's experience in the late eighties suggests that its transformation may have come at the cost of sacrificing much of the value added that was contributed by a cooperative form of organization. In 1988, LANA's management requested another obligatory capital contribution, arguing forcefully that the very survival of the cooperative was at stake. The cooperative's 214 active members were now almost evenly divided between farmer and worker members, and most of the small-scale farmers had departed. Yet in general assembly, the measure failed to gain even the necessary simple majority required since the 1986 by-law changes. This impasse suggests that in a firm such as LANA, heavily dependent on a social base of support, rational and efficient management would do well to include more than the balance sheet in its calculations. A broader understanding of efficiency in LANA might have encouraged concessions to internal groups, which, though sacrificing a measure of short-term profit, could have ensured adequate support in a genuine financial crisis. Instead, the management's exclusive approach to policy-making may well have diminished LANA's capacity to face threats to its survival.

Second, were LANA's small farmers incapable of making their own rational interpretation of their own and the firm's situations? The nature of economic rationality continues to be widely debated today in economic anthropology (Dalton 1968; Plattner 1989) and economic sociology (Granovetter 1990; Swedberg, Himmelstrand, and Brulin 1990). Regardless of whether one sees rationality as a formal (undersocialized) or substantive (oversocialized) phenomenon, researchers have plausibly demonstrated that peasant behavior is patterned and is based on a reasoned analysis of interests, whether those be individual or communal, political, cultural, or economic. The LANA members' rejection of attempts to restructure their operations or to reduce their autonomy was not necessarily irrational. These small farmers originally formed the cooperative in an attempt to save their diversified farms through gaining secure access to markets and technical services. They gradually became convinced that the cooperative failed them on both counts. Pricing policies subordinated the farmers' interests to those of the industrial manufacturing process. Technical extension was oriented toward convincing farmers to abandon the very way of life they wished to preserve.

The issue arises, of course, of whether the farmers could have interpreted LANA's structural situation according to their own terms and still have maintained the cooperative as a viable economic unit. As unfortunate as LANA's turn away from its small-scale farmers was, was it not inevitable, given the state of the Basque agrarian sector and its insertion into a larger framework of global economic restructuring? The crux of the CLP's analysis appeared to be that the fate of the Basque *caserío* rested solely on the question of its efficiency. Yet the fate of the peasant and the family farm has long been debated without a definitive conclusion (Buttel 1983; Chayanov 1986; Friedmann 1986; Kautsky [1899] 1988). Davydd Greenwood found that the abandonment of the Basque *caserío* is not necessarily a result of its alleged inefficiency but is associated with a complex of cultural factors (Greenwood 1976). Ironically, the bank's own analysis of efficiency also drew on a cultural and social analysis. But its analysis was based on an ideal of the Basque small-scale farmer, sharply contrasted with an equally ideal agrarian industrial firm. According to the bank, the *casero* was rooted in a stagnant past, incapable of progress and furthermore, incapable even of reasoned analysis. This analysis of the small farmer's social and cultural context may well have underestimated the *caserío*'s resilience and ability to transform itself in unexpected ways.

Etxezarreta, for example, argues that doomsayers do not adequately appreciate the unpredictable consequences of the *caseríos'* insertion into an industrial and urban context: "It is not the same to predict the future of agriculture in a little industrialized region and where the land has no alternatives other than agrarian use, as it is to signal the probable transformation of the sector in a zone of intense industrialization that provides an important market for land with flourishing expectations and provides industrial employment to the owners, without their having to contemplate migration" (Etxezarreta 1979, 85).

What is clear is that in LANA, alternatives for the small farmer were not seriously sought after. Alternatives for small farmers pursued with significant success elsewhere in Spain (Taylor 1989) have included intensive greenhouse agriculture, intensive poultry, pig or beef production (often in collaboration with grain cooperatives) or spun-off and scaled-down marketing and insurance activities. The Mondragón agrarian group EREIN itself, of which LANA was a member, came to encompass beef cattle fattening, calf-raising, greenhouse vegetable, and other agrarian cooperative ventures, all organized from the top down, according to the agrarian industrial ideal, and some originating under the organizational aegis of LANA itself. In addition, accepting the reality of part-time agrarian production on the Basque family farm (Etxezarreta et al. 1983) rather than dismissing it, might have constituted one step toward developing profitable activities appropriate for existing LANA members. Instead, one member of the CLP's staff summed up LANA's principle development criteria: "It is a question of marketing. . . . If the people are said to need cheese, then we will look for producers to deliver us the milk we need. A consequence of that conception is that industrial interests are going to prevail a little more" (Van der Broek and Van der Schoot 1983, 50).

A rhetorical strategy based on an idealized image of the cooperative as an agrarian industry, modeled closely on its urban counterpart, precluded a discussion of LANA's development trajectory that might have promoted a more even balance among the interests of existing participants. Rather, the ideal's departure from a market demand priority, rooted in idealist visions of the competitive, rationally managed firm and of the stagnant, conservative, irrational peasant, limited the terms of debate and narrowed the range of possible responses to LANA's need to survive as a firm. In so doing, LANA may have transformed itself into a streamlined agrarian firm capable of competing in its chosen economic sectors. But it may well have done so at the cost of sacrificing its commitment to the original ideal of the Mondragón industrial cooperatives of putting "the human being at the center of production" (FAGOR Central Social Council 1988).

NOTES

1. The Alto Deva is the district in which Mondragón is located.

2. This ambivalence with a one person-one vote system is not merely the artifact of LANA's internal politics but also existed elsewhere in the Mondragón cooperative complex. Indeed, Mondragón's one person–one vote system was instituted in the early seventies in order to comply with changes in Spanish cooperative law. A "qualified voting system" had previously provided for members to exercise one to three votes, depending on the nature of their jobs (Copreci General Assembly 1972).

REFERENCES

Abercrombie, Nichlas, Stephen Hill, and Bryan S. Turner. 1980. *The Dominant Ideology Thesis.* London: George Allen & Unwin.

Altmann, Norbert, Manfried Deiss, Volrer Dohl, and Dicter Sauer. 1991. "The 'New Rationalization'—New Demands on Industrial Sociology." *International Journal of Political Economy* (winter): 42–60.

Amunarriz, José Ramón. 1975. *Agriculture associative en Guipúzcoa et en Nararre.* Paris: Centre de Recherches Cooperatives, Ecole de Hautes Etudes en Sciences Sociales.

Biggart, Nicole Woolsey. 1991. "Explaining Asian Economic Organization. Toward a Weberian Institutional Perspective." *Theory and Society* 20 (2): 201–32.

Block, Fred L. 1990. *Postindustrial Possibilities: A Critique of Economic Discourse.* Berkeley: University of California Press.

Booth, David. 1985. "Marxism and Development Sociology: Interpreting the Impasse." *World Development* 13 (7): 761–87.

Burke, Kenneth. 1969. *A Rhetoric of Motives.* Berkeley: University of California Press.

Buttel, Frederick H. 1983. "Beyond the Family Farm." In *Technology and Rural Social Change,* ed. Gene F. Summers, 87–107. Boulder, Colo.: Westview Press.

Cadenas, Alfredo, and Antonio Fernández. 1988. "La internacionalización del sector agroalimentario español durante la década 1975–1985: Una aproximación temática y factual." *Agricultura y Sociedad* 49.

Caja Laboral Popular. 1975. *Los Caseríos de la Cuenca del Deva. Análisis Socio-económico. Mondragón, Spain: CLP* Dept. Desarrollo Regional, mimeo.

———. 1977. *Sondeo del sector de la alimentación. Tomo II: Hacia una política de actuación de CLP.* Mondragón, Spain: CLP, mimeo.

———. 1983. *La promoción del empleo y Caja Laboral Popular.* Mondragón, Spain: CLP, mimeo.

———. 1984, *Memoria de las actividades de producción agroalimentaria en el grupo cooperativo asociado a Caja Laboral Popular y sus expectativas ante el ingreso del estado español en la C.E.E.* Mondragón, Spain: CLP, mimeo.

———. 1985. *Actuación de CLP en el sector rural.* Mondragón, Spain: CLP, mimeo.

———. 1987. *Criterios para fijar una política de promoción en el sector agroalimentario.* Mondragón, Spain: Area de Promoción Agroalimentario, CLP, mimeo.

Chayanov, A. V. 1986. *The Theory of Peasant Economy.* Madison: University of Wisconsin Press.

Copreci, S. Coop. Various years. *Copreci General Assembly Minutes.* Aretxabaleta, Spain: Copreci, mimeo.

Corbridge, Stuart. 1990. "Post-Marxism and Development Studies: Beyond the Impasse." *World Development* 18 (5): 623–39.

Dalton, George. 1968. "Economic Theory and Primitive Society." In *Economic Anthropology: Readings in Theory and Analysis,* ed. Edward E. LeClair Jr. and Harold K. Schneider, 143–67. New York: Holt, Rinehart and Winston.

Daly, Glyn. 1991. "The Discursive Construction of Economic Space: Logics of Organization and Disorganization." *Economy and Society* 20 (1): 79–102.

DiMaggio, Paul. 1990. "Cultural Aspects of Economic Action and Organization." In *Beyond the Marketplace. Rethinking Economy and Society,* ed. Roger Friedland and A. F. Robertson, 113–36. New York: Aldine de Gruyter.

Etxezarreta, Miren. 1977. *El caserío vasco.* Bilbao, Spain: Fundación C. de Iturriaga y M. de Dañobeitia.

———. 1979. "La crisis del caserío." *SAIOK* 111 (3): 58–87.

Etxezarreta, Miren, and Lourdes Viladomiu. 1989. "The restructuring of Spanish Agriculture, and Spain's Accession to the EEC." In *The International Farm Crisis,* ed. David Goodman and Michael Redclift, 156–82. Hong Kong: Macmillan.

Etxezarreta, Miren, et al. 1983. *La agricultura insuficiente: La agricultura a tiempo parcial en España.* San Sebastián, Spain: Instituto de Estudios Agrarios, Pesqueros y Alimentarios.

Etzioni, Amitai. 1988. *The Moral Dimension: Toward a New Economics.* New York: Free Press.

FAGOR Central Social Council. 1988. *Declaración de principios*. Mondragón, Spain: mimeo.

Friedland, Roger, and A. F. Robertson. 1990. "Beyond the Marketplace." In *Beyond the Marketplace: Rethinking Economy and Society, ed.* Roger Friedland and A. F. Robertson, 3–49. New York: Aldine de Gruyter.

Friedmann, Harriet. 1986. "Patriarchy and Property: A Reply to Goodman and Redclift." *Sociologia Ruralis* 26 (2): 186–93.

Friedrich, Paul. 1989. "Language, Ideology and Political Economy." *American Anthropologist* 91 (2): 295–312.

Gaudier, Maryse. 1988. "Workers' Participation within the New Industrial Order: A Review of Literature." *Labour and Society* 13: 313–30.

Granovetter, Mark. 1990. "The Old and the New Economic Sociology: A History and an Agenda." In *Beyond the Marketplace. Rethinking Economy and Society,* ed. Roger Friedland and A. F. Robertson, 89–111. New York: Aldine de Gruyter.

———. 1992. "Economic Institutions as Social Constructions: A Framework for Analysis." *Acta Sociologica* 35: 3–11.

Greenwood, Davydd. 1976. *Unrewarding Wealth: the Commercialization and Collapse of Agriculture in a Spanish Basque Town*. London: Cambridge University Press.

Greenwood, Davydd J., and José Luis González-Santos. 1991. *Industrial Democracy as Process: Participatory Action Research in the FAGOR Cooperative Group of Mondragón*. Stockholm: Van Gorcum, Assen/Maastricht.

Gusfield, Joseph R. 1981. The Culture of Public Problems: Drinking-Driving and the Symbolic Order. Chicago: University of Chicago Press.

———, ed. 1989. *Kenneth Burke: On Symbols and Society*. Chicago: University of Chicago Press.

Kautsky, Karl. [1899] 1988. *The Agrarian Question*. London/Winchester: Zwan.

LANA, S. Coop. 1973. *Boletín informativo*. Oñate, Spain: LANA, mimeo.

———. 1980. *Egoera Orokorraren Asterketaren Ikuspegia. Síntesis del diagnóstico de situación general.* Iraila, Spain: LANA, mimeo.

———. 1981a. *Conclusiones del tema: Organización medios humanos*. Mondragón, Spain: LANA, mimeo.

———. 1981b. *Organización de los organos de dirección y sociales*. Mondragón, Spain: LANA, mimeo.

———. 1986a. *Epe Luzera Plana. Plan a largo plazo, 1986–1990*. Mondragón, Spain: LANA, mimeo.

———. 1986b. *Proyecto de estatutos sociales tipo de la cooperative LANA.* Mondragón, Spain: LANA, mimeo.

———. Various years. *LANA General Assembly Minutes.* Oñate, Spain: LANA, mimeo.

———. Various years. *Plan de gestión.* Oñate, Spain: LANA, mimeo.

———. n.d. Untitled internal document. Oñate, Spain: LANA, mimeo.

Mauleón Gómez, José Ramón. 1989. "Los cambios de la explotación familiar según el tipo de familia: Explotaciones de leche en el país vasco." *Agricultura y Sociedad* 52: 99.

Plattner, Stuart, ed. 1989. *Economic Anthropology.* Stanford: Stanford University Press.

Robertson, Roland. 1988. "The Sociological Significance of Culture: Some General Considerations." *Theory, Culture and Society* 5: 3–23.

SUSTRAI. n.d. " 'LANA' Koperatiba-Taldea Hedatza-Aldian." *SUSTRAI* 3: 58–60.

Swedberg, Richard, Ulf Himmelstrand, and Goran Brulin. 1990. "The Paradigm of Economic Sociology." In *Structures of Capital: The Social Organization of the Economy,* ed. Sharon Zukin and Paul DiMaggio, 57–86. Cambridge, England: Cambridge University Press.

Swidler, Ann. 1986. "Culture in Action: Symbols and Strategies." *American Sociological Review* 51: 273–86.

Taylor, Michael. 1989. "Structure, Culture and Action in the Explanation of Social Change." *Politics and Society* 17 (2): 115–62.

Taylor, Peter Leigh. 1989. Estudio sociologico de COPAGA. Report prepared for COPAGA, S. Coop, Lérida, Spain.

———. 1991. "Rhetoric, Restructuring and Economic Democracy in Three Spanish Production Cooperatives." Ph.D. diss., Cornell University.

Van der Broek, Hanspeter, and Tejo Van der Schoot. 1983. *LANA: Entre el caserío y la calle.* Mondragón, Spain: mimeo.

Vandergeest, Peter, and Frederick H. Buttel. 1988. "Marx, Weber, and Development Sociology: Beyond the Impasse." *World Development* 16 (6): 683–95.

Whyte, William Foote, and Kathleen King Whyte. 1991. *Making Mondragón: The Growth and Dynamics of the Worker Cooperative Complex.* Ithaca, N.Y.: ILR Press.

Part II

People In and Out of Nature

4

In the Name of Nature: Ecology, Marginality, and Rural Land Use Planning During the New Deal

E. Melanie DuPuis

The 1930s saw the introduction of ecological concepts into U.S. public policy discussions concerning rural land use. A new group of thinkers, in particular Aldo Leopold, argued cogently that humans should live in harmony with, not in control of, nature. The idea that nature, acting through its potentials and constraints, had a role to play in the formation of society quickly became part of public debate concerning the use of natural resources. Environmental historians have treated the advent of policy in the name of nature as a sign of public enlightenment (Nash 1982; Terrie 1985; Merchant 1989; Worster 1977). These historians treat environmentalism as a reaction to the urbanization and industrialization of society. What they often ignore is the fact that the environmental movement was itself a product of, and gained its predominant support from, urban industrial political interests.

As Samuel Hays noted over thirty years ago, "The moral language of conservation battles differed markedly from the course of conservation events" (Hays 1959, 1). This chapter shows that this difference between "language" and "event" has been substantially bound up in the intimate relationship between the growth of ecological thinking and the urbanization of U.S. society. New Deal land use conservation planners found their main basis of support in rapidly expanding urban populations. They quickly took up the idea of ecology in their justification of increasingly interventionist government policies dealing with rural land resources. This intimate relationship led to a skewing of the idea of ecology as it was used to justify rural land use and conservation planning policies. In the name of saving nature, rural land use planning policies intensified the agricultural use of land and separated the rural landscape into agriculturally "modernizable" land, and land to be reforested and preserved as recreational areas or wilderness.

Many historians have described the earlier, nineteenth century, viewpoint on human–nature relationships, specifically the agrarian ideal that humans should eliminate wilderness and cultivate the landscape to the greatest possible extent (Marx 1964; Nash 1982; Terrie 1985). From this cultural point of view, the individual was morally responsible for developing and utilizing resources for society. Misuse of resources was therefore an individual responsibility. The cultural concept of personal moral responsibility, when applied to natural resources, meant that land owners were morally responsible to use their ingenuity to discover the best way to use their own resources. In the small-scale rural societies of the eigthteenth and early nineteeth centuries, the agrarian ideal was the most commonly accepted form of understanding nature (Marx 1964).

Nevertheless, the agrarian concept of individual moral responsibility could not provide answers for New Yorkers who were concerned about decades of aggressive timber harvest that had left areas such as the Adirondacks open to fire and watershed damage. Historians have described the evolution of attitudes that led to the creation of a forest preserve in the Adirondacks (Nash 1982; Terrie 1985). Nash argues that environmentalists, in order to gain support for the creation of a park, took advantage of the common perception that loss of Adirondack timberland would dry up the Erie Canal and other navigable waterways. Yet, whether the intention was preservation of wilderness or preservation of watershed, historical accounts indicate that the source of support for the creation of the Adirondack Park was primarily urban (see Nash 1982, 116–21). Even the common explanation for the need to preserve wilderness had urbanization at its source: wilderness would serve as a retreat from "trials, tribulations and annoyances of business and every-day life in the man-made towns," as New York City attorney David McClure stated at the 1894 New York State Constitutional Convention, arguing in favor of the amendment that guaranteed permanent protection of the Adirondacks (Nash 1982, 120). At the century's turn, John Muir had touted the idea of preserving wilderness to function as a respite from civilization. The move to a collective form of response therefore provided a way for urban people to intervene in rural land use issues. However, urban people experienced rural areas primarily as visitors to the wilderness, as viewers of the landscape, and as consumers of its agricultural produce. Rural land use and conservation policies therefore revolved increasingly around meeting urban expectations based on their experience. In this scenario, urban people turned to collective action through governments, that, in turn, claimed responsibility for mediating the human–nature relationship.

Of course, urban environmental constituencies were themselves the product of a growing mass-production economy. Therefore, while both Leopold and Muir were farmer's sons, public discourse about the environment grew up in an urban, industrial social context. Rural land use planning policies were a product of this intimate relationship, and this ultimate contradiction, between environmentalism and urbanization. As a result, policies to "save" nature were based primarily in the urban experience of nature—as visitor and consumer.

The effect of this contradiction was rural land use policies that actually promoted the growth of intensive industrial dairying in New York State and the demise of a less intensive, and perhaps more sustainable, form of dairy agriculture. As this chapter shows, policies implemented in the name of nature in fact promoted the transformation of New York agriculture into an intensive industrial system by separating land into land that was modernizable—capable of being intensively used—and land that was slated for reforestation as wilderness.

New York State as Metaphor

The history of New York State land use policy typifies the contradictions described above. New York State was at the forefront of the social and conceptual changes that accompanied urban, industrial society. Yet the state was also substantially agricultural—it is still the third largest producer of milk products in the nation. New York had at an early point experienced the ravages of intensive logging operations, watershed destruction, soil erosion and farm abandonment. As a consequence, New York was one of the first states to implement policies to conserve wilderness land—beginning with the creation of the Adirondack Park in the 1880s—and to plan the use and conservation of rural land (Terrie 1985; Nash 1982). New York was also one of the first states to implement agricultural policies in the context of, and with the political support of, a growing, powerful, urban constituency (Colman 1963; DuPuis 1993).[1] For these reasons, the political and social changes happening in that state were precursors to what would quickly happen in the nation as a whole, particularly when the governor of New York became the president of the nation. Many of the rural land use and conservation policies developed in New York State became the blueprint for FDR's national programs (Slichter 1959) and, later, for post-war international rural land use programs (Gilbert 1993).

Franklin D. Roosevelt's own career reflected this transitory period. In his political campaigns, Roosevelt represented himself as an upstate gentleman farmer—despite his full membership in the New York urban elite—and ran for office as a reformer, despite grudging support from that target of reform: Tammany Hall (Ellis et al. 1957). Following the legacy of his cousin, Theodore Roosevelt, and as an avid forester on his own Hyde Park estate, Roosevelt was for several decades the state's major proponent of conservation, particularly reforestation, and rural land use planning. Rural land use/land conservation planning established itself as a professional pursuit under Roosevelt's gubernatorial and presidential administrations (Gates 1960). In addition, as many historians have noted, Roosevelt used his experience as governor of New York State to experiment on many different social programs, including rural land use policies, which later became a part of the New Deal (Slichter 1959; Ellis et al. 1967).

FDR spoke about "the land problem" and his proposed solutions from the time when he was a senator in the New York State legislature in the 1910s through his New Deal presidency. Following Roosevelt's speeches and policies throughout this period therefore provides an unique opportunity to follow changes in public perception concerning the role of government intervention in human–nature relationships, the decline in the agrarian viewpoint, and the growth of the use of ecological rhetoric to justify government intervention.

The first two sections of this chapter draw on speeches and letters by Roosevelt between 1912 and 1937, examining the transformation of his rhetoric—from agrarian to ecological—during this period. These sections also draw on contemporary state and federal reports on land use planning, reforestation, and submarginal farm policies. The examples document how government experts used ecological rhetoric to justify a particular form of rural land use and conservation planning that involved classifying land according to ideal uses and restructuring the rural landscape into land either appropriate for modern industrial agriculture or land that was unmodernizable and therefore to be reforested into wilderness areas.[2]

The third section examines the nature of rural resource struggles in New York State during this period and shows how the birth of an ecological narrative—and the death of a moral agrarian narrative—emerged with the development of a new constellation of urban-based political interests. The final section examines the consequences of this change in policy and ideology and assesses whether these policies fulfilled the concept of ecology as expounded by the period's foremost environmental thinker, Aldo Leopold.

Agrarian Moral Ingenuity and Rural Repopulation Policy

As environmental historians have noted, the idea of environmental "conservation" of wilderness did not exist until the end of the nineteenth century. The public ideal was a "middle landscape," neither wild nor urban, cultivated by human ingenuity and effort (Terrie 1985; Nash 1982; Marx 1964). The public discussion of the use of Adirondack land in the nineteenth century is a prime example of this attitude. Even the Adirondack High Peaks were explored with the intention that they would eventually come under cultivation (Terrie 1985; see also Jacobs 1989). At this time, the prevailing public view remained that most land, no matter how steep or rocky, should be settled and that it was the responsibility of the settler to figure out the best way to gain a living from that land. "Wherever it was found, wilderness implicitly condemned the slack spirit of the few settlers in the neighborhood. Any American landscape unadorned by the cottages, neatly tilled fields, and well-tended livestock of an agricultural population was simply incomplete" (Terrie 1985, 24). At the national level, the nineteenth-century public view held that public ownership of land would eventually die out as the last of the frontier was finally sold and put to private use (Gates 1976).

Not until the 1880s do public accounts note that Adirondack farmers might find it hard to eke out a living in that terrain, no matter what ingenuity they possessed. During this time period, it is important to note, New York was the most successful agricultural state in the nation (Gates 1960; Jacobs 1989). The extent and dispersion of the state's population and agricultural activity at the time was part of this success. A quarter of a million farmsteads occupied nearly 24 million acres of land. Therefore, despite some concerns about problems of cultivating areas with very poor soil resources, the successful land use model involved an increasingly dispersed pattern of settlement, and the accompanying agrarian ideal of personal ingenuity, effort, and moral duty. The moral duty was to perpetuate the increased expansion of human intervention in nature—to turn the wilderness into garden (Nash 1982; Marx 1964).

By the end of the nineteenth century, a new pattern of settlement had begun, involving increased urbanization of the state's population. Farm abandonment became a serious concern for the state's political leaders (Jacobs 1989). Nevertheless, early solutions to what was known as "the land problem" remained wedded to the idea of increasingly dispersed forms of settlement and agrarian moralist forms of responsibility. The attitude toward exhausted or eroded land echoed this view; poor agricultural results continued to be blamed on the individual farmer, not on an individual farm's resources.

Franklin Roosevelt's early speeches reflect this agrarian moral viewpoint. Roosevelt's early correspondence as a state senator indicate a public expectation that he would continue his cousin Theodore Roosevelt's interest in environmental conservation issues (Nixon 1957). In one of his earliest public speeches (1912), FDR addressed "the land problem," placing the responsibility for these problems squarely on the shoulders of farmers: "The owners of 50 or 100 years ago took from the soil without returning any equivalent to the soil" (Nixon 1957, 19). While diplomatically referring only to past generations of farmers, Roosevelt condemned this group for being selfish, taking from nature without making a return. Farmers had not only injured the land, they had also injured the entire state community by abusing the land: "Today the people in the cities and the people on the farms are suffering because the early farmers gave no thought to the liberty of the community" (Nixon 1957, 19). Farmers, through their selfishness, had deprived others of their freedom. This was a serious charge.

While Roosevelt presented himself as a rural "upstate" politician, in fact, the condemnation of farmers reflects a prevalent urban viewpoint of that time. Between World War I and the 1920s, food prices rose rapidly (Cochrane 1979). Urban consumers were angry about these rising prices and blamed farmers for not growing enough food. For example, New York dairy farmers were under constant pressure at the time to either provide more milk or to allow more milk to come in from out of state (Spencer and Blanford 1977). The "land problem" was therefore part of a broader context in which food supply was not keeping up with a growing urban population. Roosevelt's indictment of farmers accuses them of failing, morally, the rest of society because of their inadequate handling of their lands. The farmers simply "gave no thought" to their moral duty of proper cultivation. Their responsibility, therefore, was to think correctly, to use their personal ingenuity, and to discover the proper way to utilize these lands.

Reflecting this belief, Roosevelt's proposed solutions to the land problem at that time involved, first, the redemption of farmers into careful, thoughtful tillers of the land and, second, the repopulation of abandoned farm areas by farmers willing to work hard enough to make these farms "pay." For example, in response to a letter portraying the seriousness of the land problem, Roosevelt argued for government policies that encouraged the settlement of foreign farmers on these lands, noting, "In my own County of Dutchess, for instance, a good many foreigners have come in in the past few years and have taken up small holdings or abandoned farms, and by intensive cultivation and hard work have made good" (Nixon 1957, 44). He referred often to a farmer's responsibility to maintain soil fertility. Hard-working foreigners, such as those solving labor scarcity problems in factories at that time, were envisioned as the people who would also provide the effort necessary to make these lands produce.[3]

The Ecological Idea of Natural Harmony and the Policy of "Planned Abandonment"

By the 1930s, the attitude toward rural land use problems had changed. From the turn of the century, a few groups, such as the Country Life Commission chaired by Cornell Dean Liberty Hyde Bailey, began to note that some plots of land did not offer a good living no matter how hard a farmer worked or what form of cultivation he or she pursued (Jacobs 1989). By the early twentieth century, the public understood that rocky upland areas, such as the Adirondack High Peaks region, would never be cultivated. As the rates of farm abandonment rose in the 1910s, people began to realize that some of this land was never meant to be cultivated in the first place. Support for repopulation of abandoned farm lands waned, replaced by a more laissez-faire approach.

The mid-1920s, however, marked a turning point in rural land planning in New York State, toward more state intervention in rural land use (Jacobs 1989). New York State farm prices had begun a precipitous decline, particularly in comparison with factory wages, which continued to rise (Slichter 1959). In 1926, the New York State Commission on Housing and Regional Planning also released a regional plan for New York State, the first statewide regional plan in the United States (Jacobs 1989). This plan advocated direct state involvement in the "planned abandonment" of what planners referred to as "marginal or submarginal" rural land (Jacobs 1989). The plan recommended that the state take upon itself the role of determining which land was suitable for permanent cultivation and which land should be taken out of cultivation, purchased with public funds and reforested. That same year, the board of directors of the Chenango County Farm Bureau asked the College of Agriculture at Cornell to study the farm abandonment problem in one of the county's townships. The result of that study was the first detailed land classification map in the country, a mapping process that eventually covered all the agricultural counties in the state.[4] The goal of these maps was to "rate the land according to its agricultural possibilities, to classify the roads in its vicinity and to determine where electrical lines should be located to serve the farms remaining in these areas" (Ladd 1932, 306).

Roosevelt and the New York State Legislature put the purchasing power of the state behind an effort to make the classification of uses recommended in the maps a reality. The Hewitt amendment appropriated over $1 million, and scheduled the appropriation of more funds for the purchase of land classified as "submarginal" (Jacobs 1989). While Roosevelt's speeches continued to reflect a re-populationist bent, historian Gertrude Slichter has demonstrated that the policy machinery necessary for Roosevelt's proposal to resettle families on abandoned farms did not exist, while the state financial and administrative resources to classify and reforest submarginal lands were plentiful. She argues that this difference between rhetoric and policy on repopulation continued in Roosevelt's national administration (Slichter 1959).

In fact, Roosevelt's rhetoric began to change in a subtle but important way once he gained national office. His speeches on land use problems no longer emphasized individual moral blame for land use problems. Instead, Roosevelt began to evoke ideas of natural harmony to explain the problem. For example, in a 1931 speech shortly after his election as president, he states: "The green slopes of our forested hills lured our first settlers and furnished the materials of a happy life. They and their descendants were a little careless with that asset. Those who found abundance in New York State were no different from the rest. Now we have great barren areas where productive forests once stood" (in Nixon 1957, 87). While continuing to receive some blame for land conservation problems, Roosevelt no longer accused farmers of being thoughtless or irresponsible, only "a little careless." Roosevelt also softens the blame by noting that New York's farmers were no different from many others who were "lured" into thinking that the nation's resources were infinite.[5] Rather than deride them as thoughtless individuals, Roosevelt portrays settlers as misguided by the pure abundance of the state's resources. In the conceptualized human–nature relationship behind Roosevelt's rhetoric, nature had begun to play a role.

Although Roosevelt now absolved the farmer of individual blame, the farmer was also no longer part of the solution. It was no longer individual moral ingenuity but government land use experts who had become responsible for the solution to the land problem. The speech presented two alternative forms of land use in submarginal farm areas: "productive forests" and the hill farmer. This comparison implied that the hill farmer was the less productive alternative.

By the mid-Depression years, "blame" for conservation problems had entirely disappeared from Roosevelt's speeches. The reports coming out of his land planning agency, the National Resource Planning Board (NRPB), no longer mentioned careless farmers in their description of eroded land. Instead they focused on the condition of these lands and the lives of people who lived on them. According to the major NRPB report on rural land problems, "the decline of rural civilization" was due to "pathological modes of [land] use" (NRPB 1934b, 181). This "maladjustment" in land use had led to a "socially degraded existence" for the occupants of these lands "as a result of their inadequate income, poor schools and roads, and infrequent contacts with outside civilization" (NRPB 1934a:182). The solution, according to these New Deal planners, was the "rehabilitation" of families by moving them off of these poor lands (NRPB 1934b, 183).

The idea that "the land problem" was a pathology—and that land use planning was the cure—was echoed frequently in public documents on the issue during this period. For example, one article on the benefits of land utilization studies stated that submarginal areas "make government expensive and inefficient, encouraging poor schools, bad roads, remote and feeble government, and low levels of community life" (Gee 1934, 357). If land use were planned in the light of land classification studies, "areas of sparse settlement, and low taxable wealth values would not be allowed" (Gee 1934, 357). Government land use planning officials made the diagnosis that the relationship between humans and the environment was diseased and that the government, as doctor, needed to provide the cure.

For example, a 1935 New York State Planning Board report presented the state not only as healer but as protector. Entitled *Submarginal Farm Lands in New York State,* it portrayed farmers in poorer soil areas as victims of shady land speculators. According to the report, most of the residents of these farms were people who had been tricked into buying land that could not produce and who were therefore trapped in lives of grim poverty because they could not sell their land. Selling the farm to another, however, did not solve the problem, because it left "another family marooned on the island of want" (Lane 1935, 13). By purchasing the land, the state would both "rehabilitate" people who had made this mistake and protect other people from repeating this process. Like the national report, the New York State report recommended the "rehabilitation" of these families through resettlement.

The report seldom mentions farm practices. Rather, it states that "large areas of the state are not contributing adequately to its welfare" (Lane 1935, iii), thereby focusing blame on the land itself rather than on the farmer. Space itself had become the "noncommunitarian" factor, and the farmer simply a passive victim of the land. In fact, marginal farmers in this report are seldom referred to as farmers at all, but as "persons who did reside in the poorer agricultural lands" (Lane 1935, iii).[6]

This reallocation of blame also shifted the identity of marginal land inhabitants from farmer to victim and shifted policy from repopulation to removal. Under the agrarian ideal, the inhabitants of these lands were farmers, whose responsibility it was to change their farm practices. Yet, from the planners' ecological perspective, these people were simply the victims of poor land resources, and the speculators who sold the land to them. Therefore, the only solution was to reverse the situation by removing people from the land.

According to these reports and speeches, the pathology exhibited in these cases was an inability to obtain a "modern" standard of living (NYSPB 1935). To New York State land planners, marginal farm lands were an "island," a remote and inaccessible place where people were trapped away from the "mainland" of modern life. Therefore, the only way to rehabilitate these people was to remove them from the land.

Like the New York State Planning Board report, the National Resources Planning Board report on rural land use planning, along with other federal land planning documents, spoke often of resettling families on better land, or into resettlement projects. In fact, very few families were actually resettled on better agricultural land (Clawson 1981), which indicates that the rhetoric of "rehabilitation" was less important to New Deal planners than the goal of restructuring rural land use.

Ecology

Historians generally trace the birth of ecology as a concept to Aldo Leopold's writings on human–nature relationships in the 1920s. Nash (1982) refers to him as the "prophet" of the ecological viewpoint. Leopold's lifework on the relationship between humans and nature eventually evolved into a concept he called "the land ethic."[7] Disagreeing with certain professional conservation practices in the field, such as the shooting of wolves, Leopold argued that the conservationist's ethical role was to work with nature rather than control it. In his writings, Leopold describes the core of the ecological ideal: that humans must adapt to natural systems and should allow wilderness to exist on its own terms.

Leopold's idea of a "land ethic" in fact combines the agrarian and ecological points of view: personal morality is still the essential factor, but the ethical standard has changed from exploitation to adaptation. Leopold was extremely ambivalent about the efficacy of state intervention in the relationship between humans and nature (Meine 1988). He advocated state intervention only when absolutely necessary. It is important to point out, however, that Leopold first developed his viewpoint while serving as a government conservation official. He began developing these concepts as a state forester and, later, as a professor at the University of Wisconsin, a state land-grant school. Therefore, Leopold's own social position involved a connection, and contradiction, between the natural view and the national view.

As Roderick Nash documents in his book *Wilderness and the American Mind* (1982), the ideas of ecology and of conservation ethics quickly took hold of public discourse on land conservation policy. However, there is a vast difference between Leopold's ideas of ecology and the land ethic and the way that these ideas were used in New Deal land use planning policy. Leopold advocated the idea of dealing with nature on its own terms, while land use planning rhetoric made nature an independent actor, arbitrating the shape of social life as mediated by planning efforts.

Roosevelt's speech presenting the NRPB report (1934a) to Congress utilizes these new ecological concepts, but in the service of promoting increased state intervention.[8] He begins by stating, "During the three or four centuries of white man on the American continent, we find a continuous striving of civilization against Nature. It is only in recent years that we have learned how greatly by these processes we have harmed Nature and Nature in turn has harmed us" (Nixon 1957, 341–42). Roosevelt once again absolved farm settlers from blame for this situation: "for they found such teeming riches in woods and soils and waters—such abundance above the earth and beneath it—such freedom in the taking, that they gave small heed to the result that would follow the filling of their immediate needs" (Nixon 1957, 342). After exonerating those who misused resources, Roosevelt turned to ecology: "The throwing out of balance the resources of Nature throws out of balance also the lives of men. We find millions of our citizens stranded in village and on farm—stranded there because Nature can not support them in the livelihood they had sought to gain through her" (Nixon 1957, 342). In this speech, Roosevelt redefined the land problem as an imbalance between the human spirit of freedom and nature's limits and gave government land use planning programs the responsibility for restoring this balance.

Roosevelt's ecological rhetoric, unlike Leopold's, directly linked human adaptation to nature to building the national state. In a self-conscious way, the NRPB report renames the concern with "natural resources" to a concern with "national resources." Roosevelt's speech explains the difference between these two terms: "If the misuse of natural resources alone were concerned, we should consider our problem only in terms of land and water" (Nixon 1957, 342). However, both human and natural resources are of concern—leading to the definition of a "National Resource" problem:

"We as a Nation take stock of what we as a Nation own. We consider the uses to which it can be put. We plan these uses in the light of what we want to be, of what we want to accomplish as a people. We think of our land and water and human resources not as static and sterile possessions but as life-giving assets to be directed by wise provision for future days" (Nixon 1957, 343).

In New Deal land use planning, therefore, the ecological and the national idea became intertwined: we must restore our balance with nature and we must do so through government planning for the national welfare. Roosevelt thereby made national government responsible for nature, nation, and modern life. Roosevelt, in his use of ecological rhetoric, redefined human–nature relationships, removing humans from nature to create wilderness and then putting both nature and humans under the direction of the nation-state.

In many ways, New Deal conservation rhetoric, based ostensibly on ecological ideals, was a form of backdoor Social Darwinism based on "nature" as described and classified by government experts.[9] Yet, many of the concepts used by land use planners, such as the idea of "pathological land use," echo Leopold's writings. Therefore, while Leopold did not promulgate his ecological viewpoint in support of New Deal land planning, he promoted a change in conceptual viewpoint that was used to promote its programs.

Marginality

The link between ecology and increased state intervention through land use planning was the concept of "marginality." A history of the land utilization program defined "submarginal land" as "land low in productivity, or otherwise ill-suited for farm crops, which falls below the margin of profitable private cultivation" (Wooten 1965, 1). Planners, in other words, defined nature as marginal to a particular agricultural economy if it did not yield profits equivalent to those of a modern farm. The margin in this case was the economic margin. However, sociologists also had begun to use the term "marginal" to describe people left behind by, or unable to cope with, progress (Park 1928). It was a short step from the argument that farmers on low-resource lands were economically marginal to the argument that these farmers were socially marginal as well. In fact, discussions of the concept of marginal land, and of marginal farmers, tended to link the economic with the social definition of marginality. Lane's description of marginal farmers living on an isolated island, and Gee's description of "sparseness of settlement" as unhealthy, echoed the prevailing social viewpoint that this isolation was an obstacle to modern development.

As a specific example, the "Land Classification Tour" of Connecticut Hill, Tompkins County—sponsored by Cornell University Agricultural Economists in October of 1933—merits a close examination. This was just one of many tours that Cornell University put on in New York State's agricultural counties, primarily for county officials. The tour consists of a list of numbered stations and comments at each of these stations. An abridged version of the tour is printed in Figure 4-1.

The tour begins outside of Ithaca, in Enfield. The first stations point out certain state reforestation projects in the local state park, and compare them to the "slowness of reforestation by nature" (stations 2 and 3). Station 7 begins a list of farms described as problematic. The first farm had changed hands many times; the second farm had paid off its mortagage through insurance paid on a burnt barn. Another man's mortgage was turned down because his farm was on poor "class I and II" land,[10] illustrating how Cornell's classification system was used by banks to redline farms on poor soils. A number of stations note that these are mainly part-time farms. Station 14 notes that the last owner had committed suicide. While never labeling these farms as "marginal," the tour notes both economic characteristics (lack of profit) and signs of social instability.

Stations 12 and 13 focus on school expenses. One school district consists of only one child; hauling children to school in other districts has been expensive. Stations 21–33, on Bald Mountain, continue the description of social, economic and fiscal problems resulting from these settlements. Few of the settlers had previous farm experience, the land yielded little to the country in the form of taxes,[11] excessively high prices had been paid for land, school expenses were high, incomes were low, insured property had a tendency to burn down, many owners worked part-time off the farm, and a descendant of an original settler had died in a state of decay.

Stations:

1. LEFT. Buttermilk Falls.

Across railroad enter land class V.

Turn Right, enter land class III.

At top of hill as we go under 2 telephone wires, land class II is on the right and land class I on the left.

2. (STOP). Top of hill, LEFT. Red pine plantation on state owned land in Enfield Park; trees have been set about 10 years; the soil is Groton gravelly loam. Land class I. Compare pines on left with idle land on right.

3. LEFT. Beyond old entrance to Enfield Park notice young pine plantation about 5 years old.
Leaving Enfield Falls we pass through class II land. On the left notice the slowness of reforestation by nature.

Bearing left to Connecticut Hill, class III land comes to the highway on the right.

Turning sharp right, we cross a corner of class III land and then re-enter class II. Notice natural reforestation on left.

4. RIGHT. Red school house. Enfield No. 10.
Turn left. Park development and outside work may keep these houses occupied. Back fields on these farms may be available for reforestation.

5. LEFT. 94 acres assessed at $1750. The owner also owns and operates No. 6, 169 acres assessed at $2925.
Spends most of his time farming.

7. RIGHT. 45 acres assessed at $650. The present owner bought the place last spring for $622.50. The barn had no roof. He fixed the barn and expects to house 350 pullets this winter. He works out with his tractor and thresher. He has farmed most of his life, and before coming here share rented a place near Enfield. The former owner bought the farm on contract, and held it for about 5 years. The farm has changed hands 4 or 5 times in the last 20 years.

8. RIGHT. 100 acres assessed at $1300. The present owner came from New York City and bought the place 3 years ago for $800. He is an Englishman and his wife a Finlander. He has put in a cow stable, built over the house and put in a pumping system. He also has limed the land.
Ithaca Savings Bank loaned him $1700 on a first mortgage and $630 on a second mortgage. His barn burned last spring and that paid off his first mortgage. He wanted to borrow $2300 from the land bank this spring – $1500 to build a barn and $800 to clear up other debts. The local appraiser approved the loan because a hard road is going to be put through here. The land bank appraiser turned down the loan because the farm was on class I and class II land.

9. LEFT. 69 acres assessed at $700. The present owner came from Wisconsin about ten years ago. Part of the time he has worked at the Morse Chain Works . . .
Leave class II land and enter class I.
Notice Connecticut Hill ahead. This was the third area studied in the land utilization survey work of the college.
This study resulted in the game refuge purchase.

. . .

12. ON ROAD TO LEFT. Where only child in Newfield district No. 14 lives. . . . In 1931–32 the mother of the child was the trustee of this district and the father was paid $446 for hauling the child to school, which was 2 miles from home . . .

14. RIGHT. Snyder, the last of the original settlers, shot himself last spring. He was 76 years old. The farm had been in the family about 120 years.

15. Game Preserve.

16. (STOP). LEFT. Pine plantation, about 5 years of age.
Turn left. It is suggested that this road be closed or be used only for forest or recreational purposes.
Near the bottom of the steep hill note the sudden change in land as we go from class I to class IV . . .

18. Valley. While the strip of class IV land is too narrow to provide enough land for a real good farm, the region is improving and alfalfa is now being grown. The soil is Groton gravelly loam. *(continued on next page)*

Figure 4-1.
Land Classification and Utilization Tour, Connecticut Hill (abridged).
Source: New York State College of Agriculture, Ithaca, 18 October 1933.

(*continued from previous page*)

Note that this class IV land has not yet been provided with electric current. A class A electric line extension has been suggested . . .

Bald Mountain

Starting up the hill we enter class II land.

21. RIGHT. 77 acres. Owner, who is a descendant of an original settler, moved off from the farm in 1895. The farm has not been operated since 1923. A year ago the house was made partially habitable and is now occupied by an unemployed relative of the owner. He does not even have a garden.

22. LEFT. 162 acres, assessed at $2100. Town and county taxes last year $37 and school taxes $10. In 1925 the taxes were $33 and $34. The present owner is a Lithuanian who bought the farm in 1927 from the Strout Agency for "a little less than $5000." Previous to that he was a coal miner in Pennsylvania, and read about the farm in a paper published in the Lithuanian language. He had no previous farm experience. At the end of the first year he was much discouraged and relisted the farm with the Strout Agency. He hauled cream out once a week and said, "I got paid for the trip but nothing for the cream." At the present time he has a source of income other than farming.

Previous to the present operator, the farm was owned by two railroad men from Ohio. They bought the farm in 1923 for $6900 ($1900 cash) which included the farm, machinery, livestock and household goods. It was estimated that $5000 was for the land and buildings. The total receipts on this farm in 1925 were $562, and the labor income $-308. The outside income of these two railroad men was $5,940 over three years. They spent $700 on the house in 1926.

Previous to the railroad men, the farm was owned by an Ithaca professional man. He put sheep on the farm at $18 a head and sold them at $2. He limed the land, sowed alfalfa, and fixed the buildings.

23. RIGHT. 97 acres assessed at $800. Town and county taxes last year $14 and school tax $4. The present owner is a Lithuanian who came here from No. 25. He came to No. 25 nine years ago from the coal mines in Pennsylvania with no farm experience. He read the advertisement of the Strout Agency in a paper published in the Lithuanian language. He bought No. 25 – 119 acres for $2500 ($1500 cash). Six years ago the house on No. 25 burned (it was insured). He bought No. 23 – 97 acres for $500. The house on No. 23 was not habitable at that time. Now has six cows and sells some cream, butter, veal calves and surplus cows. This year he has 100 hens, two acres of potatoes, 3 acres of rye, and a little buckwheat, and between 15 and 20 tons of hay in the barn on No. 23. This is the "old timer" of the region; he has been here 9 years.

In 1925, when the present owner was on No. 25, he had total receipts of $1220 and a labor income of $-227 . . .

No. 23 was idle from 1922 to 1927. The previous owner was an old man who was a descendant of the original settlers. He had no near relatives. The part of the house where he lived fell into the cellar so he moved to the other part; when that fell into the cellar he moved into the barn . . .

28. LEFT. 146 acres assessed at $500. Town and county tax this year $9, and school tax $2. The present owner is a mail man whose only interest in the place is that he bought it cheap and thinks he can sell it for more.

The previous owner was a farmer from the Cortland Valley who thought all the land needed to make it equal to the Cortland Valley was to farm it right. His departure shows that he found his mistake. Before that the farm was owned by a widow about 50 years old with an orphan grandchild. She put $1000 left to the grandchild into the place . . .

31. LEFT. 160 acres. This farm is now owned by a valley farmer, who does a small amount of farming in connection with his farm in the valley.

The previous owner was an Ithaca feed dealer who attempted to demonstrate model farmng with a tractor. He bought the farm from the Federal Land Bank. This was one of the early land bank loans and was made to a negro chef. This farm was foreclosed long before the depression started. At the time of foreclosure the Land Bank had about $1200 in the place.

(continued on next page)

Figure 4-1.

Land Classification and Utilization Tour, Connecticut Hill (abridged).
Source: New York State College of Agriculture, Ithaca, 18 October 1933.

(continued from previous page)

32. (STOP). RIGHT. Natural pine growth. Note how slowly the pines have extended up the hill after 20 years of idleness . . .

33. LEFT. The present owner is a Russian who has come here recently. The previous owner committed suicide. The farm was vacant from 1922 to 1926 and perhaps later.

As we come off Bald Mountain, notice the farms on class IV land in the valley.

Brooktondale

34. 115 acres assessed at $5200. The state and county taxes during the past year were $92 and the school tax $26. This farmer has 9 cows and 500 hens. His 55 acres of cultivated land is mostly on Chenango gravelly silt loam. This farm is in class IV. In 1929 his total receipts were $5010 and his labor income $338. The houses on this farm have all modern improvements . . .

Ellis Hollow . . .

38. RIGHT . . .Willow Glen. Turn right. Notice the good farm of Alton Mott on the corner. At the end of the road turn left. Notice the farm of Carl Mott, master farmer, and the other good farms on this road.

41. These farms on good land do not change hands nearly so rapidly as farms on poor land.

Cross railroad. Note Grade B milk plant on right.

42. Within one mile of West Dryden, land class II is on both sides of the road.

45. LEFT. City man who came from Bradford, Pa. last spring. Just living here. No farming. Born in Finland.

46. RIGHT. 47 acres. Farm owned and operated by a widow and her 7 small children. Born in Finland. Here 7 years.

47. LEFT. Operator is a widow. Lived here all her life. 45 acres. Farming. Barn that burned since last May has been rebuilt.

50. LEFT. Carpenter. Born in Finland. 120 acres. Here 13 years. Full time farming in 1932, as he had no carpenter work.

51. Building a short distance on road to right. 70 acres. The Land Bank made a loan of about $1500 on this farm in 1927. In 1930 the farm was bought for $1000 on contract by the son of the man on No. 50 because "the farm was cheap and nearby."

52. Red barn with ventilators a short distance on road to left. No farming. About 100 acres. Present occupants moved here last spring from No. 53. Now on poor relief. Native born.

54. LEFT. Operator born in Finland. 85 acres. Full time farming here for 11 years. Several children to help. Painted barn himself. Came to Canada in 1887, and was a laborer and moulder previous to coming here. Paid $4000 for place in 1922.

Totals from 1927 records for farms 47, 50, 53, and 54.

10 acres corn for grain	400	bu. ears
12 acres silage	39	tons
2 1/4 acres potatoes	313	bu.
38 acres buckwheat	927	bu.
20 acres oats and barley	490	bu.
10 acres oats	250	bu.
6 3/4 acres barley	154	bu.
1 1/4 acres wheat	14	bu.
104 acres hay	112	tons
204 1/4		

Figure 4-1.

Land Classification and Utilization Tour, Connecticut Hill (abridged).
Source: New York State College of Agriculture, Ithaca, 18 October 1933.

Station 28 describes a farmer who had moved from the fertile Cortland Valley to buy this farm, thinking that all the land needed was to "farm it right." However, as the economists show, this point of view, the old model of agrarian ingenuity, was now clearly a mistake. Station 33 notes another suicide.

Stations 34–41 pass through fertile "class IV" lands. Tour comments note modern buildings, long terms of residence, high incomes, master farmers, and then note where electrical extensions and road improvements need to be made to these farms. The tour also notes the presence of a grade A milk plant in the area and a consolidated school.

The last set of stations, 42–55, part of the town of West Dryden, once again describes farms on poorer soils. The tour comments repeat stories of foreclosure, part-time farming and barn fires. However, there are a number of differences between the farms described here and the ones on Bald Mountain:

1. Land quality was somewhat better in this area, with some class III land.
2. A grade B milk plant was located in the area, an important distinction, as the next section will describe.
3. A number of these farms were milking cows. The implication of the table is that these farms are not producing enough to be worth the expense of state infrastructure. In fact, the average dairy herd—eight cows per farm—on these farms approximated the average size milking herd statewide at this time. In addition, these farms produced a wide variety of grains, corn and potatoes.
4. A number of the farms were recently bought by Finnish immigrants, also an important distinction pertinent to the discussion in the next section.
5. Farm buildings, while not portrayed as modern, have been well cared for. Two stations note owners repainting their barns. Another barn was rebuilt. A number of children are working the farms with their parents, indicating future continuity of farming.

While never specifically referring to the occupants of these low-resource areas as "marginal," the tour portrays all of the problems of marginality referenced by Roosevelt Administration rhetoric. This tour represents the upland pasture-based hill farm as illustrative of the kinds of maladaptations between humans and nature that planners—echoing Leopold—described as "pathological." The viewpoint presented here echoes Roosevelt's own rhetoric, that some people had foolishly expected too much of nature and that nature, in return, had determined their rather unhappy fate. Seen from this point of view, the only solution to the problem was for state planners to examine the natural potential of land and to readjust land use according to these potentials. This was the goal of land utilization planning.

From an "ecological" viewpoint, New Deal planners argued, correctly, that some land was never meant to be farmed—that nature, to a great extent, determined how land could be used. However, as this tour indicates and the following section shows, ecological rhetoric legitimized policies that deemed only one form of agricultural production as ecologically adaptive, namely the intensive system, and deemed other forms of agricultural land use as pathological. Land use planning policies, based on this viewpoint, worked primarily to determine which land could be agriculturally "modern"—that is, intensely cultivated—and which land was incapable of achieving this status. The policy solution was the eradication of other forms of farming—and living—through planning. Implementation either involved planning infrastructure improvements to avoid these areas, identifying these areas for banks and encouraging them to redline loans to these areas or, in some cases, use of national Resettlement Administration funds to remove people from these areas (DuPuis 1991, 1993; Jacobs 1989).[12]

Marginality: A Social or a Political Problem?

Uncovering the political purpose for this skewing of the ecological viewpoint requires asking the question: if the West Dryden farmers chose to pursue modest lives through extensive land use, why, in the name of nature, did they need to be resettled? The answer requires understanding two major shifts in political power in New York State during this time period: the shift from farmers as a whole to intensive farmers and the shift from rural to urban political interests.

From Farmers as a Whole to Intensive Farmers

Discussions about milk prices, farmer militancy, and rural land use planning all left out the fact that there were two types of dairy market systems in the state: (1) the extensive system in which farmers, usually those with poorer land resources, minimized input costs and (2) an intensive system in which farmers, usually on the better lands, made heavy investments to increase milk production per cow (DuPuis 1991, 1993). Land use patterns for these two systems were significantly different. Extensive systems depended on a seasonal supply of pasture grasses, usually on hilly lands. Intensive systems relied more on feed crops and depended on good-quality land to grow these crops. Intensive farms generally sold their milk to grade A fluid processors for urban milk markets. Extensive farms sold their milk primarily to grade B or manufacturing processors such as cheese factories (DuPuis 1991, 1993).

These two systems survived concurrently because of a strong set of spatial market boundaries between them. Until the 1920s, these market boundaries were set by the limitations of transportation technology: farmers could only wagon-carry milk a few miles to a railroad "milk train" which then carried milk to distant urban markets. Farmers near train transportation tended, therefore, to be part of the intensive system. Farmers far from train transportation, which also tended to be the upland, poorer resource areas, tended to be part of the extensive system. The layout of cheese factories, fluid milk processing plants, and train tracks in Chenango County in 1906 (Figure 4-2) illustrates this geographical separation. Table 4-1 shows that cheese factories also were more likely to be located in poorer soil areas and that grade A fluid milk processing plants tended to be located in areas with high-quality soils.

In the 1920s, truck transport, later exacerbated by low Depression prices, broke down this technological boundary and forced farmers competing through high yields into the same market as those competing through low inputs. Intensive farmers could not recover the costs of their capital-intensive investments when competing directly with extensive farmers, particularly in the spring, when extensive farmers produced more of their milk.[13]

At the same time, institutional support for intensive farming was on the rise, with the growth of new agricultural organizations that spoke increasingly for the interests of intensive farmers. For example, Cornell agricultural economist, George Warren, addressing a luncheon of the American Farm Economic Association, lauded the coordination of the large farm organizations, such as the Grange, the Farm Bureau and the state dairy cooperative, the Dairymen's League, "so that farm problems are thoroughly discussed, and when a conclusion is reached, it represents agriculture. Formerly, there were not sufficient facilities for discussion, nor for expression. Anyone who was born on a farm was assumed to speak for agriculture. This is no longer the case" (Warren 1930, 360). Farmers, in other words, spoke with one

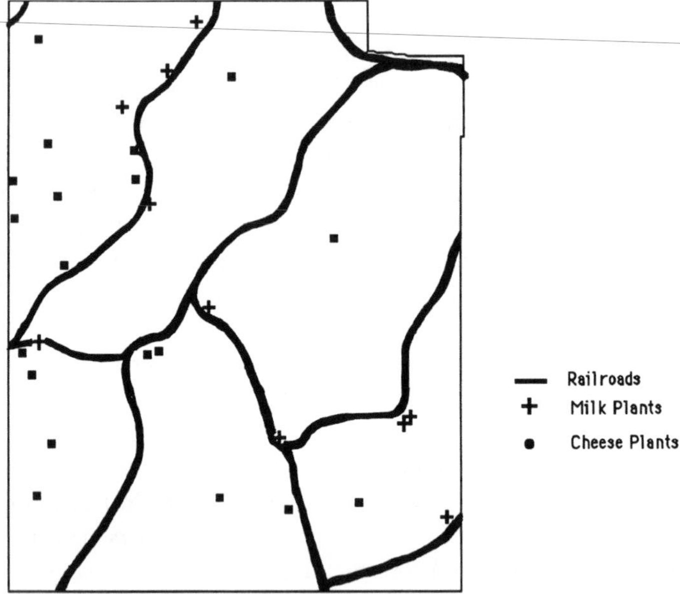

Figure 4-2.
Map of Alleghany County, New York, milk plants, cheese factories, and railroad tracks, 1906. *Source:* New York State Department of Agriculture 1906.

voice and this voice belonged to the farm groups whose members were primarily the larger, more intensive commercial farmers.[14]

The result was a land use planning policy designed to restructure land use patterns to promote intensive farming by eliminating the competitive threat posed by extensive farms, often located just up the hill. Cornell Cooperative Extension instituted what it called "a statewide campaign for the removal from the market of the unfair and unnecessary competition of milk produced at a loss" (Cooperative Extension policy statement quoted in Colman 1963, 276). Cornell University's cost-of-production studies focused on the poor resource base of extensive farms and, using the yield-competitive criteria of intensive farming, "proved" that extensive farmers were not receiving adequate income or return on equity. This type of analysis justified policies that assumed extensive farms were less productive than trees and that extensive farms should therefore be replaced by forests.

Those places classified as "marginal" and not as "permanent" farm areas, therefore, tended to be hill farming regions where extensive dairy farms predominated. While these farms may not have had the same prosperous air

Table 4-1

Location of Rural Market Milk and Cheese Plants by Soil Quality: New York Townships, 1940

Dairy plant type	*Soil quality (percent share of plant locations)*		
	POOR	FAIR	GOOD
Market milk (Grades A and B)	12	37	51
Cheese	22	60	18

Source: DuPuis 1991.

and successful look of highly capitalized intensive winter dairies, and many may have been abandoned due to rising tax rates, heavy mortgages, loss of markets, mismanagement and other factors, extensive dairies were an alternative form of agriculture adapted to the lower carrying capacity of hill regions.

Only a few rural land planners, particularly in the Western Range states, argued that there was an alternative between intensive agriculture or reforestation and that extensive pasture-based agriculture could be a successful adaptation to environments with lower carrying capacity (Renne 1936; Jacobs 1989).[15] However, in the minds of Cornell officials, land fell into only two categories: that which was suitable for "permanent" modern farming and that which was suited only for forests.[16]

In fact, extensive dairying and intensive dairying had coexisted for decades in upstate New York, along with a third type of land use: subsistence farming. Subsistence farmers had often worked part-time, for local industry or as laborers on other farms. These three farming economies had, in fact, grown out of the agrarian moral ideal that had directed farmers to use their ingenuity to determine how their own particular land resources could provide a living. Ingenuity had led to overexploitation of land in some cases. It had also led to the widely held assumption that there was more than just one way to farm, and that how one farmed depended on the resources one had—not only the quality of the soil but also other factors such as access to local markets, inputs, alternative sources of income, and the age and size of one's family.

The cheese manufacturing sector, and its pasture-based dairy supply system, had been an extremely successful agricultural economy. New York's system of associated cheese factories had dominated world cheese markets from the 1860s to the 1880s, exporting during many of those years over 100 million pounds of cheese, primarily to Britain and Canada. Known as the "American system of associated dairying" it was widely imitated from the 1860s to the end of that century and was considered the institutional predecessor of the cooperative system (Alvord, 1900). By the turn of the century, these cheese factories were primarily producing for a home market. Yet, the growing home market was for fluid milk and farmers with better land resources had turned to producing milk for fluid milk processing plants. Many cheese factories had become combination grade B milk/manufacturing plants, like the one located in West Dryden on the Tompkins County Tour. These plants made manufactured products when supply to the fluid milk market was plentiful and sold milk into the fluid market when supply was low.

Land use planners, however, did not acknowledge the existance of more than one form of dairy economy in New York State. Instead, they declared this form of land use "marginal" because it did not produce the profitable returns of the intensive industrial farm economy serving urban milk markets. Returns to extensive farming were small, but they were steady, as opposed to returns to intensive dairy operations that were higher but tended to be highly variable (DuPuis 1991).

Steady but low returns, however, require steady but low land prices. But World War I had made land prices skyrocket. Agricultural disruption caused by the war in Europe created a great demand for American commodities there and very high commodity prices for American farmers. As a result, U.S. land prices also rose rapidly and led to heavy borrowing to cover land purchases. By the 1920s, however, European agriculture had recovered and prices dropped, but farmers still had to repay mortgages for land bought at inflated prices. By the 1930s, this price/loan repayment squeeze had led to heavy economic dislocation in agriculture that was only exacerbated by The Depression (Cochrane 1979).

Therefore, the heavy mortgage failure, cited in the Tompkins County Land Classification Tour as a reason for removing farmers from low-resource lands, was as much due to historical factors as it was to the triage process that land use planners attributed to nature. However, land planners seldom broached the idea that the problems experienced in West Dryden were part of an unusual historical (not natural) situation brought on by a World War. Admitting this possibility would have also meant admitting that New York State uplands could be successfully farmed extensively, given the right knowledge and ingenuity. The ecological turn in thinking on human–nature relationships—which put nature as sole arbiter of agricultural land use and profitability as nature's sign of ecological adaptation—precluded this perspective.[17]

Urban Consumers

New Deal land use planners' idea of ecological adaptation was part and parcel of a new form of thinking that went along with the development of a mass-production agricultural economy. With a substantial agricultural industry and a rapidly growing urban consumer population, New York State reflected, and in many cases prefigured, what was about to happen to the nation as a whole. The skyrocketing population growth of New York City early in the early twentieth century had a serious effect on the power balance between rural and urban political interests in the state.

A constellation of urban interest groups developed a common agenda that led to advocating a new rural land use policy based on planned abandonment. These groups had three major goals: (1) cheap food, (2) protection of navigation, and (3) preservation of wilderness for recreation.[18] Urban consumers had been politically active concerning food issues in the late 1800s (Duffy 1974). At first, food safety was the prominent issue, and pure milk campaigns are prominent in histories of the Progressive Movement in New York City, where the "pure food" and anti-food adulteration movements were born (Duffy 1974).[19] By the 1920s, however, shortages of supply, resultant high prices, and the need to feed a rapidly growing population of immigrant factory workers moved the concern from the quality of milk to its price. By the 1930s, the *New York Times* printed "one news story on milk every second day and an editorial every two months" (Spencer and Blanford 1977). Public investigations expressed sympathy with militant farmers' "milk strikes" for higher milk prices but also insisted that the consumers' milk price could be cheaper. These investigations quickly turned from the politically difficult question of unfair "trust" profits to the more simple question of inefficiencies in milk transport (DuPuis 1991, 1993; Spencer and Blanford 1977).

Urban industrial and recreational interests also competed with low-input dairy farmers for the use of rural lands, particularly low-resource lands. These interests included the lumber and construction industries, watershed protection interests, recreation-park interests, as well as those who advocated rural land conservation as wilderness. Urban groups that supported the preservation of navigable waters, flood control, and drinking water supplies were some of the first groups to advocate reforestation of upland areas. For example, under the growing public assumption that forest cover helped to control watersheds, groups concerned about preserving Hudson River navigability were instrumental in the establishment of the Adirondack Park, which contained the river's headwaters (Nash 1982). Urban interests in wilderness recreation also played a major role in reforestation policy in New York State. These groups lobbied for more park facilities and supported state land purchase and reforestation efforts as a way to gain greater recreational resources (Nash 1982).

State Ecology: Rural Land Use Planning

Land utilization planning was the tool used to restructure rural land use. This process examined rural resources and separated these resources, through mapping, into "permanent" farm areas—those areas that were capable of using modern farm equipment and those that were not. This type of intervention in rural resource use was only possible with the growing capacity of state technocratic agricultural and environmental institutions, such as land use colleges and forestry agencies. As Roosevelt put it in his NRPB report speech, "The development of science, leaping forward, has taught us where and how we violated nature's immutable laws and where and how we can commence to repair such havoc as man has wrought" (Nixon 1957, 342). The idea of resource planning, stemming from Gifford Pinchot and the 1890s Conservation Movement, took a more active form with the development of technical capacities in these institutions. Public ownership of nonagricultural lands was the primary form of conservation planning until the 1930s (Wolcott 1934). However, legislation such as Title III of the Bankhead-Jones Act of 1937 authorized "the purchase by the national government of submarginal lands in order to insure better land use in depressed areas" (Wolcott 1939, 114).

New York's land use classification program emphasized discovering which land was modernizable and which was marginal. The classification method focused on soil class but also considered factors like the condition of farm buildings in an area (Hill 1932). The land use classification system mapped where intensive dairy production was possible. Agricultural economists mapped the entire landscape of New York State, dividing land "into five classes ranging from land earmarked for public ownership and early reforestation to land rated for permanent retention in agriculture" (Guttenberg 1976, 482). No other state mapped its agricultural land as intensely, or as repeatedly, as did New York State.

Figures 4-3 and 4-4 are maps of the area described by the Tompkins County Land Classification Tour. Figure 4-3 is a map of the land according to its classification and according to the "Types of Farming" that predominated in the area. The map classifies most of the agricultural areas as dairy; however, land classes I and II are blank, as if to indicate that these are not farm areas. Arrows point to the Bald Mountain and West Dryden areas described in the Tompkins County Land Classification Tour.

Figure 4-4 is a map showing suggested electrical power line extensions in the area. No line extensions are suggested for the Bald Mountain and West Dryden areas. One of the reasons commonly given for not extending electrical lines was sparseness of settlement. However, as the tour indicated, both of these areas were heavily settled.

Using these maps, Cornell land grant and other state officials used various means to discourage the continuation of production on marginal land. According to one history of the university, "Utility companies, bankers, and other businesses extending credit as well as agencies involved in allocating public resources for school and highway construction were informed that investment in land classes one and two were poor risks when this land was to be used for agricultural purposes" (Colman 1963, 460). Cornell also provided land classification maps to those planning future infrastructure extensions such as electric distribution lines and road improvements. Only land classified as "permanent" farm land "was to be developed as highly and served as adequately as possible with good roads, schools, and recreation and health facilities" (Guttenberg 1976, 482–83). As Figure 4-4 shows, agricultural land not classified as permanent was deliberately excluded from plans for infrastructure extensions.

Land use planning policy documents themselves are silent concerning the implications of spatial restructuring on alternative forms of dairy land use. Instead, conservation—specifically reforestation for recreation, soil conservation, watershed improvement, and wildlife preservation—was continually cited as the major rationale for land use planning in New York State. While land use planning policies may not have been enacted specifically to restructure the dairy industry, in fact, affected interest groups were not unaware of the implications of conservation policies on the structure of dairy agriculture in New York State.

For example, Cornell worked closely with the New York State Farm Bureau's Committee on Land Utilization, Roads and Electrification as well as with the Farm Conference Board's Farm Light and Power Committee,

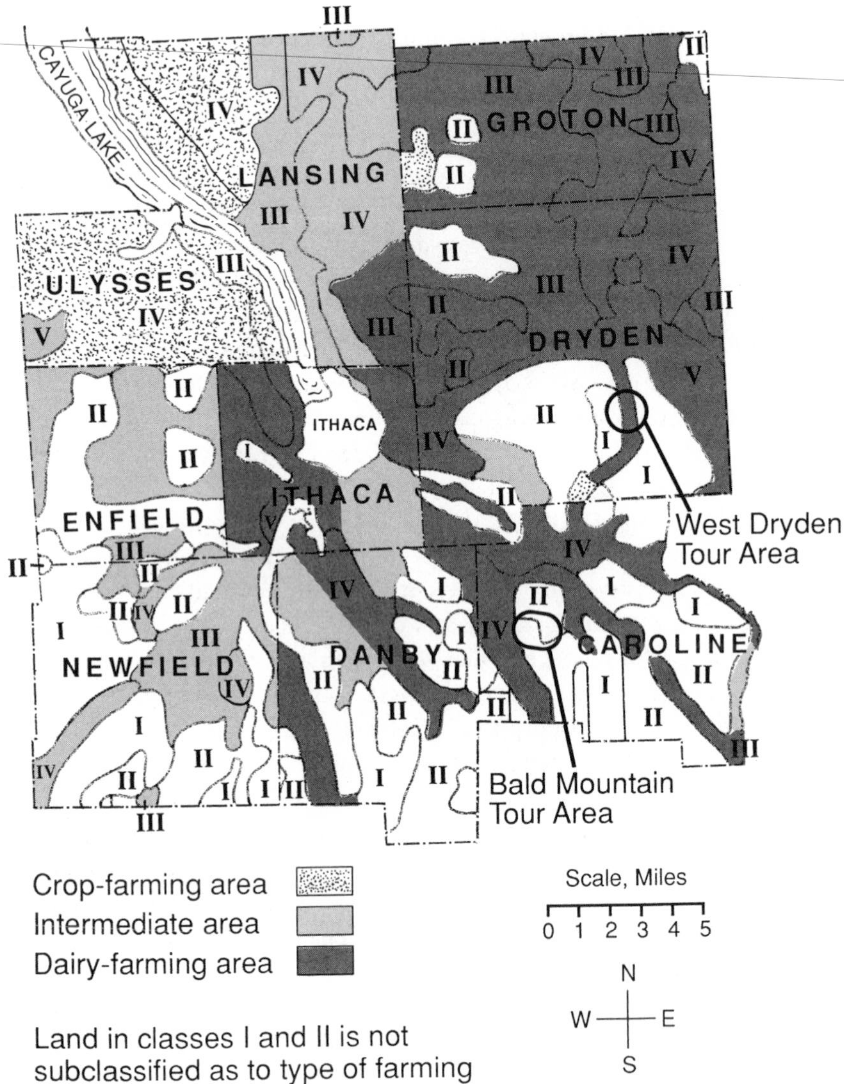

Figure 4-3.

Land classification map of Tompkins County, New York, showing land classes and types of farming areas. (facsimile of original map). Land in classes I and II is not subclassified according to type of farming. *Source:* Lewis 1934, 56.

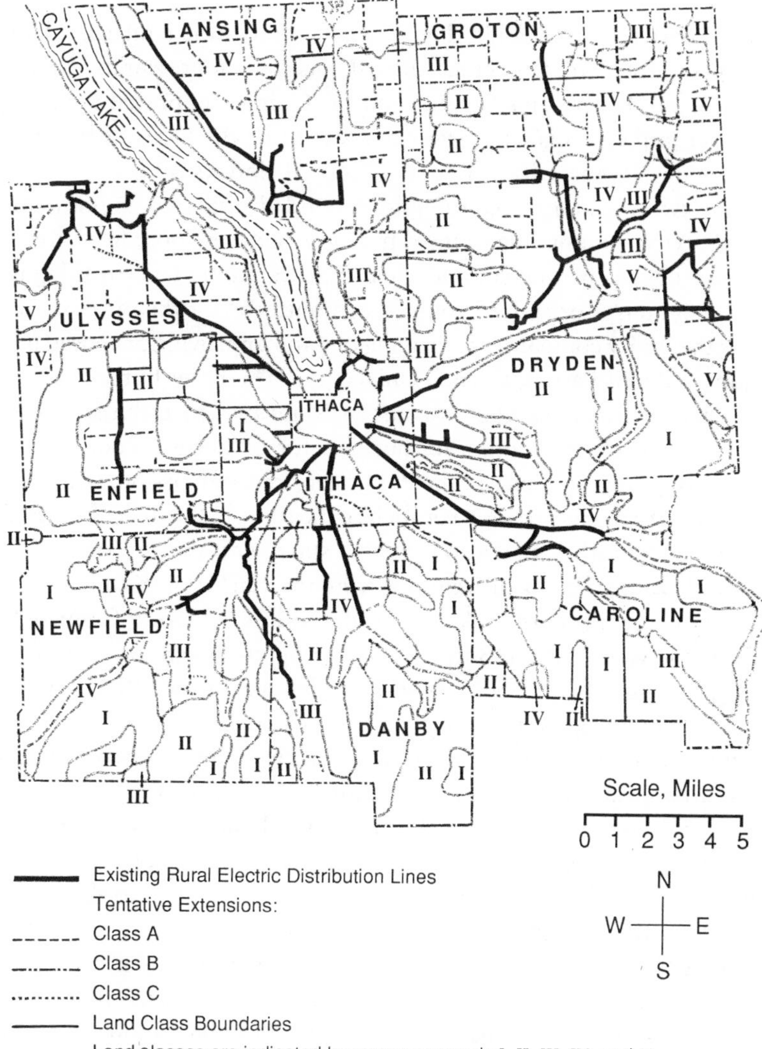

Figure 4-4.

Map of Tompkins County, New York, showing land classes and proposed electric distribution line extensions. Land classes are indicated by roman numerals I, II, III, IV, and V. *Source:* Lewis 1934, 48.

which advised Cornell and Albany officials on rural land use planning. Members of the Farm Conference Board, including representatives from the Farm Bureau, Dairymen's League, and the Grange supported the idea that only land in the permanent farm class was to be the focus of better infrastructure development (Burrit Papers, Cornell University).

These two committees continually reminded utility companies and the Public Service Commission of the differences between those farm areas that were classified as permanent and those that were not. The Farm Light and Power Committee organized country committees "for the purpose of contacting the utility companies and laying out and approving proposed line extensions" (Burrit Papers, Cornell University). The Farm Bureau also had a great deal of say in the appointment of Maurice Chase Burrit, a Cornell Agricultural Economist and a former director of Cornell Cooperative Extension, as a Commissioner of the Public Service Commission, which was in charge of approving lines for rural electrification.[20] Burrit had drafted the Cornell Cooperative Extension policy statement that recommended a "statewide campaign for the removal from the market of the unfair and unnecessary competition of milk produced at a loss" (cited in Colman 1963, 276). At the Commission, Burrit was a strong proponent of land planning through control of rural electrification, as letters between Burrit and Farm Light and Power Committee officials make clear.[21]

Reforestation programs in New York State were therefore part of a struggle by urban, industrial and state planning elites to gain control over the state's rural resources. New York rural land planners actively rejected the idea of two dairy systems in the state and consequently favored a policy of "publicly directed abandonment" (Jacobs 1989).[22] Therefore, policies to eliminate marginal farms in fact eliminated the extensive dairy system (DuPuis 1991, 1993).[23] New York state planning professionals, to gain support for rural reforestation policies, labeled low-resource pasture-based farm systems first as "submarginal" usurpers of public resources and later as victims of land use "pathologies" against nature. Instead, planners advocated public forests as moral revitalizers for urban recreationists.

Assessment

The contradiction between urban society and ecological thinking is embodied in the idea that nature is an actor independent of society. This concept enabled public officials to separate nature from society and to place the responsibility for the ecological use of natural resources under the aegis of The State. As a result, government became the primary engineer of the relationship between society and nature. Government experts assumed responsibility for observing nature's potentials and constraints, but only within the model of a particular economic system of resource use.

Aldo Leopold's own thinking did not conform to these views. He emphasized that human adaptation should involve a variety of human relationships to nature and that government should not be the primary engineer of human–nature relationships. His own viewpoint encompassed some aspects of the agrarian ideal: that the proper use of natural resources was first and foremost a personal responsibility, and that government should intervene only in those cases where individual moral responsibility had broken down. New Deal land use planners, in contrast, asserted that the state was responsible for designing human relationships with nature and that coercive planning policies, in the name of saving nature, could fulfill that role.

As Nancy Lee Peluso shows in Chapter 5, conservation programs in the Third World, often with the support of international environmental organizations, use ecological rhetoric to assert a coercive and hegemonic role over the livelihood of rural people. Many of the officials who implemented the post–World War II international rural development and conservation programs had been involved in implementing the U.S. rural land use planning policies of the 1930s (Gilbert, 1993). However, few have paid attention to the social and political context around the development of U.S. rural land use and conservation policies. Instead, historians have primarily portrayed the development of these policies as sign of progress toward a more environmentally conscious viewpoint.

Nevertheless, as this chapter shows, there are many parallels between the social justice implications of U.S. rural conservation planning policies developed in the 1930s and the problematic conservation planning scenarios that we see in the Third World today. In both cases, poor people on low-resource land have lost out, in terms of both loss of livelihoods and access to resources. This has resulted in the demise of rural economies that functioned as alternatives to the mass-production industrial economy based on intensive resource use. It is therefore myopic to criticise Third World elites and their use of ecological rhetoric to justify coercive rural land use and conservation policies without looking at how these policies functioned in the land of their origin. In fact, like their Third World counterparts, national and regional urban-based elites in the United States used the growing state apparatus to gain control over rural land use, particularly in those regions where rural economic restructuring required spatial restructuring as well. In both cases, the result has been to discourage more sustainable forms of local resource use in favor of large-scale industrialized resource "management" that has not been environmentally benign.

Despite these parallels, historical studies of U.S. conservation controversies have focused almost exclusively on controversies between Pinchot's "wise use" policies and John Muir's "preservationist" idea of national forests (for example, see Nash 1982; Worster 1977). Both sides of that debate assume that forests are the best use of low-resource lands, that governments should own more of this land, and that a "conserved" forest, whether used wisely or preserved, contains no permanent inhabitants. Reforestation policy has left us with a remarkable legacy of parks, forests, and recreation areas. Yet discourse on reforestation policy has left blank any consideration of alternative land use possibilities or any questioning of what resources were actually "saved."

Did planned abandonment policies actually save rural resources? Was the balance between nature and civilization achieved by removing farmers from hill lands? As others have noted, New Deal farm and conservation policies assisted in the mechanization, intensification, and industrialization of agriculture nationally (see McClellan 1991, for a review of studies on the effect of New Deal agricultural policies). In New York State, the spatial restructuring brought about by land classification and planning policies assisted in the full transformation of dairying into an intensive industrial system, dependent on purchased inputs, fertilizer, pesticides, and heavy capital equipment. In addition, corn is a highly erosive crop compared to forage grasses. From a long-run viewpoint, it is evident that the move to corn crops in the valleys and lower hills has not necessarily been an improvement over pasturing cows on the hillsides. Also, farms with high cow-density have become major sources of pollution, unless large investments are made in manure control systems. High-producing cows are also continually pushed to their systematic brink, leading to higher incidence of disease. Therefore, in an attempt to maintain a balance with their own social and political construction of "nature," land use planners may have eliminated a dairy system that many ecological agriculturalists today might argue is better adapted to New York's resource base. In an attempt to create "permanent" farm areas, rural planners may have eliminated a "sustainable" farm system.

To some extent, this analysis takes a traditional political economy approach, looking at the "true interests" behind ecological rhetoric in New Deal land use planning. However, this analysis is also cultural, illustrating a much more interactive relationship between words and deeds. Modern dairy agriculture could not have developed without the development of the concept of marginality and the use of ecology to describe the problems of marginal agriculture. New York State land use planning, as reflected in Roosevelt's speeches, links ecology to modernity, expertise, and state intervention. Experts treat extensive upland farmers as marginal not because they were committing suicide or because they were on relief, but because nature will not allow them to become the modern farmers in the valley below.

The development of the modern dairy state in New York depended on the elimination of alternative dairy economies through policies that declared the human–land relationship in these economies as unhealthy and unecological. Instead, these policies advocated "conserving nature" as an alternative use of these lands. Environmentalists and food safety groups are increasingly calling for regulation of the intensive dairy systems that these policies encouraged. In retrospect, it appears that ecological land planning for agricultural "health"—justified through the use of ecological rhetoric—reorganized land use to allow for the development of a dairy system that is ecologically "unhealthy."

This study points out the problems inherent in both the agrarian and the ecological viewpoints concerning nature as used in rural land use policy discourse. Nature is neither passively domesticated into society, nor is it entirely separate from society. As William Fisher notes in Chapter 6 of this volume, biologists have been reconceptualizing the idea of environment, away from something that is "out there" to be adapted to, and more in terms of its being part of a dynamic relationship between organism and its "niche." We as social scientists should be asking whether it is time to reconceptualize our use of environmental concepts—particularly our idea of nature. We also need to be vigilant concerning the role of state planners and environmental officials to ascertain whether policies carried out in the name of nature are in the name of a just society as well.

NOTES

1. The only previous instance of government intervention in rural land use was the creation of Yellowstone National Park in 1872 (Nash 1982). Previously, the government had played a role primarily in the disposal and settlement of, not control over the use of, rural lands.

2. As Geisler (1982) demonstrates, earlier forms of land use planning as centralized government control pre-dates what Bosselman and Callies (1971) called the "quiet revolution" in land use control that occurred in the 1960s.

3. As Hinrichs notes in Chapter 9 of this volume, rural inhabitants did not always welcome new settlers with different ethnic backgrounds.

4. National land use classification did not begin until 1932 (Wooten 1965).

5. Interestingly, the farmer was given responsibility for the problems of poor lumbering practice, with no mention of the commercial lumbering industry.

6. Michael Bell, in Chapter 2 of this volume, argues that explanations for the decline in New England agriculture also focused excessively on land resources.

7. Leopold's most developed presentation of these ideas appear in his best known work, *A Sand County Almanac,* which was published in 1947; however, he began writing in the 1920s about what he then called "the conservation ethic."

8. I have no direct proof that Roosevelt was aware of Leopold's article on conservation ethics or any of his previous articles on wilderness before making the 1934 speech; however, Nash (1982) documents that Leopold's ideas were widely received by this time.

9. Jacobs (1989) argues that rural "planned abandonment" policies were based in Social Darwinist precepts.

10. Land classification categories are not the equivalent of soil classification categories. In land classification, lower numbers represent poorer land.

11. State officials repeatedly emphasized that the farms on poor lands could not pay adequate taxes. However, local tax issues involving these lands have not since been resolved (Wooten 1965).

12. A portion of Tompkins County did eventually become a Resettlement Administration project.

13. The Agricultural Marketing Agreements Act of 1937 recognized the differences in these two dairy systems and instituted a legal boundary which replaced the earlier technological boundary. This legislation set higher prices for farms selling to fluid markets, to reimburse these farmers for the extra investment they had to make to sell to these markets. Farmers outside of these milk marketing areas operated in an unregulated system.

In dairy states such as Wisconsin and California, state officials were able to use milk market legislation to create strong boundaries between the two dairy systems. In New York, physical topography, the size of the urban market, and a commitment by state officials to regional rather than local cooperatives increased the difficulties of setting a strong market boundary between the two dairy systems (DuPuis 1991, 1993).

14. See McConnell (1953) for an analysis of U.S. farm organizations at the national level and their emphasis on representing the interests of larger commercial farmers.

15. In fact, Western land utilization projects in general concentrated on moving land out of crops and into pasture (Wooten 1966). As Nash (1982) and others ex-

tensively document, Western ranchers have historically been a politically powerful group with a strong voice in Western conservation policy. Resettlement would not have been a politically viable option in that region, although recent "Buffalo Range" proposals could be considered a modern version of this idea.

16. In other states such as Wisconsin, the question of "farms or forests?" was widely controversial. DuPuis (1993) compares the political land use planning interests as they affected dairying in New York, Wisconsin, and California and concludes that states with a less politically powerful urban population had land use policies that were more open to the continuation of extensive dairy agriculture.

17. In fact, land use planners did spend considerable time classifying agricultural areas according to ideal types of farming. However, areas that were classified included only those with highly fertile soils.

18. Marsden et al. (1991) and Hinrichs (Chapter 9 in this volume) discuss the political ramifications of the growing recreational consumption of rural land by urban people.

19. "Swill milk" city dairies attached to city breweries, where cows subsisted entirely on brewery waste, were breeding grounds for disease. Some opponents of this system went so far as to attest of the milk: "out of 100 children fed with it, 49 die yearly" (quoted in Gates 1960).

20. For example, on 13 February 1939 Burrit wrote to Farm Light and Power Committee General Secretary, Edward S. Foster: "I recognize that it is the support of organized agriculture that has had a great deal to do both with my original appointment and with the reappointment" (Burrit Papers, Cornell University).

21. For example, in a letter dated 3 June 1937, Edward S. Foster (see above note 20) wrote to Burrit concerning his recent address to the Telephone Association: "I think your suggestion that the Telephone Companies give more thought to land utilization surveys in developing their lines is particularly fitting. It is our belief that every farm in the permanent farming areas of the state must eventually have access to good roads, good schools, electric power, telephone service, and R.F.D. (Burrit Papers, Cornell University Archives, Box No. 2414).

When farmers in the hill farm areas began to demand access to infrastructure services as well, in a letter dated 13 March 1940 Foster suggested that Burrit talk to utility officials: "If you get an opportunity to do so I think it would be well to talk with Mr. Buckman and Mr. Kelsey with reference to questions which have been raised in Chenango County. I should dislike very much to have these extension plans jeopardized by any attempt to counsel electrification of all farms in Classes 1 and 2" [the low-quality soil land classes] (Burrit Papers, Cornell University Archives, Box No. 2414).

22. As one New York State Planning Board report states: "Seldom is it profitable to engage in a type of farming which differs radically from that in neighboring ar-

eas. Those areas classed as submarginal cannot compete either with the regions where radically different types of farming prevail, or with the fertile and productive farming areas right in their own neighborhood" (Lane 1935, 4).

23. New York State land planning policy was also unusual in that, unlike other states, decisions were carried out by a small number of officials. In contrast, land planning in other states such as Wisconsin involved institutionalized public input and participation by the farmers and other local people through county land use planning committees. In addition, land classification by Wisconsin county committees concentrated primarily on land that was tax delinquent at the time, rather than on economists' predictions whether particular areas had the resources to remain in farming in the future (Guttenberg 1976, 483).

References

Alvord, Henry. 1900. "Dairy Development in the United States." In *Yearbook of the United States Department of Agriculture, 1899,* 381–98. Washington, D.C.: U.S. Government Printing Office.

Bosselman, Fred, and Callies, David. 1971. *The Quiet Revolution in Land Use Control.* Washington, D.C.: Council of Environmental Quality.

Burrit, Maurice Chase. nd. Papers. Cornell University Archives, Ithaca, N.Y.

Clawson, Marion. 1981. *New Deal Planning: The National Resources Planning Board.* Resources for the Future. Baltimore: Johns Hopkins University Press.

Cochrane, Willard W. 1979. *The Development of American Agriculture: A Historical Analysis.* Minneapolis: University of Minnesota Press.

Colman, Gould. 1963. *Education and Agriculture: A History of the New York State College of Agriculture at Cornell University.* Ithaca, N.Y.: Cornell University Press.

Duffy, John. 1974. *A History of Public Health in New York City, 1625–1866.* New York: Russell Sage Foundation.

DuPuis, E. Melanie. 1991. "The Land of Milk: Economic Organization and the Politics of Space in the U.S. Dairy Industry." Ph.D. diss., Cornell University, Ithaca, N.Y.

———. 1993. "Sub-National State Institutions and the Organization of Agricultural Resource Use: The Case of the Dairy Industry." *Rural Sociology* 58 (3): 440–60.

Ellis, David M., James A. Frost, Harold C. Syrett, and Harry J. Carman. 1957. *A History of New York State.* Ithaca, N.Y.: Cornell University Press.

Gates, Paul W. 1960. *The Farmer's Age: Agriculture, 1815–1860.* New York: Holt, Rinehart, and Winston.

———. 1976. "An Overview of American Land Policy." *Agricultural History* 50 (1): 213–29.

Gee, Wilson. 1934. "Rural Population Research in Relation to Land Utilization." *Social Forces* 12 (3): 355–59.

Gilbert, Jess. 1993. "Democratic Planning in the New Deal: The Federal-County Agricultural Planning Program, 1938–1942." Paper presented at the Center for Agrarian Studies, Yale University, New Haven, Conn., March 1993.

Guttenberg, Albert A. 1976. "The Land Utilization Movement of the 1920s." *Agricultural History* 50: 477–90.

Hays, Samuel. 1959. *Conservation and the Gospel of Efficiency: The Progressive Conservation Movement, 1890–1920.* Cambridge, Mass.: Harvard University Press.

Hill, F. F. 1932. "Land Classification Tour." Department of Agricultural Economics and Farm Management, New York State College of Agriculture, Cornell University, Ithaca, N.Y., mimeo.

Jacobs, Harvey. 1989. "Debates in Rural Land Planning Policy: A Twentieth Century History from New York State." *Journal of Rural Studies* 5 (2): 137–48.

Ladd, Carl E. 1932. "Land Planning in the Empire State." *New Republic,* 3 August, 306–7.

Lane, Charles. 1935. *Submarginal Farm Lands in New York State.* Albany: New York State Planning Board.

Lewis, A. B. 1934. *An Economic Study of Land Utilization in Tompkins County, New York.* A.E. Bulletin No. 590. Department of Agricultural Economics, Cornell University, Ithaca, N.Y.

Marsden, Terry, Jonathon Murdoch, Philip Lowe, Richard Munton, and Andrew Flynn. 1991. *Constructing the Countryside.* Boulder, Colo.: Westview.

Marx, Leo. 1964. *The Machine in the Garden: Technology and the Pastoral Ideal in America.* New York: Oxford University Press.

McClellan, Steve. 1991. "Theorizing New Deal Farm Policy: Broad Constraints of Capital Accumulation and the Creation of a Hegemonic Relation." In *Towards a New Political Economy of Agriculture,* ed. William H. Friedland, Lawrence Busch, Frederick H. Buttel, and Alan P. Rudy, 215–31. Boulder, Colo.: Westview Press.

McConnell, Grant. 1953. *The Decline of Agrarian Democracy.* Berkeley: University of California Press.

Meine, Carl. 1988. *Aldo Leopold: His Life and Work.* Madison: University of Wisconsin Press.

Merchant, Carolyn. 1980. *The Death of Nature: Women, Ecology, and the Scientific Revolution.* San Francisco: Harper and Row.

———. 1989. *Ecological Revolutions: Nature, Gender, and Science in New England.* Chapel Hill and London: University of North Carolina Press.

Nash, Roderick. 1982. *Wilderness and the American Mind,* 3d edition. New Haven, Conn.: Yale University Press.

National Resources [Planning] Board. 1934a. *A Report on National Planning and Public Works in Relation to Natural Resources and Including Land Use and Water Resources with Finding and Recommendations.* Washington, D.C.: U.S. Government Printing Office.

———. 1934b. *A Report on National Planning and Public Works in Relation to Natural Resources and Including Land Use and Water Resources with Finding and Recommendations: Part II, Report of the Land Planning Committee.* Washington, D.C.: U.S. Government Printing Office.

New York State Department of Agriculture. 1906. *Butter and Cheese Factories, Milk Stations and Condenseries in the State of New York.* Bulletin no. 8. Albany, New York.

Nixon, Edgar B., ed. 1957. *Franklin D. Roosevelt and Conservation, 1911–1945.* Franklin D. Roosevelt Library, Volume I, 1911–1937. Hyde Park, N.Y. General Services Administration, National Archives and Records Service.

Park, Robert. 1928. "Human Migration and the Marginal Man." *American Journal of Sociology* 33 (6): 881–92.

Peluso, Nancy Lee. 1993. "Coercing Conservation: The Politics of State Resource Control." *Global Environmental Change* 3 (2): 199–217.

Slichter, Gertrude Almy. 1959. "Franklin D. Roosevelt's Farm Policy as Governor of New York State, 1928–1932." *Agricultural History* 33 (8): 167–76.

Spencer, Leland, and Charles J. Blanford. 1977. *An Economic History of Milk Marketing and Pricing, 1800–1933.* Volume I (amended version). Columbus, Ohio: Grid.

Terrie, Philip G. 1985. *Forever Wild: Environmental Aesthetics and the Adirondack Forest Preserve.* Philadelphia: Temple University Press.

Warren, George. 1930. "A State Program of Agricultural Development." *Journal of Farm Economics* 12 (3): 359–66.

Wolcott, Leon. 1939. "National Land-Use Programs and the Local Governments." *National Municipal Review* 29: 111–19.

Wooten, H. H. 1965. *The Land Utilization Program, 1934 to 1964: Origin, Development and Present Status.* Agricultural Economic Report No. 85. U.S. Department of Agriculture, Economic Research Service. Washington, D.C.: U.S. Government Printing Office.

Worster, Donald. 1977. *Nature's Economy: A History of Ecological Ideas.* New York: Cambridge University Press.

5

"Reserving" Value: Conservation Ideology and State Protection of Resources

Nancy Lee Peluso

How does resource valuation affect the ways people "construct" the countryside? How do different resource users define and value wilderness, wild places, or untamed places in contrast to cultivated, "improved," tamed, and mapped areas? What sorts of places are viewed as productive, which are inaccessible? All these concepts are defined by different and changing experiences of social context and history. From the perspective of a state,[1] a ruling group, or an extractive enterprise, human activities can be better controlled (managed) in tamed areas. Centralized or bureaucratic efforts to control nature characterize non-Western as well as Western societies, in colonial, precolonial, and contemporary time frames. When centralized states attempt to control distant regions, effective physical control may be impossible. In such cases, it becomes important to the managing agency to control resources by controlling the discourse of resource management.

"Wild" areas, unsupervised by sufficient territorial guards, are dangerous spaces; the people living there pose real or imagined threats to authorities, who may depict the people, like the resources, as "wild." For example, government authorities may call people who use resources without government permission "wild settlers," "poachers," "squatters," even "bandits"; using graphic terms that invoke destruction, such as "slash-and-burn farmers," has the same effect. These terms do not necessarily denote specific activities, but rather the legitimacy or source of authority for action. Settlement, game hunting, agriculture, clear-cutting, or burning may all be permitted land uses by government-authorized users. The terms are politicized by their application to particular *users* rather than *uses*.

This extract has been adapted from an article first published in *Global Environmental Change,* Vol. 3, No. 2, June 1993, pp. 199–217, and is reproduced here with the permission of Butterworth-Heinemann, Oxford, U.K.

Different constructions of the countryside and its human and natural components are different versions of history. The telling of "natural" or environmental history is not immune to ideology, idealism, or moral judgment—all of which have political consequences. In this chapter, I argue that the elimination of people from natural history changes the ways that resources are perceived, defined, valued, allocated, and used, and can ultimately undermine conservation.

Human agency—specifically the investment of labor—in the creation of nature frequently imparts rights of either "ownership," or access/usufruct. This is as true in many non-Western cultures as in those whose traditions have evolved from Judeo-Christian and Lockean bases. Many times indigenous people have controlled their resources for hundreds of years before any state claimed them. The lack of acknowledgment of humans' roles in creating natural environments is a political statement—involving the decision to recognize people's rights and obligations, and their access to or control over "natural" resources.

This chapter draws on two case studies to explore the ways that resources may be redefined, valued, and subsequently managed, and to examine both the politics and political consequences of valuation. In both cases, the states have initiated efforts to "develop" at least some portion of the populations against whom they now use or threaten with violence.[2] In both cases, however, development efforts have been secondary to security efforts and have largely ignored the political-ecological contexts and origins of local resource use (see, for example, Western [1984], Kiss [1990], Anderson and Grove [1987], Peluso [1992a], Peluso and Poffenberger [1989], Barber [1989], Dove [1983, 1986]).[3] The cases illustrate how international (read: Western-based) conservation groups can purposely or inadvertently contribute to adverse political consequences for local resource users in promoting certain conservation and development strategies. Changes in the ways resource users and uses are perceived and described (narrated) by powerful resource managers, in both colonial and contemporary settings, contribute to the choice of management strategies and their justification. In extreme cases—such as those illustrated here—international conservation groups may contribute to state violence in the name of conservation, resulting from their efforts to see resource territories protected and to create "stability" in a state's capacity to govern. At the same time, conservation can become part of a state's strategy to control people and territory.

A state or state agency's capacity to enforce this construction of tamed and wild places, and of legitimate and illegitimate users, has both political and economic consequences, affecting the state's perceived legitimacy locally and internationally. Resource control, resource protection, and even resource mapping overlap with the goals of some conservation organizations, and can be appropriated by the state. Particularly in nation-states which have been formed from a conglomeration of relatively separate or different ethnic groups with different types of social organizations, the ability of state leaders to enforce their policies and define resource use varies widely. Sometimes a state's successful imposition of its will on its constituents depends on the means of social control and the relative effectiveness of those means in achieving state agendas, including particular forms of resource management and use.

By depicting resource users (the local ones) as wild, destructive, (or "illiterate," "uneducated," "backward," or "noninnovative"), state resource management agencies think that they can justify their use of militaristic environmental protection. Oftentimes, the language of conservation policies, position papers, environmental impact statements, and so on fuels violence unintentionally and unjustifiably. For example, humans are often referred to collectively and pejoratively as predators; all human uses of resources are included in this category. Resource uses such as grazing and farming are called destructive and devastating when they are done on marginal lands or at high population pressures; they are likened to irresponsible logging and mining activities. Equal blame for tropical deforestation is often accorded to agriculturalists and loggers, although both the rate, extent, and permanence of their "destruction," and the kinds of benefits the two groups derive from resource use—and the morality of their actions—are entirely different. Humans as producers, especially small-scale producers, are rarely discussed in these high-level policy pieces or in designing global strategies (Pinedo-Vásquez, Zarin, and Jipp 1992) . Managed diversity, for example, is hardly discussed in the current fervor of concern over losses of biodiversity, even in habitats (such as mangroves) that have clearly been occupied by humans for decades or centuries (Padoch, pers. comm.).

Because states and local groups value resources for different reasons or end uses, their interests in resources sharing a common spatial territory are also likely to differ. For example, a forest has a different value and a different set of end uses depending on whether it is standing or exploited for its timber. Choosing a use for land rich in both topsoil nutrients and gold deposits will likely benefit different actors or interests and will result in the creation of different landscapes.

Valuation strategies created by, or favoring, the state often disenfranchise local people who have long histories of local resource use and may have played significant though unrecognized roles in creating wild habitats (Peluso 1994). Many such strategies change who has access to and control over local resources. At the local level, the boundaries of state control are nearly always contested, as the state comes up against the political ecological histories of local resource use patterns. Local social relations of resource use and their histories affect the state's capacity to implement its plans. This is one way a state or state agency gets involved in local relationships, and in local politics of property relations and resource access.

In some cases, local resistance to these changes becomes so intense that violence is used both to protect and to appropriate the resource (Peluso 1992a). The state, with its monopoly on the "legitimate" use of violence, may use violence against competing resource users in the name of conservation, for both ecological and economic interests, and as a means of protecting its political sovereignty (Peluso 1992a). Local people's strongly vested interests in their resources may lead them in turn to violently contest state intervention. New forms of valuation, and the violent defense of valuable resources, can cause degradation and defeat conservation goals.

The state's interests in controlling both discourse and resource use are primarily two: power—which includes both control and the capacity to govern—and economics. Power struggles are constantly played out in the course of resource allocation, resource control, and resource access. Resource control increases a state's social control (Barber 1989; Peluso 1992a). Whereas previously economic power gave states greater legitimacy in the eyes of the international community, now it is the ability to control resources that does so, although often with competing "constituencies." In an international arena, the state may use conservation, economic, and sovereignty arguments to justify the coercive exclusion of certain groups from valuable resources. When the outcome of coercive resource management coincides with the goals of outside conservation groups, those factions of the state that produce the results may gain or strengthen the latter's financial and ideological support. Some states or state interests appropriate the conservation concerns and the discourse of environmentalism as a means of eliciting support for their own control over productive natural resources.

Competitions over arenas of legitimacy are played out in multiple dimensions at different scales: within the state itself (among its agencies, ministries, and political factions); within various international arenas (among groups variously interested in natural resource/commodity trade, production, and conservation); and in the countryside (where the resources are located and where local users may be competing both with outsiders and among themselves for access to local resources).[4]

State resource managers may use coercion to establish control over people and territory just as conservation and economic arguments are used to keep people away from valuable resources. When state actors use coercive means of gaining resource control, it is often when their own control of the resource is questioned or challenged by other resource users and when coercion is considered either the last resort or the easiest means of establishing control over people and territory. The military is never a neutral player and is generally driven by goals, methods, and ideologies deriving from the central power, that contradict the needs of marginal groups such as pastoralists and swidden cultivators. It is precisely these types of marginal people that governments have difficulty controlling. Having the military establish control over state-claimed territories and the resources therein serves this political purpose as well as that of environmental protection.

Oftentimes, conservation groups augment the financial and physical capacities of Third World states or state agencies to protect resources with "global" value. Wise global resource management constitutes the high ground of conservation discourse, one which is virtually impossible to dispute. Some international environmental organizations, perhaps inadvertently, justify coercive-protective actions on the basis of their outcomes, such as the preservation of the world's biological heritage, with no view to the means used to achieve these goals (Deudney 1990). The urgency called for to defend endangered species, endangered habitats, or whole ecosystems is a common component of the discourse of conservation (McNeeley et al. 1988). Conservationists often depict their agendas as being in the common interest of everyone equally, constructing an imagined, homogenous, "global community." However, violence in the name of resource control also helps states to control people, especially recalcitrant regional groups, marginal groups, or minority groups who contest state resource claims or otherwise challenge the state's authority. The states in question may apply the tools and equipment they use to establish their resource sovereignty beyond the conservation end points envisioned by international conservation facilitators, and appropriate the moral ideology of global conservation to justify state systems of resource extraction and production. Conservation groups' acceptance of coercive approaches to conservation can thus backfire and lead either to damaging extractive relations with the environment, or violent conflict that degrades the environment.

The extraction of valuable resources such as oil and other minerals, timber, or even some agricultural products, just like the commercial exploitation of rare resources for their tourist and scientific value, is a revenue-generating strategy embraced by most national governments. States generally allocate rights to extract or protect resources in ways that benefit the state itself (in generating revenues to reproduce itself) as well as for the proverbial "greater good of society" (a parallel concept to the "global community"). For this reason, states are often not interested in international conservation groups taking a role in national resource management, especially if the state's decision-making power is curtailed by environmental, rather than economic, considerations. This may lead to the conservation groups' taking on economic arguments—for example, that marketing natural products will preserve them in the wild—even though these arguments have little basis in the history of large-scale commercial exploitation of the rainforest.

Even where international environmental nongovernment organizations (NGOs) or states try to "develop" competing resource users at the local level, the sacrifices people must make in lifestyle, autonomy, or real economic gain may make the transition a difficult, if not impossible, undertaking. If such efforts fail to establish state control and ensure conservation, both states and international environmental groups may call for coercion as a necessary means to the end of environmental protection.

As the case studies below show, however, international intervention or support does not guarantee the realization of conservation goals. Both valuation and increasing the state's capacity for resource control may increase local resistance or rebellion against further state or international controls on local resources. But even if the state's use of violence leads to increasing resistance from local resource users, and conservation goals are not achieved, state actors may not "lose." By using conservation rhetoric for legitimacy with outside environmental groups, the state may succeed in strengthening its capacity to govern via the use of force (Tilly 1985; Migdal 1988). The means of violence and the ideologies of state stewardship of global resources, obtained directly or indirectly from the international conservation community, may facilitate the state's enforcement of its claimed right to govern.

The Case Studies

Of the two cases chosen to illustrate this trend, the clearest and most extreme is that of Kenya and its wildlife conservation areas. I examine the evolution of the alliance between the international conservation community and the Kenyan state agencies that make wildlife protection policies in reserves and parks. The Indonesian case focuses on Java, where a parastatal agency manages luxury hardwoods. In both cases the state's control of these land-based resources using coercive management techniques is examined. I relate the use of coercion to the origins of the state's claims on those resources, the nature of competition for those resources, and the effectiveness of state policies when coercion is used (Blaikie 1985, 83). I also examine the relationships between coercive state resource management and other aspects of state–society relations (Skocpol 1985, 9–11). Finally, I explore the role of international environmental groups in explicitly or implicitly supporting coercive state resource management.

Kenya

The resources discussed in this section are the lands set aside for national parks and wildlife reserves and resources within those lands (wildlife, pasture, and water).[5] Colonial and contemporary governments in Kenya have excluded the traditional users of these lands, the Maasai, Kamba, Orma, and pastoralists of other ethnic groups, from access to these lands to various degrees over the past century. State claims to nearly two-thirds of traditional Maasai lands were first made by the British colonial state at the turn of the twentieth century. In 1904 the Maasai, who used to occupy all the land from Mt. Kenya in the north to the border with (and into) what is today Tanzania, were resettled in two reserves. Several years later, the inhabitants of the northern reserve were resettled again in an extension of the southern reserve. By 1912, they were confined to an area of approximately 38,000 square kilometers (Lindsay 1987). The British allocated some of the Maasai's traditional lands to European planters whose activities were believed by colonial officials to be "more productive" (Collett 1987, 138). This view of relative productivity had two meanings, each differently beneficial to the British. First, the uses to which the Europeans put the land—cultivation of both subsistence and cash crops—were valued more highly than Maasai use of the land for grazing. Production methods of plantation agriculture were viewed as much more advanced than pastoralism. Second, the taxation of settled farmers with annual measurable production was easier than the taxation of mobile pastoralists. Thus in terms of both the relative modernity of a land use and its potential for revenue production that benefited the colonial state and the new settlers it was there to protect, the value of particular land uses affected the ways in which much of the land in the colony was allocated.

At this time, however, the British did not subscribe to the theory that the Maasai could not coexist with wildlife. In 1906 they created the Southern Game Reserve—a wildlife reserve *within* the Maasai reserve—because the Maasai were not believed to threaten wildlife, having coexisted with the region's wild game for thousands of years (Collett 1987, 140 citing Eliot 1905, 278–79; Lindsay 1987, 152 citing Cranworth 1912, 310). Rather, the colonial government first established game reserves as a means of extracting revenue through taxes and permits from the massive slaughter of East African wildlife by European hunters (Collett 1987, 140; MacKenzie 1987).

Not until the 1940s and 1950s did the colonial government succumb to pressures from game hunters and some conservation groups to set aside rangeland exclusively for wild game. Changing the ways in which conservation efforts were discussed—rather than speaking in terms of the reallocation or revaluation of resources—helped the state pursue another political-economic purpose: sedentarizing the Maasai and again, allocating some of their land to European colonial farmers and Kikuyu agriculturalists, again, as an easier means of controlling local populations and their production for surplus extraction (Collett 1987, 142).

For the Maasai, sedentarization meant changing their migratory cattle-raising practices. The Amboseli Basin, occupying some 3,200 square kilometers of both the Maasai Reserve and the Southern Game Reserve, had been an important source of water during the dry season for both the wildlife in the region and for the migratory Maasai and their cattle. The colonial government had constructed dams and boreholes to provide water for Maasai cattle outside the Amboseli Basin. As the number of Maasai cattle increased, as they continued to migrate to areas where wild game also sought drinking water, and as hunters threatened wildlife in a different manner, conservationist interests grew more concerned that the wildlife dependent on the Basin waters was threatened. Along with big game hunters, conservationists pressured the colonial government to create reserves where human use would be more restricted. The Southern Game Reserve was abolished in 1952 and four smaller reserves were created, including a new reserve outside the area of the old Southern Game Reserve, called Maasai Mara. In the 1950s, hunting was first outlawed within these reserves, although the government issued permits for hunting outside the reserves. Hunters thus continued to benefit from the new arrangements, as the reserves were meant to ensure the continued breeding of the game species. The

Maasai were not so fortunate: the change in the way that their practices were represented—as competitive, rather than complementary—and the conjuring of the "wilderness devoid of humans" myth—were used to justify keeping them out of the reserves. In the early 1960s, livestock grazing was forbidden in an 80 square-kilometer area of the Amboseli reserve—directly threatening Maasai lifestyles and livelihoods (Lindsay 1987, 153–55).

The Maasai did not so easily give up their traditional patterns of migration to seasonal water supplies, and there were no water development efforts sufficient to permit them to do so. Pasture quality, and therefore the land's capacity to support both wild and managed grazers, is affected both by water availability and by grazing itself. Research has shown that grazing often stimulates grass productivity, depending on the soil moisture status at the time of grazing, because grazing maintains the vegetation "in an immature, rapidly growing state similar to that at the beginning of the rainy season" (McNaughton 1985, 259). Without appropriate water supplies, the Maasai either would have to watch their cattle die or resist the laws and graze their cattle inside the park.

Meanwhile, another international development increased the state's direct interest in the protection of wild game and the reservation of parklands—the increase in wildlife-oriented tourism beginning in the 1960s. Some tourism revenues, including hunting fees, were given to various Maasai district councils as an incentive to win their acceptance of the reserves (Western 1984, 305; Lindsay 1987, 154). Fees and revenues grew throughout the 1960s and early 1970s, after Kenyan independence. Not all district councils, however, truly represented the interests of the people in the immediate vicinity of the reserves and parks. In Amboseli, for example, the Kajiado District Council, 150 kilometers from the park boundaries, received park revenues. Maasai herdsmen living near the park received nothing (Lindsay 1987:155).

The value of wildlife tourism soon became clear to the central government. In 1974, the government designated 488 square kilometers of the Amboseli Basin as a national park, while still negotiating with the Maasai. In 1977 this area was reduced to 390 square kilometers, which was gazetted as a park and would remain livestock-free. A de facto buffer zone was to be established around the core area of the park, and group ranches—a brand-new form of social organization imposed on the Maasai—were established to further the government's continuing intentions to sedentarize the tribe (Lindsay 1987, 156–57). In addition, the Maasai were expected to allow wildlife to graze on these ranches in exchange for a "wildlife utilization fee," which was supposed to compensate them for losses of water and grazing area to their own livestock (Kiss 1990, 72). But fees, which did not always find their way into the hands of the local Maasai, were meager compensation for the forced transformation of livelihoods, lifestyles, and cultural values (Collett 1987, 145).

By 1989, tourism in Kenya was contributing about 20 percent of the nation's total foreign exchange (Knowles and Collett 1989, 452). By 1991, tourists were spending some $50 million a year to view elephants and other wildlife (Chadwick 1991, 11). In this way, as Knowles and Collett have pointed out, the creation of national parks to protect wildlife not only separated the Maasai from their livestock production base and created a mythical nature devoid of humans for tourist consumption; it also provided the government with the financial means to "develop" and "modernize" the Maasai (Knowles and Collett 1989, 452). Moreover, "National Parks and Game Reserves are never justified solely in terms of the economics of tourism: both the conservationists and national governments support the creation and maintenance of these areas *by moral arguments based on the need to conserve wildlife and the intangible benefits that conservation confers on humanity*" (Collett 1987, 129; emphasis added).

The discourses of the state and the environmentalists are thus linked: wilderness is a place to be observed but not used, but both intangible benefits to "humanity" (the global community) and tangible revenues can accrue to the state from the observers. Any acknowledgment of the historical role that local people have played in creating the habitats frequented by the elephants might justify their rights and entitle them to much more of the revenues.

The plans for development of the Maasai in Amboseli have not worked as well as they have in Mara. Some blame the failure on the basic conflict in the lifestyles of the Maasai and their unwillingness to allow outsiders to make decisions about their lives and their uses of resources. Collett, for example, claims that the main reason that the provision of water supplies outside the park has not achieved the government's development goals is the preference of the Maasai for a migratory, pastoralist lifestyle (Collett 1987, 144). However, a recent report by the World Bank indicates that there were also significant technical problems:

> [The conflicts] may be attributed . . . to failure to implement the agreements, to the lack of an official written agreement outlining the management responsibilities of the different parties and

> policy changes. The water pumping system, financed by the New York Zoological Society and the World Bank, worked well for a few years and then began to fail due to technical and administrative problems which were not corrected by the central Government which had built it. An inadequate water supply left the Maasai little option but to return to find water inside the Park. The problems were aggravated by a drought in 1984, in which the Maasai lost a substantial part of their livestock and received no assistance from the Park authorities. The wildlife utilization fees were paid regularly until about 1981, then the payments became sporadic without explanation to the Maasai. The agreement for group ranches to retain a portion of Park entry fees fell through, perhaps due to administrative changes. . . . Anticipated income from tourism did not increase as quickly as expected. . . . Construction of new lodges and viewpoint circuits on group ranch lands did not materialize as expected. Finally, the 1977 hunting ban eliminated anticipated income from safari hunting license fees. (Kiss 1990, 72)

The restriction of their principal means of livelihood was probably a major reason that some Maasai began killing rhinoceros and elephants in protest. A decade later, some allegedly began collaborating with ivory poachers. They also resisted further appropriation of their access rights by increasing their use of the area surrounding the livestock-free zone, and later demanded tenure rights to all these lands (Western 1982, 304; Lindsay 1987, 155). Neither these protests by the Maasai nor the increase in grazing area, however, have been the primary reason for wildlife loss in the region. As discussed below, their proximity to the resource, lack of a strong political voice, and the rising crescendo of global concern for African elephants have implicated the Maasai and other pastoralists in the "ivory wars."

In the early 1980s in particular, the government began to reconstruct the deep-seated, historical conflicts over land and resource rights in Kenyan national parks and reserves in terms of a government mandate to stop the poaching of wildlife, especially elephants and rhinoceros. Major international environmental organizations, including the Worldwide Fund for Nature, the African Wildlife Foundation, World Conservation International (WCI), the International Union for the Conservation of Nature (IUCN), Conservation International, and the National Geographic Society publicized the poaching issue and its threat to global and African biodiversity. The efforts of these and other environmental groups led in 1985 to the creation of the Convention on International Trade in Endangered Species (CITES). By 1991, 105 of 110 world nations signed the CITES declaration to ban the raw ivory trade in their effort to protect elephants in Asia and Africa (Chadwick 1991, 14).

A great deal, however, has been left out of the international discussion of the poaching issue, and neither the origins nor the implications of the proposed solutions to the "poaching problem" have received the critical analysis they merit. Two gaps in the conservation community's discussion are particularly glaring. The first is the lack of historical perspective on the political and ecological contexts within which parks were created to protect wildlife, and the resulting dismissal of both local people's and their ancestors' roles in creating particular environments. Customary uses of park land are viewed either with suspicion, if they are still permitted, or as crimes. Local people's uses of so-called wild areas are represented as a departure from the past, as "encroachments." The elimination of people from natural history is part of the dominant wilderness discourse.

The other gap in the international poaching discussion is the failure to consider the political-economic implications of providing arms and equipment to protect wildlife. In April 1989, Richard Leakey became the director of Kenya's Wildlife Service.[6] Leakey was renowned for having fired administrative and field staff believed to be involved in the illegal ivory or rhino horn trade, for giving raises to underpaid and overworked park rangers, and for arming these rangers with automatic rifles and helicopter gunships in order to wage war more effectively on the poachers invading Kenya's national parks. Wage war they did: within two years of his taking over, more than one hundred poachers were killed, many of them with no chance for discussion or trial. The rangers were licensed, like military in a state of emergency, to shoot-to-kill on sight (Chadwick 1991, 26–31). The Wildlife Service also reclaimed direct control over the Maasai Mara Reserve, where the combination of wildlife management with local participation and benefits had reportedly been more successful (Kiss 1990, 71). The government claimed that the reserve had been inadequately maintained and was deteriorating, denying earlier reports that elephants and rhinoceros populations within this park had been increasing while antipoaching costs were virtually negligible (Kiss 1990, 71, 74).

The questions here are obvious. Who are the poachers and from where do they derive their claims and their support? Why were they able throughout the 1970s and much of the 1980s to eliminate, according to the World-wide Fund for Nature, some four-fifths of Kenya's elephant population (McNeeley et al. 1988, 1)?

In their campaigns to save animals, international conservation groups aggregate people with very different sorts of claims into the general category of "poachers." A letter to members from the WWF, for example, depicts poachers as follows: "Some poachers, tribesmen displaced from traditional occupations by drought or civil war, use primitive methods to kill elephants and transport tusks. But most use high-powered weapons and even airplanes and various sorts of poisons" (World Wildlife Fund 1989, 6).

The tribes to which all these "tribesmen" belonged is not immediately clarified. The reader is led to certain types of conclusions from the language of the letter, however. For example, "poachers" are always bad guys, whatever their motives. Those "tribesmen" poachers who use poison, airplanes, and high-powered weapons clearly have the most distasteful of motives as discussed here. The only other motive for elephant-killing offered here is employment displacement. The reader's potential empathy for these people is displaced by the use of the words "primitive weapons," invoking an image of spears, and "traditional occupations," implying a lack of contemporary relevance. Both the technology of poaching and the complex circumstances including, among others, ethnic variation, an interplay of class and ethnic variables, and locally specific histories of resource use and claim are deemed secondary to the fact that elephants are being killed.

Later in the letter, Somalis, both "tribesmen" and "officials," are specifically implicated. In reference to ivory tusks sold or stockpiled within Somalia, the letter says, "These tusks were not legally confiscated. Instead, they probably were poached from Kenya's nearby Tsavo National Park by well-equipped Somali tribesmen, then smuggled out of Kenya with the complicity of Somali officials." The Somali president himself also apparently wrote a letter guaranteeing his government's purchase of ivory tusks from neighboring countries (World Wildlife Fund 1989, 8, 9). Not all ethnic Somalis live within the political boundaries of Somalia, however, and the complexity of ethnic relations, as described in more detail below, is submerged in the rhetoric of urgency and militancy.

The WWF does not specifically accuse the Maasai of killing wildlife for ivory, but implies that their increasing populations are an equal if not greater threat than poaching to the survival of the elephants and other wildlife. They never mention that thousands of elephants were slaughtered by European and American hunters in the late nineteenth and early twentieth centuries for their ivory and for stuffing and display (Mackenzie 1987, 43–44). Nowhere in their letter to WWF members about the poaching problem is it mentioned that the Maasai and other pastoral and hunter-gatherer groups coexisted with elephants and other savannah wildlife over thousands of years, or that people—as well as elephants—have played an important role in creating and maintaining the contemporary savannah habitat that supports them both (Collett 1987, 130–36). Rather, the letter implies that the presence of the Maasai is a new phenomenon to which elephants must adapt: "One broad cause of the decrease in elephant numbers is surely the advance of human populations into *their* habitat. . . . To some extent, elephants are able to adapt to the growing presence of pastoralists such as Kenya's Maasai" (World Wildlife Fund, 1989, 4, 5; emphasis added).

Chadwick, writing for *National Geographic,* is more guilty of inappropriately aggregating all types of people as poachers, and therefore confuses the sources of "the poaching problem":

> Tusks became a sort of underground currency, like drugs, spreading webs of corruption from remote villages to urban centers throughout the world. . . . The seventies saw the price of ivory skyrocket. Suddenly, to a herder or subsistence farmer, this was no longer an animal, but a walking fortune, worth more than a dozen years of honest toil. . . . Ivory was running above a hundred dollars a pound, and officials from poorly paid park rangers to high ranking wildlife ministers had joined the poaching network. . . . [In addition,] poaching gangs, including bush-wise bandits called *shifta* from Somalia, armed with AK 47 assault rifles, were increasingly turning their guns on tourists. This has all but shut down Meru National Park in the north. (Chadwick 1991, 24).

What is wrong with this description is its "snapshot" of a contemporary situation, with the camera angled in such a way as to keep the background out of focus. The protagonists in the picture are considered equally culpable, regardless of the roots of their involvement, their power to prevent its happening, their public stance, or the historical basis of their claims to being where they are in relation to the wildlife and the lands. Both the average reader and the writer of the article are unfamiliar with the social history of these "wildlife habitats" and this gap in understanding is neither missed nor deemed necessary. Readers, like the writer, are most likely to empathize with the victims in this conflict—the tourists and the elephants they are viewing "in the wild." The story, after all, is about people against nature. The people *for* nature, the heroes, are not the local people who lived alongside wildlife for thousands of years before their lands were appropriated by colonial and contemporary state agencies and carved into parks. The implicit heroes are the conservationists and their armies who rout all manner of poachers, whether or not they carry rifles.

Moreover, the human victims of this scenario are not the villagers locked between a violent state and violent outsiders, but tourists. Local people are faulted in two ways. First, because of their proximity to the parks and the logic that they must be helping outside poachers with no traditional claims to the park lands. In addition to the lack of evidence for this insinuation, it is also highly unlikely that any "peasant farmer" sees one hundred dollars for any pound of ivory he had a hand in obtaining.

Chadwick hints at the motive underlying the involvement of certain state and would-be state actors in this conservation drama: "To currency-strapped governments and revolutionaries alike [ivory poaching] was a way to pay for more firearms and supplies. In the eighties Africa had nearly ten times the weapons present a decade earlier, which encouraged more poaching than ever" (Chadwick 1991, 24).

However, peasants and "tribesmen" bear the final responsibility for encroachment on the elephants' habitat—the areas from which they were excluded not many decades ago—because of the ultimate villain: population growth. "Ultimately, though, people, not poachers, and [population] growth, not guns, pose the most serious long-term threat to the elephant's survival" (Chadwick 1991, 14).

To counter the effects of these two very different types of enemies, it is necessary to increase the power of the "good" government officials, particularly those working in the parks. As the WWF letter explained, "Anti-poaching forces have been traditionally paid poorly, had insufficient training and equipment, and were understaffed. Moreover, they rarely enlisted the aid of nearby villagers by offering them economic incentives" (World Wildlife Fund, 1989, 7).

Underlying this statement are the assumptions that (1) park rangers are not involved in poaching and that (2) economic incentives alone should be sufficient to enlist the assistance of villages with completely different claims on the resource. Believing that "the only long-term security for elephants in Africa lies in strengthening national capabilities in wildlife conservation and management, WWF and its partners (IUCN, TRAFFIC, and WCI) began providing "emergency assistance to key African wildlife departments," improving ranger incentives and providing antipoaching equipment and training. In addition, to their credit, WWF and other groups sought "to ensure that protected areas benefit from the income generated through access fees" (World Wildlife Fund 1989, 10). Leakey also requested assistance from the African Wildlife Foundation, which AWF provided, including airplanes and vehicles for antipoaching patrols in Tsavo National Park (African Wildlife Foundation 1989, 5). Though it is a relatively small operation, AWF occasionally takes a more direct role in coercive wildlife protection by "mounting extra patrols when an emergency arises" (AWF 1989, 3). That these aircraft, radios, vehicles, night-goggles, and other antipoaching equipment might serve another purpose besides conservation has, however, been a secondary consideration in view of the emergency status of the quest to protect these wildlife. And yet, in an article appearing in January 1989, three months before Leakey's takeover and the subsequent high-powered, highly publicized crackdown on poaching, reports from Kenya showed how the government was already using its mandate to protect and manage resources to assert its authority (*Africa Confidential* 1989, 6–7).

For example, ostensibly to settle a dispute over grazing rights between Somali and Borana groups residing in the north, the government sent in police, army helicopters, military aircraft, and the paramilitary General Service Unit. Over 600 people were detained and "large numbers" were killed in the course of the current incident (*Africa Confidential* 1989). The conflict is not a new one: a 1984 clash had left 2,169 people dead, and in 1987 some 200–300 Home Guards, none of them Somali, were armed "to assist in policing grazing rights and local disputes" (*Africa Confidential* 1989).

Many of these disputes date from the time that the Kora National Reserve was created, when Somali pastoralists were excluded from access to parklands for grazing. Whole communities of Somalis were resettled onto arid lands in Borana districts. In the course of their resettlement, they were deprived of pasture and water for their livestock. Seeking these resources in the vicinity of the reserve, they were harassed by the Kenyan security forces in the same manner as alien Somalis who travel long distances from their country, some of whom are engaged in the smuggling trade. The government's harassment of both settled and nomadic Somalis in the region was couched in conservation rhetoric, but dated back at least to the region's efforts to secede from independent Kenya in 1967.[7] In the course of the 1984 clash near the Kora reserve, it was reported that "under the state of emergency, security forces have powers to act without warrant and detain without specific reason . . . clean-up operations are commonplace" (*Africa Con-*

fidential 1989). Moreover, officials involved in the political security operations were integrated into the government's antipoaching operations.

Clearly, the historical bases of resource conflict and claim differ in northern and southern Kenya, although a thorough exploration of their origins is beyond the scope of this article. However, the historical politics of resource management in each region have not evolved into separate management policies for the present. Inside and outside the parks, the Kenyan government under both Presidents Jomo Kenyatta and Daniel Arap Moi has been plagued by corruption. Under the former regime, powerful government officials were allegedly involved in ivory, rhino horn, and charcoal smuggling. Moi sought to illustrate his commitment to conservation by publicly burning millions of dollars' worth of tusks. But his militaristic style of governance, through widespread citizen surveillance and violence, and his government's rampant corruption have recently led World Bank and bilateral donors to put a hold on Kenyan aid. Thus the financial assistance of environmental NGOs are now even more coveted by the state and more contradictory under the circumstances.

The question here is whether a coercive conservation strategy, allying the international environmental NGOs with the Kenyan government, is at all sustainable—not to mention ethical—in the medium to long term. Both indigenous people with claims to resources now encompassed by parks and outsiders seeking easy enrichment by ivory poaching are treated in the same manner: with threats and violence. Moreover, although equipment, funds, and ideology may be donated with the intention of protecting nature, these can be used directly or indirectly by the state to serve its other political ends, that is, to exert control over recalcitrant human populations as well as territory and wildlife. Wildlife conservation and the territorial requirements of the large charismatic mammals being protected, fit comfortably into a broader state strategy of controlling its people. In this way, the Kenyan government's public commitment to preserving wildlife for tourism and research serves both the economic and political interests of the Kenyan government, while its long-term effectiveness as a conservation strategy is as questionable as the ethics of a militaristic approach.

Indonesia

Through the Ministry of Forestry, the Indonesian state maintains control over the management of production forests under two different forms of what it calls sustained yield management. On Java, production forests are organized into state-managed forest plantations, some of which are over one hundred years old. Peasant farmers living near production forests and forest reserves have been formally excluded from all but the most limited forms of access to the forest lands since Java was first governed by the Dutch colonial state at the turn of the nineteenth century. Outside of Java, most forest management by the state is indirect: the Ministry of Forestry leases large tracts of forest to concessionaires who are responsible for management. Some Outer Island forests are directly managed by state concessions. In addition, the nature of local people's legal and customary access to the forest varies widely.[8]

The resources discussed in this section are the forests and lands in Java officially classified as state production forest. As in the Kenya case, the state forest management agency, the State Forestry Corporation, has historically viewed forest-based peasants as "threats" to the forest (and to the state's management goals) largely because of their subsistence activities. State timber management policies threaten forest-based peasants' livelihoods because of their restrictions on local people's access to agricultural land, their development of agroforestry systems, and their exclusion from shares in the revenues generated from the long-term plantation production of trees.

Most production forestry in Java consists of the plantation production of timber (primarily teak, *Tectona grandis,* mahogany, *Switenia macrophylla,* and rosewood, *Dalbergia*), and tree resins such as rosin (from *Pinus merkusii*) and copal (from *Agathis spp.*). The current management system was originally established by the Dutch colonial government in the mid to late nineteenth century, after some two centuries of increasingly centralized controls on the natural forest and fallow agricultural lands of the island. Most forest lands in Indonesia were declared the property of the colonial state in 1870, as a result of the *Domeinverklaring,* a decree defining and separating private and state property. Included within the state lands were any formerly cultivated lands that had been in fallow for more than three years. The declaration remained effective after independence in 1945 in that the lands recognized as the domain of the state remained the same. The Forestry Law of 1967 also confirmed the status of certain lands as state forest lands.

As did the Dutch, Indonesian state foresters in Java directly manage the forests; production forests are under the jurisdiction of a parastatal forest enterprise, the State Forestry Corporation (SFC). Employees of this parastatal make and implement detailed management plans to establish, maintain, and harvest forest products. They also retain a monopoly on the exchange and transport of all primary production of teak, the species that occupies less than one-third of the lands controlled by the SFC but contributes 92 percent of the SFC's annual income.

Although Java's forests cover some 3 million hectares, or nearly a quarter of the island, they tend to be scattered, rather than occupying large contiguous areas. Most forests are surrounded by densely populated, predominantly agrarian settlements. Two-thirds of these forests are classified as production forests. More than 20 million people—a fifth of the island's population—inhabit more than 6,000 forest villages (villages adjacent to or enclosed by state forest lands) making them subject to the SFC's jurisdiction. The only legal access villagers have to production forests and their products is for the collection of deadwood for fuel and the collection of some naturally occurring nontimber forest products. Some nontimber products, such as resins, are grown in state forest plantations and "owned" by the SFC. Villagers are hired to collect these products and to plant and nurture the trees. Nontimber forest products available to villagers are further limited in number or variety because of the monocropping of forest trees in plantations.

The tree plantations, regardless of whether timber or resin is their primary product, only absorb village labor at selected points in the plantation's life-cycle. During reforestation of clearcut tracts, selected villagers gain access to land for the first two or three years of the forty to eighty year life-cycle of the primary forest species, using the land between newly planted rows of trees to plant agricultural crops. Local labor is also absorbed at the end of a tract's life-cycle, when all the trees in the tract, representing an allegedly sustainable proportion of the district's total forest base (one-fortieth, one-sixtieth, or one-eightieth of the district's total forest area), are clearcut. A few day laborers are hired in certain years or seasons to help thin or clear brush during the thirty-seven to seventy-seven years between planting and harvesting of timber trees. In resin-producing forests, after plantation establishment, trees require nine or so years to begin producing enough resin to tap; local people are then hired by the SFC to tap resin for the SFC until the trees are harvested twenty to forty years later (depending on the species and the market). Thus, whether in timber or resin-producing areas, employment opportunities are not regular throughout the life-cycle of the plantation tract. The most valuable timbers, such as teak, have the longest life-cycles (sixty to eighty years) and provide the fewest employment opportunities for local people between planting and harvest. For many forest villages, however, these forest plantations dominate the local production landscape. Moreover, villagers' access to reforestation land and to forestry employment is controlled entirely by local staff of the SFC.

Longer-term involvement of villagers comes in "social forestry" areas. Social forestry is essentially a movement in international forestry that seeks to empower forest villagers and other local forest users to make forest management decisions. Many forms of social forestry involve some kind of joint management between professional foresters and forest villagers on state or private lands. Until 1991, social forestry was being applied on approximately 20,000 hectares of SFC land, with another 250,000 hectares deemed appropriate for expansion of the model. In Java, social forestry is defined rhetorically as a movement to involve forest-dwelling people as management partners, but only on certain forest lands. In practice, this has meant many extremely degraded forest lands, or those lands over which the SFC has the least control (Peluso 1992a).

Social forestry is not implemented in mature forest areas where teak harvest is under way or planned within the next twenty years. Most social forestry sites are located where the SFC has been unable to reforest its lands with trees whose production will benefit the SFC. Thus villagers derive no financial benefits from planting or maintaining the long-rotation, valuable teak timbers that most benefit the SFC. Another aspect of the implementation of social forestry in Java is that the "partnership" between forest villagers and the SFC does not mean that villagers really take part in decision-making or planning. Though the success of social forestry has been spotty (Peluso 1992b), there are some real opportunities for joint management and mutual benefit from reforestation. Unfortunately, similar endeavors at joint management in the most productive and most valuable teak forests of Java do not exist. Repressive modes of management and state domination of benefits characterize the large productive forests.

There are two types of forest protection in Java: preventive and repressive. State forestry policy clearly directs foresters to use both modes of protection to secure the forest's territorial borders and the standing trees. Preventive measures include the usual patrolling of forest lands; getting to know forest villagers; checking the permits of students, scouts, tourists, researchers, and officials from other administrative branches; checking forest product transport permits; and supervising "people who have a traditional relationship with the forest" (Peluso, 1992b, 9). Social forestry is also included among preventive means of forest security. Repressive measures are employed when preventive measures fail to check theft or forest damage. The policing of these forests, and a militaristic style of forest security, have always been critical components of forest management in Java.

Forest police began patrolling the forests of Java in the late nineteenth century. The best foresters were often former soldiers (Peluso 1992a, 73).[9] Indeed, their training and bureaucratic organization were modeled after the military, as had been the case in Germany where Dutch foresters were trained (Peluso 1992a, 46–56). In independent Indonesia, in 1962, President Achmad Sukarno authorized arming the forest police with pistols. Symbolically, this meant that they were put on a par with the military and the police; no other institutions, state or private, and no civilians are allowed to own firearms under Indonesian law. While lack of funds in the early years precluded the arming of all forest police, today nearly all forest guards in the teak forest districts carry guns.[10]

The police functions of these foresters are written into forest policy, and justified because they are meant to protect strategic resources claimed by the state: "Police security activities in the forest . . . according to Government Regulation No. 28, 1985, are designed to secure and guard the rights of the state to the forest lands and forest products" (Darmosoehardjo 1986, 5). Despite the foresters' alleged commitment to social forestry in other parts of the Javanese forest, police methods still prevail in the most productive forests. One reason foresters give for the continuation of repressive forest protection has been the foresters' perceived need to contain the increasing public discontent with the exclusive management system. An important effect of the general discontent, however, has been that armed foresters rarely, if ever, actually fire on forest villagers. Their guns are effectively little more than symbols of government-sanctioned forest control. In this way the Java case differs significantly from the Kenya case.

While field foresters rarely, if ever, use their guns, the infrastructure of forest repression in Java has grown substantially within the past 15 years. Forest security is implemented at several levels of intensity, from the forest police who operate at the same level as labor foremen (*mandor*); to the Special Forest Police (*Polisi Chusus Kehutanan,* or PCK) who are a level higher, equivalent to forest guards (*mantri*); and the Long-Distance Patrols (*Patroli Jarak Jauh,* or PJJ), also called BRIMOB, like the mobile brigades of police and military that they imitate. The PJJ operates as a sort of forest SWAT team. The first of these forest-policing mechanisms originated under the Dutch, the second under Sukarno, and the third is the creation of the SFC. The evolution of the forest police to include paramilitary operations to retrieve teak and teak "thieves," represents the most critical change in the nature of territorial forest control since the colonial period (Peluso 1992b).

The training and operations of forest guards reflect the importance of police methods in forest management. Both forest guards and the special forest police receive at least three months of training in police tactics and criminology; both groups carry guns and engage in military and paramilitary-type exercises during various training periods throughout their careers. In many teak forest districts, forest guards spend as much of their time engaged in high-powered security activities—stake-outs and the like—as in planning reforestation, logging, thinning, or forest labor organization. The territory over which a forest guard has jurisdiction is called a "forest police resort" and administratively is on a par with the administrative territory of a village head. The long distance patrols' operation units consist of three to five special forest police, several representatives from either the local military post or the nearest police station, or both, a representative from the forest district office, a driver and an all-terrain vehicle. The team is driven into a forest area close to an area of suspected teak theft; the unit members synchronize watches and scatter to seek illicit wood and suspects.

Not only are these security functions part of the routine of forest protection; they are part and parcel of the state's strategy for social control throughout the island. According to the head of forest security and agrarian affairs for the SFC:

> Conscious of the burden of implementing [forest management] tasks and the strategic position of the State Forestry Corporation in serving the country and in the development of our people, particularly within the scope of [our] participation in directing socio-political security and safety in Java, an island which has traditionally [and] historically acted as a barometer of political hegemony and power in the archipelago, all SFC troops are expected to play fundamental roles as Security Agents capable of detecting political, economic, social, cultural, and military troubles among the people. . . . Unlike other businesses . . . the SFC has a special mission related to the conditions of the territory it manages. These conditions have resulted in the SFC's being an enterprise with two functions. (Darmosoehardjo 1986, 1)

The politico-military functions of these state foresters has led many of them to perceive and describe themselves as state heroes, protectors of state resources. This attitude is clearly intended—and encouraged—by both forestry and political security policy-makers.

One contradiction that influences the forest security system is that foresters have jurisdiction over trees and forest territory while jurisdiction over the people lies with the civil administration: subdistrict officers, village heads, and others. Although all part of a common state structure, the loyalties and interests of civil administrators do not always coincide with those of the foresters. Formal barriers to alliances exist, for example, in the policy preventing the implementation of long-distance patrols in a village without the explicit, on-site approval of the village head. The foresters' primary response to this snag in security operations has been to forge formal and informal alliances between themselves and civil administrators at all administrative levels from the central offices in Jakarta to overlapping district offices, to the village-forest police resort units. Although the details of this program would extend beyond the scope of this discussion, it is important to note that, at least in theory, the forestry–civil administrative alliances also include alliances with local military and police offices.[11] Moreover, in the past decade, more and more former military officers are being "elected" to village head positions, putting in place officials who have a history of specific interests in bureaucratic, state-directed control of village people and resources.

Although the government has developed social forestry programs for some disenfranchised forest users in Java, these concessions pale in comparison to the gross profits earned by the timber industry. Moreover, as in Kenya, these development efforts benefit the state more than the local people in many ways. Social forestry opportunities in Java are located on degraded forest lands, that the SFC had largely given up for lost. Any increased production of forest species benefits the state, and the SFC never gives up its rights to control those lands. The most repressive approaches to forest protection are applied in most valuable and productive forests, that is, the oldest teak forests, and not on degraded land. The preventive mode of social forestry is not applied where repressive forestry is deemed appropriate and necessary.

The Java case differs from Kenya in the way that state resource management bodies interact with international conservation interests. While conservation groups do not arm the Indonesian government in an effort to help protect tropical forest habitats, they do play a role in legitimating the state's use of violence to protect its claims to the nation's natural resources. For example, such groups lobby for "sustainable forestry," and define sustainable plantation forestry in exclusionary terms traditionally used by Western foresters or ecologists. In other words, they neither acknowledge nor consider the role of people in creating or managing so-called natural environments, or the rights their labor or proximity to resources may have imputed them prior to the establishment of a bureaucratic resource management agency. Rather, conservation groups tend to look at the formal, scientific, externally planned aspects of forest management and the ecological outcomes in determining whether a forest product is eco-politically correct.

Furthermore, the international conservation agenda is always framed in terms of its "urgency," calling for rapid action to save either critical species or their habitats. While this is indeed an important consideration, I would argue that appropriate rural development and social forestry types of projects cannot be developed quickly, need to be flexible—particularly in the early stages—and will not take the same form in different settings. Moreover, "urgency" is susceptible to the possible interpretation that "under any circumstances" certain resources must be protected. International complacency toward this attitude in some state resource bureaucracies thus lays the groundwork for acceptance of the most expedient means of resource protection, even if this involves repression.

Most recently, the Rainforest Alliance's certification of Java teak as part of its "smart wood" program has provided the SFC with international legitimation for its management of mature teak (Rainforest Alliance 1991). As a direct result of this certification, businesses in the so-called green market, including many "environmentally correct" gardening catalogues, have begun to endorse Java teak. Consider the following trademark explanation from a recent Smith and Hawkin gardening catalogue: "The Plantation Teak™ from which we make our teak benches, chairs, and tables does not come from rainforests. It is carefully grown on tree farms in Java, and its harvesting is certified as being beneficial to the economy and the ecology of the region" (Smith and Hawkin 1991, 38). Their message is that teak is acceptable if it is not extracted from rainforests (as is teak from parts of Thailand and Burma, for example).[12] The catalogue ignores the critical social sustainability questions such as the conditions or claims of teak laborers and teak forest villagers and the means of protecting mature teak. Instead, it makes a bland (and unsubstantiated) comment about plantation teak production being "beneficial to the economy of the region."

One of the reasons that Java teak has been certified as "smart wood" is that the SFC has started a social forestry program and shown a willingness to involve local people in forest management. However, as illustrated above, social forestry is only one means of forest security, and not the approach taken in those forests where plantation teak is currently being harvested for sale to Smith and Hawkin and other green marketeers. In ascertaining that the state has complied with a loose set of "social sustainability criteria" developed by the rainforest group, no consideration is given to the fact that "sustainable management" includes forest "SWAT teams" and a management philosophy that explicitly (and unabashedly) includes both repressive and preventive components. Thus, by ignoring the totality of the teak production system, the conservation group, in concert with the green market, legitimizes coercive forest management. Given the long history of this type of management in Java, it is not surprising that the SFC chooses to continue these practices when faced with increasing international pressure to quickly conform to global conservation goals. In addition, the international criticism of Indonesian forest mismanagement in the Outer Islands—clearing forest for resettlement (Schwartzman 1986), replacing mixed tropical forest with monoculture oil palm and rubber plantations, and the general criticism of the impacts of both selective harvesting and clear-cutting on tropical forest stands—has only increased the SFC's desire to show how much better managed forest plantations are in Java. Urgency, expediency, and international recognition of plantation teak help justify the historical forms of forest control.

Conclusion

In the first of a series of publications entitled *Conserving the World's Biodiversity,* a consortium of the wealthiest mainstream environmental organizations and the World Bank detailed an extensive analysis and a set of strategies to protect the world's biological resources from their most ubiquitous predator: humankind (McNeeley et al. 1988). The authors, all scholars or environmental policy analysts, based their concerns on solid science, documenting the demise of certain components of the environment. On the other hand, many of the policy prescriptions were uncomfortably imperialistic, if not naive. Most disturbing was a section toward the end of the document, which was entitled "The Special Case of the Military." The section lists a number of indicators to support its contention that conservationists worldwide would do well to "systematically" approach "national defense services . . . to provide their support for positive action in the conservation of biological resources" (McNeeley et al. 1988, 131). Although every one of the nine indicators listed raises questions about their validity and about the ethics of justifying military involvement in conservation, two indicators have particularly disturbing implications related to the arguments presented above.

> The military is concerned primarily with national security, and it is increasingly apparent that many threats to national security have their roots in inappropriate ways and means of managing

natural resources; the military might therefore reasonably be expected to have a serious interest in resource management issues.

> As conflicts between people and resources increase in the coming years, the military will require detailed understanding of the biological, ecological, social, and economic issues involved if they are *to deal effectively with these conflicts.* (McNeeley et al. 1988, 131; emphasis added)

These assertions are disturbing in that they imply that the state and its security forces are neutral mediators in conflicts over natural resources. And while the latest in this series does not explicitly mention these military options, paramilitary "solutions" are still widely discussed, condoned, and planned for implementation.

The examples given here are part of a growing body of evidence showing that wherever the state directly claims, controls, or manages land-based resources, state organizations and individual state actors have strong vested interests in the commercial exploitation of resources. Their control over the territories within which the resources occur, and over the people living within them, is a major aspect of their strategic territorial controls. Militaries, paramilitary organizations, and state agencies often create or exacerbate resource-based conflicts by their participation in protective activities, their involvement as actors, or their coercive tactics. It is far from clear, therefore, that "the various national military establishments operate for the benefit of their respective nations" in regard to conservation, as the authors of *Conserving the World's Biodiversity* claim (McNeeley et al. 1988). Just as some military leaders can be co-opted to work for the sake of conservation agendas, the resources and ideologies of conservation groups can be co-opted for separate military agendas. Once coercive conservation tactics are accepted, such co-optation is nearly impossible to prevent.

In both the Java and the Kenya cases, the structures of control and the means of violence are not spreading from the natural resources sector to the rest of society. Rather, they originate in the institutions of social control that already dominate civil society, and are applied to the control of natural resources by and for the state. A major difference exists, however, in that Kenya is actively using force, including the killing of suspicious people found in parks (that is, not tourists), without trial or formal confirmation of their assumed guilt in poaching. Such tactics are not part of the SFC's management, although fear of such action is in many cases sufficient to enforce the state's will.[13] In both Kenya and Indonesia, outside conservation groups help to legitimate the state in two ways: first, by pressuring the state for rapid action on conservation issues, motivating state managers to be coercive; and second, by negotiating the pace and form of resource management and economic development on the terms of the state and outside conservationists, not on the terms of local people.

By failing to venture beyond the concept of thinking globally and acting locally, the writers of international conservation initiatives often brush aside or simply ignore the political implications of empowering states to coercively control access to natural resources. The environmental community's tacit or explicit support of coercive conservation tactics has far-reaching consequences, not all of which will benefit the environment in the long run. First, local resistance to what are perceived as illegitimate state claims and controls over local resources may lead to and even heighten violent response, resource sabotage, and eventual resource degradation (Blaikie 1985; Hecht and Cockburn 1989; Guha 1990; Peluso 1992a). Second, the activities of the outside environmental community may in fact be weakening the position of local resource claimants with less firepower than the state. While some conservationists are also “arming” local nongovernment organizations with symbolic and financial support, more likely, their ultimate goal in doing so would be as much to influence state policy as to empower local resource users. Third, whether for intensive state-controlled production or preservation for tourism revenues, valuation of resources often disenfranchises local people with long histories of subsistence resource use and some trade. State controls over commodified resources both empower the state and legitimate its use of coercion to protect “its” resources. Finally, even if the state's use or threat of violence does not guarantee the achievement of conservation goals, state actors may not “lose.” The means of violence and the ideologies of state stewardship of globally important resources, both obtained directly or indirectly from the international conservation community, may facilitate the state's enforcement of its claimed right to govern.

For all these reasons, the ethics underlying the spread of Western conservation ideologies require close reexamination, while programs to provide military equipment as part of their enforcement or “management” package, should be stopped. Professional environmental organizations need to examine the potential misuse of their resources for nonconservation purposes, and need to understand the long-term socio-political consequences of careless policies. In particular, the escalation of violence around valuable resource territories, and the losses of local resource control and local people's knowledge of resource management bode ill for biodiversity. Only by seriously considering how local people will tangibly, immediately, and for the long-term benefit from conservation activities will the protection of these resources be ensured. Unfortunately, coercive conservation can also strengthen or extend a state's military capacity—not only with the weapons of enforcement but also with new "moral" justifications to legitimate coercion in enforcing a narrowly defined "global community's" environmental will. Urgent action encouraged in the hope of alleviating urgent problems can become a burden, not a blessing, in the long term.

NOTES

Acknowledgments: Thanks are due to Ken Conca, Howard Dick, Dan Deudeny, Melanie DuPuis, Ann Hawkins, Ronnie Lipshultz, Christine Padoch, Jesse Ribot, Matt Turner, Peter Vandergeest, Charles Zerner, and the anonymous reviewers for their comments on earlier versions of the paper. Its shortcomings, of course, remain my own.

1. In general, following Skocpol, I use a Weberian definition of states as "compulsory associations claiming control over territories and the people within them. Administrative, legal, extractive, and coercive organizations are the core of any state" (Skocpol 1985, 7). However, although it is simpler to discuss "the state" as if it were a homogenous entity with common purpose under all circumstances, it should be understood that the use of this term does not imply homogeneity. See, for example, Evans (1979).

2. A complete discussion of the interactions between incentives and coercion in resource management is beyond the scope of this paper (compare Menzies and Peluso 1991).

3. Discussion of the militaristic aspects of conservation is less common and remains the key focus of this essay.

4. For example, conflicts at UNCED over rights to cut tropical forests and sell tropical timber versus preserving the world's primary sources of biological diversity, conflicts between nations and within the international environmentalist community over hunting elephants and ivory sales, conflicts between officials in forestry departments responsible for conservation versus those who manage production forests, mapping changes, violations of logging and antilogging permissions, and so on.

5. Other land uses in the areas discussed include capitalist wild game ranching, commercial cattle ranching, and irrigated wheat farming. The consideration of all these land uses in this paper is not possible. The focus here is on lands claimed by state resource management agencies but contested by rural people.

6. In late 1993, Leakey resigned his position as head of the Wildlife Service. Developments leading up to his resignation and those immediately subsequent to it are beyond the scope of this essay.

7. Previously, the colonial government had also had difficulty in establishing its authority.

8. The diversity of "Outer Island" forest circumstances makes a discussion of these forest management systems beyond the scope of this essay.

9. Using former soldiers as foresters was also a common practice in the forest districts first annexed by the United East India Company in eighteenth-century Java and is not uncommon today.

10. Forest guards carry guns only in the teak forests because of the high value of the teak trees. Guns are not carried by guards in pine or other types of non-teak forest in Java.

11. On the formation of these intrastate alliances between the center and peripheries of power, see Barber (1989), Peluso (1992a), Hart (1986).

12. In the first catalogs to use this environmental justification for their marketing sources, the company mentioned that they bought their Java teak through Thailand. This comment was written separately from the note on its certification both because the supplying of teak from Thailand hardly fit the eco-claims of the company and because of the implausibility of Java teak being sold to Thai middlemen for sale to the United States.

13. This is due to recent events in Java's agrarian history to which many forest-based peasants were witnesses, including the killing of people associated with (then-legal) communist groups in the 1960s and the execution of various petty and major criminals in the early 1980s (known as "the mysterious shootings," or *penembakan misterius)*.

REFERENCES

Africa Confidential. 1989. "Kenya: Crackdown on Somalis." 30 (1): 6–7.

African Wildlife Foundation. 1989. "1989 Was a Very Good Year: Annual Report." *Wildlife News* 25 (2): 5.

Anderson, David, and Richard Grove, eds. 1987. *Conservation in Africa: People, Policies, and Practice.* Cambridge, England: Cambridge University Press.

Barber, Charles. 1989. "State, People, and the Environment: The Case of Forests in Java." Ph.d. diss., University of California, Berkeley.

Blaikie, Piers. 1985. *The Political Economy of Soil Erosion in Developing Countries.* London: Longman.

Chadwick, Douglas H. 1991. "Elephants—Out of Time, Out of Space." *National Geographic* 179 (5): 11–24.

Collett, David. 1987. "Pastoralists and Wildlife: Image and Reality in Kenya Maasailand." In *Conservation in Africa: People, Policies, and Practice* ed. David Anderson and Richard Grove. Cambridge, England: Cambridge University Press.

Cranworth, B.F.G. 1912. *A Colony in the Making*. London: Macmillan.

Darmosoehardjo, Djokonomo. 1986. "Penguasaan teritorial oleh jajaran Perum Perhutani" (manuscript). Jakarta: Perum Perhutani.

Deudney, Daniel. 1990. "The Case Against Linking Environmental Degradation and National Security." *Millennium: Journal of International Studies* 19 (3): 461–76.

Dove, Michael. 1983. "Swidden Agriculture and the Political Economy of Ignorance." *Agroforestry Systems* 1 (1): 1–15.

———. 1986. "Peasant versus Government Perception and Use of the Environment: A Case Study of Banjarese Ecology and River Basin Development in South Kalimantan." *Journal of Southeast Asian Studies* 17 (3): 113–36.

Eliot, C. 1905. *The East African Protectorate*. London: Edward-Arnold.

Evans, Peter. 1979. *Dependant Development: The Alliance of Multinational, State, and Local Capital in Brazil*. Princeton: Princeton University Press.

Guha, Ramachandra. 1990. *The Unquiet Woods: Ecological Change and Peasant Resistance in the Himalaya*. Berkeley: University of California Press.

Hart, Gillian. 1986. *Power, Labor, and Livelihood*. Berkeley: University of California Press.

Hecht, Susanna, and Alexander Cockburn. 1989. *The Fate of the Forest: Developers, Destroyers, and Defenders of the Rainforest*. New York: Verso.

Kiss, Agnes. 1990. *Wildlife Conservation in Kenya*. Washington, D.C.: The World Bank.

Knowles, Joan N., and D. P. Collett. 1989. "Nature as Myth, Symbol, and Action: Notes Towards an Historical Understanding of Development and Conservation in Kenyan Maasailand." *Africa* 59 (4): 452.

Lindsay, W. K. 1987. "Integrating Parks and Pastoralists: Some Lessons from Amboseli." In *Conservation in Africa: People, Policies, and Practice*, ed. David Anderson and Richard Grove. Cambridge, England: Cambridge University Press.

MacKenzie, John. 1987. "Chivalry, Social Darwinism, and Ritualized Killing: The Hunting Ethos in Central Africa up to 1914." In *Conservation in Africa: People, Policies, and Practice*, ed. David Anderson and Richard Grove. Cambridge, England: Cambridge University Press.

McNaughton, S. J. 1985. "Ecology of a Grazing Ecosystem: The Serengeti." *Ecological Monographs* 55 (3): 259.

McNeeley, Jeffrey A., Kenton R. Miller, Walter V. Reid, Russell A. Mittermeier, and Timothy B. Werner. 1988. *Conserving the World's Biodiversity*. Washington, D.C.: Worldwide Fund for Nature.

Menzies, Nicholas K., and Nancy Lee Peluso. 1991. "Rights of Access to Upland Forest Resources in Southwest China." *Journal of World Forest Resources* 6 (1): 1–20.

Migdal, Joel. 1988. *Strong Societies, Weak States: State-Society Relations and State Capabilities in the Third World.* Princeton: Princeton University Press.

Peluso, Nancy Lee. 1992a. *Rich Forests, Poor People: Resource Control and Resistance in Java.* Berkeley: University of California Press.

———. 1992b. "Traditions of Forest Control in Java: Implications for Social Forestry and Sustainability," *Natural Resources Journal* 32 (4): 1–35.

———. 1994. "Fruit Trees and Family Trees in an Indonesian Rainforest: Property Rights, Ethics of Access, and Environmental Change." *Theory and Society* (under review).

Peluso, Nancy Lee, and Mark Poffenberger. 1989. "Social Forestry in Java: Reorienting Management Systems." *Human Organization* 48 (4): 333–44.

Pinedo-Vásquez, Miguel, Daniel Zarin, and Peter Jipp. 1992. "Economic Returns from Forest Conversion in the Peruvian Amazon." *Ecological Economics* 6: 163–73.

Rainforest Alliance (New York). 1991. "The "Smart Wood" Certification Program." manuscript.

Schwartzman, Stephen. 1986. *Bankrolling Disasters: International Development Banks and the Global Environment.* San Francisco: Sierra Club.

Skocpol, Theda. 1985. *States and Social Revolutions in France, Russia, and China.* Cambridge, England: Cambridge University Press.

Smith and Hawkin, Ltd. 1991. *A Catalog for Gardeners.* 38 (summer).

Tilly, Charles. 1985. "War-Making and State-Making as Organized Crime." In *Bringing the State Back In,* ed. Peter Evans, Dietrich Rueschemeyer, and Theda Skocpol, 169–91. Cambridge, England: Cambridge University Press.

Western, David. 1982. "Amboseli National Park: Enlisting Landowners to Conserve." *Ambio* 11 (5): 304.

———. 1984. "Conservation-Based Rural Development." In *Sustaining Tomorrow: A Strategy for Conservation and Development,* ed. F. R. Thibodeau and H. H. Field. Hanover, N.H.: University Press of New England.

World Wildlife Fund. 1989. "A Program to Save the African Elephant." *World Wildlife Fund Letter* no. 2:6.

6

Native Amazonians and the Making of the Amazon Wilderness: From Discourse of Riches and Sloth to Underdevelopment

William H. Fisher

The process by which particular environments come to be descriptively labeled is exceedingly complex. In the case of the Amazon, one cannot speak only of an autochthonous development, the growth of scientific knowledge, or human understanding, but of a global exchange of competing enterprises and meanings. Current descriptions of the Amazon as a region defined, above all, by its natural characteristics have made it difficult to appreciate some rather dramatic changes in what the perception of the Amazon as a particularly "natural" area might mean. While the weight of the environment in explaining the state and potential of the Amazonian economy has been preponderant throughout the present and past century, the concept of modernization and concomitant "development" ideology transformed an area that merely awaited "civilization" into one that was refractory to it and thus best characterized as a "wilderness." This chapter considers the changing meanings of the environment in Amazonia in light of successive attempts to organize the area to supply raw materials for a world market and to modernize its industries, communications and social organization. As this chapter shows, the social construction of the Amazonian environment has shaped the avenues of political influence open to indigenous peoples living there.

It is worthwhile reemphasizing along with the editors of this volume that the meanings associated with "environment" are both changing and highly contingent. This is in part a result of the way that meanings come to be assigned or contested in the realm of discourse. It is by now a truism that acts of classification are fraught with power since such acts never merely define and assign meanings but, as importantly, exclude potentially relevant meanings from consideration. Even that which appears as a matter-of-fact and timeless descriptive usage does not take place in a social vacuum. The discipline of ecology would seem to be the source of many of the conservation prescriptions sought by those of us who seek to reverse trends toward destruction of the environment. However, science is itself part of a wider culture. Not only do commonsense terms such as "nature" and "rural" contain implicit social assessments and policy implications; technical descriptions along scientific lines may help complete the social definition of environment, as Melanie DuPuis shows in this volume, by lending the validity of science to contingent classifications of the world. Looking at the way ecologists define "environment" invites us to consider how the social construction of environment is embedded in scientific practice itself and leads us to consider directly some of the hidden implications of looking at the world in terms of "developed" and "underdeveloped" regions.

I wish, first of all, to build on the ideas of evolutionary biologists Levins and Lewontin (1985) concerning the relationship between organism and environment. Although their formulation is conceived as a necessary emendation to classical Darwinian theory, for our purposes they forcefully explain why the environment cannot be treated as a preexistent "thing" standing on its own. To describe an environment as "rich," "lush," "forbidding," or, perhaps even "complex" involves the fallacy that an environment is simply "there," confronting beings that attempt to survive within it. Levins and Lewontin argue that the view that treats the environment as presenting constraints and possibilities to which organisms must adapt is surely wrong. They illustrate the difficulty of what they take to be the majority position within ecology by pointing out the impossibility of defining an ecological niche for an organism before that organism actually exists.

> The description of the niche of a bird, for example, is a list of what the bird eats, of what and where it builds its nest, how much time it spends foraging in different parts of the trees or ground, what its courtship pattern is, and so on. That is, the niche is described always in terms of the life activity of the bird itself. This is not simply a convenience but an implicit recognition that niches are defined in practice by the organisms in the process of their activities. But there is a contradiction here. If the metabolism, anatomy, and behavior of an organism define its niche, how can a niche exist before the species, so that the species can evolve into it? (p. 98)

The problem in describing an ecological niche underlines the difficulty of describing an "environment" in the abstract. In describing an environment, organisms themselves always determine the relevant features. Levins and

Lewontin (1985, 99) illustrate this with an example of a tree. Tree bark is part of a woodpecker's environment as is an insect-eater while stones at the tree's base are not. For a thrush that feeds on snails whose shells it smashes, the stones are present, but the tree may be excluded. Adaptive problems and solutions are not objectively posed by the environment and solved by the organism—they emerge from the activities of the organism in particular environments. This has profound consequences for description of the environment since "the environment is not a structure imposed on living beings from the outside but is in fact a creation of those beings. The environment is not an autonomous process but a reflection of the biology of the species" (Levins and Lewontin 1985, 99).

This imperative to explicitly link description of the environment with specific activities of organisms is associated with a view of evolution and ecology that reintegrates the organism and environment as processes actively creating one another. For human beings, the relation between individual organism and environment does not exhaust the processes to be considered since these necessarily involve social organization as well. Social organization mediates human interaction with the environment, and groups of socially organized humans form the primary subjects of the kinds of mutually constitutive processes between organism and environment referred to above. Even in the simplest human societies, from the technological point of view, human activities are never a result of purely individual volition. By way of example, we can see that it is a particular cultural expression of social organization rather than species biology or individual will that mandates that youngsters of some Amazonian peoples collect turtle eggs while their mothers garden and their fathers make manioc flour. This is not to deny that individual differences in ability or biological differences associated with age or sex play a part in the assignment of social roles. However, "society" and "environment" never confront one another as seamless wholes. Activities of individual humans never duplicate one another in their entirety but conform to social roles that differentiate the distribution of human–environment interactions.

Thus there is no ecosystem to be described in the absence of attention to differently organized human endeavors (although surely this statement should be more explicit regarding the scale of such activity and the different sorts of bounded processes that might best be considered as part of smaller or larger ecosystems within a region). Authors throughout the centuries have been impressed with the luxuriant nature of the Amazon. In the absence of attention to the social context that defines both human practices and concomitant environments (note that these are necessarily plural if we consider different social roles!), we will tend to interpret awe at the Amazon's teeming diversity as a primordial human reaction to the vastness of nature, rather than looking at what is obscured by such expressions of rapture and amazement. In contrast, we should explicitly consider the aims of those authors who describe the Amazon, placing them in the historical and cultural context necessary for understanding the full content of these aims.

Many political initiatives against degradation of tropical forests enjoin the public to listen to the "voices from the rainforest" (for example, Gennino 1990). However, the heralding of indigenous peoples as "natural" allies against environmental destruction and indigenous knowledge, in particular, as a potentially fruitful alternative to destructive development practices holds a special irony. This irony is highlighted by a longer historical view of the course of the conquest in the Amazon. Looking through the foggy frame of development (or antidevelopment) ideology, we see that this discourse locates indigenous peoples outside social and economic processes leading up to the present. In fact, Native Amazonians have been subsidizing "development" and other economic projects not of their own initiative in the Amazon for almost 400 years. They have been paid in various currency: decimation by disease and overwork, mass migrations, destruction of a way of life, violence and physical annihilation (for example, see Hemming 1978, 1987; Ferguson 1990). It is almost inevitable that in the latter half of the twentieth century the Amazon Indian should be resurrected as the "guardian of the forest," because, no longer needed as labor, they can now serve the ideological role of defining an alternative to development.

This is an inadequate framework within which to contextualize the multiple voices of native Amazonians. The salience of the "environmental connection" is a result of a particular history and constraints placed on native peoples. The absence of historical contextualization tends to make Indians intelligible to a Western audience in terms of their relations with the environment rather than with a larger system of social relations. This has consequences for the political options open to indigenous peoples in pursuing their own agendas.

In this respect it is worth recognizing that, in its particulars, the course of events in different localities in the Amazon do not simply reflect the broader trends of the boom-and-bust cycles. That is not to say that local events are impervious to global or regional trends. What it suggests is that indigenous peoples were not engaged in an abstract historical trend but were making alliances, defending territory, or trying out new subsistence or trading strategies, depending on local circumstances. To this day, indigenous identity continues to be forged in both local happenings and processes operating over large areas of the globe. Local history is important precisely because it refuses to assimilate indigenous peoples as mere symbols of opposition to a certain model of development and asks questions about events of continuing importance for indigenous identities. What, for example, impelled the indigenous Mundurucú to venture en masse from fairly safe redoubts to attempt an attack on the state capital of Belém, and what motives had the equally indigenous Apinagé for acting on their own to thwart the thrust of the attack? What reasons lay behind the Pau d'Arco Kayapó's decision to settle alongside the nascent Dominican village of Conceição do Araguaia while their Gorotire Kayapó brethren chose to isolate themselves and later resist? To pose questions such as these (even if answers are not easily forthcoming) means to depart from large-scale history and partially undermine broad analyses of discourse such as the one in the first part of this chapter that supported my claim about the imaginative shift in the industrializing West regarding the Amazon. Yet both sorts of analyses come together precisely in the political struggles of indigenous peoples to maintain their ways of life. Indigenous peoples are a product of both the inner forces that they have acknowledged as part of their history and tradition and the broader climate of public opinion to which their appeals are formulated. This climate of public opinion is the result of widespread changes in perception that have resulted in the current propensity to see issues of environmental destruction in terms of economic development.

The rest of this chapter explores the specific hypothesis that the decline of the rubber boom in the Amazon after 1910 helped lead to a change in the way that the Amazonian environment was presented and inscribed in the popular imagination of the industrialized world. During the boom, per capita incomes in the Brazilian Amazon climbed 800 percent and regional population grew more than 400 percent (Barham and Coomes, 1994). Rubber wealth gave the capital of the Amazon the first electric street lighting in a large Brazilian city in 1896, a modern trolley system, extensive telephone service, and piped water, while approximately 1,675 ocean-going steamships docked at its port during 1910, 900 miles upriver from the coast (Burns 1980, 334; Weinstein 1983a, 192). The decline in rubber prices was dramatic, however, once plantation rubber began to be cultivated in Asia from seeds smuggled out of the Amazon. The price of rubber plunged to below $1.20 per pound in November 1910 from a high of about $3.00 per pound in May of the same year. The result was a massive wave of bankruptcies over the next few years. Rubber production declined dramatically over subsequent decades but without any sort of dynamic growth in other sectors of the Amazon. The Amazon entered a long period of stagnation.

In the popular imagination of North America, Europe and even Brazil, the Amazon region emerged from the rubber boom wilder and more intractable than previously thought. A contrast of travel accounts after 1910 with those of 60 or so years before suggests that the imaginative shifts that accompanied the rubber bust contrasted with those that preceded the boom. The rather staid narratives of early vintage, such as the straightforward packaging of Alfred R. Wallace's mid-nineteenth-century work *A Narrative of Travels on the Amazon and Rio Negro, of the Native Tribes, and Observations on the Climate and History of the Amazon Valley* ([1853] 1969) or William H. Edwards's 1847 work *A Voyage up the River Amazon,* give way to twentieth-century sensationalism. The penetration of a forbidding frontier is the subject of both Fritz Krause, the German explorer, who published his *In den Wildernissen Brasiliens* in 1911, and Theodore Roosevelt, whose *Through the Brazilian Wilderness* appeared three years later in 1914. "Forest" is no longer descriptive enough for the threatening Amazonian habitat; "jungle" with all its attendant air of menace is far preferable as is well illustrated by the subtitle of Alcot Lange's (1912) *In the Amazon Jungle—Adventures in Remote Parts of the River, Including a Sojourn among Cannibal Indians.*

Foreigner's views of the Amazon predominate in the existing literature on the Amazon, in which the Amazonian environment is evaluated as to its potential for activities (particularly those bringing progress and wealth) in terms understandable to its authors and readers. Remarkable changes had taken place in between 1850 and 1910, and expectations for the kinds of productive activities suitable for the Amazon changed accordingly in the interim. Given Brazil's colonial past, it is not surprising that these expectations were explicitly linked to the part that the Amazon would play in the global economy.

The rubber boom itself must be placed in the context of a history of boom-and-bust cycles that linked Brazil with the wider world since the early 1500s. For several centuries after Brazil's occupation by Portugal, Brazilian products constituted about two-thirds of the mother country's export trade with other countries (Burns 1980, 72). One of the difficulties in reconstructing an understanding of Brazilian colonial society is that foreign trade is much better documented than domestic trade (Prado 1971, 265–66). During the 1700s Brazil provided about 80 percent of the world's gold supply, during the period 1550–1650 most of the world's sugar, and during the end of nineteenth and beginning of the twentieth century most of the world's rubber supplies. Between 1895 and 1899, Brazil had 66.8 percent of world production of coffee (Flynn 1979, 7). Over several centuries the land, lives, and survival of indigenous peoples in Brazil have often been affected by economic pressures literally world-wide in scope.

Between 1850 and 1912, "for more than 60 years the rubber goods industry—a key sector of economic growth in the industrializing nations—received all or most of its basic material from the Amazon valley" (Weinstein 1983a, 9). Yet it is towards the end of this period that depiction of the region comes to stress neither its natural wonders nor its riches but its intractability to certain kinds of economic enterprise. The failure of a capitalist socioeconomic model to take hold in the region made the idea of the Amazonian wilderness appropriate. The difficulties of transforming social relations and introducing cattle, communications, and export agriculture as well as wage labor in the extractive industries produced an authentic backwater and validated the Brazilian north's character as a hostile environment.[1] Agricultural and manufacturing efforts in Brazil's south were successfully transforming society and the landscape, whereas in the north, the socioeconomic structures that existed prior to the rubber boom and that supported rubber production stubbornly resisted such radical changes (see for example Weinstein 1983b, 1986 for attempts to introduce capitalist relations of production in the rubber industry). Thus it was the idea of development, or rather the lack of development, that transformed the Amazon into a wilderness.

Our current conception of the Amazonian environment owes much to the backdrop of the specific model of economic development against which it is viewed. While "development" covers a plethora of overlapping meanings, in the Amazonian context, "discovery," "occupation," and "modernization" are currently seen as the essential components of changes that will accompany the intensification and rationalization of both agriculture and the extraction of raw materials. I take this particular mindset to be reflected in what I call "development discourse." However, there were alternative models and courses of action which hinged on different assumptions about the environmental and human potential of the region in the past century. A look at localized social and economic links forged on the frontier reveal that different discourses about the environment and progress can be interpreted as representative of conflicting economic strategies. Nonetheless, as will become clear in the course of this chapter, development discourse that highlights the progressive occupation and rationalization of the Amazon represents something new with respect to the worldview of nineteenth-century Amazonians. As would be expected, the latter espoused different views, depending on their respective emphases on mercantilism, landholding, cattle ranching, or export agriculture. None of these views, however, contained prescriptions for modernization as the basis of their outlook. Weinstein (1983a, 35–38) reports on the initial reluctance of the elite in Pará to encourage the rubber economy, since it was feared that this would contribute to a decline in already existing agriculture, which was believed to be the basis of true long-lasting prosperity.

As Bunker (1985) points out, boom-and-bust cycles based on extractive products not only eliminate other kinds of productive activities but also result in a collapse of social organization and its productive base in such a way as to make it very difficult to assemble the preconditions necessary for a subsequent upswing after a collapse. After the rubber boom the subsequent decline of strategies based on extractivism paralleled a rise in "development" ideology. Native Amazonians became all but invisible in the discourse of development at the same time as they were being marginalized even further economically with the shrinking of extractivism (industries based on the extraction or harvesting of natural products). What I hope to make clear is that the "discourse of development" is not only understood as a discourse that contains specific modernizing prescriptions for economic progress; it is above all, a way of perceiving that is largely taken for granted. This mode of perception is so ingrained that it colors the act of environmental description and shapes our commonsense contemporary acceptance of the connection between "Indianness" and ecology.

In fact, the tendency for some sectors of the Paraense elite to discourage or downplay the expansion of rubber extraction at the onset of the rubber boom echoed century-old polemics regarding the negative effects of the extractive industries on the productive infrastructure of the colony. Consistently and whenever possible throughout the colonial period, Indian labor was forcibly directed toward extractive industries which often required long collecting trips. Historians MacLachlan (1973) and R. Anderson (1976) stress the harm that overemphasis on collecting forest products caused to the development of stable populations and settlements in the area. This often worked to the detriment of local agriculture which was constrained by the organization of collecting expeditions. Because of its profitability, even active discouragement by local officials, such as limiting the number of canoes in use, proved to be ineffective at changing the priorities of profit-seeking colonists. When the Directorate system was instituted in 1758, Indian villages were placed under secular government authority, and each village director received one-sixth of the profits generated by the village. Since forest collecting tended to be the most profitable activity, it continued unabated. Finally, in 1780 collecting in common was banned so that the government would have enough native labor available to maintain the state apparatus (MacLachlan 1973, 210). Ross (1978, 194) argues convincingly that the lack of self-sufficiency in food production common to many areas of the Amazon today was a result of the disequilibrium caused by the stress on extractive industries. Not only did such industries make certain kinds of agriculture impractical, but they also produced the towns and urban centers dedicated to serving as commercial intermediaries for the extractive products that required food imports.[2]

The recent studies by Bunker (1985), Schmink and Wood (1992), and Hecht and Cockburn (1990) focus precisely on the political-economic and institutional histories of the extractive economy dominating the Amazon basin. These works make clear that neither current efforts to develop/conserve the Amazon nor past boom-and-bust cycles of extractive economies in the region can be understood with reference to historical events internal to the Amazon itself. For centuries regional policies have been formulated outside of the region. Regional products were destined for overseas markets. Evaluation of the needs of the area's inhabitants or of the area's stability were totally subordinated to the attempts to organize the extraction of wealth.

It is against this backdrop that indigenous peoples must fight the high-stakes battles for their land, traditions, and often their very lives. To avoid falling into the trap of a simple-minded association of Indianness and environmentalism, no matter how benevolent and reform-minded the public intentions, means paying attention to both local histories and broad cultural trends. The rest of the chapter can give no more than a hint of the complexities involved. I begin by contrasting nineteenth century and twentieth-century rhetoric of entrepreneurship inspired by the awesome nature and seemingly stunted social world of the Amazon and distinguishing between Brazilian and foreign variants. Then I discuss the history of a particular region on the Southern fringes of the Amazon, the Araguaia-Tocantins basin, where both reality and rhetoric diverged substantially from the broader trends. Eventually even in this region, rhetoric overcame and shaped reality in respect to the way indigenous people were viewed by Brazilians and international observers. The result is that current appeals for indigenous rights are wedded to the discourse of environmental activism which itself is a reflection of the development paradigm.

Foreign and Brazilian Observers of the Amazon in the Nineteenth Century

During most of the colonial period Brazilian territory remained closed to foreign exploration. From 1817 to 1820 the German botanist and zoologist team of Martius and Spix were the first non-Portuguese explorers permitted to explore the Brazilian Amazon. In the decades following the declaration of independence of the Brazilian north from Portugal in 1823, tremendous pressure was exercised on Brazil by Britain and the United States to allow international travel on the Amazon (Chaumeil 1992). By mid-century, foreign exploration expeditions to the Amazon increased in number, especially British and North American ventures, but also French and German, as these powers sought to extend their influence over the region. In 1866 a decree permitting international navigation on the Amazon was signed and the Brazilian Companhia de Navigação e Comércio do Amazonas, incorporated in 1853, came under British ownership as the "Amazon Steam Navigation Company."

The copious prescriptions for progress that grace travel accounts of the period thoroughly depended on what was envisioned as the mainstay of the economic future. Industrious agriculturalists clearly loomed large in the imagination of most outside observers. The historical substrate of these outsiders' visions seemed to be quite differently formed from those of Brazilians. Foreign travelers to the Amazon in the nineteenth century, such as Edwards (1847), saw the slothfulness of the natives as the chief impediment to regional progress. Henry Bates ([1864] 1962, 162), the botanist, echoed this assessment: the native population suffers from "incorrigible nonchalance and laziness . . . [which] alone prevented them from surrounding themselves with all the luxuries of a tropical country." The natural scientist Agassiz (1888) with a more imperialist bent mirrored similar thoughts that the advent of progress would only occur "when the banks of the Amazons will teem with a population more vigorous than any it has yet seen—when the twin continents will shake hands and Americans of the North come to help the Americans of the South in developing its resources." These viewpoints reflect an agrarian view of wealth and economic "progress." They reflect as well the outpouring of immigrants from Europe which amounted to over 50 million between 1820 and 1930 (Crosby 1986, 5). Although only a small minority found their way to the tropics, there was hope that this flow of European humanity could be at least partially diverted to the tropical Amazon, where bountiful nature provided the substrate for human industriousness that could produce wealth. The description of the environment as "rich" in light of the poverty of the region provided forceful evidence of the "sloth" of the natives. Within this equation, human vigor and application was the missing variable.

Foreign travelers from abroad quoted here were less sensitive to the antecedents of the landscape they glimpsed than their Brazilian counterparts. In contrast to foreign reports, the economic changes in nineteenth-century Amazonia noted by Brazilian observers represented a decline from the previous period when there was ample native labor. They were aware that productivity had actually been higher in the previous century. For example, João Henrique de Matos described the places he visited during his trips along the Rio Branco and Rio Negro in 1842–43. "The greater part of its settlements were deserted by their inhabitants, and today it is impossible to establish their whereabouts for they have hidden themselves in the tangled forests in order to exempt themselves from the onerous enlistment service, from the country's plunderers, and from those thirsty for power" (Matos 1979, 146). The town of Manaus (today capitol of the state of Amazonas, then the Vila da Barra do Rio Negro) was also observed to be in a similar state of decadence and abandonment, with "everything in total ruin and shortly all these edifices will disappear; and already the tiny leftover ceramic works does not operate, for want of an administrator (Administrador da Recebedoria) to work with" (Matos 1979, 148).

Brazilian observers linked the failure to achieve economic prosperity to the government's inability or shortsightedness in preventing the decline of native settlement along the main waterways. Consistently, nineteenth-century travelers in the Amazon speak of the decadence and abandonment of former productive centers. The fact that a particular region was relatively unknown or unexplored was never put forward as the cause for the existing economic state of affairs. Exploration of the area was necessary to achieving administrative control and such control was a parallel process to economic revival rather than the impetus for development. Even those authors who effectively described uncharted routes in documents labeled *roteiros* usually presented their endeavors as aimed at facilitating existing ventures. They aimed to facilitate travel and communication by enhancing existing economic enterprise rather than by presenting the discovery of new resources as the key to economic improvement.

Neither nineteenth-century formula for economic progress, whether stressing the need for immigration or a resurrection of past successes, highlighted the environment itself as the main roadblock to the achievement of wealth. When natural surroundings enter into consideration, they are most commonly judged as favorable; the characterization of the environment as a daunting or as an inhibiting factor is absent. Discussions of local inhabitants in these works often take the form of racial stereotypes and their differing abilities to adapt to the exigencies of civilization and also climate. Even in this respect the disposition towards sloth among natives is rooted in racial traits rather than the environment's effect on human beings. Bates ([1864] 1962, 109), for example, in discussing the constitution of indigenous Amazonians says "There is something in their constitution of body that makes them feel excessively depressed in the hot hours of the day, especially inside their houses. Their skin is always hot to the touch. They certainly do not endure the heat of their own climate so well as the whites. The negroes are totally different in this respect; the heat of midday has very little effect on them, and they dislike the cold nights on the river."

If some Indians were ill-disposed to strenuous work, their absence was also lamented. Although the instability of settlements was blamed on the innate shiftlessness of their inhabitants, as seen above, the oppressive demands of forced labor were also recognized. Accusations of nomadism were often tantamount to accusations of "paganism," since nomadism effectively curtailed organized Christian worship. There is no small irony that even indigenous peoples who cooperated with rural officials should be derided for their nomadic lifestyle in nineteenth-century accounts, since colonial administration increased the need for many indigenous peoples to be more mobile. It made mobility far more prevalent through the decimation of populations along the floodplain where highly productive agriculture was once well established. Populations inhabiting inland areas not only had to practice more extensive agriculture but also had to be mobile enough to exploit diverse and often widely spread game, fish, and wild plant resources. Increased warfare, both between Europeans and Indians, and also between indigenous groups themselves as a result of population displacements and Europeans' demands for slave labor also forced populations to move. The administrative failures of the Directorate Indian villages forced many peoples to flee as well. Unlike current models of human ecology that stress the adaptiveness of mobility within many tropical environments (see for example Meggers 1971 for an early classic presentation), Indian mobility in the nineteenth century was derided because it made for an elusive labor force, regardless of the ends to which their labor was used. However, native mobility was not only viewed as detrimental to economic and religious administration but also clearly seen by Brazilian observers as a result of a specific history or indigenous personality rather than as a consequence of environmental limitations.

Use of frontier discourse is absent in the accounts of Brazilians and most foreign explorers in the nineteenth century. When we do encounter frontier analogies, as in the references to the U.S. West in the writings of the Brazilian Euclides da Cunha ([1906] 1976) early in the twentieth century, they seem to have the modular qualities that B. Anderson (1983) claims aided the spread of national ideologies.[3] During most of the nineteenth century, the model of the frontier as the cusp of vitality and innovation was unsuitable for wholesale adoption into the very different Brazilian conditions. A situation almost inverse to that of the United States obtained over most of Brazil. With the decline of mineral prospecting at inland sites, the population flow had been away from the interior into concentrations along the coast during the early parts of the nineteenth century. The Amazonian pattern consisted of pulses of expansion and retraction following the rise of production of a particular extractive product and its subsequent exhaustion. Given this background, it is conceivable that only the advent of modern development ideology created the context for Brazilians to adopt a frontier rhetoric to describe the dynamics of Amazonian settlement. The idea of the frontier elaborated along with national expansion of the United States was appropriated for the Brazilian project of consolidation of its control over Amazonian territory only in the present century.

Twentieth-Century Constructions of the Amazonian Environment

The underdeveloped character of the Amazon was finally ratified by the recognition of the central role it could play as a supplier of raw materials to industrializing nations with new industrial needs. The Amazon possessed resources whose importance became newly emphasized in the 1970s. The constraints of the environment in allowing efficient and profitable access to raw materials and land becomes paramount in descriptions of development. Efforts to mobilize factors of production, labor and capital, are stymied by difficult access to resources. The attempt to exploit resources and make them available to global industrial usage begins what has been called the "second conquest of the Amazon." The 1972 report *The Amazon: Its Treasures Are Being Revealed* sums up the prevailing attitude:

> The importance of the Amazon jungle is decisive, above all for Brazil. Not so much for its present economic role . . . it is contributing less than 4 percent to the Brazilian Gross National Product—but for its potential wealth: it has 79.7 percent of the country's lumber reserves, 81 percent of its fresh water, half of its iron ore deposits, nearly 100 percent of tin deposits, 93 percent of its aluminum, and the largest deposit of rock salt in the world, estimated at ten billion [American] tons. The Amazon region also possesses what is thought to be the largest oil deposit in the world. . . . It is only recently, however, that effective measures have been taken to open up this great treasure-house, with the [Brazilian] Federal Government's decision to take real steps towards the occupation and "conquest" of the region. *Up to recently, the problems and difficulties of the Amazon area, while discussed at length, were never really faced, in any concrete way by the succeeding governments.* (cited in Davis 1977, 32 [emphasis added])

The "problems and difficulties" in the area are interpreted as problems "of the area"; the geographic locating of the problem thus conceals its social basis (see Short 1991, 110, for examples of this kind of semantic displacement). Clearly it was new forms of wealth to be appropriated that led to the stress on "occupation" and "conquest" in the context of development, rather than any objective "natural" status as a bona fide wilderness. In this scenario, exploration and discovery became synonymous with "development" in ways they never had before. Politically, this was immeasurably aided by the characterization of the area as a wilderness. The emphasis on the Amazon as an untouched natural area implied that what was hidden by the wilderness had to be simply uncovered. The notion depoliticizes development as a process: the unknown is conquered and unpeopled lands are occupied. Hidden in this formulation, of course, is the idea that the appropriation of new forms of wealth are responsible for the changing social relations in the region. Development is presented as a conquest of nature and occupation of the wilds. Simultaneously, and as part of the same ideological shift, the histories of indigenous peoples are concealed. They are concealed not in the sense that they no longer exist or that scholars no longer write about the Amazon, but in the sense that indigenous people's defense of their way of life is not sought in their history but in their relationship with and attachment to their natural surroundings.

Economic Cyles in the Araguaia-Tocantins Region

However, indigenous peoples were not simply inhabiting the wilds and avoiding contact with "civilization." In the backlands of Brazil they provided the basis for most of the productivity and accumulation of wealth by settlers and traders. The story of Amazonian economic development must include the many different kinds of encounters between indigenous peoples and larger social networks, which, in turn, are often themselves linked to trends that are global in scope. To illustrate this, I focus on describing contemporary observations of economic activity, indigenous people, and nature in Araguaia-Tocantins regions on the south central fringe of the Amazon basin and how these observations changed with the economic transformations following the rubber bust (see Figure 6–1).

Both rubber and Brazil nuts are extracted from this area, along with other wild products collected for market. It has also been the site of cattle ranches and missionary activity. While diverse groups of indigenous peoples are represented, those of the Gê linguistic stock are particularly numerous. This region is the ancestral homeland of important indigenous political activists in contemporary Brazil, such as the Kayapó and the Shavante.

The natives of the region of southern Pará, and Goiás, and Maranhão lived through various economic cycles. The first consisted of *bandeiras,* or armed military companies in search of gold, slaves, or trade that continued throughout the seventeenth century. These were followed by another hundred years during which inland prospecting expanded and then violently retracted. The opening of navigation of the Tocantins and Araguaia running through the territory to Belém and the subsequent closing of these rivers between 1737 and 1782 was decreed by the crown in order to better control trade and the royal tariffs collected on trade, and particularly to avoid gold smuggling. The effect was to decrease access to the area from the north during half a century. During the nineteenth century in Goiás (formerly spelled Goyaz) and southeastern Pará, after the decline of mining in the previous century, there was the development of different kinds of commercial ventures, mostly agricultural and ranch exports such as cotton, salt, and cattle.[4]

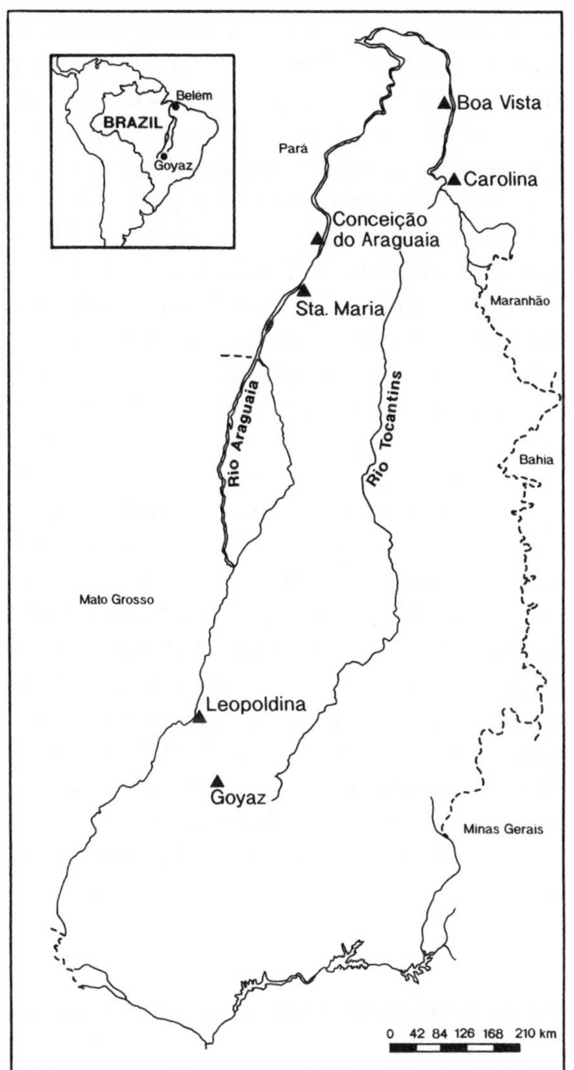

Figure 6–1

Former state of Goyaz prior to repartition. *Sources:* Joseph 1907; Bartholomew 1957; Pedroso 1993. Map illustration by Sondra Jarvis.

These were primarily based on the expansion of river trade between Goiás and Belém along the Tocantins and Araguaia Rivers, although a prominent trail led eastward from the province through the Indian village of Duro, established during the ban on river transport (Dole 1973, 29). The collecting of wild products from the area, collectively called *drogas do sertão,* also expanded during this time. Wild products included clove bark, cinnamon, vanilla, salsaparrilha, cacao, Brazil nuts, timber, turtles, turtle eggs, wild animal pelts, vegetable and animal oils, and manacaru (Prado 1971, 243). The rubber boom-and-bust followed at the end of the nineteenth century as well as smaller, but still significant, expansions and contractions of extractive enterprises such as Brazil nuts, wild cat pelts and other natural products. Indigenous peoples were indispensible in the successes of all these enterprises. They were even party to the struggle between Portuguese loyalists intent on preserving Brazil's colonial status and those opting for independence. As in North America, Indians fought on sides representing both independence and continued colonial rule over the colony. The two most interesting military men to record their observations of northern Goiás (now the Brazilian state of Tocantins) were Cunha Mattos and de Paula Ribeiro, both of whom sought out native allies. Throughout centuries, within the Amazon's south-central fringe, indigenous peoples took on diverse roles as military allies, laborers, guides, suppliers of food, and often the providers of the necessary infrastructure, paths, shelter, portages, and ports. Throughout the ups and downs and shifting emphases of the local economy on the Amazon's southern fringe and despite the rebellions that challenged rule by the elite in other parts of Brazil, natives of the region continued to figure in the plans for the area's renaissance.

Indian Labor and Infrastructure as the Key to Wealth to Nineteenth-Century Goiás

Like observers along the central waterways of the Amazon, those of the Goiás interior such as Cunha Mattos ([1824] 1874), Silva e Souza ([1812] 1874), and Alencastre (1864–65) lamented the province's decline in the early nineteenth century. Cunha Mattos ([1824] 1874, 285) pleaded for the introduction of capitalists into the province. The historian Furtado (1963) in his assessment of the early nineteenth century in Goiás contends that during this time the incoming migrants were technically inept, unskilled, and unable to contribute to the economic development of the area. Descriptions of Brazil's interior, while extolling the potential richness of the area, did not call attention to the intractability of nature nor to its impenetrable mysteries. Clearly, whether or not the area was defined as wilderness had little bearing on the challenges to inland settlement and prosperity.

In the Brazilian literature of the mid-nineteenth century it is sometimes difficult to understand the continued use of terms implying that native peoples are "savages" (*selvagem* or *silvícola*), given their evidently close and extended contact with national society. In fact, what is referred to is less a racial category than a description of adherence to "civilized" or "Christian" ways of life. In the accounts of Goiás and Pará, even those indigenous people who maintain trade and contact with missionaries and traders and may profess some Christian faith continue to be referred to as "savages." It appears that the criterion of fixed settlement becomes more important than peaceful intercourse or profession of religious faith in the definition of a savage. Of course, one of the prime aims of missionary activity was precisely the establishment of fixed settlements, ostensibly to permit systematic indoctrination of religion through schools and religious observances. However, the economic logic was also compelling. Only a fixed settlement could be counted on as a dependable source of labor or supplies. Thus the missionary conception dovetailed perfectly with the goal of economic progress based on a particular kind of export agriculture that the government officials were attempting to stimulate. Indigenous lifestyles were at odds with the efforts of missionaries and the provincial government, which encouraged fixed settlements, as well as with those of other interests who enforced mobility through labor drafts for collecting expeditions often lasting many months. For many of the Gê-speaking peoples of the region, social life was not so easily adapted to either scheme since it depended on the organization of both village activities and periodic nomadic forays, often associated with rituals. Both settled and nomadic sides of community organization were exercises in complementary forms of traditional sociality (Maybury-Lewis 1979). The Gê peoples inhabiting the great central plateau of Brazil spent a great deal of time away from their base villages on seasonal treks and in doing so acquired some of the foraging and survival skills extolled by administrators of Goiás. While prejudice against indigenous peoples is clearly reflected in the writings of the nineteenth century, it does not seem to be a lack of Christian faith or total reliance on their immediate environment that brings censure as much as a refusal to adopt a sedentary lifestyle and thus be subject to both the laws and labor demands of civilization.

In terms of the coercion of indigenous labor and the use of food, travel, and transportation as well as raw materials generated by Indians peoples, the experiences within the Araguaia-Tocantins region present both significant similarities and differences with other Amazonian areas. An important variable was that fixed settlements of numerous indigenous peoples were undertaken by the government rather than by religious missions even before the expulsion of the Jesuits in 1759. Another critical variable was the ability of many indigenous peoples to continue to function as a community in their dealings with elements of Brazilian society. The geographical location between cattle, mining and extractive pioneer fronts allowed indigenous peoples a bit of room for maneuver. A large number of indigenous peoples were successful in maintaining their collective identities in spite of periods of contact with colonial and post-colonial society sometimes amounting to hundreds of years.

The administrators of Goiás looked towards indigenous labor as the key to economic activity in their own region. This is starkly evident from an examination of the rhetoric of economic progress employed by the former president of Goiás, Couto de Magalhães, who wrote a popular and prominent book, O *Selvagem,* published in 1876, about the different indigenous peoples of the Brazilian interior:

> The Amazon valley by itself is a larger territory than that of the great European states. Its population, which is small, exports around 20,000 contos.
>
> And these 20,000 contos derive from rubber, salsa, brasil nuts, cacau, copaíba, wild animal skins and in general products collected from nature by tapuias of Brasil and the neighboring republics. . . . If the Amazon valley did not possess the Tapuia [or semi-integrated natives], it would currently be one of the poorest regions of the country, while, with the Tapuia, and precisely because he is semi-barbarous and is able to carry out these industries, the region is one of the most productive that we possess." (Magalhães [1876] 1975, 23—my translation)

The former president goes on to include cattle herding as another activity that would be unsuccessful without native labor. Moreover, indigenous peoples should be the instruments of further extending the dominion of Brazil to their as yet unintegrated brethren: "the principal instrument of riches is neither the white nor the black race. . . . The manual labor, the elaboration of riches that there depends totally on the extractive industries is exclusively daughter of the natives who in the past were pacified in that valley by bodies of interpreters, indispensable auxiliaries of civilization and of the missionary" (Magalhães [1876] 1975, 25).[5]

This is not an isolated expression of optimism but is found stated in similar terms throughout this period. We find that the Amazon is presented in keeping with the Portuguese colonial project in which natives are not affected by development but instead are central to the whole enterprise. In the nineteenth-century accounts cited above, complaints of the decadence of the Amazon region were invariably linked to the reduction of productive activity and to the decimation or flight of native inhabitants. Thriving native communities were a necessity for economic development.

The stance of Couto de Magalhães toward the integration of natives into the regional economic project coincides with the exaltation of Indianism as a symbol of Brazilian national identity. This tide of nationalist ideology reached its peak between the years of 1840 and 1875. Writers, poets, historians, and other members of the intelligentsia agreed on the desirability of basing Brazilian national culture on an endogenous native tradition in preference to their Portuguese or European heritage (Burns 1968, 44). It would be a mistake to write off Couto de Magalhães's thought as mere verbiage rather than authentic public policy proposals, even though his praise of "tapuias," or detribalized indigenous peoples, stands in sharp contrast to North American observations during the same period. In fact, Couto de Magalhães's discourse might best be read as a reaction to those cited who advocated the replacement of Brazil's native population as a way out of the existing impasse. The assumptions shared by both sides about the environment and the kinds of economic activities that represented progress underscore the fact that positive evaluation of the native population became one way to signal a clear differentiation of national self-interest. In addition, as part of the Brazilian military, Couto de Magalhães had witnessed the aggression against Paraguay (1865–70) in which the wholehearted support and participation of the indigenous Guaraní for the cause of Paraguay provided staunch resistance against the combined might of Brazil, Uruguay, and Argentina. Finally, in his search for models to generate wealth, Magalhães, like those chroniclers of Goiás before him, Silva e Souza, Alencastre, and Cunha Mattos, quite consciously sought to recreate and extend the modest successes of the previous century in Amazonia.

At the beginning of the nineteenth century in Goiás the provincial government and the Portuguese crown hoped to stimulate agriculture and commerce in the aftermath of the precipitous drop of wealth and population in the mining regions. The 50,000 nonindigenous inhabitants of the territory at the time was a striking drop from the population at the height of the mining boom.[6] The interior of Pará and Amazonas saw similar declines. In 1850 these areas were less populated and less prosperous than a century before (Abreu 1954, 276). It was not only the royal Portuguese decree of 1785 banning manufacturing in the colonies that inspired policies to generate agricultural production and commerce (compare Furtado 1963), but the success of the missionaries in the Amazon during the mid-eighteenth century that oversaw the production of at least sixteen large farms, six cattle ranches and more than sixty villages of Indians or Tapuias. As an economic model these villages loomed large in the minds of nineteenth-century observers. They "produced large quantities of flours, cotton, sugar, sugar-cane rum, and cacao. They made salted fish and produced capital . . . using the riches of the forest, cutting timber, making boats, while women spun cotton and wove cloth" (Azevedo 1930, 228–29 in Moreira Neto 1988, 23). Natives were portrayed by influential nineteenth-century observers as responsible for the kind of diverse and sustainable production that provincial leaders felt could fuel the Goianian economy and effectively employ its water resources for transport.

The plans to revive the economy of the Goiás captaincy involved the stimulation of settlements along the rivers that could then be integrated into a system of river trade connecting Goiás with Belém, the capital of Pará. At the beginning of the 1800s, the outgoing governor of Goiás, D. Francisco de Assis Mascarenhas, wrote to his successor, Delgado Freire, that agriculture and commerce with Pará are the hopes for expansion, and tax breaks would encourage settlement to that end. "The instructions given to Don João Manoel de Menezes in the memo of the Secretary of State of Overseas Affairs of January 10, 1799 recommend especially to this governor the navigation of the Araguaia and Tocantins Rivers and commerce between this Captaincy with that of Grâo-Pará. The Royal Letter of January 7, 1806 in response to my 'officio' of October 7, 1804 conceded exemption of the ten percent tax for 10 years to those who would establish themselves along the banks of these rivers up to a distance of 3 leagues from them" (Mascarenhas 1843, 180–89).

The project of establishing consistent water communication between Goiás and Pará was a continual, and frustratingly unattainable, objective for successive administrations throughout the nineteenth century (Dole 1973). If the project was ultimately unsuccessful, the technical engineering of hard-to-navigate stretches, the unavailability of financial resources to undertake these infrastructural reforms, the lack of political coordination between the administrations of Pará (formerly called Grâo-Pará) and Goiás, and the fairly low level of population and exportable production in the area were all partly responsible. Where river trade was continually maintained through private initiative along the Tocantins, the participation of indigenous peoples was central to its success. Although government efforts focused primarily on the Araguaia, with the building of outposts that could serve as supply depots for trading vessels, here as well indigenous peoples played a central role both as laborers on the boats and as furnishers of supplies, including wood needed for steamboat power.

Although various accounts cite native hostility as the chief cause for the sparseness of river travel (for example, Cunha Mattos [1824] 1874, 285) what in fact transpired was that, with some encouragement, the very peoples that were the sources of the supposed offenses against Pará-bound river commerce made possible the limited success it did enjoy. Native peoples both rode the boats and supplied them with provisions and firewood. The French explorer Francis de Castelnau (1949, 348), who traveled in the service of his compatriot's interests in the commercial potential of the Araguaia, describes the role played by the Apinagé who lived near the juncture of the Tocantins and the Araguaia when he made his descent in 1844. "These Indians are diligent workers and it is they, with their vast plantations that feed, not only the people of Boa Vista, but also the personnel on the boats that navigate the Tocantins until the Post of São João. They pride themselves also of being excellent rowers, many of them having made the trip all the way to Belém of Pará. For this long journey that can take from six to eight months, they receive by way of payment an ordinary shotgun worth five or six francs."

Another indigenous people, the Karajás, also assisted Castelnau during his voyage. They, too, were key players in river transport. Ruffin Theodoro Segurado (1848), who followed an itinerary similar to Castelnau in 1847, was well received in numerous villages of the Karajás, and it is doubtful if his trip downstream to Pará would have been at all possible without their assistance. Segurado's party also met Shamboiá relatives of the Karajás; some Shavante people and at least four Apinagé were part of his crew. Neither Castelnau nor Segurado seemed to be aware of the history of government-level contacts with the Karajás (from at least 1775 and perhaps earlier, see Fonseca [1775] 1846) nor that some Karajás previously had agreed to settle in the government-sponsored village of Nova Beira and were consequently transferred in 1780 to the village São José de Mossamedes to live alongside the Kayapó (Chaim 1974, 121). Instead, Segurado speculated that the Shamboiá leader, Carô, who appeared quite familiar with Brazilian customs, may have been a fugitive from the state of Pará. However, he mentions chief Carô's acceptance of settlers, missionaries, and river transport and emphatic rejection of any construction of military outposts. The Indians had previous distressing experiences with such an outpost, Santa Maria do Araguaia, built in 1812. In a formidable show of unity, Santa Maria had been destroyed the following year under joint attack by the Karajás, Shavante, and Sherente. The abuses of the garrison were generally acknowledged to have provoked such a legitimate reaction. The Indians Segurado met spoke Portuguese, possessed arms, were trading partners with the Apinagé, and inquired of him if fighting continued in the north, presumably a reference to the Cabanagem revolt (1835–40 in Pará) and possibly the Balaiada revolt (1838–41 in Maranhão).

In terms of regional trade, military preparedness, and concern with the potential impact of distant events, the Karajás were clearly products of social processes that far transcended the boundaries of their own villages. While quite hospitable to wayfarers, they vigorously resisted the establishment of military garrisons along the expanse of the Araguaia, and it was not until 1861 that another garrison was established to take the place of Santa Maria.[7] In 1871 with the introduction of steam-powered transport, Friar Sigismundo was sent to organize the Karajás specifically to supply food for steamboat navigation along Araguaia. "For a time the settlement at São José was a 'centre of evangelisation,' with bands of Karajá camped on the wide beaches nearby while steamers, plied the empty *[sic]* Araguaia. All along the Araguaia, the Karajá were encouraged to bring logs for the steamers' boilers and were to be paid in tools, tobacco, clothing and salt" (Hemming 1987, 394).

With identical intentions of enlisting Indian aid, Couto de Magalhães founded a school, Colégio Isabel, at Leopoldina in the same year, 1871. In the preface of the second edition to his book, *Viagem ao Araguaya* ([1863] 1977), Couto de Magalhães (p. 25) asserts that all the tribes of the Araguaia region were represented at the school's founding: "immediately there entered twenty children of both sexes from the Shavante, Gorotires, Kayapós, Karajás, Tapirapés and three from the extinct tribe of the Guajajará." Magalhaes envisioned a future when, although the area to the west of the Araguaia would still be settled by Indians, each village would house at least several youths educated in Portuguese and prepared to assist any colonists or others aiming to bring economic progress to the region. To the twentieth-century reader this may appear more on the order of a Utopian dream than a clear-eyed prescription of government policy. In fact, this ideal was often a fair description of the kinds of encounters documented in the above cited works of Castelnau,

Segurado and others and probably also seemed partially capable of recapturing some of the dynamism of the extractive economies of the past century in the Amazon, especially given the growing trade in rubber in the second half of the nineteenth century.

If indigenous communities provided support for transport, they also formed the basis of settlements up and down both the Araguaia and Tocantins Rivers. The Krahó people along the Tocantins were essential to the founding of the settlement called São Pedro d'Alcântara. The mediator of this process was the trader Pinto de Magalhães. He recognized that the system of chiefly authority characteristic of the Gê language speakers, such as the Kayapó, Krahó, and Shavante among others, permitted the chief to act as a conduit for manufactured goods which in turn would be redistributed.[8] The separation of kinship relations and "public" chiefly office served the Gê in good stead. Following their own organizational principles they were able to form political alliances while not accruing kinship obligations with outsiders. Pinto de Magalhães (1852, 52) presents this form of transaction as if it were his own rather than an indigenous innovation: "I adopted the system of preserving them under the sight and governance of their own chief; to him, I make clear what he should do with his people, and show them the products and deeds I seek. He docilely listens and, without hesitation, orders his followers who execute whatever orders I have determined; immediately, there is obedience."

Along the Araguaia, the principal settlements for extractive activities as well as other sorts of production were "Pau D'Arco, Shamboiá, Santa Maria and Sant'Ana da Barreira (Ianni 1979, 11). Not coincidentally, the first two names also refer to two groups of indigenous peoples, the Pau D'Arco Kayapó and the Shamboiá Karajás. In all of these settlements farmers, cattle herders, fishermen, and Brazil nut and latex collectors settled in proximity to Indian villages. The French explorer Henri Coudreau, while in the service of the Pará state government, described the expansion of cattle production across the Araguaia and mentions that the cattle herders (many obviously of indigenous extraction themselves) followed the paths made by the Kayapó to lead their cattle safely. He specifically cites the village of Sant'Ana da Barreira as subject to periodic inundations, especially to the great ten-year floods. Because of this the population tended to move toward the interior although they feared Kayapó attacks. The cattle searched out pastures and the farmers trailed along afterwards. "A definitive settlement would have to be close to the river, yet not subject to constant flooding and have both good pasture and farming land in close proximity. The inhabitants of Barreira—folks of the people, of little instruction but much good sense—understand this perfectly. In this way, with total willingness, they threw themselves, along with Frei Gil, into the task of exploring the fields *(cerrados)* and the bush of the Lower Pau D'Arco region where they wish to guarantee a good permanent installation, safe from flooding and at the same time within reach of the General Fields of the Kayapó and of the villages of these Indians" (Coudreau 1897, 150).

Necessary Savages

The uncertain position of Indians in discourse reflects their contradictory social position. State adminstrators of the backland economy relied on indigenous communities at best partially under its control. As presented in the passage cited from Coudreau, the motivations of the settlers are unintelligible because, while they will not look for a suitable site because of fear of Kayapó attack, they also insist that the suitable site must be in proximity to the village of the Kayapó. This fear of dealing with the independent power of native communities in the face of continued reliance on these communities informs and shapes many of the documents and accounts of the period. Not only, as mentioned above, is there the continued derogatory reference to "savages", but language of the time is liberally sprinkled with references to the *insultos* of the aforementioned "savages." These "insultos" are often unaccompanied with reference to any particular transgression, leading one to surmise that the very inability of frontierspeople or forces of the state to regulate the behavior or power of indigenous communities in itself constituted an insult to properly constituted religious and civil authority. Hemming (1987, 399) reports how even fears of Indian attack along the Verde and Bonito tributaries of the Araguaia in Southern Goiás in 1880 did not provoke unilateral condemnation against the Kayapó from authorities because of the mistreatment these peoples were known to have suffered at the hands of settlers. Province President Sousa Spinola praised the Kayapó stating, "They are the best rowers on the Araguaia, robust and audacious workers. If they have attacked us, they have also been treated mercilessly by the Christians. Your Excellency cannot imagine how many atrocities our people have committed against the Indians, even recently."

Autonomous communities of indigenous peoples thus both furnished instrumental labor for the transportation and extractive industries, but remained outside direct social control. As Sousa Spinola recognizes, they are not "our" people, they were not subject to all the regulations of the state, and moreover they retain the autonomy to choose either some form of cooperation or armed attack as means to achieve their collective goals. As a group the northern Kayapó, like the southern Kayapó who alternately rowed or attacked, were, in fact, not of a single mind as to their collective goals. Northern Kayapó settlements separated on the basis of disparate attitudes towards elements of the national society infiltrating their lands.

The instrumental participation of autonomous indigenous communities in mainstream economic activities of the time was repeated over and over again within the area of the Araguaia and Tocantins during the nineteenth century. Further examples could be supplied, such as the Shavante of Salinas, the Akroa and Shikriabá Shavante of Duro, the Javaé Karajás and other indigenous peoples who also furnished their labor power to agricultural and transportation concerns. I do not wish to downplay the manner in which what appeared to be generally good will on the part of indigenous people was so often rewarded with disease, betrayal, forced settlements, or the fomenting of conflict between different indigenous groups. A sad example is given by the Pau d'Arco Kayapó, who befriended the Dominicans and laid the basis for the town of Conceição do Araguaia. They were totally obliterated by smallpox, the last remaining survivors dying in the 1940s. In contrast, the Gorotire Kayapó, who lived some distance from the settlements of Araguaia, gave rise to numerous thriving communities. What I wish to reiterate with these selected examples is that indigenous peoples were not relegated to a peripheral frontier, either rhetorically or practically, during the 150-year period between the decline of mining in the mid-eighteenth century and the precipitous decline of the rubber industry early in the present century.

Frontier Rhetoric and Economic Decline on the Early Twentieth-Century Araguaia

The town Conceição do Araguaia was established because the Domican missionary Frei Gil Vilanova was able to convince the Pau d'Arco Kayapó to settle along the town boundary. Accounts of the town are crucial to help pinpoint the juncture at which Indians were relegated to a particular position vis-à-vis the environment. Between 1897 and 1912, the inhabitants of Conceição devoted themselves primarily to the collection of rubber latex. One can see the importance not only of Indian labor but of infrastructure in the form of paths, gardens, and settlements to the economic enterprise. Frei José M. Audrin, a Capuchin missionary, notes in his memoirs written in 1911 that "the roads leading to the forests with latex crossed territories inhabited by Indians, being the case that some crossed through their villages. Mule trains and tappers contracted young natives, fooling them with ridiculous promises" (Audrin 1963, 184).

While it is possible to see the evidence of native economic activity in this passage, a unique twentieth-century construction characterizes the way it is framed. Natives are but an appendage or a feature of the environment. This rhetorical shift is prompted not by any change in the native's contribution but by the changing subject that constitutes the environment: that is, the area's underdevelopment. This is the same descriptive frame that makes it possible for Indians in the late twentieth century to be listed among the environmental impediments that must be taken into account for successful completion of a hydroelectric facility in the modern development plans of the Brazilian state electric utility, ELETROBRAS (Castro and Andrade 1988, 7). In Audrin's formulation, rubber tapper's roads passed through Indian villages as if by chance. In fact, rubber tappers and mule trains followed trails built by the natives themselves. Not only was transportation facilitated, but in native villages they could trade for food and also recruit labor for next to nothing. This rhetorical shift is emblematic of Amazon's status as a wilderness. This perspective, which sees development happening to, rather than by means of, natives, is possible because in the twentieth century untamed wilderness represents not only a state of nature but a state of society: social relations are assimilated to relations with nature. It is in this ideological environment that natives can be treated along with other plants and animals in assessing the environmental impact of hydroelectric projects. It is this perspective as well that makes Indians part of the environmental solution to a scenario not of their making.

As it presents itself, the case is not one in which Indians were consigned to a periphery merely because the extractive industries in which they played a central role gradually receded. Instead, the shift in discourse is part of an economic and ideological attempt to supplant these activities through modernization. To this end it was necessary to exclude indigenous peoples from any apparent role in the "progress" of the region. Clearly, if the new impetus for progress enters from outside the region in the form of modernization, it follows that indigenous and other local inhabitants must be forcibly roused from their lethargy by energetic stimuli from the very Brazilian society from which they are excluded. The recognition of an indigenous role in even nascent economic activity implies the possiblity of alternative courses of development. After all, Couto de Magalhães's view represents a contemporary competing paradigm or policy against which the new reigning paradigm was constructed. The final result was that, after more than a century of involvement in the central economic activities of the province of Goiás, indigenous communities found themselves on the outside of the centers as redefined by modern development ideology.

Conclusion

> But the story of the modern Brazilian Amazon frontier is at bottom a story of conquest. Viewed through the cool glass of history, this is only the most familiar sort of human ritual, the occupation of one more of the world's "waste spaces" and the coming to terms with the commandments of a new climate and ecology.
>
> Mac Margolis,
> *The Last New World,* 1992

> I envisage the conquest of the Amazon as a continuation, in time and in space, of the conquest of Goiás and Matto Grosso. When a dense and intelligently coöperating civilization has developed on the high plateau where the southern affluents of the Amazon have their sources, the frontier will roll northward decade by decade—century by century, perhaps—but it will roll! . . . It will be battle. Each advance will be planned with infinite care and detail. The determined engineers and sanitarians of a farsighted government will make their reconnaissance of the terrain ahead of the shock troops, whose battle losses will be heavy enough in any case. Every inch gained will be consolidated by an army of agriculturalists, herdsmen, and mechanics.
>
> Roy Nash,
> *The Conquest of Brazil,* 1926

The language of conquest, of a wilderness frontier being pushed outwards by the forces of progress is numbingly familiar. The applicablity of such language to the Amazon has retained its commonsense quality at least since the collapse of the rubber export economy over seventy years ago. While the Brazilian Amazon experienced incredible economic growth during the rubber boom, this led neither to sustained economic growth nor to a reshaping of the social order or dominant forms of social organization. The subsequent failure to modernize or modify social organization was seen as a failure to build on the commercial success of the rubber boom.

But who are the actors in this universal drama of frontier occupation, a seemingly permanent sideshow to empire- and nation-building throughout the twentieth century? The metaphors of war feature prominently (occupation, shock troops, advance, conquest), but while the protagonists are human beings, they, in turn, represent the far more impersonal forces of modernization and civilization. Looming as foe and adversary is "waste space" or "untamed wilderness." This point of view is at odds with both the texture of local histories as exemplified by discussion of the Araguaia-Tocantins above and the assessments of the environment by many competent and learned observers in the nineteenth century before the rubber boom. How do commonsense ideologies of today become so removed from the commonsense of previous generations as well as from the experiences of specific regions?

Support for the paradigm of frontier penetration made difficult by an unfamiliar Amazonian environment is not hard to locate; the forces of modernization have made much less headway (to continue the metaphor) than governments, planners, and hundreds of thousands of colonists and entrepreneurs would have hoped. They have seen their dreams of wealth and financial independence devoured by the immense and difficult terrain of the Amazon Valley. The "ecological" critique of development is traceable to such a conundrum; it essentially asks why the visions of early optimists were never realized and why environmental destruction so closely accompanies most attempts at "development." Betty Meggers (1971) has coined the phrase "counterfeit paradise" to underline the small potential for dense human populations and the forms of intense production envisioned by modernizers. Together with modernization ideology, the environmental movement also takes the central problem (and hence also similar notions of social agency) as one of "development" and offers alternative solutions that are less destructive of the environment.

Wallace ([1853] 1969) reminds us that, in general, nineteenth-century attitudes had little to do with conquest and much to do with competency of administration and racial characteristics of populations:

> It is a vulgar error that in the tropics the luxuriance of the vegetation overpowers the efforts of man. Just the reverse is the case; nature and the climate are nowhere so favorable to the laborer.

> What advantages there are in a country where there is no stoppage of agricultural operations during winter, where the least possible amount of clothing is the most comfortable, and where a hundred little necessities of a cold region are altogether superfluous. With regard to the climate, I repeat, that a man can work as well here as in the hot summer months in England, and that if he will only work three hours in the morning and three in the evening, he will produce more of the necessities and comforts of life than by twelve hours' daily labor at home.
>
> I fearlessly assert that here the primeval forest can be converted into rich pasture and meadow land, into cultivated fields, gardens, and orchards, containing every variety of produce, with half the labor, and what is of more importance, in less than half the time that would be required at home, even though there we had clear instead of forest ground to commence upon.

These were not the claims of the ignorant: Wallace was one of the most learned naturalists of his day and, along with Darwin, co-discoverer of the evolutionary theory of natural selection. In Wallace's vision, neither discovery nor modernization—linchpins of the frontier wilderness paradigm—are really fundamental to this vision of progress. The land is there to be worked and wealth awaits those who do so successfully.

An important shift in understanding occurred when the Amazon environment itself began to be described from a perspective that took for granted the goals of modernization and development that served the needs of manufacturing. With this shift came an idea that the Amazon could best be described as a wilderness. The main actor of economic development ceases to be a process initiated by inhabitants of a region and is instead generated by expansion of a frontier that overruns and incorporates both the environment and indigenous inhabitants. This is only possible with an imaginative shift in perception that defines the relevance of the environment with respect to modern techniques or strategies of economic development. I suggest that if the Amazon is seen today primarily as a wilderness, this is the result of a specific history. If the earlier cited titles of books published before and after the rubber boom are any indication, in the Western imagination, the Amazon has become more (not less) of a wilderness—more wild and unruly, more representative of nature's domain with the passage of time. This change in perception, ushered in with the twentieth century, was in all probability linked to the plethora of cultural and technological changes experienced during this period (Kern 1983; Lefebvre 1974). As part of this imaginative shift, indigenous peoples disappear from the social history of the area and from the policy recommendations of local administrators only to be later resurrected as part of the natural attributes of the wilderness region. On a local level we can see not only policy changes regarding the need to involve local indigenous populations[9] but also Indians vanishing as economic actors only to reappear later as part of the landscape in Audrin's account cited above.

The chief reason indigenous peoples are today able to employ their relationship with the environment in political contexts is that the association between ecology and native peoples is fairly well ingrained in the popular imagination of the industrialized world. The shift in discourse describing the Amazon only partially reflected internal regional processes, although it was and is used as a weapon to marginalize indigenous and *caboclo* (Amazonian rustic peasant) populations.

Removal of indigenous people to the frontier in Brazil was less a physical removal than a substitution of the central impetus for economic growth. If the adoption of a new discourse did not substantially change the relationship of indigenous people with lower-level brokers for the extractive industries, it proved to have a substantial impact on the political space in which Indians could receive a hearing for their collective interests. In fact, well into the twentieth century, Kayapó relations with Brazil nut and rubber backland bosses who directed extractive enclaves continued in a very similar vein (Fisher 1994). The move toward modern development of the Amazon has all the hallmarks of a hegemonic process as defined by Laitin: "The coercive forging and institutionalization of a pattern of a group activity in a state and the subsequent idealization of that schema into a dominant symbolic framework that reigns as common sense" (Laitin 1986, 13). This institutionalization of the new ideology necessitated a rejection of competing ideologies on one hand and a marginalization of Amazon's rural population, including indigenous peoples, on the other. The definition of "development" in these ideological circumstances necessarily centered on the effort, with the help of modern productive techniques and social relations, to dominate an intractable environment. It seems inescapable that the rhetorical shift assimilating indigenous people to the environment was part of a struggle to relegate rural indigenous people to the background status of recipients of economic innovation rather than groups with distinct interests that involved certain kinds of control over social and environmental resources, such as access to ecological niches, markets for what they produce, and health care. It is no accident that Native Amazonians' attempts at political engagement with a larger world have recently been framed for governments and the wider public in terms of a focus on the environment, problems of ecology, and economic development. Previously, native Amazonians had to seek the furtherance of their political agenda in other kinds of rhetoric and other kinds of actions.

The adoption of modern development ideology ensures that native peoples were assimilated to their surroundings in such a way that Western concerns have become attributed to them. In contemporary perspectives, natives are affected by development when development overruns their land and changes their relationship with their natural habitat. Thus their relationship with their environment becomes an overriding concern in much the same way that frontier development, primarily seen as "coming to terms with the commands of a new climate and ecology," becomes the privileged method of defining environment. The status as an underdeveloped region defines the subjective perspective from which the environment is viewed. In the same way that Levins and Lewontin (1985) point out that an ecological niche depends on and shapes an interacting subject, the aims of modernization define the relevant environmental parameters. With development as subject, an environment is created as its object. Native peoples, their social relations, and their habitat become defined as variable elements that are molded by a process whose initiating and conscious impetus has been appropriated to a particular model of economic growth.

The intricacies of development are not simply a matter of technical or social problems that are surmountable by vocational or sensitivity training. One can never focus solely on economic and ecological processes to understand development. One must also study the historically rooted ideological processes through which a world view comes to assert itself with such persuasiveness that all other phenomena become assimilated to a field irresistibly defined with respect to its major terms. From another point of view, the hegemonic process has defined not only a powerful view of the Amazon and its inhabitants in terms of an economic process but also the space within which indigenous communities can resist attempts to strip away resources and identities that are the basis of their continued distinct existence. Direct calls for elementary social justice and self-determination may not be as effective for indigenous peoples as appeals directed toward saving the wilderness. However, the political effectiveness of environmental appeals depend precisely on the fact that they derive their meaning from pervasively held ideas about indigenous peoples contained in development ideology. Ironically, in at least parts of the Amazon, this ideology itself is an artifact of the modern imperative to marginalize indigenous peoples.

NOTES

Acknowledgments: I thank Janice Alcorn, Larissa V. Brown, Janet Chernela, Brian Ferguson, Dave Hess, Marco Lazarin, Mindie Lazarus-Black, Melanie DuPuis, Peter Vandergeest, and Elayne Zorn for comments on forerunners to this essay. I alone am responsible for the argument as it now stands. My thanks go as well to Sondra Jarvis for her map illustration.

1. In the present volume Melanie DuPuis points to a striking parallel in New York State in which land unsuitable for intensified farming and milk-producing techniques came to be defined as marginal or submarginal and therefore subject to reforestation and conservation as wilderness areas.

2. This and all subsequent translations are my own.

3. Anderson (1983) posits that the model of national identity forged by newly independent nations in the New World was appropriated for self-conscious pragmatic use by dynastic empires in nineteenth-century Europe and later by leaders in the post-colonial Third World as a ready-made model for the creation of their own official national ideologies.

4. Products exported along the fluvial system at the time included raw and processed cotton, cotton cloth, tobacco, quinine, leather soles, sugar, aguardente (raw sugar-cane rum), soap, lard, dried meat, guava paste, beans, manioc flour, rice, wheat and quince preserves (Dole 1973, 45–46).

5. While slavery was not prohibited until 1888, the overseas slave trade was halted in 1850 below the Equator. Trade connecting the north (above the Equator) with the south of Brazil now trafficked more in the slave trade. While there may have been greater pressure to enlist native labor, the conditions under which this was accomplished depended on how much coercion could be exerted on native individuals or groups. Presumably traditional indigenous communities that retained a large degree of self-sufficiency and autonomy had an advantage in this regard.

6. This is strikingly low given that the captaincy of Goiás then also included the territory now called the Miner's Triangle or *Triangulo Mineiro,* which was only ceded to the sate of Minas Gerais in 1816 (Prado 1971, 446). The population of Brazil, excluding Indians independent of colonial authority, is thought to have been approximately 2 million in 1800 (Alden 1987, 286).

7. The tragic response of the government was to populate the newly established garrison with convicts. The President of Goyaz state, Gómes Siqueira, wrote to the post commander in 1866 to "seek to prevent the [Indians] from having much contact with your soldiers or ill-educated people, so that they have no reason to complain

about us but will instead become convinced that we esteem them" (after Hemming 1987, 396). The president also sought to stop the traffic in Kayapó children. In 1881, President Leite de Morais disbanded the garrisons, hoping to win the Indians over by trade. He admired the Karajás' cooperation with the steamer's need for wood fuel.

8. There are numerous Gê ethnographers who have paid attention to some of the implications of extended contact, including Maybury-Lewis 1965 and 1965/66, Melatti, 1967, Nimuendajú 1939, 1942, 1946, Verswijver 1982, 1985.

9. Compare Pacheco (1979) for discussion of a similar process involving changing relations between dominant modes of rubber extraction and *caboclos* (the Amazonian peasantry whose way of life draws on many indigenous traditions).

REFERENCES

Abreu, Capistrano de. 1954. *Capítulos de história colonial.* Rio de Janeiro: Briguiet.

Agassiz, J.L.R., and Elizabeth Cabot Agassiz. 1888. *A Journey in Brazil.* Boston: Houghton Mifflin.

Alden, Dauril. 1987. "Late Colonial Brazil." In *Colonial Brazil,* ed. Leslie Bethell, 284–343. New York: Cambridge University Press.

Alencastre, J. M.P. 1864. "Annaes da província de Goyaz." *Revista Trimensal do Instituto Histórico, Geográphico e Ethnográphico do Brasil* 27 (2): 5–186, 229–349; [1865], 28 (2): 5–167.

Anderson, Benedict. 1983. *Imagined Communities: Reflections of the Origin and Spread of Nationalism.* London: Verso.

Anderson, Robin Leslie. 1976. "Following Curupira: Colonization and Migration in Pará, 1758 to 1930 as a Study of Settlement of the Humid Tropics." Ph.D. diss., University of California at Davis.

Audrin, José M. 1963. *Os sertanejos que eu conhecí.* Rio de Janeiro: Livraria José Olympio.

Barham, Bradford L., and Oliver T. Coomes. 1994. "Reinterpreting the Amazon Rubber Boom: Investment, the State, and Dutch Disease." *Latin American Research Review* 29 (2): 73–109.

Bartholomew, John, ed. 1955–1959. *The Times Atlas of the World. Volume 5, The Americas.* Mid-century edition. London: Times Publishing Co.

Bates, Henry W. [1864] 1962. *The Naturalist on the River Amazons.* Berkeley: University of California Press.

Bunker, Stephen G. 1985. *Underdeveloping the Amazon. Extraction, Unequal Exchange and the Failure of the Modern State.* Urbana: University of Illinois Press.

Burger, Julian. 1987. *Report from the Frontier: The State of the World's Indigenous Peoples.* London: Zed Books.

Burns, E. Bradford. 1968. *Nationalism in Brazil: A Historical Survey*. New York: Praeger.

———. 1980. A History of Brazil, 2d edition. New York: Columbia University Press.

Castelnau, Francis de. 1949. *Volume I. Expedição às regioẽs centrais da América do Sul.* São Paulo: Ed. Nacional (Col. "Brasiliana") [original French edition 1850–1]

Castro, Eduardo Viveiros de, and Lúcia M. M. de Andrade. 1988. "Implicações sociais da política do setor elétrico." In *Hidrelétricas do Xingu e os povos indígenas,* ed. L.A.O. Santos and L.M.M. de Andrade, 7–23. São Paulo: Comissão Pró-Indio de São Paulo.

Chaim, Marivone Matos. 1974. *Os aldeamentos indígenas na capitania de Goiás.* Goiás, Brazil: Editora Oriente.

Chaumeil, Jean-Pierre. 1992. "De Loreto à Tabating a D'une frontière l'autre: Antagonisme sur l'Amazone au XIXe siècle et après." *L'Homme* 32 (2-3-4): 355–75.

Coudreau, Henri. 1897. *Voyage au Tocantins–Araguaia: 31 décembre 1896–23 mai 1897.* Paris: A. Lahure, Imprimeur-Editeur.

Crosby, Alfred W. 1986. *Ecological Imperialism: The Biological Expansion of Europe, 900–1900.* Cambridge, England: Cambridge University Press.

Cunha, Euclides da. [1906] 1976. *Um paráiso perdido. Reunião dos ensaios amazônicos.* Petrópolis, Brazil: Editora Vozes.

Cunha Mattos, Raymundo José da. [1824] 1874. "Chorográfia histórica da província de Goyaz." *Revista trimestral do Instituto Histórico, Geográfico e Etnográfico do Brasil, Rio de Janeiro.* (1874) in Volume 37, part 1: 213–398; (1875) in Volume 38, part 1: 5–150.

Davis, Shelton H., 1977. *Victims of the Miracle: Development and the Indians of Brazil.* Cambridge, England: Cambridge University Press.

Dole, Dalísia Elisabeth Martins. 1973. *As comunicações fluviais pelo Tocantins e Araguaia no século XIX.* Goiás, Brazil: Editora Oriente.

Edwards, William H. 1847. *A Voyage up the River Amazon.* Philadelphia: G. S. Appleton.

Ferguson, R. Brian, 1990. "Blood of the Leviathan: Western Contact and Warfare in Amazonia." *American Ethnologist* 17 (2): 237–57.

Fisher, William. 1994. "Megadevelopment, Environmentalism and Resistance: The Institutional Context of Kayapó Indigenous Politics in Central Brazil." *Human Organization* 53 (3): 220–32.

Flynn, Peter. 1979. *Brazil: A Political Analysis.* Boulder, Colo.: Westview Press.

Fonseca, Alferes José Pindo da. [1775] 1846. Copia da carta que escreveu ao Exmo. General de Goyaz, dando-lhe conta do descobrimento de duas nacões de índios. *Revista do Instituto Histórico e Geográphico Brasileiro* 8:376.

Furtado, Celso. 1963. *The Economic Growth of Brazil; A Survey from Colonial to Modern Times,* trans. Ricardo W. de Aguiar and Eric C. Drysdale. Berkeley: University of California Press.

Gennino, Angela. 1990. *Amazonia: Voices from the Rainforest: A Resource and Action Guide.* San Francisco: Rainforest Action Network.

Hecht, Susanna, and Alexander Cockburn. 1990. *The Fate of the Forest: Developers, Destroyers and Defenders of the Amazon.* New York: HarperCollins.

Hemming, John. 1978. *Red Gold: The Conquest of the Brazilian Indians.* London: Macmillan.

———. 1987. *Amazon Frontier: The Defeat of the Brazilian Indians.* Cambridge, Mass.: Harvard University Press.

Ianni, Otavio. 1979. *A luta pela terra,* 2d edition. Petrópolis, Brazil: Editora Vozes.

Joseph, Paul Marie. 1907. *Histoire et Géographie: Atlas Classique Vidal-Lablanche.* Saint-Michel, Paris: Librairie Armand Colin.

Kern, Stephen. 1983. *The Culture of Time and Space: 1880–1918.* Cambridge, Mass.: Harvard University Press.

Krause, Fritz. 1911. *In den Wildernissen Brasiliens.* Leipzig: R. Voightlander.

Laitin, David. 1986. *Hegemony and Culture: Politics and Religious Change among the Yoruba.* Chicago: University of Chicago Press.

Lange, Alcot. 1912. *In the Amazon Jungle: Adventures in Remote Parts of the River, Including a Sojourn among Cannibal Indians.* New York: G. P. Putnam's Sons.

Lefèbvre, Henri. 1974. *La production de l'espace.* Paris: Maspero.

Levins, Richard, and Richard Lewontin. 1985. "The Organism as the Subject and Object of Evolution." In *Dialectical Biologist,* 85–106. Cambridge, Mass.: Harvard University Press.

MacLachlan, Colin M. 1973. "The Indian Labor Structure in the Portuguese Amazon: 1700–1800." In *Colonial Roots of Modern Brazil,* ed. Dauril Alden, 199–220. Berkeley: University of California Press.

Magalhães, Couto de. [1876] 1975, *O selvagem.* Belo Horizonte, Brazil: Livraria Itataia Editora.

———. [1863] 1977. *Viagem ao Araguaya,* 2d edition. São Paulo: Companhia Editora Nacional.

Magalhães, Francisco José Pinto de. 1852. "Memoria sobre a descoberta e fundação da povoação de S. Pedro de Alcantara, apresentado ao Governador da Capitania de Goyaz Fernando Delgado Freire de Castilho em 3 de janeiro de 1813." [Report on the discovery and founding of the settlement of S. Pedro de Alcantara, presented to the Governor of Goyaz, Fernando Delgado Freire de Castilho, on 3 January, 1813]. In *A Carolina ou a definitiva fixação de límites entre as províncias de Marãnhao e Goyaz,* ed. Candido Mendes de Almeida, 44–58. Rio de Janeiro: Typ. Episcopal de Agostinho de Freitas Guimaraes. [The original work does not bear the name of the author.]

Margolis, Mac. 1992. *The Last New World: The Conquest of the Amazon Frontier.* New York: W. W. Norton & Co.

Mascarenhas, D. Francisco de Assis. [1809] 1843. Carta escripta pelo mesmo senhor no dia em que deu posse do governo da capitania de Goyaz a Fernando Delgado Freire de Castilho, nomeado seu successor. *Revista do Instituto Histórico e Geográphico Brasileiro.* 5:58–69.

Matos, João Henrique. 1979. Relatório do estado atual de decadência em que se acha o alto Amazonas. Revista do Instituto Histórico e Geográfico Brasiliero. Rio de Janeiro 325:143–180.

Maybury-Lewis, David. 1965. "Some Crucial Distinctions in Central Brazilian Ethnology." *Anthropos* 60:340–58.

———. 1965–66. On Martius' distinction between Shavante and Sherente. *Revista do Museu Paulista,* São Paulo n.s., 16:263–88.

———, ed. 1979. *Dialectical Societies.* Cambridge, Mass.: Harvard University Press.

Meggers, Betty. 1971. *Amazonia: Man and Culture in a Counterfeit Paradise.* Chicago: Aldine.

Melatti, Julio Cezar. 1967. *Indios e criadores. A situação dos Krahó na área pastorial do Tocantins.* Rio de Janeiro: Monografias do Insituto de Ciências Sociais da UFRJ.

Moreira Neto, Carlos de Araújo. 1988. *Indios da Amazônia, de maioria a minoria (1750–1850).* Petrópolis, Brazil: Editora Vozes.

Nash, Roy. 1926. *The Conquest of Brazil.* New York: Harcourt, Brace & Co.

Nimuendajú, K., 1939. *The Apinayé.* Washington: Catholic University of America Press.

———. 1942. *The Šerente.* Los Angeles: Frederick Webb Hodge Anniversary Publication Fund.

———. 1946. *The Eastern Timbira.* University of California Publications in American Archaeology and Ethnology, Volume 41. Los Angeles: University of California Press.

Pacheco de Oliveira Filho, João. 1979. "O Caboclo e o Brabo: Notas sobre duas modalidades de força-de-trabalho na expansao da fronteira Amazônica no século XIX." *Encontros com a Civilização Brasileira* 11:101–40.

Pedroso, Dulce M. R. 1993. Master's thesis, Universidade Federal de Goiás, Brazil.

Prado, Caio Jr. 1971. *The Colonial Background of Modern Brazil.* Berkeley: University of California Press.

Roosevelt, Theodore. 1914. *Through the Brazilian Wilderness.* New York: Charles Scribner's Sons.

Ross, Eric B. 1978. "The Evolution of the Amazon Peasantry." *Journal of Latin American Studies* 10 (2): 193–218.

Schmink, Marianne, and Charles H. Wood. 1992. *Contested Frontiers in Amazonia.* New York: Columbia University Press.

Segurado, Dr. Ruffino Theodoro. 1848. "Viagem de Goyaz ao Pará." *Revista Trimensal de História e Geographia* 10:178–212.

Short, John R. 1991. *Imagined Country: Society, Culture and Environment.* London: Routledge.

Silva e Souza, L. A. da. 1874. "Memória sobre o descobrimento, governo, população e coisas notáveis da Capitania de Goyaz." *Revista do Instituto Histórico e Geográphico Brasileiro,* 13:429–510. [Original was written in 1812.]

Verswijver, Gustaaf. 1982. "The Intertribal Relations between the Juruna and the Kayapó Indians (1850–1920)." *Jarbuch des Museums für Völkerkunde zu Leipzig* 34:305–15

———. 1985. "Considerations on Mekragnotí Warfare." Ph.D. diss., Faculteit van Rechtsgeleerdheid, Belgium.

Wallace, Alfred Russel. [1853]. 1969. *A Narrative of Travels on the Amazon and Rio Negro, of the Native Tribes, and Observations on the Climate and History of the Amazon Valley.* New York: Greenwood Press.

Weinstein, Barbara. 1983a. *The Amazon Rubber Boom, 1850–1920.* Stanford: Stanford University Press.

———. 1983b. "Capital Penetration and Problems of Labor Control in the Amazon Rubber Trade." *Radical History Review* 27:121–40.

———. 1986. *The Persistence of Precapitalist Relations of Production in a Tropical Export Economy: The Amazon Rubber Trade, 1850–1920.* In *The Roots of Class Formation in an Industrializing World.* Contributions in Labor Studies, No. 17, ed. Michael Hanagan and Charles Stephenson, 55–76. New York: Greenwood Press.

7

Reverence Is Not Enough:

Ecological Marxism and Indian Adivasis

Amita Baviskar

The Indian environmental debate is an argument in the cities about what is happening in the countryside

Ramachandra Guha, "Prehistory of Indian Environmentalism: Intellectual Traditions"

New Delhi. 28 January 1992. The Chief Minister of Gujarat, Mr. Chiman Lal Patel, asserted that work on the Sardar Sarovar Project was proceeding apace. Mr. Patel was in Delhi to receive the Independent Review team sent by the World Bank to evaluate the environmental and rehabilitation aspects of the Project. In a meeting with the press, Mr. Patel said that any objective appraisal of the Project would show that it was scientifically planned to harness the river Narmada to permanently solve the water problems of Gujarat. The government of Gujarat had designed a truly enlightened rehabilitation package for dam-oustees. Opposition to the Project was limited to some misguided environmentalists.

Press Release, Government of Gujarat

I was in Anjanvara, a village of Bhilala tribals in the area to be submerged by the Sardar Sarovar dam. It was late in the evening and I was sitting outside the hut of the pujara (priest), watching him roll a bidi. We were talking about gods. The pujara said, "People think of Narmada as bigger than all the gods, bigger than the earth. She can grant all that anyone desires." "Then why aren't you better off? Why doesn't she give you all that you want?" I asked. "But we live in the belly of the river," said pujara. "Sometimes she listens to us and sometimes she doesn't.

Amita Baviskar

Environmental movements in India assert that their ideology incorporates an all-encompassing critique of environmentally destructive "development." Such movements also claim that this critique is writ large in the actions of those marginalized by development, by the indigenous people who have, in the past, lived in harmony with nature. According to the intellectuals of the environmental movements, indigenous people combine reverence for nature with sustainable management of resources. Because of their cultural ties to nature, indigenous people are exemplary stewards of the land. I was moved by such beliefs when I began research in western India, examining the experience of a Bhilala tribal community that has organized in opposition to the construction of a dam that threatens to displace them from their homeland.

My expectation that I would encounter a community that lived in harmony with nature, worshipping it and using its resources sustainably, turned out to be both true and false. During research, my neat theoretical framework linking nature–culture relationships to political critique, action, and change, crumbled into an untidy jumble of contradictions. The dissonance between the depiction of tribal people in scholarly writing on the subject, and the everyday lives of tribal people, led me to ask the questions that run through this essay: Does the lived reality of "indigenous" people today allow the formulation of a critique of "development"? What is the tribal relationship with nature today? How do people, whose struggles are the subject of theories of liberation and social change, perceive their own situation?

We can see the contradictions inherent in the tribal relationship with the nation by placing the tribe's present predicament in the context of the Bhilala tribe's history of state domination. These contradictions permeate Bhilala consciousness as well as their practices. Given the problematic nature of tribal resource use, how accurately are the lives of tribal people represented by intellectuals in the environmental movement who speak on their behalf? Only when we have a clearer understanding of the politics of representation can we forge an effective alliance between intellectuals and "indigenous" people that is more just to people and to nature.

Development and the Ideology of Indigenous Resistance

The Model of Development

The last forty years of the postcolonial era have seen the growth of industry around the world, as newly independent nation-states have embarked on a program to bring prosperity and progress to their citizens. In India too, the independent state mobilized massive amounts of private and public capital to build the infrastructure—transport, communications, power, and steel—that would be the basis of a strong, self-reliant economy. This model of development had been tested and proven in Europe and North America. Jawaharlal Nehru, Prime Minister and the first architect of India's reconstruction, was also convinced that industrial and urban growth was essential to free the country from the shackles of colonialism.

This high-minded intent has been undermined from the start by its own contradictions. The attempt to achieve modern industrial growth was based on two interrelated processes: (1) the unchecked use of the earth's natural resources, and (2) the transformation of people, often against their will, into a dispossessed working class. The ideology of "national development" legitimizes exploitation by promising that industrial growth is universally beneficial and desirable. The pursuit of growth necessitates large injections of capital into the national economy for developing industrial infrastructure—an investment that is often financed by foreign funds. A typical instance of such state expenditure aimed at fostering economic growth is the Narmada Valley Project in western India—a gigantic scheme to harness the waters of the river Narmada for irrigation, power generation, and drinking. The project is funded by the World Bank, bilateral aid, and the Indian states.

The Ideology of Indigenous Critique

The attempts by members of the elite to exploit in the name of development are challenged and resisted by the people that development seeks to marginalize. In India, among the many kinds of struggles against national development, one in particular has received increasing scholarly attention in the last fifteen years of resistance in the form of social movements. Even though social movements tend to be small and localized compared to trade unions and peasant parties, which probably have larger followings, social movements have more often become the subject of scholarly treatment. This academic shift, similar to the one that occurred in Europe, is due as much to the resurgence of this form of protest as to the intellectuals' own ideological disillusionment with electoral politics and mainstream socialist politics. As Kothari argues, social movements are "really to be seen as part of an attempt at redefining politics at a time of massive attempts to narrow its range, different from electoral and legislative politics, which [have] relegated large sections of the people outside the process of power" (Kothari 1988, 46).

Intellectuals argue that the new social movements are formulating a far-reaching critique of the ideology of development, rejecting its claims that the ever-increasing exploitation of humans and nature constitutes "progress," and reshaping people's ideas about what is socially good and desirable. Intellectuals also believe that this critique extends to a repudiation of the underlying cultural values that are privileged by the ideology of development: the ecological hubris of trying to attain mastery over nature, the Economism that ranks profit over all else, and the pursuit of technological expertise, which prevails over other, more Egalitarian and "organic," ways of knowing the world.

By espousing new social movements, intellectuals seem to have surrendered their interest in state power as an arena of struggle because of the failure of progressive mass-based parties to form stable governments at the national level. Several reasons are offered for this: party politics are corrupt and compromised; they contain inherent tendencies towards centralization; in any case, new institutional spaces are opening up at the grassroots.

The surge of Indian scholarly interest in social movements parallels the interest in Green movements that occurred in Western Europe about the same time. But while the European experience has been called a shift from "red" to "green"—that is, from Marxism to environmentalism—the Indian political process seems to be tinted by both hues. The struggle over nature, for example, has an inherent class dimension because nature also provides resources, which are the bases of production. Unlike Europe, where ecological crisis is perceived as a universal threat to biological survival, conflicts over nature in India tend to follow closely the battle lines between those who produce and those who own the means of production (Ramachandra Guha 1988, 2578).

However, in one respect, scholarly interest has moved away from the consideration of one set of productive resources to another, which had earlier been peripheral to the concerns of political organizations. From an examination of conflict in the factory and the field, intellectuals have moved to study conflict revolving around forests and rivers—a shift that is sometimes perceived to be a move toward a "green" agenda of ecological sustainability.

According to Ramachandra Guha, the environmental critique in India springs from three ideological streams (Ramachandra Guha 1988). The first, which he calls "Crusading Gandhian," upholds the precapitalist and precolonial village community as an ideal of social and ecological harmony.

It criticizes the domination of modernist philosophies such as Rationalism and Economism and propagates an alternative philosophy, which has roots in Indian tradition. The second stream, called "Appropriate Technology," is influenced by socialist principles but reconciled to industrial society. It emphasizes the liberating potential of resource-conserving, labor-intensive technologies. The third stream, "Ecological Marxism," holds that political and economic change must predate ecological concerns, and collective action aimed at systemic transformation must come first. This stream is philosophically at odds with Gandhian values because of its overall faith in the emancipatory potential of modern science and technology.

While conceptually separate, these ideologies have been influential in modifying each other. The Gandhian critique of modern science has muted the Marxists' celebration of technicism, while the Marxist analysis of exploitation has compelled the Gandhians to incorporate a more egalitarian perspective on social change.

Guha's categorization of the ideological bases underlying Indian environmentalism can be extended to include yet another stream, similar in its values to the Gandhian, but rooted in a different tradition: the belief that the cultural beliefs and practices of "indigenous communities" constitute a critique of ecologically destructive development and provide an alternative vision of a sustainable human–nature relationship. Like "environment," the word "indigenous" is hard to define. The term is problematic outside its original context of the Americas where, historically, there has been a sharper differentiation between "natives" and European settlers. The use of "tribe" as an alternative is also difficult because of the porosity of the boundary between "caste" and "tribe," both of which have existed side by side for centuries in India. I shall avoid controversy by using *Adivasi* (literally "original dwellers"), a widely accepted Indian term.

Environmentalists who follow the stream of indigenous critique claim that, over centuries of living sustainably with nature, Adivasis have acquired a deep knowledge and understanding of ecological processes so that they are ideal natural resource managers (Shiva and Bandyopadhyay 1990, 77). Thus, scholars of social movements say that "rural women and indigenous people . . . still retain the aranya sanskriti (forest culture) which is based on the 'creative interdependence between human evolution and the protection of forests' " (Parajuli 1991, 179). Vandana Shiva, the well-known spokeswoman of Indian environmentalism, and J. Bandyopadhyay reiterate this theme when they speak of the cultural lessons of diversity and democratic Pluralism learned by Asian societies "modelled on the forest." They claim that the concept of

> the forest as the source [of life] also means that forests and trees must be treated as sacred. The sacred is inviolable: its integrity cannot be violated. If Asian civilizations have survived over centuries it is because they learnt to be like the forest, sustaining both the forest and the culture through time. . . . For these cultures, all life, both human and non-human, is in symbiosis. Human society is not predatory but in rhythm with the forest. (Shiva and Bandyopadhyay 1990, 67, 77)

This basic view that Adivasis are sustainable managers has gained wide acceptance today among intellectuals writing about development and resistance. They say that Adivasis exemplify "the life-enhancing paradigm" (as opposed to the modern "life-destroying paradigm"), where "renewability is the primary management objective" (Shiva and Bandyopadhyay 1990, 74). Taylor (1990, 184), for example, declares that

> all serious studies of natural resource use by indigenous peoples show that their traditional ways are brilliantly conservationist. . . . Theirs is an ecological wisdom that is intricately woven into the very fabric of their cultures; for the most part it is not an articulated, conscious "body of knowledge" . . . Their entire way of life expresses an ecological wisdom that enables them to take care of their forest environment.

This view of the Adivasis as "ecologically noble savages" is not unique to India; it is frequently voiced among conservationists concerned about saving the forest. In Europe, the concept of "noble savage" represented the idealized vision of Rousseau, Thomas More, and others, about the inhabitants of the New World. The belief that Native Americans "lived in close harmony with their local environment" was resurrected in this century among conservationists. Paralleling Shiva and Bandyapadhyay's conceptualization, the modern world was seen as being divided into "two systems, two different irreconciliable ways of life: the [Native American] world—collective, communal, human, respectful of nature, and wise—and the western world—greedy, destructive, individualist, and enemy of nature" (from a report to the International NGO Conference on Indigenous People and the Land 1981, quoted in Redford 1991, 46).

North American "Deep Ecologists" also believe that Adivasis in forests everywhere are conservationist. Deep Ecologists see their philosophical principle of "biocentrism" (as opposed to "anthropocentrism") realized in

Eastern religious traditions and, at a more popular level, by "primal" indigenous people in non-Western settings who, through their material and spiritual practices, subordinate themselves to the integrity of the biotic universe they inhabit. The coupling of (ancient) Eastern and (modern) ecological wisdom apparently helps consolidate the claim that Deep Ecology is a philosophy of universal significance (Guha 1989b, 73–76).

This romantic view of the East is a mirror image of the "scientific" view taken by many Western "Orientalists" (Inden 1986; Guha 1989b). In both cases, the East constitutes the "other"; it is defined by a uniquely spiritual, nonrational "essence," even though this essence is valorized quite differently by the two schools. The romantic and the Orientalist both believe that Eastern people exhibit a spiritual dependence on nature that is symptomatic of, on one hand, their prescientific and backward self, and on the other, their ecological consciousness and wisdom. Both views are monolithic, simplistic, and have the same effect—intentional in one case, perhaps unintentional in the other—of denying agency and reason to the East. Indian environmentalists such as Shiva and Bandyopadhyay repeat this structural dichotomy.

Environmentalists believe that our hope for the future lies in the knowledge and belief systems of the Adivasis. The wisdom of "indigenous" people has contemporary relevance, for it is inherently ecologically sound, as demonstrated in their sustainable survival strategies (Redclift 1987, 153). This wisdom forms the philosophical foundations of present-day social movements of people who resist and challenge the dominant ideology of development. Adivasis, who have been marginalized by development, can mount a comprehensive critique of this ideology and, through the example of their ecologically wise culture, can present an alternative vision of a sustainable, ecologically respectful, coexistence with nature. Such an alternative or cultural critique is realized today through social movements.

A Research Agenda

The above-mentioned theories have been influential in the formulation of my research hypothesis. I expected that Adivasis were acting politically in response to their experience of development—a process that has resulted in the alienation of their natural resource base and their consequent cultural impoverishment. I expected to find that the conflict between social movements and the state is not simply that of differing interests but, more profoundly, that of differing values. As a people fully incorporated into neither the state nor the marketplace, Adivasis drew upon traditional values such as reverence for nature as the source of their cultural critique of development and the basis of their resistance. This resistance would not be merely reactive; through it, Adivasis would also construct a creative alternative to the dominant and destructive system of development, based on their tradition of living sustainably with nature.

The ongoing struggle of the Adivasis in the Narmada valley in central India seemed to be a living example of the resistance of "indigenous" cultural communities to development. The Indian government plans to dam the River Narmada, harnessing its water for irrigation and power generation. The reservoir of the dam will submerge an area of forested hills, displacing the Adivasis who derive their livelihoods from this environment. The Adivasis' fight against displacement seemed to be intrinsically an environmental movement—after all, they were the ones who worshiped nature and used it sustainably. While the dam was both a part of and symbol of development, the movement against the dam seemed to embody both the idea of cultural resistance and an alternative to development. This alternative extended to the very mode of political action in which Adivasis engaged: a decentralized, grassroots mobilization that challenged the state's authority to act "on behalf" of the people. The Narmada Bacoh Andolan (Save Narmada Movement) represented the marginalized, uncorrupted "alternative political culture" of the Adivasis.

My intention was to go to the Narmada Valley and, by living with the Adivasis, to observe their relationship with nature and to determine how this relationship changed with their experience of development (including the dam) and their struggle to create an ecologically sustainable and socially just alternative world. On my arrival in the Narmada Valley, I discovered a somewhat different reality. I had earlier believed that the movement against the dam was the only way in which Adivasis acted politically. Instead, I found that they were also organized into a Sangath (union), which fought for Adivasi rights to land and the forest. Moreover, this did not represent the full extent of Adivasi politics; people also participated with enthusiasm and great energy in waging and settling village-level feuds about honor. Fieldwork revealed that there were several different levels of politics, and that it was essential to incorporate all of these into the study in order to better appreciate Adivasi life.

More disconcerting, though, was the rapid discovery that Adivasi life was not at all what I had imagined it to be. My expectation of encountering a community that lived in harmony with nature, worshipping it and using its resources sustainably, turned out to be both true and false. My neat (in retrospect, suspiciously so) theories linking nature–culture relationships to political critique, action, and change therefore disintegrated. The disjuncture between my romantic notions of Adivasis, based on scholarly writing on the subject, and the facts of the everyday lives of Adivasis, compelled me to question the accuracy with which the environmentalist critique of development represents the lives of people who are thought to be at the forefront of environmental movements. While I have analyzed this issue in relation to the Bhilalas of Alirajpur who live in the planned submergence area of Sardar Sarovar dam, it bears upon the lives and struggles of Adivasis elsewhere, who share a past and a present of development and resistance.

Summary of Findings

Over the centuries, Adivasis have constantly fought an unequal battle against outside oppressors: the state and the market. Although power has changed hands from time to time, being wrested from the Marathas by the Mughals, from the Mughals by the British, and from the British by the Indian nationalists, the Adivasis have experienced only a steady erosion of their material base and their cultural autonomy (Baviskar 1992). National independence and new development projects did not significantly alter this process; the universalizing claims of the benefits of development were meaningless to people who did not identify with the concept of "India" or "Our Independent State." The lives of Adivasis continued to be ruled by Bazaarias—bureaucrats and traders—as their resources were appropriated by the state; they were compelled to enter into market relations and to live under the hegemony of Hindu caste ideology.

Resistance to this domination took the form of frequent uprisings, when Adivasis would swoop down from the hills to which they had been driven and attack the villages of the plains. These Adivasis were bandits whose raids were a constant trial to colonial powers engaged in maintaining "law and order," but their ability to challenge the overall authority of colonial power was limited by their circumstances. Their tendency to importune their rulers for just settlements and their willingness to present injustice as grievances before the state indicated that, however grudgingly, the Adivasis accepted colonial domination.

This history of domination has shaped the present-day lives of Adivasis in the hills. They have carved out an identity and an existence that distinguishes them from their more Hinduized counterparts in the plains, even as they have felt the tug of the Hindu mainstream. Their isolation in the forested hills, relatively distant from centers of power, has enabled them to maintain a distinct language, religion, and material culture that sets them apart from Hindus, although they have been influenced by Hindu values of caste hierarchy. Adivasi identity is expressed in the unity of the village community, defined by the clan, which stretches back in time to include previous generations and which inhabits a particular physical space. The village is remarkably egalitarian in terms of land ownership, and forest resources are held in common. Households pool their strength together for labor-intensive tasks, and there is no differentiation between landowners and laborers. The community is ruled by the ideology of reciprocity.

At the same time, the tradition of generosity toward one's kin contains within it both calculation and conflict, as shown in the arrangements of marriage. The clan comes together to negotiate the purchase of a bride, guided by the desire to drive a hard bargain and, at the same time, buttress its power and prestige. The rites of wedding symbolize the corporate unity of the clan as it acquires another female to carry forth its name.

The village community is defined in relation to the geographical site upon which it exists. The economy is based on an agricultural cycle that revolves around the use of the land, livestock, forest, and river—a dependence that is acknowledged and secured through rituals of worship. Yet the apparent continuity of economic life is being undermined by ecological deterioration. The appropriation of the forest by the state has forcibly confined Adivasi cultivation to friable hill slopes, gradually eroding the livelihoods of the people. At the same time, nevad—illegal Adivasi fields in the forest—provide a steady stream of income for corrupt officials who extort bribes for looking the other way.

Today, the state justifies its continued ownership of the forest with the need for environmental conservation. However, previous destruction of natural resources by the state has so exhausted the environment that even the modest demands of impoverished people trying to make a living can potentially deplete natural resources beyond repair. The slow decline of the once relatively self-sufficient hill economy has resulted in people being unwillingly drawn into the ever-widening circles of commodification of their produce as well as their labor. Constrained by their lack of control over their resource base, people lead contradictory lives, mining their future for the present.

At the level of their beliefs about nature, too, Adivasi understanding is contradictory. On one hand, the Adivasis' reverence for nature suffuses their everyday lives; they make strenuous efforts to secure the cooperation of nature through rites of propitiation. But respect for nature, whose uncertainties rule their fate, does not translate into a set of sustainable resource use practices. Beliefs about nature do not address ecological degradation. People living on the very edge of survival cannot entertain a concern for degradation of resources. While impoverishment and powerlessness compel people to carry on as usual, leaving little room for action that will deal with environmental deterioration, inaction is also in part a consequence of beliefs and practices carried through from the past into the present-day context. People think that the forest will always be there, and that it will regenerate itself, or that the spirits that control nature can be appeased through sacrifice—a belief that acknowledges the power of nature over human beings.

Although this humility is a welcome contrast from the arrogance of industrialism, it is not equivalent to an understanding of how the problems of ecological degradation should be managed. In the context of depleted natural resources, reverence is not enough.

The relationship between nature, Adivasis, and the developmental state is also expressed through more secular collective action such as that of the Sangath, the trade union of Adivasi peasants. However, apart from political action against the state, Adivasis also engage in feuds, where the village community mobilizes to defend its honor against other villages. Feuds are something of an analytical anomaly, for they are not about matters that fit into a theory of politics structured around development and "resistance." When Adivasis fight each other, they are usually driven by concerns such as the maintenance of caste taboos, the avenging of drunken insults, and the management of recalcitrant women.

The social values guiding these feuds—patriarchal honor and caste purity—indicate that Adivasi politics do not always embody the principles of progressive thought. These frequent conflicts show that the Adivasi community is not an idyll of harmony and cooperation and has its own share of dissent and friction. For various reasons, this level of action tends to be ignored by scholars interested in assimilating Adivasis into the politics of resistance. However, these concerns are held to be highly important by villagers, all of whom participate actively in their pursuit. Significantly, women can use the dominant values of local politics to gain a degree of freedom denied to them otherwise: for example, by eloping with a lover, they can defy the power of their husbands and fathers over them.

The notion of "community" is transformed by the work of the Sangath trade union, which seeks to bring together people as Adivasi, united against the state, fighting to secure access to the land and the forest. The activists of the Sangath are important as mediators who provide resources that Adivasis did not have before, and as agents engaged in the task of changing people's consciousness, creating the conditions for self-reliant resistance. The Sangath's experience of collective action has been mixed: although its members have succeeded in staving off the state's attempts to take over nevad fields, and have gained a degree of clout that discourages corruption in local officials, the trade union's agitational politics have prevented them from effectively taking over the institutions of local government. The Sangath's agenda has been limited both by the repressive and bureaucratic power of the state and by a lack of resources. However, through links with similar organizations in the region, the Sangath has harnessed local efforts into a more general struggle between Adivasis and the state over natural resources and democratic rights.

The Andolan movement has focused even more explicitly on a critique of development, fighting against the injustice of the state's appropriation of natural resources from people in the Narmada Valley. It has successfully united the disparate constituencies of Bhil and Bhilala Adivasis in the hills and prosperous Patidar (upper caste) landowners in the Ninar plains, transcending caste, class, and party affiliations, and forging a common front against the Sardar Sarovar Project. The popular movement in the valley among people threatened with displacement has attracted worldwide attention and support and has lead to additional criticism of other aspects of the project. The Andolan has been embraced by the intelligentsia for its critique of development and the "national state" and for its attempt to create an "alternative political culture."

There are, however, a number of problems with this attempt to portray the popular movement in the valley as representing a critique of development. First, the great differences in the social basis of the movement are disregarded, in particular, the class basis of the Andolan movement in the Nimar plains. The plains are dominated by Patidar capitalist farmers, whose mode of production is the antithesis of ecological sustainability and social justice. The people of the valley, Patidars as well as hill Adivasis, have continued fighting for their land, unconcerned by the niceties of theoretical frameworks and abstract political analyses. This has led to debate within the Andolan itself between the movement in the valley and its urban-based supporters, about ideological coherence and the long-term perspective of the movement.

Second, the urgency of stopping construction of the dam has meant that all kinds of strategies be adopted, including endorsing candidates from mainstream political parties whose ideology may contradict the espoused goals of the movement. As a result, the Andolan's attempt to challenge liberal democracy through mass mobilization aimed at creating an "alternative political culture" has proved difficult. The Andolan characterizes the state apparatus as illegitimate and repressive. It tries to repudiate dominant political values through the moral pressure of passive resistance and espouses village self-rule based on participation and decentralized power. However, the need to achieve rapid results has compelled activists to set aside these stances temporarily for a program of more pragmatic action that is more in keeping with the realities of dependence on the state in the villages of Nimar. In order to fight against the fast-rising dam, the Andolan has brought together many disparate groups and ideologies, knitting them together in a political coalition that has been remarkably effective.

The three levels of politics—local feuds, Sangath, and Andolan—together demonstrate the possibilities as well as limitations in the ways that the collective action of hill Adivasis fits into a structure of development and "resistance." While people's experience of development has certainly placed them in opposition to the developmental state, the movement from objective conditions for opposition to an ability to articulate an alternative vision of ecologically sustainable life achieved through "alternative politics" has been more difficult. How closely do Adivasis themselves resemble their portrayal as sustainable resource managers? To what extent can their politics be projected as an environmental movement? To answer these questions, we must also examine the different interpretations of the notion of "environment" and the meanings that it holds for different people.

Interpretations of "Environment" and Ideology

Earlier I argued that the appropriation of nature and labor was intrinsic to capitalist development—an inherently resource-intensive and socially inegalitarian process. Therefore the struggle against development involves people marginalized by its processes. This is quite different from the way in which the relationship between development and environment is understood by national political elites.

In India, environmentalists tend to be depicted as "boys and girls": irresponsible and immature. Vidyut Joshi, for example, uses this tactic by calling Sangath activists "youngsters," despite the fact that the average age of the "youngsters" is thirty-five. (Joshi 1991, 70). At a conference on the Narmada conflict held in New York in March 1992, pro-Narmada bureaucrats persistently patronized Andolan activists by referring to them as "our young friends." In the words of Amarsinh Chaudhary, former Chief Minister of Gujarat, environmentalists are "boys and girls" interested in saving "tigers and trees."

The Gujarat government, on one hand, has consistently refused even to acknowledge the existence of the Andolan and the widespread movement against displacement in the valley, merely reiterating that criticism of the project was limited to "a few environmentalists" and could therefore be dismissed. The environmentalists have been further marginalized and referred to as "ecofundamentalists" (Sheth 1991, 73). Such an understanding of what is "environmental" echoes the thoughts of those who see development as an essentially benign process, marred only by few regrettable externalities such as environmental pollution. They percieve "tigers and trees" as trivial concerns, luxuries that elites can afford to indulge in, since they have already gained the benefits of development. This interpretation of the conflict as "environment versus development" has prevailed in government discourse.

The Sangath and the Andolan, on the other hand, have stressed the inseparability of ecological sustainability and social justice. Development is destructive because it works against social distribution by reallocating resources from the poor to the rich. The Andolan critique of the dam discusses its environmental dimensions—its impact on upstream and downstream ecosystems and on soils in the command area—and yet these effects are understood primarily in terms of their human consequences. The Sangath's politics, which deals directly with the issue of Adivasi control over the land and forest, is also based on this analysis of development. The Sangath and the Andolan understanding of environmental conflict can be summed up in the following manner:

> Social movements of poor people are very often struggles for livelihood and they are ecological (whatever the idiom in which they express themselves) insofar as they express objectives in terms of ecological requirements for life. . . . They are also ecological in that . . . they attempt to take environmental resources out of the economic sphere, out of the generalised market system. (J. Martínez Alier, quoted in Watts n.d., 23)

Yet there is a noticeable difference between people's perceptions of what they are fighting for: on one hand, basic subsistence denied by the state, and on the other, the claims made by intellectuals who postulate that "indigenous" resistance is a comprehensive critique of development based on the "traditional" Adivasi way of life. Although the ideology that perceives environmental conflict in terms of sustainability is external to Adivasi consciousness, it is employed strategically by the movement in the valley to gain the sympathy of urban supporters.

The complexity of ideology—a result of the mingling of the public and the private and of claims about sustainability and claims about subsistence—can be best unraveled by locating ideologies among the various social groups. The ideology of development and resistance cannot "sail through history innocent of any references to real individuals and the lives they lead" (Sayer 1987, 95). In particular, it is important to distinguish between the people in the Narmada Valley and their intellectual supporters. It is the Adivasis—not agents in the abstract, but definite socially and historically located individuals—who have ideas, whose subjective understanding guides their collective action and gives it meaning and shapes their world. We cannot simultaneously hail Adivasis as agents of history, while dismissing their consciousness and their everyday life.

In the final analysis, the relationship between social being and social consciousness can only be elucidated historically, over time, through empirical investigation of how (in Marx's words) "people make their own history, but not of their own free will; not under circumstances they themselves have chosen but under the given and inherited circumstances with which they are confronted" (Marx and Engels [1852] 1963, 15). To ignore how the historical circumstance of domination constrains consciousness leads to the misrepresentation of Adivasis by intellectuals. In representing Adivasis as living sustainably, and acting politically, inspired by a critique of development based on their "traditional" values, intellectuals often romanticize subaltern forms of experience and culture, "granting them a heroism that makes it difficult to understand 'unheroic' decades" (Roseberry 1989, 46). Roseberry argues that if we make much too direct a connection between people's experience and the meanings that we feel they must attribute to it, we ignore the political implications of the way in which meaning and experience are separated in the context of domination. In addition, we ignore the ambiguity and contradictory nature of experience itself and the fact that ambiguous experience can only produce a contradictory consciousness (Roseberry 1989, 46). Thus, we cannot automatically "read off," or read into, the everyday experiences of Adivasi life an ideology that is derived from an external critique of development.

At issue here is the difference between the beliefs and practices of Adivasis and of those who speak "on their behalf." Instead of assuming a congruence between these two sets of ideologies, we must explore how differences may be united in a synthesis that gains from the normative vision of the intellectuals and, at the same time, incorporates a more realistic view of Adivasi life. Intellectuals are, after all, also agents of change, and their words carry more weight in certain settings. By inhabiting a particular social moment that is shaped by traditions of critical discourse, intellectuals bring to present struggles a historical richness. They have provided the theoretical framework to link the social movement in the Narmada Valley with movements elsewhere in the world. Yet their eloquent championing of Adivasi resistance has tended to obscure some of the difficulties that Adivasis have encountered in their attempt at resistance—namely, the fact that environmental degradation is embedded in overall political and economic structures that are hostile to sustainable resource use by Adivasis.

Under these circumstances, there is a contradiction between the Adivasis' reverence for nature and their unsustainable resource use. The only limited claim that we can make on their behalf is to assert that Adivasis are "environmentalists by default." That is, their present resource use can be called sustainable only if we compare it with the vastly more destructive practices of the state and the market. In relation to the ecological devastation wreaked by the state in the Narmada Valley—first deforestation, and now the ultimate solution of drowning the land—the Adivasis' use of resources appears miniscule in its impact. Thus Adivasis are not the perfect stewards of the land, but in this grossly imperfect world, they come closest to that ideal.

But by ironing out the imperfections, not only in resource use practices but also in the easy invocation of "community" joined in an "alternative political culture" in opposition to development, intellectuals allow themselves to be "blinded by the glare of a perfect and immaculate consciousness" (Ranajit Guha 1988, 84). Committed inflexibly to the notion of resistance as a generalized movement against development, they underestimate the power of the brakes put on resistance by the circumstance of domination.

To paraphrase Ranajit Guha, the objective of intellectuals and scholars of social movements is to take the history of insurgency from the continuum that is the progressive march of development and rearrange it along an alternative axis of a campaign for "sustainability and social justice." However, this too amounts to an act of appropriation that excludes the Adivasis as the conscious subjects of their own history and incorporates them as only an element in another history with another subject. Just as it is not Adivasis but development that is the real subject of these theories, in a similar way, the abstraction called "indigenous" or "peasant-tribal" is an ideal, created to replace the real historical personality (Ranajit Guha 1988, 77).

> For once a peasant rebellion has been assimilated to the career of . . . the Nation or the People [or against Development], it becomes easy for the [scholar] to abdicate the responsibility [s]he has of exploring and describing the consciousness specific to that rebellion and be content to ascribe to it a trancendental consciousness. In operative terms, this means denying a will to the mass of the rebels themselves and representing them merely as instruments of some other will (Ranajit Guha 1988, 83).

The Politics of Representation

The privileging of elite consciousness, which divides the world into "Development" and "Resistance," does endow the struggles over land, forest, and river with legitimacy in the eyes of environmentalists elsewhere. And, by linking local struggles into a global context, such appropriation is strategically important. Why does the image of the Adivasi resonate so powerfully in certain minds? The image has come to symbolize a normative vision of ecological wisdom—an inspiring quality for environmentalists in today's world, searching for cultures that embody a more respectful way of living with nature. Nevertheless, however noble the cause, appropriation leads to a mediation of the Adivasi consciousness by that of the scholar. The discourse of the general theory of development does not allow people to speak for themselves; it tends to be deaf to people's own understanding of their predicament. This is problematic because it slights the other, equally valid concerns of Adivasis, which answer to a different logic—of patriarchy, caste, honor. These areas of politics that are autonomous from development tend to be marginalized, even though, ironically, they come closest to constituting truly "indigenous" "alternative political culture."

Intellectuals speak of the hegemony of development and how its myth of universal gain and progress, in which everyone believed for a time, has been shattered (Parajuli 1991). However, if development was the god that failed, it was never an Adivasi god. People were never enchanted by the myth of development—how could they be when they only experienced its crushing exploitation? There could be no disillusionment when people had no illusions in the first place. The assimilation of Adivasi struggles into an antidevelopment agenda neglects history—that people have always fought against outside oppression, on their own terms. Their history of resistance long predates the advent of development.

The present theoretical treatment of Adivasis reifies "the grassroots" and is an idealization of people's actual life, a representation that is vulnerable to refutation. Their low-impact use of nature in earlier times was probably as much adventitious as it may have been deliberate; Adivasis were limited by demography and technology from using resources destructively. It therefore becomes hard to say whether their "traditions" can be uncritically extolled as epitomizing sustainability, and what potential they hold as an ideal in the present, vastly changed, context. We cannot frame the Adivasi past (or present) as a "natural economy"—a starting point for a historical process that is a counterpoint to development; we have to come to terms with its disordered reality to create a more equal basis for cooperation.

Romanticizing the Adivasis trivializes their problems and refuses to acknowledge that at present their ability to mount a critique has been vastly eroded by their subordination. While intellectuals as well as people in the valley stress that priority must be given to a need-based economy—a wholly sound basis for reorienting natural resource management—this in itself is not enough. The scale of the degradation of land and forest requires a massive effort calling upon financial, technical, and organizational resources—a magnitude that has been achieved so far only by the state. This leads us to reconsider seriously the strategic choices made by movements that seek to stay clear of the sphere of party politics, moving instead toward a reengagement in political struggles aimed at controlling state power, at least at the local level.

Idealization overstates the transformative potential of Adivasis acting in small, localized movements and tends to downplay the power of dominant classes. It also underestimates the help and cooperation that is needed to challenge this domination—a shame, since intellectuals, with all their resources, not the least of which is their commitment to the cause of fighting oppression, are so well situated to provide that help. Idealization ignores the role of outside activists, whose presence empowers local peoples' struggles and transforms their consciousness. The activists mediate between Adivasis and those who write about them; their perspective influences the intellectuals' view. This dialogue holds the potential for a fruitful coming together and crossing over.

Conclusion

A general argument about the theory of development and its environmental impact posits that development will be resisted in the form of environmental movements. This formulation, while perfectly valid in the abstract, becomes problematic when examined more closely in the context of a real set of conditions, the Narmada Valley, and a real set of people, Bhilala Adivasis. Glossing over the contradictions of people's lives is a tactic that prevents action toward their possible resolution. Intellectuals' reduction of the "grassroots" to no more than a medium for alternatives to development denies the very real impact that a people's history has had on their present conditions. Our task cannot be simply that of rediscovery or excavation of a pristine "indigenous" way of knowing the world; we must also deal concretely with problems in people's understanding and actions. If we do not respect people's understanding of what they are fighting for, we contravene their history, their strengths and weaknesses, their truths. An appreciation of subjectivity is not simply an issue of representation, for representations are after all regimes that act upon the world. From an abstract, idealized expectation about Adivasi politics, the environment and development, we come to a need to understand local struggles on their own terms, to work to strengthen them, and to recognize their limitations.

Earlier I discussed the distinctive character of Indian environmentalism, where the Red project of changing the relations of production, and the Green project of using nature sustainably, are merged to create an ecological "landscape of resistance." As the case of Bhilala Adivasis in the Narmada Valley shows, the conflict over nature has several manifestations, from organizing to protect access to local forests to the world-renowned movement against Sardar Sarovar Dam. The ability to mobilize across these different, yet connected, levels of action can be understood in terms of the relationship between local communities, activists, and intellectuals—groups united in a common cause yet embedded in different social contexts and moved by different ideologies.

In the case of the Narmada Bachao Andolan, fighting against the dam and other forms of destructive development has necessitated the mobilization of a panoply of strategies that span the ideological spectrum of environmentalism. Critics of the dam employ arguments challenging the wisdom of large, capital-intensive projects, calling for the use of appropriate technology. The issue of the displacement of a vast population raises questions about the social distribution of costs and benefits, implicitly drawing upon an ecological Marxist understanding of the nature of development. At the same time, the attempt to engender an "alternative political culture" opposed to the developmental state and mainstream politics builds on Gandhian traditions of decentralized and nonviolent collective action. However, the urgency of fighting on all fronts has compelled the Andolan movement to reconcile constituencies and ideologies that are sometimes at odds, leading to an alliance that, despite its successes, retains elements of unease.

The work of the Andolan complements that of the Sangath in its attempts to bring about a more deep-rooted transformation of consciousness. The Sangath's more long-term outlook and more modest scale of operations allow it to engage more thoroughly in the task of organizing people against the state that has alienated their natural resources. While insurgent consciousness is inextricably tied to the issue of livelihood, and action against the state is motivated by the desire to safeguard the ecological basis of survival, popular mobilization requires a change of identity. From a preoccupation with the politics of honor, people come together as Adivasis, unified by their common experience of exploitation. Thus, although the ideology of the Sangath is broadly ecological Marxist in its orientation, circumstances cause it to address the issue of identity based on cultural values other than class.

These streams of ecological consciousness are joined together by yet another strand—the cultural traditions of Adivasis—to form a powerful, visionary critique of development that, despite the contradictions embedded in its lived reality, promises to inspire environmental action in the future. The three aspects central to Adivasi life—the gods that are nature, land and forest, community—hold the potential to form a challenge and an alternative to development when supported by the help of activists and intellectuals who listen and observe as much as they speak and write. It is our task to transform understanding into action and aid, and together forge a future that is more just—to people and to nature.

REFERENCES

Baviskar, Amita. 1992. "Development, Nature, and Resistance: The Case of Bhilala Tribals in the Narmada Valley." Ph.D. diss. Ithaca, N.Y.: Cornell University.

Guha, Ramachandra. 1988. "Ideological Trends in Indian Environmentalism." *Economic and Political Weekly* 23 (49): 2578–81.

———. 1989a. *The Unquiet Woods: Ecological Change and Peasant Resistance in the Himalaya.* Berkeley: University of California Press.

———. 1989b. "Radical American Environmentalism and Wilderness Preservation: A Third World Critique." *Environmental Ethics* 11 (1): 71–83.

———. 1992. "Prehistory of Indian Environmentalism: Intellectual Traditions." *Economic and Political Weekly* 27 (1, 2): 57–64.

Guha, Ranajit. 1988. " The Prose of Counterinsurgency" In *Selected Subaltern Studies,* ed. R. Guha and G. C. Spivak, 45–88. New York: Oxford University Press.

Inden, Ronald. 1986. "Orientalist Constructions of India." *Modern Asian Studies* 20 (3): 401–46.

Joshi, Vidyut. 1991. *Rehabilitation—A Promise to Keep: A Case of SSP.* Ahmedabad, India: Tax Publications.

Kothari, Rajni. 1988. *State Against Democracy: In Search of Humane Governance.* Delhi: Ajanta Publishers.

Marcus, George E. 1990. "Contemporary Problems of Ethnography in the Modern World System." In *Writing Culture: The Poetics and Politics of Ethnography,* ed. James Clifford and G. E. Marcus. London: Oxford University Press.

Marx, Karl, and Friedrich Engels. [1852] 1963. *The Eighteenth Brumaire of Louis Bonaparte.* New York: International.

Parajuli, Pramod. 1991. "Power and Knowledge in Development Discourse: New Social Movements and the State in India." *International Social Science Journal* 43 (127): 173–90.

Redclift, Michael. 1987. *Sustainable Development: Exploring the Contradiction.* London: Methuen.

Redford, Kent H. 1991. "The Ecologically Noble Savage." *Cultura1 Survival Quarterly* 15 (1): 46–48.

Roseberry, William. 1989. *Anthropologies and Histories: Essays in History and Political Economy.* New Brunswick, N.J.: Rutgers University Press.

Sayer, Derek. 1987. *The Violence of Abstraction: The Analytic Foundations of Historical Materialism.* Oxford: Blackwell.

Sheth, Pravin. 1991. "The Politics of Ecofundamentalism." In *All About Narmada.* Gandhinagar, India: Directorate of Information, Government of Gujarat.

Shiva, Vandana, and J. Bandyopadhyay. 1990. "Asia's Forests, Asia's Cultures." In *Lessons of the Rainforest,* ed. Suzanne Head and Robert Heinzman, 66–78. San Francisco: Sierra Club Books.

Taylor, Kenneth I. 1990. "Why Supernatural Eels Matter." In *Lessons of the Rainforest,* ed. Suzanne Head and Robert Heinzman, 184–95. San Francisco: Sierra Club Books.

Tilly, Charles. 1985. "War Making and State Making as Organised Crime." In *Bringing the State Back In,* ed. Peter B. Evans, Dietric Rueschemeyer, and Theda Skocpol, 169–91. New York: Cambridge University Press.

Watts, Michael. n.d. "Sustainability and Struggles over Nature: Political Ecology or Ecological Marxism?" mimeo. Berkeley: University of California.

8

Caribbean Environmentalism: An Ambiguous Discourse

Barbara Deutsch Lynch

> The environmental movement has begun to undermine the social consensus for growth, development, and the promotion of commodified relations with the land. It must now directly engage in social debate, for the culture of nature—the ways we think, teach, talk about, and construct the natural world—is as important a terrain for struggle as the land itself.
>
> Alexander Wilson, *The Culture of Nature*

> Feminist history in the broadest sense requires that we look at history with egalitarian eyes, seeing it anew from the viewpoint not only of women but also of social and racial groups and the natural environment, previously ignored as the underlying resources on which Western culture and progress have been built.
>
> Carolyn Merchant, *The Death of Nature*

Environment as a Social Construction: Contest and Ambiguity

Environment and Environmentalism as Contested Terrain

Two 1992 media events, the UN Conference on Environment and Development (UNCED) in Rio de Janeiro and the Quincentennial of Columbus's landfall in Hispaniola, revealed with unusual clarity that *environment* (the physical landsape, its biota, and its landforms) and *environmentalism* (awareness of, concern for, and action in the name of the environment) are cultural constructions subject to conflicting interpretations and that control over these interpretations is at the heart of contemporary political struggle in Latin America and the Caribbean.

The political, even cognitive, distance between UNCED and the Global

Forum (and the difficulties in forging consensus on specific issues within the latter) revealed a widening rift within the environmental movement, separating those sitting in official assemblies who favored global, generally conservationist approaches to resource management and the myriad social movement organizations networking under tents and in the open air—some hawking appropriate technologies and others insisting on linking environment to social justice. The problematization of the Columbian encounter is perhaps best symbolized by the monumental, cruciform Lighthouse for Columbus (Faro a Colón) in Santo Domingo, Dominican Republic. The lighthouse, whose construction displaced thousands of residents and whose operation entails conspicuous consumption of scarce power, has served as a focal point for protest against Dominican development programs and has drawn attention to the victims of that development, from the decimated Taíno and deracinated Africans to the dispossessed Dominicans.

Both of these events demonstrated the importance of culture, class, and position in the global economy in shaping the ways in which peoples know landscapes and biota, define environmental problems and threats, propose solutions, and act to counteract perceived threats. Both made visible the ways some social movement organizations are appropriating landscape and environment as symbols of resistance in their struggles to improve the social and physical terms of their integration into national societies and global economies, while others focus on landscape change as a symptom of decline of an older and better social order.

To accept the environment and environmentalism as cultural constructions that vary according to context does not deny the reality of the physical landscape or negate the importance of concerns about its destruction, but rather suggests that attention to difference in environmental constructions may offer new possibilities for creating more habitable places. Conversely, failure to understand the cultural contexts in which environmentalisms are embedded all too often perpetuates, if not aggravates, social injustice as well as environmental degradation. In this chapter, I draw attention to differences within environmental discourse by focusing on the environmental perspectives coming from Hispanic communities in the island Caribbean and their counterparts in the United States.[1] I suggest how these perspectives may have been shaped by race, class, and national identity; how island Caribbean environmental perspectives are modified in the process of migration; and how these perspectives reframed in the North inform projects to change the face of both worlds. I focus on the cultural production of the islands' peoples, with particular emphasis on literature and reference to the environmental content of indigenous social movements.

Ambiguity in Environmental Discourse

To analyze cultural productions for their environmental content is to uncover ambiguities often suppressed in mainstream environmental discourse. This suppression has had two unfortunate consequences. One is the fragmentation of the movement into a growing number of unambiguous positions that represent the perspectives of smaller and smaller subsets of environmentalists, whether deep ecologists, ecofeminists, or spiritual ecologists (Merchant 1992). A second is the muting of other voices—environmental perspectives that grow out of everyday experience.

The term environment itself is ambiguous and can be construed both as landscape, complete with geological and life forms, and as a spatial arrangement of meaningful places—a map. When viewed as landscape, particular features may be highlighted or allowed to recede into the background, sharply drawn or blurred, depending on the viewer. An obvious example is the conquistadors' skewed perception of the islands as a source of both mineral wealth and the manual labor to extract it—a vision that obscured and devalued agricultural elements in the landscape. Less obvious are the blind spots of conservationists who seek to preserve forest remnants on the islands but fail to consider the possible contributions of cultivation practices to existing biodiversity. Whether a landscape is regarded as friendly or hostile, empty or peopled, endangered and needing protection or underutilized and awaiting development may have more to do with who is using it than how it is being used (see for example DuPuis in this volume). Therefore, perceptions of the landscape are very much tied to the racial and ethnic understandings of the beholder.

This is also true of maps. Whether recorded or cognitive schemas of relationships among places, maps may sanction land uses favored by dominant groups or guide the movements of others through alien territory. Hegemonic maps imply the need to protect resources and territory from others, usually from the poor or people with different cultural values. Scientists and surveyors draw lines around places deemed susceptible to non-sanctioned uses; these lines become boundaries, and the areas that they confine are defined as zones with specific allowable uses (Peluso 1993). In contrast, the cognitive maps of subordinate groups in society are more likely to chart routes of access to resources over which they have a moral rather than a formal claim. Acceptable uses of any given landscape will vary according to season, time of day, and need.

These ambiguities inherent in the social construction of environment, either as landscape or as map, generally go unacknowledged in natural science, much of social science, and policy statements, because ambiguity makes the task of problem definition more complex. And these ambiguities are rarely flagged by the chroniclers of the environmental movement. Yet, attention to ambiguity is fundamental to an understanding of difference within environmental discourse, and therefore it is essential to chronicle the movement as viewed from the periphery as well as from the center.

Constructing Chronicles of Environmental Thought

Elsewhere (Lynch 1993), I argue that to make different environmental discourses audible, one must give them a history—a pedigree. While the history of environmental thought in the United States and Western Europe is amply documented, the contributions of Latino writers to its development are largely unacknowledged.[2] Chroniclers of northern environmentalism (for example, Nash 1973, 1990; Williams 1973; Marx 1964; Burch 1964; Bramwell 1989; Worster 1977) have traced the history of the movement through literature and philosophy, but the various intellectual histories of environmental or ecological thought and activity that have appeared since the early 1960s almost uniformly restrict their focus to the United States and/or Northern Europe and lack any discussion of Southern European, let alone Latin American discourse on nature. These histories, together with polemics of writers like Rachel Carson, Garrett Hardin, Paul Ehrlich, Donella Meadows, and the wilderness paeans of Henry David Thoreau, Aldo Leopold, Sigurd Olsen, and Edward Abbe have come to constitute the canon of U.S. environmental thought.

Rural sociologists investigating environmental perspectives (often dismissed as "attitudes") have tended to work with reference to this canon and to frame their research from the perspective of mainstream environmentalism.[3] In the 1970s, other perspectives on environment began to enter the sociological consciousness, albeit at its fringes, as development sociologists working in Asia and Latin America came into contact with the work of ecological anthropologists (for example, John Murra, Stephen Brush, Brooke

Thomas, Harold Conklin, Andrew Vayda, Bonnie McKay), who emphasized the utility of indigenous knowledge and the long-term sustainability of indigenous resource management strategies. In the 1980s change accelerated, due in no small part to the contributions of feminist and Third World scholarship. Carolyn Merchant (1980), seeking to understand the subjugation of women in Western societies, identifies a number of conflicting images of nature and their associated value systems. Somewhat later, the writings of South Asians (for example, Agarwal 1986; Guha 1989; Shiva 1989) and native Americans (for example, Leslie Marmon Silko) received increasing attention from environmentalists and social scientists.

In the United States, Edelstein (1988), Levine (1982), Brown and Mikkelsen (1990), Bullard (1990), and Cepek (1993), by shifting their focus to local environmental social movements and issues of environmental justice, have done much to open the discipline to considerations of divergent environmental perspectives, and in 1991, the United Church of Christ Commission for Racial Justice provided a forum for defining environmental racism. Southwestern geographer Laura Pulido (1992), sociologist Devon Peña (Peña 1992; Peña and Gallegos 1993), and activists María Varela and Antonio Manzanares of the Ganados del Valle cooperative are seeking to redress the failure of North American and Northern European environmentalists to recognize Latino cultures of nature and the environmentalism rooted in these cultures. But their own perspectives are regional as are the issues they address. The environmental discourses of Caribbean peoples bear little resemblance to those of Chicanos and Mexican-Americans in the Southwest in the same way that immigrant workers and their descendants differ markedly from Southwesterners and Puerto Ricans whose consciousness was informed by foreign domination and progressive loss of rights or access to their homelands. Moreover, environmental movements that have grown out of farmworkers' exposure to poison in California fields are quite different from those occasioned by nostalgia for an earlier hacienda society.

To borrow Scott's (1990) terms, the apparent discordance of peripheral voices reflects the plurality of hidden transcripts and the forced homogeneity of the official ones. This plurality undermines the methodological utility of looking for different perspectives on environment by asking of others a directed set of questions framed within one's own cultural perspective.[4] It is similarly difficult to arrive at an adequate understanding of environmental debates in the Caribbean by reading formal government documents, NGO reports, or academic writing. Because the language of policy statements and scientific writing generally conforms to outsiders' expectations, it often conceals that which is distinctive in Latino environmental understandings. In contrast, fundamental environmental questions and preferences are likely to be most precisely and accessibly expressed in fiction, poetry and narrative, in art, in the built landscape, and in the theater of social movements. From these expressions one can gather pieces of different environmental discourse with which to begin construction of an alternative chronicle of the environmental movement.

Fortunately, in recent years, the cultural production of the Caribbean has been extraordinarily rich and to a large degree focused on questions of regional identity and the maintenance of that identity in new surroundings. At the same time, as elsewhere in the region, the focus of social movements has shifted from the workplace and the state to the neighborhood and the municipality, and this shift has been accompanied by an emphasis on urban and rural landscapes. For this reason, I have chosen emphasize these forms of cultural production in the following discussion of the construction of Caribbean Latino environmental discourse.

Chronicling Caribbean Environmentalism: Elements of a Discourse

In attempting to chronicle Caribbean environmental thought, I have tried to avoid imputing to other voices the logic of Northern environmental rhetoric, yet, in emphasizing difference, I did not want to lose sight of possible points of comparison between Caribbean and Northern environmental discourse. I have therefore chosen to organize the following discussion around three elements of environmental discourse which, I believe, transcend cultural boundaries: (1) the construction of ideal landscapes against which environmental degradation can be measured, (2) explanations of environmental decline, (3) understandings about the relationship of landscape to nation and ethnicity.

The contents of these elements differ insofar as they reflect the life experiences of different groups in society. Caribbean environmental perspectives have been profoundly conditioned by (1) migrations from Europe and Africa to the Greater Antilles; (2) the cultural and intellectual traditions shaped these migrations; (3) landscape transformations wrought by a development process that was largely dictated by external forces and characterized by rapid urbanization, free-trade zone industrialization, rationalization of agriculture, and the rise and decline of island paradise boom towns; and (4) migration to the United States and other countries of the North. Cuba, Puerto Rico, and Hispaniola were all characterized by extremely early settlement and decimation of indigenous populations, repopulation with Africans and Canary Islanders, persistence of a Spanish colonial presence well into the nineteenth century,[5] a two-phased reconfiguration of the agricultural landscape to accommodate artisanal and later industrial sugar production, and direct U.S. military occupation to support the second phase of this reconfiguration. Caribbean environmental discourse almost always contains elements of reaction against the economic domination of sugar and the political domination of the U.S. marines.[6]

The logic of the plantation economy necessitated involuntary migration within the islands as dedication of prime lands to sugar cultivation moved food production and the few remaining indigenous food producers to steeply sloped, inaccessible lands. Plantation slaves often cultivated clandestine subsistence plots on the fringes of the plantations, while runaway slaves or maroons continuously replenished the population already in the hills.

While the pace of plantation development varied from one region to another, it invariably led to the transformation of the agricultural landscape in fertile, low-lying lands. In the hills, the *conuco,* the Taíno root crop–dominated polycultural system, evolved into an agriculture in resistance, and palenques, fortified settlements, were constructed as bases for trading with, raiding, and defending hill dwellers against the plantation and colonial forces. The informality of the conuco and palenque stood in sharp opposition to the ordered plantation, but it was the maroon economy on which the subsistence of the islands ultimately depended (Price 1979; Montejo 1993; Pulsipher 1990). Thus, the transformation of landscapes into endless oceans of cane came to be associated with progress, order, and the whiteness of refined sugar, while root-crop cultivation on steep, inaccessible hillsides was associated either with an increasingly Arcadian pre-Columbian past or with Africanness—darkness, disorder, and rebellion. Coexisting with these patterns of plantation and palenque, sugar and conuco, were enclaves of smallholder production for export—coffee, tobacco, cacao, and ginger—as well as large cattle enterprises. In the past decade, these subcultures of peasant production—the *guajiro* in Cuba, the *jibaro* in Puerto Rico, and the Cibao coffee cultivator in the Dominican Republic—appeared in Caribbean environmental discourses to symbolize non–Afro-Caribbean opposition to the culture of sugar.

A second critical element in defining landscape and nation in the Spanish Caribbean has been the transforming role of United States military forces, whose presence in the three islands coincided with and supported a further rationalization of the agricultural landscape. On Hispaniola, for example, the marines defined the Haitian-Dominican border, carried out cadastral surveys, and built roads that penetrated into the heart of the island. The marine presence, in turn, facilited industrialization and rapid expansion of sugar production on the Dominican side of the island. The introduction of industrial sugar mills in the Dominican Republic, Cuba, and Puerto Rico meant bringing more land into sugar cultivation, including the conucos that had fed plantation workers. Cadastral surveys facilitated this transfer. At the same time, small independent commercial producers lost political clout and saw their regions decline in terms of prestige and services. The environmentalism of resistance born of conquest and slavery continued, but alongside it arose an environmentalism that stemmed from nostalgia for a landed leisure rudely disrupted by the expansion and industrialization of sugar production.

Acknowledgment of the islands' common historical elements—African roots, dependence on maroon agriculture, and eventual subjugation to the order of industrial sugar production—has depended to a large degree on the ideological necessities of recent political and economic regimes. Moreover, the seemingly infinite variations in the spatial expressions of these historical events and the sharply divergent political histories of Puerto Rico, Cuba, and the Dominican Republic in the past half century account for the complexity and ambiguity that is inherent in Caribbean social thought—a complexity that colors Caribbean Latino perspectives on environment.[7]

In Puerto Rico, the sugar economy peaked early. In the 1930s, reforestation initiatives and the work of the Civilian Conservation Corps contributed to the shaping of a Puerto Rican conservation ethic (Valdez Pizzini, pers. comm. 1993). In the 1950s, incentive-based industrialization initiatives forced Puerto Ricans to face the untoward environmental effects of heavily polluting industries (López 1987). In the past 25 years, export agriculture has played a secondary role in the island economy, the importance of smallholder agriculture has diminished, and forest cover has been increasing.

In contrast, the Dominican sugar boom of the late nineteenth and early twentieth centuries was followed by a second boom in the early 1970s. Both periods of expansion were accompanied by land consolidation processes that drove small producers into the woods, but the latter boom also displaced large cattle producers and was fueled by a large influx of Haitian labor. Collapse of the second sugar boom has been followed by new forms of plantation agriculture and contract production for export (Raynolds 1991) and the continuing relegation of food production to steeply sloped lands (Rosario 1993).

The plantation economy that developed in Cuba during the nineteenth century was superseded by industrial sugar production following the defeat of Spain in 1898. Here, too, rationalization of sugar production was accompanied by a strong U.S. military presence, although in a less direct form than in Puerto Rico and the Dominican Republic. The U.S. response to the 1959 revolution ensured that Cuba's dependence on sugar would continue unabated until the present. Preferential treatment for sugar exports by Eastern European nations once helped to support the social programs that have been the source of Cuban stability since 1959. Despite sweeping changes in Cuba's trade relationships with Eastern Europe and widespread dissatisfaction with the results of high-tech agriculture, Cuba's dependence on sugar has, if anything, deepened since the mid-1980s. Sugar is not only Cuba's primary source of foreign exchange, but its byproducts are now being used for fertilizers, cattle feed, and fuel.

Perceptions of the forest, too, vary from one island to another, although in all three, they are intimately tied to military domination and resistance—both individual and collective. The raiding and survival experience gained by Cuban maroon Esteban Montejo served him well in the Cuban revolutionary army. The Sierra Maestra forest reserve, the redoubt of Fidel Castro's forces during the revolution, has benefited from revolutionary nostalgia and, now, enjoys an international reputation for its successful strategies for the incorporation of resident peoples in its management plan. Conversations with ecologists and conservationists in Cuba's Institute for Ecology and Systematics, the Academy of Sciences, and COMARNA (The Coordinating Agency for Environment and Natural Resources) suggest a definition of ecology that encompasses human use—and in particular small-scale agriculture. In contrast, the association between insurgency and forests in the Dominican Republic led to a draconian forest policy in the 1960s. In recent years, these policies have been enforced with increasing vigor and capriciousness, causing a deep rift within the environmental movement (Lynch 1994). The Luquillo National Forest in Puerto Rico, managed by the U.S. Forest Service, is associated with secret activities of the U.S. military in popular lore. Nonetheless, it remains a potent symbol of Puerto Rican nationalism. Thus, in all three islands, the association between forest protection and military activity lies just below the surface of environmental discourse, but due to their divergent histories, the quality of this association differs from island to island.

While resistance to the plantation economy and military occupation has supplied much of the symbolic content for environmental discourse,

Caribbean environmentalism is still very much a response to development processes that also vary widely among the three nations. Puerto Rican development was marked by early migration of largely unskilled rural people to San Juan and the United States in the late 1940s, followed by Operation Bootstrap and the relocation of some highly polluting pharmaceutical and chemical plants to the island. Pressure on agricultural land has diminished with the advent of federal assistance programs. Cuba and the Dominican Republic have remained largely dependent on agriculture both for foreign exchange and food self-sufficiency. With the loss of assistance from Eastern Europe, Cuba has undergone a forced transition to low-input agriculture and is developing significant research capacity in this area (Rosset 1994). In contrast, poor pest-management practices in the Dominican Republic have resulted in rapid proliferation of insect pests, rapidly rising rates of pesticide poisoning and reproductive disease, and loss of competitiveness in international markets (Murray and Hoppin 1992). These phenomena, in turn, have heightened local environmental awareness.

While resort development is now being encouraged in Cuba, its beaches and mangroves have suffered less than those in Puerto Rico and the Dominican Republic, and the relatively pristine environment of its cays support the highest rate of endemism in the Caribbean. A salient feature of Dominican development has been the rapid proliferation of free-trade industrial zones, whose industries insist on exemption from Dominican environmental and occupational health and safety statutes and dump toxic effluents directly into rivers. Landscape changes resulting from development are particularly stark for migrants who return only on an occasional basis. A number of these migrants, particularly in the Dominican Republic, invest in reshaping rural landscapes in an attempt to give life to their memories.

In sum, the elements of Caribbean environmental discourse were constructed and reconfigured within a common historical context. However, within that broader context, divergent political histories and migrant experiences have produced different explanations of environmental degradation and their attendant understandings of risk. The following discussion looks at some of the ways that Caribbean Latino writers have shaped the building blocks of environmentalism—the ideal landscape, explanations of environmental degradation, and landscape and national identity—and shows the relationship of these shapes to the social and historical contexts in which these authors have written. The discussion then looks at how migrants' experiences transformed these elements and how these new perspectives have influenced individual actions and social movements within the Hispanic Caribbean community in the North.

The Ideal Landscape as a Starting Point

A Puerto Rican official in the New York City Department of Environmental Protection recently complained that many of his compatriots were more interested in creating Eden than they were in confronting the concrete environmental problems that the city was facing. Indeed, environmentalism often seems to concern itself with recuperaing the idyllic landscapes of an imaginary past, an aboriginal state imagined by colonial writers. The Eden to which the official alluded referred to an ideal landscape located in Western Christianity, but also to the 1492 encounter and the discourse on the "state of nature" that this encounter engendered. Descriptions of the aboriginal landscape left by the conquistadors, the friars, and the indigenous pupils of the friars reflected in part the genuine wonder and amazement of the Spaniards—as in the case of the voyage of Alvar Núñez Cabeza de Vaca. However, these descriptions were also promotional writings (López de Gomara), political manifestos (Bartolomé de las Casas, the journals of Christopher Columbus), and justifications for land claims (Columbus). By the late sixteenth century, Andean and Mexican chroniclers began to syncretize European and indigenous cosmologies. Whatever their original purpose, however, the writings of Columbus, Las Casas, Gonzalo Fernández Oviedo, Diego Durán, Cabezade Vaca, Garcilaso de la Vega, Guaman Poma and their implicit or explicit origin myths have become part of Latino cultural baggage. Among peoples of the Hispanic Caribbean, the idea of prehistory came from the earliest chronicles—Columbus, Las Casas, and Oviedo. These chronicles portray the aboriginal state as a lush, tropical, fruitful populated environment. The ideal landscape is the shaded, storied polycultural garden replete with root crops, tobacco, coffee, and tropical fruits; its stewards were the peaceable Taíno. In this landscape, the productive and the natural were inseparable.[8]

This conceptualization of the ideal landscape was incorporated into opposition accounts of conquest and European Humanist and Enlightenment social critiques (for example, Michel Eyquem de Montaigne, Jean-Jacques Rousseau). In the late nineteenth and early twentieth century, these images were picked up by colonial elites who, left behind by the rationalization and industrialization of sugar production, were nostalgic for agricultural landscapes that included horticultural and forested fringes. The resulting conflation of Eden and the state of nature, somehow located in a prehistoric past and populated by the Taíno, became the basis for popular histories of the islands. For example, summarizing Puerto Rican prehistory for a U.S. Latino audience, *El Diario/La Prensa* (14 June 1992) states:

> Los primitivos pobladores vienen de afuera, desarrollan una cultura propia, en la que se amalgaman las tradiciones originarias o la creación puramente autóctona. Esta viene impuesta por el nuevo medio o habitat en que se radican, produciendo unas formas culturales completamente personalizadas y diferentes de las tradiciones importadas. Ello permite hablar de una cultura arauca insular-taína y de una cultura boriqueña primitiva, o como se dice hoy, boricua.
>
> . . . Los exploradores españoles encontraron en el archipiélago antillano una sociedad perfectamente organizada y claramente definida en sus estructuras, lo que les impresionó en gran medida. Seguramente, ella es la primera que causó el impacto de lo novísimo en el mundo europeo, haciendo nacer la idea de que este estado "natural" del hombre era el perfecto, el modelo de lo que pudo ver el paraíso terrenal después de la caída de los llamados "primeros padres." La presencia, pues, del mundo taíno en la historia de los comienzos del pensamiento moderno tiene una repercusión que no debemos silenciar, pues de ella arranca, hasta el siglo XVIII, el concepto de la simplicidad de los pueblos naturales y la imagen del bon sauvage.
>
> [The primitive residents came from outside the island, developed their own culture, an amalgamation of traditions that they had brought with them and purely autochthonous creations. These last were imposed by the new environment in which they set down roots, producing cultural forms completely different from the imported traditions. It is this that permits us to speak of an araucanian, island Taíno culture and of a primitive Puerto Rican culture, or as it is referred to today, Boricua.
>
> . . . The Spanish explorers encountered in the antillean archipelago a society perfectly organized with clearly defined structures—which impressed them in great measure. Surely the encounter as a novelty in the European world, gave birth to the idea that the natural state of man was perfect, the model from

> which one could glimpse the earthly paradise after the fall of the so-called first parents. The presence, then, of the Taíno world in the history of the beginnings of modern thought has had repercussions that we cannot silence. From this model came in the eighteenth century the concept of the simplicity of natural peoples and the image of the noble savage.]

The association of the Taíno and the ideal landscape are not confined to the rhetoric of declining elites or the popular press. They also appear in serious literary efforts. Poet Martín Espada offers perhaps the most eloquent and economical expressions of Latino environmentalism in "Colibrí" (Espada 1990, 34). He locates Eden in Boricua, before

> The Spanish conquered
> with iron and words:
> "Taíno" for the people
> who took life
> from the plátanos in the trees,
> those multiple green fingers
> curling around unseen spears,
> who left the rock carvings
> of eyes and mouths
> in perfect circles of amazement . . . .

The garden, then, has distinct temporal connotations. It is located in the historic past at one of two junctures: either the moment of European penetration or the entrance of capitalism under protection of the marines. One ideal landscape is associated with the Taíno population and agriculture, both of which were conveniently destroyed at Conquest. The Taíno are the perfect stewards of the ideal landscape: the imagined world of the Taíno is limitless, precisely because Taíno reality is so ephemeral, existing only in a few remaining petroglyphs and artifacts, and, possibly, as well diffused and diluted genetic and cultural traits. Taíno contributions to the garden are acknowledged, but rarely are those made by Afro-Caribbean peoples on the margin of the plantation system, still less those made by maroons or *cimarones* who created the garden in the shelter of the woods. For the remnants of a planter aristocracy, the garden is associated with a period prior to the North American domination of the agricultural landscape, but not prior to the establishment of the plantation system which preceded it.

Novelist Rosario Ferré, for example, uses the garden to invoke the Arcadia of a declining Hispanic aristocracy. In *Sweet Diamond Dust* (Ferré 1988, 4–6), the garden is a landscape of nostalgia; it allows indigenous and African elements in Puerto Rican culture to merge and blossom and to produce a diverse array of pleasures for the self-made landed elite of the Spanish colony:

> the claret-red yautía as well as the paled, sherried golden one, the velvety kind that grew in Vieques, and the bristly, bearded one, which resembled a conquistador's pugnacious jaw and whose glories of the palate were sung by Gonzalo Fernández Oviedo
>
> the tumultuous tom tom taro roots, brought by African slaves on the wailing ships of death, which they named Ñáñigo and Farafanga, Mussumba and Tombuctú, in honor of their towering raven kings . . . and which we innocently reaped from our gardens as one digs out a snow-filled mammoths foot
>
> the poisonous treacherous cassava streaked with purple orchid's veins, which the Taínos and the African slaves used to drink when they were about to be tortured by the Spanish

Ferré's baroque description captures in a detached and ironic way the productivity of the garden, its sheer biodiversity, and the cultural diversity that went into its creation. Her description of the lush garden is presented as bombastic male rhetoric intended to obfuscate the problematic nature of the Puerto Rican past and to rationalize the greed of a declining planter aristocracy. Her female protagonists show the acknowledgement of cultural and racial mixture embodied in this description of the garden to be a sham in the face of concerted family efforts to whiten both race and landscape through steady expansion of sugar production and erasure of the few remaining fragments of garden. Because they understand the complexity of pre-occupation economy and society, Ferré's women can see the good as well as the bad in U.S. governance of the island.

The lush, exuberant garden, then, like the pristine wilderness, the English Arcadian landscape and the unpeopled frontier of Anglo societies, is the cultural construct that defines environmental good and allows the invention of measures of decay and standards for achievement. However, it is an ambiguous symbol whose meaning shifts with class and ethnic identification and with place of residence. It constitutes a focal point about which nationality and ethnicity are defined. But to the extent that the garden is identified with a Taíno past, it opens up the possibility of linking environmental thought to a nativism based on rejection of African contributions to island landscapes and culture.

Competing Explanations of Environmental Degradation

In Latino writings, the force behind environmental degradation may be the serpent in the garden that tempts Latinos to taste progress—to achieve, to get ahead, to poison themselves amid plenty. Degradation might also be seen quite simply, if not simplistically, as the legacy of Conquest and, later, North American domination. The deepest roots of Caribbean Latino environmentalism, then, come from Taíno resistance to Conquest—from the resistance of Enriquillo in the Central Sierra of the Dominican Republic. Developed in the twentieth century within the broader framework of political and philosophical indigenism, contemporary manifestations of this resistance are to be found in rural and urban "new social movements."

As indicated above, for Caribbean Latinos environmental degradation or decline from the ideal landscape, or The Fall, is situated in the historic past, most often at the moment of Conquest when the Spaniards destroyed Taíno society and economy deliberately, through enslavement, military conquest, and removal of indigenous populations from their lands, or inadvertently, through the introduction of European cultivars and diseases. The ecological consequences of the European "discovery" of this hemisphere were a major theme of both UNCED and Quincentennial observances, although the discussion can be traced to the writings of Sauer (1966) and Crosby (1972) in North America.

This view of decline poses problems for the non-Taíno. *Mestisaje,* the blending of genes and of culture, is a reality on all three islands, and identification of European civilization as the source of decline is problematic for islanders who look to colonial society with nostalgia. A fundamentally reactionary fraction of the environmental movement in Latin America views the self-sufficient hacienda as the ideal landscape and identifies North American economic imperialism as the culprit. It is not clear to what extent this vision of Utopia finds its way to the North.

Another stream of Latin American environmental thought shares the reactionary's view of degradation, but looks for reversal of the process in a reforging of national and ethnic identities through smallholder agrarian myths. The Cuban guajiro and the Puerto Rican jíbaro are associated with the Taíno, with fierce independence, and with an environmentally sustainable agrarian existence (Barreiro 1992; Vásquez 1992). The largely White producers of the Dominican Cibao share a similar mystique, but in this case nationalism gives way to regionialism—a regionalism that groups like the Ecological Society of the Cibao are now using to build support for environmental action. The independent heroes of these agrarian myths may be vested with Taíno ancestry,[9] but if they have African ancestors, these are seldom acknowledged. An exception is Espada's "Cordillera" (1986, 5):

> We are of mountains.
>
> Descended from
> Taíno carvings,
> Spanish watchtowers,
> African manacles,
> the jíbaro plow . . .

Yet in much of the Caribbean, pockets of Eden were maintained by maroons fleeing the plantations, escaped slaves who adapted the pre-Columbian conuco to the requirements of resistance and to their own cultural preferences (see, for example, Montejo 1993). African relationships to the landscape still appear to go largely unacknowledged in the environmental literature of the Spanish Caribbean.

Environment and National Identity

Martínez Alier suggests that environmentalism is a product of nationalism. He speaks of a "retrospective pride" about the successes of pre-Hispanic agriculture in Peru that gave rise to a popular ecological vision (Martínez Alier 1991, 630). Whether in Europe, Asia, or the Western Hemisphere, environmental thought is almost always tightly connected to the closely related concepts of homeland and landscape. Bramwell (1989), for example, locates "ecologism" within a context of Northern European nationalism and nativism. The appropriation of particular elements in the environment or patterns of adaptation to the environment as symbols of nationalism is informed both by the common construction of the ideal landscape and the divergent causal understandings of degradation. This appropriation cannot be understood in a Caribbean context without understanding the dynamics of the sugar economy and related issues of racial definition.

Ethnicity plays a curious role here, in that environmentalism is so often associated with appeals to Taíno identity in places where virtual elimination of the Taíno was one of the first acts of conquest. Puerto Ricans, for example, use symbols of the Taíno past to bolster their environmental claims (Latoni, Valdez Pizzini, and Rodríguez, 1992; Ferré 1988), but, because it is easier to make environmental claims on the basis of ethnicity as an aboriginal rather than as a mestizo or the inheritor of Taíno symbols and artifacts, broad claims based on Taíno aboriginal rights may carry very little weight compared to those of relatively intact indigenous groups like the Kayapó or the Cree.

Island Puerto Ricans can make stronger environmental claims as colonized peoples subject to a political and economic order imposed as a result of the Spanish-American War. Puerto Rican environmental agendas have frequently been tied to movements for independence and the restoration of prior rights or control over lands and water. López (1987) found that the leading environmentalists in the Puerto Rico of the 1980s linked environmental destruction to North American colonization, particularly the industrialization policies of Operation Bootstrap, and generally aligned themselves with the Independence movement. Ferré makes this connection in *Sweet Diamond Dust* (1988), but she presents a more complex picture. Environmental nationalism belongs to the aristocrats who lament the disappearance of the garden with the advance of industrial sugar production and their own marginalization as a class; the lives of the poor, in contrast, have improved measurably as a result of the political changes that produced this degradation. In the environmental arena, just as in the social, the despoiler comes to regard himself as the most effective protector.

The ambiguous relationship between colonial domination and environmental protection pervades Puerto Rican attitudes toward El Yunque, the island's highest mountain and largest rain forest (Latoni, Valdez Pizzini, and Rodríguez, 1992) and its fauna. El Yunque is, according to these authors, perceived at once as a sacred symbol of the Taíno and as a symbol of the "federal" presence, an emblem of the complicated feelings that the U.S. presence evokes on the island. For some Puerto Ricans, the Forest Service suggests unhealthy, but necessary, dependence on foreigners for resource protection. Others, notably Caminantes por La Paz and the Coalición Ambiental, have contested Forest Service's claim to superior knowledge and opposed its logging and road-building programs. But most important, "the scientists, the media, and the public alike appropriated El Yunque as a symbol of resistance, of cultural identity, of continuity of history, and national character" (Latoni, Valdez Pizzini, and Rodríguez 1991, 17).

The forest's most celebrated denizen is the *cotorra* or Puerto Rican parrot, a species unique to the island. A recent article in *El Diario/La Prensa* (14 June 1992) recommended that it replace the pan-Caribbean *pitirre* as the national bird. In making its case, *El Diario/La Prensa* claimed that not only was the bird well known to the island's inhabitants, but it was also "important for the native taínos. . . . It is also a symbol of what Puerto Rico once was, un hermoso paraíso forestal." Regaining paradise means regaining "the Taíno" in Puerto Rican culture. Conversely, invocation of the Taíno is an approach to restoring the island ecologically and reclaiming it territorially. The parrot became a compact symbol of these nested aspirations due largely to the misguided efforts of the U.S. Fish and Wildlife Service to save the remnant population by shipping it from El Yunque to Houston (Latoni, Valdez Pizzini, and Rodríguez 1992). In a climate of scientific uncertainty, a group called Friends of the Parrot (Amigos de las Cotorras) used the language of colonialism and nationalism to mobilize support for the Forest Service's position that the parrot remain in an island aviary. Latoni and coauthors suggest that "as a response to the historical appropriation of resources, science, ideology, objective discourse . . . and minds . . . by the U.S. in Puerto Rico, the group Amigos de las Cotorras proposed to appropriate the parrots through political action and symbols." But even here, the association of environment with nationalism is by no means clear. By claiming the parrot, nationalists have aligned themselves with the U.S. Forest Service, which until recently controlled El Yunque (Luquillo National Forest) as an enclave, limiting access to Puerto Ricans, but permitting clandestine and rather environmentally unsavory uses of large portions of the reserve.[10]

By 1990, the environmental movement in Puerto Rico had expanded from a critique of Operation Bootstrap and North American imperialism to a more complex, if equally critical, stance toward the North American presence as environmental protector of the island's most powerful national symbol. This broadening may ultimately permit the growth of a nonaligned Green movement on the island. Chemist Neftalí García, an Independence supporter in the 1980s, hoped to build a broad environmental coalition by running as an independent candidate in the 1992 Puerto Rican Senate race

(*Claridad,* 20 February 1992, 7). García's political evolution and that of his green supporters indicated a new willingness to build unity across traditional partisan lines in support of an environmental agenda.

The interweaving of environment and nationalism around potent symbolic landmarks in Puerto Rico permitted a far broader movement than that found in the Dominican Republic. In the latter country, the movement is sharply bifurcated along class lines. The grassroots movements of urban residents around issues of industrial pollution, water contamination and the loss of public space have gone largely unheeded in national government circles, as have myriad local NGO efforts centered on securing the rights of poor rural people to land, fuel, water, and their participation in natural resource decision-making. Meanwhile, the Dominican state continues to pursue a forest conservation strategy that involves brutal removal of small farmers from the source of their livelihood. In the Dominican context, environmental protection issues pit state against people, rich against poor, and region against region, rather than engendering national sentiments.

In Cuba, the development and innovative management of the Sierra Maestra reserve—management that has incorportated human settlement—was undertaken with nationalist concerns in mind, the Sierra Maestra being the locus from which the revolution spread in the late 1950s. Of more pressing national concern, however, are the need to develop low-input, sustainable livelihood systems for Cuban citizens and the need to subject its relatively pristine coastline and the rich biodiversity of its coastal waters to international tourist development interests in return for much needed foreign exchange.

The links between environmentalism and nationalism are more complex in the Dominican Republic, where environmentalism of a particularly conservationist stripe, coupled with violent dislocations of forest-dwellers, was used to facilitate counterinsurgency in the late 1960s and early 1970s and has more recently been used to justify tight controls over the movements of Haitian agricultural workers within the Dominican Republic. The arbitrary and harsh enforcement of forest protection decrees has, in turn, spawned new regionally based environmental organizations, linked by opposition to dislocation programs and by an interest in connecting Dominicans to their African roots and their Haitian neighbors. If the conservationist effort emphasized forest protection and reserves, the new environmental movement focuses on sustainable food production and urban habitat. Whereas the official conservationist movement was rooted in the anti-Haitian and implicitly racist nationalism of the Trujillo era, the new environmentalists emphasize the ecological unity of the island of Hispaniola and the integrity of regions within it.

Caribbean Environmentalism in the North

Different class, race, and national experiences have colored the content of environmental perspectives on the islands. The environmentalism of elites and politically vocal segments of the population has been in general associated with the preservation of particular landscapes—whether rooted in nostalgia for an old order and the creation of bulwarks against marronage and counterinsurgency, in nationalist expression, or floating in on the tide of the international conservationist impulse. The environmentalism of the poor, in contrast, tends to be rooted in claims for access to resources and the right to clean air, water, and public space (Martínez Alier 1991; Goodman and Redclift 1992). These distinctions break down in North America where, despite the persistance of class and racial difference within the migrant streams, migrants share a need to chart the new territory, to define safe and unsafe places, and to tame at least small parts of the landscape and make them their own. In the North, moreover, the initial absence of symbolic elements in the immigrant landscape makes it difficult to make environmental claims based on ethnicity or nationalism. Creation of such symbolic elements then becomes a central task of the immigrant's resettlement. For this reason, Caribbean environmental perspectives can be seen to have the following elements. These are neither necessary nor mutually exclusive: (1) a reimagining of the island of origin and its investiture of Eden-like qualities, (2) creation of regions of refuge where familiar sights, smells, and sounds stave off the pressures of an alien land, and (3) use of that base to actively create a new geography of conquest.

The Garden as a Spatial Alternative

As it migrated north with Dominicans and Puerto Ricans, the myth of the garden was submerged and became, in Scott's words, part of the hidden transcript, one that is beginning to emerge in the North in U.S. Latino fiction and in the Spanish-language press. For New York Dominican Julia Álvarez, the myth of the garden is distilled into a passionate longing for the semiwild guava. Her migrant daughter in search of roots drives to the country over the protests of her proper urban family to search out the fruit trees that invade old fields and pastures. Among the guava trees her car fails her, and, in spite of her carefully nurtured fear of the rural, she encounters the kind of human relationships that the term community implies.

Environmental concern within the homeland rises as old landscapes are despoiled or appropriated, but for those in a strange land it may focus on the desire to alter an alien landscape to make it conform more closely to the imagined homeland. Thus, U.S. Latino environmental perspectives are the products of the juxtaposition of landscapes of memory with the concrete landscapes of immigrant life. This juxtaposition lies at the core of much of Martín Espada's poetry,[11] Aurora Levins Morales's essay "Puertoricanness" (1991), Vector Hernández Cruz's poem "Snaps of Immigration" (1991), and Cristina García's novel *Dreaming in Cuban* (1992). These perspectives, defined and redefined in a context of migration, reflect the circumstances of the diaspora. Contrast, for example, García's reaction to the Cuban landscape: "There's a magic here working its way through my veins. There's something about the vegetation, too, that I respond to instinctively—the stunning bougainvillea, the flamboyants and jacarandas, the orchids growing from the trunks of the mysterious ceiba trees" (García 1992, 235) with her description of trees growing in Brooklyn: "Down the street the trees are imprisoned equidistantly in square plots of dirt. Everything else is now concrete. Lourdes remembers reading somewhere about how Dutch elm disease wiped out the entire species on the East Coast except for a lone tree in Manhattan surrounded by concrete. Is this, she wonders, how we'll all survive?" (García 1992, 129).

Aurora Levins Morales makes a similar comparison: "The mulberry trees of Chicago, that first summer, had looked so utterly pitiful beside her memory of flamboyant and banana and . . . No, not even the individual trees and bushes but the mass of them, the overwhelming profusion of green life that was the home of her comfort and the nest of her dreams" (Levens Morales 1991, 12). And Espada, with his usual economy, offers a "Puerto Rican Autopsy" (1986,11):

Winter-corpsed
in East Harlem,
opened his head
and found
a rainforest

The garden stands in contrast to another ideal landscape: the glittery Utopia of the American "growth machine" and consumer's paradise. Silvio

Martínez Palau debunks this Utopia in "El reino de este mundo II" (1986), a fictional chronicle of Harrisburg's (and the nation's) giddy obsession with the results of a radiation leak from an employment-generating factory that produces an ever-shifting set of marginally useful gadgets. In *Dreaming in Cuban,* the growth machine, run amok, appears in the guise of the Yankee Doodle Bakery, as the product of emigrée Lourdes's blind infatuation with America and the producer of unending streams of sweet rolls, which feed her obesity. In the Northern context, then, the garden is an alternative landscape that can be realized on a small scale and that can offer a small measure of peace and solace in an alien world. Within migrant communities in the North, the garden similarly has both a nostalgic function and holds a vision of the future. The garden's perfection is marred by the apple and the serpent; North American dystopias still hold the promise of a better life.

Migrant nostalgia about the "happier" rural environments of times past is often balanced by a heightened consciousness of particular patterns of environmental degradation that have impelled exodus. Nostalgia may also provoke contemplation about the root causes of those changes and differences between the landscapes in which migrants find themselves, those that they had expected to find, and those left behind. New York's *casitas* are built physical manifestations of this consciousness. Vázquez (1992) finds that by evoking a landscape of nostalgia, the casita provides a commentary on the economic processes that impelled the diaspora and as well as the inadequacies of the built environment in the new land.

Where migrants were drawn to the promise and glitter of the American economy, the ideal landscape may have little to do with what was left behind. Whether a product of necessity or force or part of a process of self-realization, of gaining knowledge of the broader world, of becoming a man or a woman, migration is often the context in which ethnicity is expressed. And, as Victor Hernández Cruz suggests in "Snaps of Immigration" (1991, 13), central to migrant definitions of ethnicity are the imagined landscapes of the past, the forces that have changed them and impelled migration, and the concrete landscapes in which cultural adjustments are constantly made:

3 When we say the tenements
our eyes turned backwards
to the miracle of scenery.
At the supermarket
My mother caressed the parsley.

Rural mountain dirt walk
Had to be adjusted to cement
pavement
The new city finished the
concrete supply of the world
Even the sky was cement
The streets were made of shit.

Migrants frequently lose attachment to place. This loss is a central theme in Oscar Hijuelo's *Our House in the Last World* (1983), whose protagonists leave Cuba as the Batista regime closes political and economic spaces. When the American-born, blond child Hector returns to revel in the garden, to eat its fruit and drink muddy water from farm puddles, the land of sunshine and flowers strikes back infesting him with *micróbios* and fear. Toward the novel's close, a postadolescent Hector drifts between his home of unimaginable ugliness on the Upper West Side of New York and a Florida landscape undergoing redesign by the Miami Cuban construction entrepreneurs, who are plotting to reconquer the island. Even as he appears to come to peace with his West Side roots, in the warm sunlight of his window, Hector is "transported by that light into another world before awareness of problems. I'm not in the apartment anymore, but in Cuba . . . Cuba radiates in through a window. Peeking out I follow the path of a long silvery hill with its trees and colorful houses. I take in the scent of the flowers and of the bakery making its soda crackers and loaves of high rising puffy bread. . . . I feel mesmerized by this notion of the past. I want it forever in my house, but it fades away" (Hijuelo 1983).

Espada captures the environmental dimension of this rootlessness, which is more acute among poor migrants, in *The Immigrant Iceboy's Bolero* (1986, 8):

"Utuado. Puerto Rico." Refugee's words.
"I can't go back.
They poisoned the country."
And the chemical gas that dissolved
in the grain of mountain leaf
has dissolved in the grain of his tongue,
so that he furies at the landlords;
General Electric, Union Carbide;
Kennecott Copper, ITT,

the rage of a bloodclot
streaked in oil refinery sky,
his eyes that other eyes avoid.

The Garden: From Ideal Landscape to Social Action

The inability to return creates new territorial needs, and these too are part of an environmental perspective—one that emphasizes the built, rather than the natural. But just as maroons and Taíno remnants needed their mountain redoubts, immigrants need their own sanctuaries and outposts, nodes for communication with peers and for articulation with the alien land. Espada expresses this need with eloquence in "Tony Went to the Bodega, but He Didn't Buy Anything" (Espada 1986). The bodega, the little store staffed by Latinos, is an outpost where one can enter into relations with the larger society, but where one can also procure the roots and fruits of the garden—yuca, yautía, sweet potato, island coffee, mangos, and avocados.

Puerto Rican casitas, family or neighborhood clubs, constitute another kind of safe place. These reconstructions of rural dwellings and landscapes replete with chickens and vegetable gardens have been springing up on empty lots in the South Bronx and other Hispanic neighborhoods. The casita itself is a symbolic recreation of the island *bohio,* or rural dwelling that serves as a school for socializing immigrant children into Puerto Rican society. Undergirding this environmental reclamation is a nostalgic association with the *jíbaro,* the small, independent peasant from the hills of Puerto Rico (Vázquez 1992). Evidence that the "jíbaro" yearning for a garden is a phenomenon that can be traced to the Puerto Rican migrant community of the 1930s and 1940s can be found in the memoirs of the thoroughly urban life of nationalist and labor activist Bernardo Vega (Iglesias 1984). Thus, the casita is not only a refuge secured by guerilla activity (Vázquez 1992), it is a sanctuary for jíbaro nationalism, replete with such cultural symbols as flags and a vehicle for transport to a rural tropical landscape of nostalgia.

A more widespread and visible part of the urban landscape in the North is the garden, which is taking on new importance as a spatial critique of urbanization. In particular, in the North American city, the garden takes on a new reality as a multipurpose Arcadian construction offering respite from the pressures of urban life; it produces food to share with family and neighbors; it offers its cultivators ties with the rural landscapes of other times and places, and it is in itself an act of rebellion against the North American definition of urban with its clearly defined zones and segregated land uses. In short, the garden transforms an alienated and alienating environment into a nurturing one. Consider, for example, the case of Daniel Pérez, a Dominican who in 1991 planted corn in a noman's land, a median strip on Broadway at 153d Street as part of his individual beautification project: "All I saw was bottles, old newspapers, garbage and weeds. I took a large garbage bag and cleared the land. I planted with the idea that this is my own little contribution, my own little Cibao" (Myers 1991b).

Remarkably, while a few ears disappeared, the crop was treated with respect by neighbors and passersby. Pérez cultivated garlic and tomatoes with the corn; the year before he had grown black beans and shared the harvest with neighbors (Myers 1991a, b). Pérez's deed was one of numerous steps, however small and tentative, taken by Latinos toward reconquest of New York City's hostile environment.[12] There have been others as well: the Crotona Community Coalition, under the leadership of Dominican migrant Astín Jacobo, turned empty lots into community gardens. New York City's Operation Green Thumb and the New York Botanical Garden's Bronx Green-Up have supported Latino gardening efforts with cheap land leases and elephant dung (Raver, 1991). The benefits that New York's Latinos claim to derive from these activities shed some insights on their particular environmental values. Puerto Rican cultivator José García learned about tomatillos from his Mexican neighbor. "Every night," he says, "I come home and work in the garden, breathe the fresh air. Sometimes I fall asleep out here. My wife doesn't even know where I am." He uses no chemicals on his crop: "Chemicals can kill the flavor. I work in the market at Hunt's Point. You see these tomatoes, so nice, but not natural. They use gas to make them red. You grow it yourself, you get something fresh" (Raver 1991).

Toward New Environmental Actions

Having begun the creation of a new urban geography that allows the maintenance of ethnicity, New York City Latinos have begun to transcend ethnic cleavages to promote environmental agendas. This is evident in Luís Garden Acosta's and Astín Jacobo's insistence in looking at the environment as a politically unifying issue in the fractious context of NYC politics. Garden Acosta, director of El Puente Community Center in Williamsburg, Brooklyn, undertook an unprecedented and difficult dialogue with the neighboring Hasidic community to secure its backing in opposition to a proposed incinerator. Astín Jacobo, Dominican president of the Crotona Community Coalition in the South Bronx, has coordinated Latino community efforts to transform the South Bronx with community housing, gardens, and lighted playing fields. He insists that these environmental efforts require cooperation across ethnic lines.

What appears to be happening in the New York City Latino community is a significant shift in environmental discourse. While environmental claims are based on the assertion of national or ethnic identity, social movement leaders are increasingly interested in environmental rights that transcend ethnicity. The organizations that pursue urban environmental agendas remain distinctly Latino, but they are increasingly motivated by a more general ideology of environmental justice. At this level, one begins to see increasing correspondence between environmental activities in the Caribbean Latino community and those of Chicanos and Hispanos in the Western United States.

At the same time, continuity in the migration process over time, frequent return trips to visit family and for tourism, and excellent communication (except to Cuba) are creating a new kind of internationalization of environmental consciousness, rooted in both nostalgia and nationalism. Diane Rocheleau (pers. comm., 26 August 1993) reports visiting a small farmer living in the Dominican Sierra. The trees once planted in his yard were grown; the adjacent field once in crops now stood in pasture. Domestic birds, pigeons and guinea fowl, ruled the yard, and small ponies fed on the pasture—a land use pattern with no obvious economic utility. When asked about the animals, the farmer explained that a relative in New York paid him to raise the birds and ponies, to reconstruct the ideal landscape in miniature—the ideal landscape as imagined from the North. Not altogether different from such idiosyncratic constructions are efforts on the part of communities in the North to increase environmental awareness on the islands. The fledgling Dominican Foundation of New York, for example, sees its goal as environmental protection within the Dominican Republic, and Cuban Americans working with the Nature Conservancy on everglades protection in Florida are now looking beyond the peninsula to address environmental concerns on the island.

Conclusion

To conclude, environmentalism in the 1990s is no longer the preserve of Northern Europe and the United States, but is pervasive and mediated by culture and position within the world order. This makes it possible to talk about Latin American, Caribbean, or Latino environmentalisms. But environmentalism is further mediated by class in the Hispanic Caribbean and, for this reason, it is an ambiguous movement. This ambiguity is more easily discoverable in high brow and popular literary production from the islands and the United States than in scientific or policy statements on environment by Latinos or through the use of standard survey techniques.

Despite class and race differences, the garden offers at least a minimal shared definition of the ideal landscape. Thus, the environmentalism of Caribbean Latinos differs fundamentally from mainstream environmentalism in the North, in the first instance because it is rooted in the garden—a profuse and exuberant landscape, but one managed with human desires in mind, rather than a pristine landscape untouched by the human species or an abstract concept like biodiversity. The garden serves as a reference point for understanding the islands' past with reference to the present and for making sense of landscape change on the islands. Environmentalisms based on other end points are largely exogenous to Caribbean societies. Moreover, as certain landforms have become symbols of nationalism or regional identity—El Yunque, the Sierra Maestra, Diego de Ocampo, the Cibao—their meanings are shared across class and racial lines. Finally, despite widely varying class backgrounds of migrants in the three national streams, the possibilities for unity within the national migrant streams are greater in exile, where the meanings of these national symbols are redefined by the migratory experience. Within the migrant community it is possible to find a common interest in investing a new alien landscape with comforting symbols of the old.

And so, in attempting to rechronicle the environmental movement from a Caribbean Latino perspective, we find, first, that the dichotomies between the natural and the civilized, the pure and the impure, the city and the country, the North and the South that undergird environmental thinking in the North begin to break down. With this breakdown, concepts such as "the garden" take on a new complexity and richness. Explanations of decline vary as they are influenced by different understandings of race and class, understandings whose meanings become somewhat blurred as landscape assumes new and perhaps more complex functions in the lives of migrants.

NOTES

1. In this chapter I use the term Caribbean or Caribbean Hispanic to refer to these communities, mindful of the fact that I exclude from my discussion environ-

mental perspectives the francophone and anglophone islands and the Atlantic coast of Central America.

2. A notable exception to this pattern of exclusion is Catalan Martínez Alier's *Ecological Economics* (1987), a study that refers to North American and Latin American discussions of Andean land use patterns.

3. Here I adopt Bullard's definition: "Historically, the mainstream environmental movement in the United States has developed agendas that focus on such goals as wilderness and wildlife preservation, wise resource management, pollution abatement, and population control. It has been primarily supported by middle- and upper-class whites. Although concern for the environment cuts across class and racial lines, ecology activists have generally been individuals with above-average education, greater access to economic resources, and a greater sense of personal power" (Bullard 1993:22).

4. See Lynch (1993). The experience of Latoni, Valdés, and Rodríguez (1992) in back translating a Forest Service questionnaire for use in El Yunque reveals not only the limits of such an approach, but the value of these limits in guiding researchers to more ethnographic approaches to data collection.

5. The Spanish colonial hold on Hispaniola was far weaker because of the power of the Haitian Republic in the early nineteenth century. It could be argued that after 1841 a reassertion of Spanish institutional and cultural forms took place as a reaction against occupation.

6. Antonio Benítez-Rojo (1992) underscores this particular hold of sugar on the Caribbean imagination from Bartolomé de las Casas to Nicolás Guillén.

7. Benítez-Rojo, a Cuban writer and literary critic resident in the United States, uses chaos, in its scientific sense, as a metaphor to convey the infinite social, political, and cultural variations on common themes in his synthetic treatment of Caribbean history and literature (1992).

8. Goodman and Redclift (1991) look at environmentalism as principally a Northern response to accelerating transformations within the productive landscape and a concomitant segregation of landscapes of consumption from landscapes of production. They correctly point to reactions against the transfer of Northern environmental logics to the reality of the South as misguided at best. However, like many other development scholars from Europe and North America, they reduce Southern environmentalism to livelihood issues and neglect the aesthetic dimensions of these movements.

9. See for example Victor Hernández Cruz's "New/Aguas Buenas/Jersey" (Hernández 1991) and Martín Espada's "Cordillera" (Espada 1986).

10. It is widely speculated that inaccessible parts of the reserve have been used for weapons testing.

11. See especially "Puerto Rican Autopsy" (Espada 1986), "Justo the Painter and the Conquest of Lawrence" (Espada 1990).

12. Accounts of Pérez's achievement appeared in the *New York Times* 13 and 15 August 1991. National Public Radio's news program "All Things Considered" covered the story 14 August 1991.

REFERENCES

Agarwal, Bina. 1986. *Cold Hearths and Barren Slopes: The Woodfuel Crisis in the Third World.* Riverdale, Md.: The Riverdale.

Barreiro, José. 1992. "Guajiro: The Natural Cuban and the Revolution." Paper presented at Conference on Environment and Latino Imaginations, Cornell University, Ithaca, N.Y., 30 April–2 May.

Benítez-Rojo, Antonio. 1992. *The Repeating Island: The Caribbean and the Postmodern Perspective,* trans. James E. Maraniss. Durham, N.C.: Duke University Press.

Bramwell, Anna. 1989. *Ecology in the 20th Century: A History.* New Haven, Conn.: Yale University Press.

Brown, Phil, and Edwin J. Mikkelsen. 1990. *No Safe Place: Toxic Waste, Leukemia, and Community Action.* Berkeley: University of California Press.

Bullard, Robert D. 1990. *Dumping in Dixie: Race, Class, and Environmental Quality.* Boulder, Colo.: Westview.

———. 1993. "Anatomy of Environmental Racism and the Environmental Justice Movement." In *Confronting Environmental Racism: Voices from the Grassroots,* ed. Robert D. Bullard, 15–39. Boston: South End Press.

Burch, William. 1964. "Nature as Symbol and Expression in American Life: A Sociological Exploration." Ph.D. diss., University of Minnesota, Minneapolis.

Capek, Stella. 1993. "The Environmental Justice Frame: A Conceptual Discussion and an Application." *Social Problems* 40:5024.

Crosby, Alfred W. 1972. *The Columbian Exchange: Biological and Cultural Consequences of 1492.* Westport, Conn.: Greenwood.

Edelstein, Michael R. 1988. *Contaminated Communities: The Social and Psychological Impacts of Residential Toxic Exposure.* Boulder, Colo.: Westview.

El Diario/La Prensa. 1992a. "Borinquén: Una tierra de inmigrantes." Suplemento de Puerto Rico, 14 June, 25.

———. 1992b. "El ave nacional de Puerto Rico." Suplemento de Puerto Rico, 14 June, 3.

Espada, Martín. 1986. *The Immigrant Iceboy's Bolero.* Maplewood, N.J.: Waterfront Press.

———. 1990. *Rebellion Is the Circle of a Lover's Hands: Rebelión es el giro de manos del amante.* Willimantic, Conn.: Curbstone Press.

Ferré, Rosario. 1988. *Sweet Diamond Dust.* New York: Ballantine.

García, Cristina. 1992. *Dreaming in Cuban.* New York: Knopf.

Goodman, David, and Michael Redclift. 1992. *Refashioning Nature: Food, Ecology and Culture.* London and New York: Routledge.

Guha, Ramachandra. 1989. *The Unquiet Woods: Ecological Change and Peasant Resistance in the Himalaya.* Berkeley: University of California Press.

Hernández Cruz, Victor. 1991. *Red Beans.* Minneapolis: Coffee House Press.

Hijuelo, Oscar. 1983. *Our House in the Last World.* New York: Persea Books.

Iglesias, César Andreu, ed. 1984. *Memoirs of Bernardo Vega: A Contribution to the History of the Puerto Rican Community in New York.* New York: Monthly Review Press.

Latoni, Alfonso R., Manuel Valdez Pizzini, and Virgilio Rodríguez. 1992. "El Yunque es nuestro" [The CNF is ours]: An ethnography of mysteries, appropriations and management in a tropical rain forest. Paper presented at the Fourth North American Symposium on Society and Resource Management, Madison Wis., 17–20 May.

Levine, Adeline G. 1982. *Love Canal: Science, Politics, and People.* Lexington, Mass.: Lexington Books.

Levins Morales, Aurora. 1991. "Puertoricanness." In *Puerto Rican Writers at Home in the USA,* ed. Faythe Turner, 12–14. Seattle: Open Hand Publishing.

López, Alfredo. 1987. *Doña Licha's Island: Modern Colonialism in Puerto Rico.* Boston: South End Press.

Lynch, Barbara. 1993. "The Garden and the Sea: U.S. Latino Environmental Discourses and Mainstream Environmentalism." *Social Problems* 40:108–24.

———. 1994. State formation, public lands, and human rights: The case of the Dominican Republic and Los Haitises. Paper presented at the XVIII International Congress of the Latin American Studies Association, Atlanta, 10–12 March.

Martínez Alier, Joan. 1987. *Ecological Economics: Energy, Environment and Society.* Cambridge, Mass.: Blackwell.

——— 1991. "Ecology and the Poor: A Neglected Dimension of Latin American History." *Journal of Latin American Studies* 23:621–39.

Martínez Palau, Silvio. 1986. "El reino de este mundo II." In *Made in USA.* New York: Ediciones del Norte.

Marx, Leo. 1964. *The Machine in the Garden: Technology and the Pastoral Ideal in America.* New York: Oxford University Press.

Merchant, Carolyn. 1980. *The Death of Nature: Women, Ecology and the Scientific Revolution.* San Francisco: Harper.

———1992. *Radical Ecology: The Search for a Livable World.* New York and London: Routledge.

Montejo, Esteban. 1993. *The Autobiography of a Runaway Slave,* trans. Miguel Barnet. London: Macmillan Caribbean.

Murray, Douglas L., and Polly Hoppin. 1992. "Recurring Contradictions in Agrarian Development: Pesticide Problems in Caribbean Basin Nontraditional Agriculture." *World Development* 20:597–608.

Myers, Steven Lee. 1991a. "Broadway's New Feature: Cornstalks." *New York Times,* 13 August, B1–2.

———. 1991b. "Farmers Unearthed: He Planted the Corn. *New York Times,* 15 August, B5.

Nash, Roderick. 1973. *Wilderness and the American Mind,* revised edition. New Haven, Conn.: Yale University Press.

———. 1990. *The Rights of Nature: A History of Environmental Ethics.* Madison: University of Wisconsin Press.

Payton, Frederick. 1990. "The Role of Potato in Sustainable Cropping Systems in the Lowlands of the Dominican Republic." International Potato Center, Santo Domingo, Dominican Republic. Unpublished report. 27 November.

Peluso, Nancy Lee. 1993. "Coercing Conservation? The Politics of State Resource Control." *Global Environmental Change* (June): 199–217.

Peña, Devon. 1992. "The 'Brown' and the 'Green': Chicanos and Environmental Politics in the Upper Rio Grande." *Capitalism, Nature, Socialism* 3:79–103.

Peña, Devon, and Joseph Gallegos. 1993. "Nature and Chicanos in Southern Colorado." In *Confronting Environmental Racism: Voices from the Grassroots,* ed. R. D. Bullard. Boston: South End Press.

Price, Richard. 1979. *Maroon Societies: Rebel Slave Communities in the Americas.* Baltimore: Johns Hopkins University Press.

Pulido, Laura. 1992. "The Complex Environmentalism of Everyday Life: The Ganados del Valle Cooperative." Paper presented at Cornell University Conference on Environment and Latino Imaginations, Ithaca, N.Y., May, 1992.

Pulsipher, Lydia. 1991. "Galways Plantation," Montserrat. In *Seeds of Change,* ed. Herman J. Viola and Carolyn Margolis, 139–60. Washington, D.C.: Smithsonian Institution Press.

Raver, Anne. 1991. "In a Mix of Cultures, an Olio of Plantings." *New York Times,* 15 August, C1, 4.

Raynolds, Laura T. 1991. "Export Substitution and the Rise of Non-traditional Agricultural Commodities in the Dominican Republic." Paper presented at the XVI International Congress of the Latin American Studies Association. Washington, D.C., 4–6 April.

Rosario, Pedro Juan del. 1993. *Informe final de los resultados del Proyecto Uso de Suelo y Producción de Alimentos en la República Dominicana.* Santiago, Dominican Reupublic: Centro de Estudios Urbanos y Regionales, Pontificia Universidad Católica Madre y Maestra and CARTEL, University of Sherbrooke.

Rosset, Peter, with Shea Cunningham. 1994. *The Greening of Cuba: Organic Farming Offers Hope in the Midst of Crisis.* San Francisco: Institute for Food and Development Policy.

Sauer, Karl O. 1966. *The Early Spanish Main.* Berkeley: University of California Press.

Scott, James. 1990. *Domination and the Arts of Resistance.* New Haven, Conn.: Yale University Press.

Shiva, Vandana. 1989. *Staying Alive: Women, Ecology and Development.* London: Zed Books

Vázquez, Oscar. 1992. "New York 'Casitas': the Discourse of Nostalgia." Paper presented at Cornell University Conference on Environment and Latino Imaginations, Ithaca, N.Y., 30 April–2 May.

Williams, Raymond. 1973. *The Country and the City.* New York: Oxford University Press.

Wilson, Alexander. 1992. *The Culture of Nature: North American Landscape from Disney to the Exxon Valdez.* Cambridge, Mass.: Blackwell.

Worster, Donald. 1977. *Nature's Economy: A History of Ecological Ideas.* Cambridge, England: Cambridge University Press.

Part III

Constructing Rurality

9

Consuming Images: Making and Marketing Vermont as Distinctive Rural Place

C. Clare Hinrichs

Instrumental ways of seeing Vermont have long shaped the construction and presentation of Vermont as rural place. The images and narratives surrounding this small New England state brim with pastoral charm, small town tranquillity, Yankee resourcefulness and, of course, natural beauty. Indeed, such representations of Vermont have been so widely and vigorously disseminated that they are easily evoked by the simple utterance of its name. In almost metonymic fashion, to speak of Vermont is to conjure up a broader vision of balanced, beneficent rurality. Yet while the name "Vermont" may signify a generic rurality, it also confers the specificity of place, suggesting that Vermont rurality is especially distinctive and worth experiencing by the tourist or consumer.

Treating rurality as an amalgam of landscape, tradition and place, this chapter examines several questions concerning the production and dissemination of images of rural Vermont. First, how did Vermont come to represent an idealized rural place? Second, in whose interest have such images been promoted? Finally, what does it mean to "preserve" Vermont, given the legacy and appeal of carefully constructed images of Vermont rurality?

The Consumption of Rurality

To understand the promotion of Vermont as distinctive rural place, it is important to consider both general trends heightening the importance of consumption in rural places and specific historical developments shaping the situation in Vermont. Various commentators have noted the recent rise in conflicting claims on rural space to fulfill recreational, environmental and aesthetic priorities, beyond the traditional ends of resource production (Cloke and Park 1985). To sketch a North American example, the interests of hikers, dirtbikers, birdwatchers, snowmobilers, hunters, homeowners and farmers (to cite only a few of the possible bases of interest) now meet, and frequently clash, in rural settings where it may once have seemed that views on "appropriate" land use were more uniform. In rural areas less than a day's drive from major metropolitan centers, the concerns of tourists, second-home owners and urban refugees have gained particular influence, in large part because such groups represent an economic infusion for otherwise strained rural economies. While picturesque scenes of tidy farms nestled in sunlit valleys may be what attracts this new, more heterogeneous mix of "stakeholders," they view the countryside not merely as space for production but also as space for their own consumption—that is, as a landscape and lifestyle amenity.

In this situation, farmers and other rural producers increasingly serve as what British researchers Paul Cloke and Nigel Thrift call "scenechangers":

> Some farmers, for example, have had the opportunity to cash in on the accumulated value of their land, either by selling for housing development or by diversifying their production to cater for the consumption requirements of the new classes of rural resident. Farming people in these places often play the contemporary role of "scenechangers" who create the ambiance of the countryside for middle-class residents and urban visitors. (Cloke and Thrift 1990, 172)

Whereas the social role of rural producers once rested largely on their actual production of food, fuel or fiber, their present social role also encompasses the presentation of idealized images of rural life, valued by groups originating from or based elsewhere. In this respect, it may now be less a question of the "farming landscape," and rather a question of "landscape farming" (Goodey 1986).

Such changing configurations of social roles and actors in rural spaces are indicative of what Belgian sociologist Marc Mormont (1990) calls "multiple locality phenomenon"—a term referring to the growing tendency for some social groups to identify with and make claims on more than one local environment. Mormont suggests that while geographical mobility has become common in post-industrial societies, more economically and politically advantaged groups tend to wield disproportionate influence in the various localities with which they identify. For example, in-migrating metropolitan-based groups, who profess a love of the countryside, often exhibit little tolerance for long-standing farming practices producing odors, noise, or possible pollution, and move quickly to enforce or establish local regulations that will ensure a scenic and "natural" landscape (Dunphy 1988; Fitchen 1991). But others who simply visit or tour the countryside wield influence as well, since their expectations and pleasures in the experience of rurality have economic implications for communities there (Urry 1990).

While the consumption of rurality has important political and policy implications, it should also be recognized as a cultural phenomenon, emerging from interpretations of rurality as an amalgam of landscape, tradition and place. Apart from any satisfaction of material needs, consumer goods and consumption practices generally serve as symbolic markers providing a social currency (Douglas and Isherwood 1979). Such symbolic distinctions of consumer culture will ultimately reproduce class structure (Bourdieu 1984). Although much recent theoretical work on consumption has focused on obvious "cultural goods," such as art, music, and fashion, rurality is as much a commodity produced for, marketed to and consumed by different class fractions. Rurality as an object for consumption, then, rests on both material instances and symbolic understandings of landscape, tradition, and place.

Cultural geographers generally agree that landscape is constituted at multiple levels, both as material practice and cultural product (Jackson 1989). Denis Cosgrove, for example, writes:

> Landscape represents an historically specific way of experiencing the world developed by, and meaningful to, certain social groups. Landscape . . . is an ideological concept. It represents a way in which certain classes of people have signified themselves and their world through their imagined relationship with nature, and through which they have underlined and communicated their own social role and that of others with respect to external nature. (Cosgrove 1984, 15)

Cosgrove argues that "landscape is not merely the world we see, it is a construction, a composition of that world" (Cosgrove 1984, 13). In this respect, the landscape concept carries within it the tensions between object and subject, matter and culture, the individual and the social. While land itself can become the object of consumption for different social actors pressing for their preferred land uses, landscape—the dominance of particular images of land and human interaction—is no less an arena for contest. The landscape concept thus embraces at once the concrete materiality of land, the social relations undergirding different land uses, and the ideological content implicit in particular images of human–land interaction, including specific rural production practices.

Bourdieu's (1984) notion of symbolic capital offers one way of thinking about the consumption value of rural images to particular class fractions. Symbolic capital refers to "a reputation for competence and an image of respectability and honourability" (Bourdieu 1984, 291) conferred by participation in particular cultural practices or consumption of certain cultural goods. While Bourdieu dwells at length on how the symbolic capital of artwork, home furnishings, or food is read and appropriated, proximity to, ownership of, or simply evocation of idealized rural landscapes can also constitute a form of symbolic capital. As Bourdieu explains, "What is at stake is indeed 'personality', i.e., the quality of the person, which is affirmed in the capacity to appropriate an object of quality" (Bourdieu 1984, 281).

For metropolitan-based class fractions now making claims on the countryside in advanced industrial countries, landscape of "quality" usually suggests some mythical, harmonious rural world. The desirability of such landscapes lies in their apparent contrast to the obviously industrial landscapes of blighted cities and bland suburbs (Williams 1990). In the United States, such rural landscapes can still be linked to a "pastoral ideal" (Marx 1964), where taming the wilderness and cultivating the land are seen as the source of moral and civic virtue.[1] However, rural ideologies are historically and culturally specific (Short 1991). Thus, a "pastoral ideal" in the United States, the romanticization of *la vieille France* in France (Bourdieu 1984, 280), the "rural idyll" in Britain (Newby 1979), the "garden myth" of Prince Edward Island (Milne 1982), or notions of *furusato* Japan (Robertson 1988) each bear the mark of specific social formations within a common idealization of rural life.

In most advanced industrial countries, idealized images of rurality (in contrast to idealized images of wilderness, which tend to deny the presence or influence of humans) usually feature land uses and rural production practices characterized by technological moderation, calm industriousness, and social harmony, or what Wilson (1992) identifies as a "working rural landscape." Such popular images of rurality often bear a historic cast, showing little mark of the technological excesses or social problems more commonly ascribed to cities and towns. In New England, for example, half a dozen Holsteins grazing peacefully on a verdant hillside form a tableau far preferable to the reality of manure management on a large modern dairy farm. Similarly, a weather-beaten board and batten sugarhouse surrounded by ancient maples hung with galvanized buckets somehow seems more "rural" than a huge, high-tech sugaring operation using plastic pipeline, vacuum extraction and a host of sophisticated processing equipment.

In this respect, idealized rural images are redolent of "tradition." Such tradition typically also features people who work hard, at once colorful, yet unobtrusive, neither complaining nor having reason to complain. The sturdy bonds of kin and the comfortable networks of small town community provide the reliable, enduring social context of such a rurality. Rather than acknowledge conflict, benightedness, or squalor, notions of "rural tradition" dwell selectively on its most sanitized, beneficent possible features.[2]

While the consumption of rurality presumes particular interpretations of landscape and tradition, it acquires additional cultural meaning through the positionality of place.[3] Specific rural places, each with its own unique mix of landscape and tradition, are by definition limited in availability and are hence to some degree exclusive. Although general images of rurality have certain consumption value, they are clearly superseded by specific images of particularly desirable rural places. Thus touring Provence, with its Roman ruins, wild hills and famed regional foods, holds far more cachet than simply touring "the European countryside." In this way, the consumption of rurality is driven first by generalized longing for landscapes and traditions seemingly opposed to those of the cities or suburbs. But beyond this, the consumption of rurality splinters along fault lines differentiating specific rural places, each struggling to distinguish itself as more appealing, essential, or enduring in its representation of rurality.

Promoting and Marketing Vermont as Rural Place

Much discussion about the consumption of rural space builds on observations about recent social change in the post-productionist countryside of the advanced industrial countries (Cloke and Goodwin 1991; Marsden 1989; Marsden, et al. 1993). However, conflicts about the use and consumption of rural space in Vermont are nothing new. Indeed, historians and other writers have noted that tourism and an orientation to recreation by outside populations have long undergirded Vermont's rural economy (Graffagnino 1991; Lipke 1991; Meeks 1986; Sherman 1991). For businesspeople and residents of Vermont, as much as for policy-makers and administrators, genuine regional pride has co-existed, at times uneasily, with an awareness of the instrumental uses to which such "regional identity" might be put.

While railroad entrepreneurs may have begun the unrelenting promotion of Vermont as a tourist destination from the 1850s onward (Graffagnino 1991), state agencies also took up such efforts well before the turn of the century. In the second half of the nineteenth century, in response to serious decline in Vermont's hillside agriculture and out-migration not just from the hills but from Vermont altogether, the state began to pursue various measures promoting the consumption value of Vermont's rural landscape to nonrural populations and the image of "Vermont" as a distinctive rural place (Graffagnino 1991). This involved constructing Vermont as a unique Yankee outpost and exemplar of pastoral New England, and then justifying the appeal of that identity to tourists, summer residents, and second-home buyers. Thus, the state's interest in developing and promoting an appealing image of rural Vermont was firmly linked to the vagaries and overall decline of its resource-based economy.

Much of the earliest such promotion was conducted by Vermont's first state legislated Board of Agriculture, created in 1870 (Rozwenc 1981). The bureaucratization and regulation of agriculture within Vermont thus occurred during a period of sufficient crisis in the rural economy that non-agricultural strategies of development might also merit serious attention. Although the Board did conduct a number of "farmers' institutes," it also prepared and disseminated reports on the resources and attractions of Vermont in an effort to attract tourists and capital. At that time, Vermont was usually bypassed by tourists who favored the more daunting wilderness of New York's Adirondacks, New Hampshire's White Mountains or inland Maine (Rebek 1982). After an unsuccessful attempt to attract Swedish farmers to Vermont for the purpose of taking over abandoned hill farms, the Vermont State Board of Agriculture launched appeals to out-of-state industries, summer visitors, and second-home buyers, specifically promoting the unique pastoral charms of the Vermont landscape, rather than trying to compete as a wilderness destination:

> The height of our mountains is exceeded by many localities, but their beauty by none, clad in green to their greatest altitude, clustered together without system or order, but in great harmony, tinted with varying hues and shades by the foliage of the forests at the different altitudes, they possess a charm and beauty peculiarly their own. . . . As seen from the mountain summits, there is the cultivated farm; the country hamlet, with

> its single church spire and country store; the manufacturing town, with the smoke from its many chimneys; the ponds and lakes nestled among the hills and mountains. (Vermont State Board of Agriculture 1892, 28)

Here the State Board of Agriculture portrays a rural landscape, offering something for everybody (natural beauty, pastoral charm, cozy settlement and viable industry), yet remaining unique and distinctive. However, the Board went beyond mere promotion in this publication and actually listed available hill farms, which it claimed would make ideal second homes in the countryside. In this respect, state promoters emphasized the pastoral and small-town heritage of Vermont, markedly different than, but not overwhelmingly distant from, urban life on the Eastern seaboard.

In addition to promoting Vermont's natural and property resources, the Board extolled the Yankee virtues of the people populating Vermont's rural landscape:

> The people of a locality are always an important consideration in the minds of persons who are to come to live among them. Vermonters are peculiar in many ways, but in nothing is their disposition more marked than in their intense love of liberty and equal rights, of liberty of thought and action, so long as it does not infringe upon the rights of another. (Vermont State Board of Agriculture 1892, 8)

Just as the Vermont landscape possesses a "peculiar charm and beauty," its denizens may be "peculiar in many ways," but admirable and unthreatening in their fundamental adherence to libertarian values. Such allusions to political traditions and Vermont state history served to reinforce a broader message, suggesting that Vermont represented typical rural values at the same time that it stood out as a distinctive rural place.

While these efforts helped to develop a tourist-based economy in Vermont, concerns with emigration and economic decline remained central for policy-makers, intellectuals and elites in Vermont. By the Great Depression, a report by the Vermont Commission on Country Life (1931) echoed even more strongly the early State Board of Agriculture's concern about attracting visitors to Vermont and developing tourism and recreation to bolster an economy, which seemed to lag behind much of the country, if not the other

New England states. In a set of recommendations, the 1931 report overwhelmingly stressed the importance of landscape and image in addressing the consumption concerns of tourists, visitors, and second-home owners:

> In the larger development of our recreational resources, which may be expected, care should be taken to avoid features that disfigure the landscape and are an offense to good taste. Nature has made Vermont a state of great natural beauty. . . . There ought to be a united effort to preserve the characteristic features of our old New England architecture, and the best in our community life. So far as possible we should keep our state free from crude and offensive advertising signs, from cheap and vulgar displays along the roadside, and from all that would offend good taste. (Vermont Commission on Country Life 1931, 132)

While the nature and validity of "good taste" are not debated, the passage suggests a canny understanding that conserving the symbolic capital in rural landscape is necessary to heighten its consumption appeal. Furthermore, preexisting traditions, such as architectural styles, begin to assume a compulsory aspect, suggesting, if not the "invention of tradition" (Hobsbawm 1983), at least its painstaking encouragement and maintenance:

> When visitors come to Vermont from the Middle West or for that matter from any section of the country other than New England, they cherish the idea of a Vermont in which there are old-time meeting houses with steeples, colonial houses, painted white with green blinds, and other characteristic features associated with new England villages and farms. It is good business and a patriotic duty to preserve a distinctive new England type. (Vermont Commission on Country Life 1931, 376)

An important thread running through the state's concern with abandoned hill farms reached beyond the specter of economic decline to include uneasiness about the incursions of in-migrating "foreign stock," particularly French-Canadians moving into Vermont from Quebec where the economy was even more depressed (Graffagnino 1991). Thus, some of the appeals explicitly targeted classes and groups deemed welcome additions to the Vermont landscape. A 1932 publication released by the Vermont Bureau of Publicity, which had taken over the promotional work begun by the early State Board of Agriculture, was structured as an open letter to "those men and women teaching in schools, colleges and universities; those who are doctors, lawyers, musicians, writers, artists—in a word those who earn their living by a professionally trained use of their brains" (Fisher 1932, 3). Almost fawning in its supplications, the booklet stresses the commonalities and compatibility between resident Vermonters and these select candidates for summer homes:

> In many ways Vermonters will seem like country cousins of yours, sprung from the same stock. At least on our side we have what seems to us a family liking for summer people of your kind. We approve of and are proud of many of your ways that some Americans find odd—such as the fact that you prefer to buy books and spend your money educating the children rather than to buy ultra chic clothes and expensive cars. That makes us feel natural and at home with you. We simply love the fact that your women folks do not feel it necessary always to wear silk stockings, and that your men folks like to wear old clothes. You value leisurely philosophic talk and so do we. We like the way you bring up your children, and we like to have our children associate with them. (Fisher 1932, 11–12)

The appeal to solid middle-class professionals, teachers, and artists reveals concern that in-migrants to Vermont have sufficient money and resources to "contribute" economically and socially to the state but at the same time not come from so wealthy or aristocratic a background that they disrupt a place that regards itself as the social province of small farmers and small-business owners. In this sense, the material marketing of Vermont—the attempt to sell land and homes to new residents—was framed and pursued in a way to ensure outcomes that would not threaten a particular rural image of Vermont.

Although the promotion of Vermont was first assumed by state agricultural agencies and publicity units, this function passed to the Vermont Development Commission at the close of World War II. The Commission's mandate was to coordinate promotion of tourism and recreation in the state and oversee industrial and agricultural development planning (Vermont Development Commission 1948). Broad economic development initiatives were firmly nested within the long-standing priority of promoting the state to outsiders. Among its first activities was the launching of *Vermont Life* (still published today), "a magazine that could take the Vermont story to a much wider audience than conventional methods of pamphlet distribution" (Vermont Development Commission 1948, 19). While "country life" magazines proliferate today, *Vermont Life* represented one of the earliest entrants in the field of rurality publications, one that through high standards of photography and homespun feature writing, would contribute considerably to the mythic interweaving of landscape, tradition, and place that constitutes the image of rural Vermont.[4]

The Symbolic Marketing of Vermont

Although the material marketing of Vermont as rural place may have been driven initially by a mix of opportunity (relative proximity to urban populations) and necessity (economic decline in resource and industrial sectors), the advent of *Vermont Life* marks the transition to greater emphasis on the symbolic marketing of Vermont as rural place. Images and ideas about Vermont—almost all centering on the rural charms and virtues of the state—are now used less to sell actual pieces of Vermont property and more to distinguish and market the goods and services that happen to be produced in Vermont. Where state promoters, both bureaucrats and entrepreneurs, once sought to attract investors and tourists, they now aim more generally to cultivate awareness and appreciation of rural Vermont by those beyond its borders (Lipke 1991).

The use of such symbolic marketing was perhaps heralded by the Vermont agricultural sector, which has long capitalized on popular recognition of and positive associations with the name "Vermont" in developing agricultural markets. Such an approach, however, was initially guided as much by necessity as by creative insight. Writing in 1945, the historian Edwin Rozwenc (1981) claimed that Vermont agricultural policy to that point had been most strongly influenced by the "poverty and particularism" of Vermont. The Department of Agriculture, which supplanted the early State Board of Agriculture, rarely commanded sufficient fiscal resources to actively develop or subsidize particular sectors. Instead, the board consistently took a more regulatory approach in concert with the different specialized commodity associations, "to encourage high standards of quality and grading in every field—poultry, apples, maple sugar as well as dairy products—as a means of developing state brands that will be accepted everywhere as a mark of excellence" (Rozwenc 1981, 190). The "Made in Vermont" label on an agricultural product thus ensured certain standards of quality, clearly linked to the positive aspects of landscape, tradition and place reinforced by more general promotion of Vermont.

In the last twenty years, the state's orientation to agriculture has, if anything, become more market-driven and more linked to symbolic promotion of "Vermont as rural place." Much of this now involves an almost proprietary rurality, where the place name "Vermont" serves as a jealously guarded trademark. Indeed, protecting the Vermont name and insuring the quality of Vermont's products remain regulatory functions that this small state takes very seriously.[5]

The furor over the Vermont label becomes understandable, given recent market research conducted by the state's Agency of Development and Community Affairs. This research confirmed that consumers associate the name "Vermont" with "purity, wholesomeness, rural values, tradition, self-reliance . . . hard work, environmental awareness and closeness to nature" (Calta 1991, C1)—that is, some contemporary version of the pastoral ideal. From the standpoint of recent trends toward diversification in agriculture, niche marketing and specialty food-processing, such findings represent an obvious angle for Vermont producers.[6] In fact, the Marketing Division of the Department of Agriculture now organizes the state's numerous specialty food producers for "Vermont" exhibits at national gourmet food fairs and trade shows (Calta 1991), most often held in major metropolitan centers such as New York, Los Angeles, or Chicago, where the rural image of Vermont engenders especially nostalgic feelings. Almost all such producers prominently include the words "Vermont" or "Green Mountain," with their clear value-adding potential, on the product labels (Schlosberg 1989). Many of these newer Vermont specialty products (for example, salsas, mustards, vinegars) could well be produced anywhere in the United States, but they follow in the footsteps of more traditional Vermont agricultural products, like cheese, apple cider and maple syrup, which the Vermont Department of Agriculture earlier linked to a homey, appealing image of "Vermont."

With the image and narrative of Vermont as a distinctive rural place compressed and packaged in the name itself, the consumption of Vermont products and services becomes a way of buying fully certified, highly desirable rurality. Furthermore, one need not necessarily visit Vermont or move to Vermont to reap the benefits or participate in the rural experience. Mail-order shopping permits symbolic appropriation of rural Vermont from a distance. One company, originally based in Vermont, but now a national concern, advertises in its catalogue a "rent a maple tree" option next to trout umbrellas and stenciled pillows: "Here in Vermont, there are few richer springtime rewards than the harvesting of pure maple syrup. If you haven't had the time or trees to gather your own, consider this creative alternative, a truly unique gift for the person who has everything or *for anyone who appreciates a traditional way of life and nature's bounty*" (emphasis added). The customer is promised at least a quart of "your very own pure maple syrup," a personalized parchment lease and reports on "your crew's sugaring activities." In contrast to simply purchasing a can of maple syrup through the mail, the "rent a maple tree" option offers the consumer a more formal claim on the Vermont landscape and the conceit of participating in its distinctive resource production practices without ever leaving home.

Instrumental uses of the Vermont place name become further apparent in perusing tourist-oriented tabloids, specialty catalogues and gourmet grocery stores. Few Vermont maple syrup producers would attempt to retail their product without the Vermont label, particularly given the state's success in linking the product with the name "Vermont," even as all neighboring states and provinces also produce maple syrup. Labels on maple syrup containers usually read "pure Vermont maple syrup," a sequence that conflates the putative rural purity of the state with the nutritional purity of the food product. In addition, as throughout the maple syrup industry, containers invariably present images of snow-covered woods where galvanized buckets hang from trees and horse-drawn sleighs collect the sap, despite the fact that modern maple syrup production technologies, which are widely used, tend to look very different (Perrin 1978).

Repetition of the Vermont place name in brand names and labeling, supplemented by references to the rural attributes that support the image, provides further evidence of the symbolic marketing of Vermont (deWit 1992). A Brattleboro, Vermont specialty juice company, for example, markets "Vermont Apple Juice," which on the front label is further identified as "Vermont pressed" and on the back label described as made from "unfiltered apple juice pressed from whole apples (Vermont's special apple varieties including Macintosh, Delicious, Empire, Idared, Rome, Crispin, Winesap and Northern Spy)." That the juice is "unfiltered," the apples "whole" and the varieties "special," simply reinforces the wholesome and natural distinctiveness of Vermont. And lest the beneficial attributes of rural Vermont remain unclear, the label explains that Vermont apple juice is "the absolute finest in flavor and richness," thanks to the "clean rural environment" of a place at some remove from "urban pollution," the "exceptional apple flavor" afforded by Vermont's northern climate, and the "attention to detail" possible on the state's small family-farms.

Specialty dairy products have also capitalized on the market appeal of the Vermont name. Ben and Jerry's Ice Cream, marketed nationwide as well as overseas, calls itself "Vermont's Finest All Natural Ice Cream," a phrase stringing together several compelling superlatives. The label of a pint of Ben and Jerry's stresses the Vermont provenance of the ice cream ("We start with lots of fresh Vermont cream"), and manages to promote rural Vermont at the same time as it appropriates it. As a company, Ben and Jerry's has a reputation for conducting business with a sense of environmental and social ethics (Calta 1991). The label announces, "We support family farms" by buying dairy products from a large Vermont milk cooperative. Stating that "family farmers are central to the heritage and quality of life in Vermont and across America," Ben and Jerry's explicitly links itself with the positive essence of Vermont rurality by serving as a champion of threatened agrarian life. However that link may benefit family farmers, it clearly also benefits the market appeal of this gourmet ice cream.

Numerous other specialty food products apply the symbolic mystique of rural Vermont to enhance market appeal. A producer of mustards, barbecue sauces, and salad dressings in northern Vermont, for example, includes "homemade in Vermont" on her labels, conferring the rustic charm of Vermont on her otherwise quite exotic and certainly not traditional Yankee fare. This is evident as well with more traditional Vermont agricultural products, often marketed now in "specialty packs," and typically including Vermont cheeses, maple syrup, and sometimes pancake mix. A small company in northeastern Vermont offered four such variety packages by mail-order and in specialty shops in the late 1980s. With names like "Vermont Country Sampler," "Vermont Triple Delight," "Vermont Yankee Sampler," and "Vermont Breakfast Sampler," they were representative of an entire genre of specialty food products based on allusions to rural tradition and the specificity of Vermont as a place. Even seasonal forest products, many of which are available throughout New England and Quebec, are marketed not so much for *what* they are, but for *where* they come from; accordingly, a mail-order ad for balsam wreaths urges, "Send a bit of the Vermont woods for Christmas."

In similar fashion, nonagricultural products and services sold throughout Vermont are qualified in advertisements and marketing as "Vermont" products and services. Thus, a T-shirt printing business takes the name "Images of Vermont," a fine crafts and jewelry boutique calls itself "Vermont Artisan Designs," a decorative ironworks is known as "Vermont Industries, Inc.," and a fine woodworking establishment has the name "Vermont Wood Specialties." Use of the place name would seem to have no particular value for people who reside in and are oriented solely to Vermont, but evocation of the Vermont name for others—tourists, second-home owners, in-migrants, even those geographically distant from Vermont—provides the imprimatur of manageable, well-managed rurality (deWit 1992). As various writers and commentators have observed, the salience and appeal of rural images seem to grow in direct proportion to popular anxiety about degeneration, crime and pollution in a seemingly separate urban world (Williams 1990). To the extent that the idea of Vermont continues to suggest a rural place that is good, clean, picturesque, and natural, and, more important, not likely to change, producers and marketers will purvey such images and consumers will readily buy them.

"Preserving" Vermont for Whom?

In June 1993, the National Trust for Historic Preservation designated Vermont as one of the eleven most endangered historic places in the United States. This was the first time an entire state had made the list (Rimer 1993). Although the designation has no particular regulatory weight, it crystallizes the tensions between "preservation" and "development" in Vermont. Yet given the legacy of promotional efforts in Vermont focused on constructing, manipulating, and disseminating particular images of the state as rural place, we must question precisely what requires preserving and for whom it would be preserved.

Nationally, Vermont is often seen as an "environmental leader" (Rimer 1993), particularly given its implementation of a dramatic land use control program known as Act 250 in 1970 (Lipke 1991). However, this and subsequent efforts to manage growth in Vermont have been highly controversial (Innes 1992). While the growing rate of land transfers and housing development that led to Act 250 has often been blamed on the completion of interstate highways through Vermont and the increase in the popularity of skiing in the 1960s (Daniels, Lapping, and Keller 1989; Kunstler 1988), it is also possible that the long history of state promotion indirectly fed a development boom not every Vermonter welcomed. Such development has had implications not only for land use, but also on the composition of the state's economy. By 1980, tourism and recreation accounted for 15 percent of Vermont's gross state product, and together comprised the third greatest source of income for the state (Meeks 1986). However, many of the jobs associated with this sector are low wage and seasonal. In short, it is questionable to what extent an economy increasingly based on tourism, recreation, and "environmental services" provides a secure livelihood for all Vermonters.

Today the various environmental and land use controls in Vermont, perhaps best exemplified by the strict banning of billboards and the regulation of signage, can be seen as having two main beneficiaries: those now living in the state, who prize its quaint, rustic ambience; and those who visit to ski, "leaf-peep," vacation, or shop (and happen to spend valuable tourist dollars). The "historic" rural image of Vermont inevitably has an upscale aspect, which is very good for in-migrating Vermonters lucky enough to live in particularly scenic communities and prepared to run bed-and-breakfast establishments or market specialty foods or crafts. Certainly some "native-born" Vermonters have also successfully launched entrepreneurial ventures, capitalizing on these tourism and recreation opportunities.

But there remain other groups of Vermonters, who have had to abandon their struggling dairy farms or have lost their jobs at General Electric or the Ethan Allen furniture plant in the wake of economic changes reverberating throughout the entire country. Many such Vermonters have no ready means of cashing in on the marketability of rural Vermont, and little direct stake in its preservation. Indeed, poverty may be the biggest impediment to starting, sustaining, and profiting from potentially lucrative businesses that trade on the appeal of Vermont as a distinctive rural place. Despite the pleasingly packaged rurality of Vermont, the state is the second poorest of the New England states after Maine (Vermont State Economic Opportunity Office 1983).

Although the state's overall rate of poverty declined somewhat between 1980 and 1990, indicators for specific social groups and places in Vermont suggest that the cozy comforts of an idealized rural Vermont may elude many of the people who need them most. For example, between 1981 and 1990, the proportion of "new families at risk for poverty" (that is, first births to unmarried teen mothers with less than twelve years of schooling) increased dramatically in the historically impoverished northeast counties as well as in southern Bennington County (Vermont Children's Forum 1994). This trend points to the persistence of rural poverty, not only in the more remote reaches of the state, but even in southern Vermont, home to elite private colleges and a brisk, sophisticated tourist industry.

In this sense, poor Vermonters appear as shadowy figures in the background of a more picture-perfect rurality, much as their substandard and often quite unphotogenic mobile homes sit on distant back roads and remote parcels around the state, at a considerable distance from the artfully restored farmhouses and picturesque villages that correspond to an idealized Vermont. For the poorest Vermonters, for the underemployed, and perhaps even for the increasingly precarious middle class, the campaign to keep Wal-Mart out of Vermont does not automatically compel allegiance.[7] Wal-Mart may represent the homogenization of American retailing, flying in the face of all that is historically rural and distinct about Vermont (Rimer 1993). But it also represents basic, affordable consumer goods, and for some, it represents needed jobs.

Although Vermont has been marketed as a package, not all of Vermont conforms to the pleasing, rural images, that are now so familiar they almost constitute cliché. All sectors of the population of this small state find themselves implicated to a degree in the legacy of promotion and marketing, but the benefits appear more unevenly distributed. To the extent that a particular rural image of Vermont remains critical to attract tourism and differentiate goods and services, there will be significant pressure to maintain Vermont as a kind of living rural museum (Thrift 1989; Wilson 1992). For this to be successful, land uses that do not fit can be controlled and activities that do can be encouraged. However, the result may increasingly be some measure of artifice, where Vermont remains eternally "Vermont," at least on the surface, while the messy work of social change and conflict simmers underneath.

NOTES

1. Marx (1964) and Cosgrove (1984) each provide extended discussion of the intellectual history, including the thought of Thomas Jefferson and Hector St. Jean de Crèvecoeur, undergirding the American pastoral ideal.

2. Barthel (1990) and Ehrentraut (1991) analyze American and Austrian examples, respectively, of how open-air museums (for example, Williamsburg, Sturbridge Village) provide formal images of rural life that dwell selectively on the less troubling elements of "tradition."

3. The notion of positionality used here extends the work of economist Fred Hirsch (1976) in a more cultural, interpretive direction. Hirsch argues that with economic growth and affluence, positional goods and services—those that are scarce in either an absolute or socially constructed way or whose value is diminished by "crowding"— are only attainable by the wealthy. Scenic land is one example Hirsch offers of a positional good.

4. A recent editor of *Vermont Life* has described his job as "keeper of the sacred myths" (Calta 1991, C4).

5. In a 1989 case widely publicized by the Vermont Department of Agriculture, its consumer assurance supervisor traveled to California to investigate sales of "maple" syrup that tasted suspiciously like corn syrup. Information about the fraud was passed on to U.S. Food and Drug Administration officials, who subsequently arrested the distributor (Tighe 1989). Even though the syrup in California was not labeled as Vermont maple syrup, it stood as a misrepresentation of an agricultural product overwhelmingly associated with the state of Vermont. See Hinrichs (1993) for further analysis of the state of Vermont's proprietary orientation to maple syrup as a commodity.

6. A recent prospectus for a new specialty-milk producers group in Vermont stated, "All Vermont food products come to market with an advantage that producers in neighboring states can only envy—their Vermont origin. As many Vermont food producers have discovered, a 'Made in Vermont' label confers an intangible perception among consumers of purity, wholesomeness, quality, rural values and trust. Vermont Family Farm Premium Milk embodies all of these values as well as an interest in preserving family farms and open land, and support for humane animal management and practices."

7. As of July 1993, Vermont was one of three states in the United States without a Wal-Mart store, a huge discount chain. The other two states were Alaska and Hawaii (Rimer 1993).

REFERENCES

Barthel, Diane. 1990. "Nostalgia for America's Village Past: Staged Symbolic Communities." *Politics, Culture and Society* 4:79–93.

Bourdieu, Pierre. 1984. *Distinction: A Social Critique of the Judgement of Taste,* trans. Richard Nice. Cambridge, Mass.: Harvard University Press.

Calta, Marialisa. 1991. "Made in Vermont: Myths You Can Eat." *New York Times,* 4 December, C1, C4.

Cloke, Paul, and Mark Goodwin. 1991. "Conceptualising Countryside Change: From Post-Fordism to Rural Structured Coherence." Paper presented at the Annual Meeting of the Association of American Geographers, Miami, Fla.

Cloke, Paul, and Chris C. Park. 1985. *Rural Resource Management.* London: Croom Helm.

Cloke, Paul, and Nigel Thrift. 1990. "Class and Change in Rural Britain." In *Rural Restructuring: Global Processes and Their Responses,* ed. Terry Marsden, Phillip Lowe, and Sarah Whatmore, 165–81. London: Fulton.

Cosgrove, Denis E. 1984. *Social Formation and Symbolic Landscape.* London: Croom Helm.

Daniels, Thomas L., Mark B. Lapping, and John W. Keller. 1989. "Rural Planning in the United States: Fragmentation, Conflict and Slow Progress." In *Rural Land-Use Planning in Developed Nations,* ed. P. J. Cloke, 152–77. London: Unwin Hyman.

deWit, Cary. 1992. "Food-Place Associations on American Product Labels." *Geographical Review* 82 (3): 323–30.

Douglas, Mary, and Baron Isherwood. 1979. *The World of Goods.* New York: Basic.

Dunphy, Paul. 1988. "The Pastoral Paradox." *Harrowsmith* 3 (May-June): 41–47.

Ehrentraut, Adolf W. 1991. "Heritage without History: The Open-Air Museums of Austria in Comparative Perspective." *Canadian Review of Sociology and Anthropology* 28:46–68.

Fisher, Dorothy Canfield. 1932. *Vermont Summer Homes.* Montpelier: Vermont Department of Publicity.

Fitchen, Janet M. 1991. *Endangered Spaces, Enduring Places: Change, Identity and Survival in Rural America.* Boulder, Colo.: Westview.

Goodey, Brian. 1986. "Spotting, Squatting, Sitting or Setting: Some Public Images of Landscape." In *Landscape Meanings and Values,* ed. Edmund C. Penning-Rowsell and David Lowenthal, 82–101. London: Allen and Unwin.

Graffagnino, J. Kevin. 1991. "Arcadia in New England: Divergent Visions of a Changing Vermont, 1850–1920." In *Celebrating Vermont: Myths and Realities,* ed. N. P. Graff, 45–60. Middlebury, Vt.: Middlebury College, Christian A. Johnson Memorial Gallery.

Hinrichs, C. Clare. 1993. "Landscapes of Production, Landscapes for Consumption: A Comparative Study of the Vermont and Quebec Maple Syrup Industries." Ph.D. diss. Cornell University, Ithaca, N.Y.

Hirsch, Fred. 1976. *The Social Limits to Growth.* Cambridge, Mass.: Harvard University Press.

Hobsbawm, Eric. 1983. "Inventing Traditions." In *The Invention of Tradition,* ed. Eric Hobsbawm and Terence Ranger, 1–14. Cambridge, England: Cambridge University Press.

Innes, Judith Eleanor. 1992. "Group Processes and the Social Construction of Growth Management: Florida, Vermont and New Jersey." *Journal of the American Planning Association* 58 (4): 440–53.

Jackson, Peter. 1989. *Maps of Meaning.* London: Unwin Hyman.

Kunstler, James Howard. 1988. "The Selling of Vermont." *New York Times Magazine,* 10 April, 52–54, 66–71.

Lipke, William C. 1991. " From Pastoralism to Progressivism: Myth and Reality in Twentieth-Century Vermont." In *Celebrating Vermont: Myths and Realities,* ed. N. P. Graff, 61–88. Middlebury, Vt.: Middlebury College, Christian A. Johnson Memorial Gallery.

Marsden, Terry. 1989. "Restructuring Rurality: From Order to Disorder in Agrarian Political Economy." *Sociologia Ruralis* 29:312–17.

Marsden, Terry, Jonathan Murdoch, Philip Lowe, Richard Munton, and Andrew Flynn. 1993. *Constructing the Countryside.* Boulder, Colo.: Westview.

Marx, Leo. 1964. *The Machine in the Garden: Technology and the Pastoral Ideal in America.* London and New York: Oxford University Press.

Meeks, Harold A. 1986. *Time and Change in Vermont: A Human Geography.* Chester, Conn.: Globe Pequot.

Milne, David A. 1982. "Politics in a Beleaguered Garden." In *The Garden Transformed: Prince Edward Island, 1945–1980,* ed. Verner Smitheram, David Milne and Satadal Dasgupta, 39–72. Charlottetown, Prince Edward Island: Ragweed Press.

Mormont, Marc. 1990. "Who Is Rural? Or, How to Be Rural: Towards a Sociology of the Rural." In *Rural Restructuring: Global Processes and Their Responses,* ed. Terry Marsden, Phillip Lowe, and Sarah Whatmore, 21–44. London: Fulton.

Newby, Howard. 1979. *Green and Pleasant Land? Social Change in Rural England.* London: Hutchinson.

Perrin, Noel. 1978. *First Person Rural.* New York: Godine.

Rebek, Andrea. 1982. "The Selling of Vermont: From Agriculture to Tourism, 1860–1910." In *In a State of Nature: Readings in Vermont History,* ed. H. N. Muller and S. B. Hand, 273–82. Montpelier: Vermont Historical Society.

Rimer, Sara. 1993. "Vermont Debates Value of Saving a Rural Image." *New York Times,* 4 July, 14.

Robertson, Jennifer. 1988. "Furusato Japan: The Culture and Politics of Nostalgia." *Politics, Culture and Society* 1:494–518.

Rozwenc, Edwin C. 1981. *Agricultural Policies in Vermont, 1860–1945.* Montpelier: Vermont Historical Society.

Schlosberg, Jeremy. 1989. "Green Mountain Mystique." *American Demographics* 11 (9):56–57.

Sherman, Joe. 1991. *Fast Lane on a Dirt Road: Vermont Transformed, 1945–1990.* Woodstock, Vt.: Countryman Press.

Short, John Rennie. 1991. *Imagined Country: Environment, Culture and Society.* London: Routledge.

Thrift, Nigel. 1989. "Images of Social Change." In *The Changing Social Structure,* ed. Chris Hamnett, Linda McDowell, and Phillip Sarre, 12–42. London: Sage.

Tighe, Michael. 1989. "Vermont Official Helps to Crack Syrup Scam." *Burlington Free Press,* 1 December, 2B.

Urry, John. 1990. "The 'Consumption' of Tourism." *Sociology* 24:23–35.

Vermont Children's Forum. 1994. *The State of Our Children: Kids Count in Vermont.* The 1993 Vermont KIDS COUNT Data Book. Montpelier: Vermont Children's Forum.

Vermont Commission on Country Life. 1931. *Rural Vermont: A Program for the Future.* Burlington, Vt.: Free Press.

Vermont Development Commission. 1948. *Biennial Report, 1946–1948.* Monpelier: Vermont Development Commission.

Vermont State Board of Agriculture. 1892. *Resources and Attractions of Vermont with a List of Desirable Homes for Sale.* Montpelier, Vt.: Press of the Watchman Publishing Company.

Vermont State Economic Opportunity Office. 1983. *Vermont Profile of Poverty.* Waterbury: Vermont State Economic Opportunity Office.

Williams, Raymond. 1990. "Between Country and City." In *Reading Landscape: Country–City–Capital,* ed. Simon Pugh, 7–18. Manchester, England: Manchester University Press.

Wilson, Alexander. 1992. *The Culture of Nature: North American Landscape from Disney to Exxon Valdez.* Cambridge, Mass.: Blackwell.

10

Real Villages:

National Narratives of Rural Development

Peter Vandergeest

In the literature and practice of rural development, both development and the village are linked to the nation. Development economists and comparative sociologists have made terms such as the "national economy," "Gross National Product," and the "national bourgeoisie" their staples. World Bank reports, United Nations reports, and cross-national studies all take the nation-state as the basic unit.

The link between rurality and the nation is indicated by the dual meaning of the word "country": rural areas, and nation. In many countries the real nation is often identified with rural villages. Thus in Thailand, one often hears that the "real" Thailand is not Bangkok, but the villages of Thailand. Villages in those areas of Thailand characterized as less touched by modernity such as the Northeast are believed to be more "authentically" Thai. In countries with substantial rural populations, making a nation generally means turning "peasants into Frenchmen" (Weber 1976), Italians, or Thais. Despite the close relationship between rural areas, nation-building, and national identity, most of the recent academic (for example, Anderson 1991, and Hobsbawm 1990) and popular debates about nationalism ignore rurality and rural peoples.[1]

In this paper I draw on examples in Thailand to describe two aspects of the relation between making and imagining rural villages on one hand, and making and imagining nations on the other. First, nation-states are based on the territorialization of administration and control, so that the village is defined spatially in the institutions of national administration. The territorial administration is the means by which villages are made, located, categorized, counted, taxed, and regulated. Second, nationalists produce historical narratives in which national identities are constructed as continuous or developing over time, so that they need to be discovered in the past as well as the present. National identity is often associated with the continuity of urban culture, language, religion, or kingship. However, because villages are also identified with past, villages often become identified with the nation, and the recovery of national authenticity becomes tied up with recovering and codifying the traditions of the village.

These two aspects of the nation, taken together, have strongly influenced the way we think about the village, and the way that the village is presented in the literature on rural development. Although they seem like opposing ways of defining the village, they converge in many important ways. In particular, both are descriptions of rural areas as seen by urban people, and they both simplify rural life by associating the village with a more primitive or pure past. They differ mostly in the value they assign to rural life, and whether it should be preserved or transformed.

These representations of the village are often better characterized as a set of moral and policy prescriptions than as accurate representations of the village and should be assessed on that basis as well as on their empirical validity. However, these prescriptions could be made more feasible, compelling, and open to diverse ideas of rural people if we recognized the great diversity and the dynamic character of rural life.

Before I consider the place of the village in Thai nationalism, I discuss the two major elements of nationhood in general terms, together with two types of knowledge on which these national discourses are based. My aim in the next section is not to pin down a definitive meaning for "nation," but to point to some central elements of nationhood as they affect the way villages are described and constructed.

Knowing the Nation

To clarify the distinction between the two elements of nationhood and nationalism, I distinguish between the two forms of knowledge on which they are based.[2] The first is modern science, which takes the form of denotative statements. That is, a modern scientific statement claims to be a true statement about an external referent (Lyotard 1984, 25).[3]

One kind of scientific knowledge that is important to a national administration is the modern map. The modern map is intended by its authors to be a set of denotative statements or symbols constructed as a direct and proportional relation to an external and verifiable referent situated in abstract time and space. Abstract time–space dimensions are "linear"; they can be divided into discrete units (seconds, minutes, meters, degrees latitude, and longitude) and measured. They are also homogeneous: any one unit can be cut out, compared, and rendered equivalent to another unit. The construction of grids allows any area to be definitively located. Geographers, surveyors, cartographers, and military officials claim to represent a real and verifiable abstract space in a specified proportion to real space, on a scale of 1,000 to 1, or 10,000 to 1, or higher. Scientists can verify whether or not the location of a particular village, township, farm, elevation, river, or road corresponds to its representation on the grid represented in the map. The space represented in modern maps differs from spaces represented in older maps, which do not claim scientific status and which do not present homogenous, linear space. In Thailand, pre-nineteenth-century maps were not situated on a grid, distance on the maps did not correspond in a consistent manner to distance in abstract space, and orientation did not follow strict rules about the cardinal directions (Winichakul 1988).

National administrations are based on exclusive sovereignty over a clearly bounded national territory. Consider the modern political world map: Each nation-state is colored in by a homogeneous color—there is no shading—and each nation-state is defined by its borders, the only discontinuities on the map. Finally, every nation-state can be definitively located by its longitude and latitude on a grid. Anderson (1991), drawing on Benjamin (1969), calls the temporality of the nation "empty and homogeneous" time. This can be extended to the spatial dimensions of the nation—these are based on homogeneous space, what I call abstract space. Empty spaces can be filled, like containers (Anderson 1991, 173–74), with people (categorized by gender, age, race, etc.), soil and forest types, minerals, crops, industries, building regulations, and so on.

In both feudal Europe and most of precolonial Asia, authority was organized on the basis of personal relations and jurisdictional sovereignty—the right to tax and administer justice over specific people (Sahlins 1989, 28). The exercise of jurisdictional sovereignty was a relation between king and subject. In both Europe (Sahlins 1989) and Southeast Asia (Kemp 1988), agreements in which kings and princes acquired and ceded jurisdictional rights to domains were rarely concerned with boundaries, and the domains over which kings and princes exercised jurisdictional sovereignty were not necessarily contiguous in space. Over time, however, sovereignty began to be expressed more in terms of territory, and the right to control what happened inside the national or colonial territory.[4] This led to strict delineation of the boundaries of a contiguous and homogeneous territory, with customs and immigration posts at the boundaries.

Boundaries were constructed not only around the nation, but around the various administrative units within the national territory. When I visit an office of the Forestry Department in Thailand and ask about the location of the forests, the officials do not talk about trees. Rather, they produce a map and show me areas delineated as forests, or perhaps as three or four different types of forest. The forest is not defined by its vegetation; thus an area that is occupied and farmed can still be classified as forest. This classification can affect the occupants, however, since the Thai Forestry Department has often tried to evict people from areas classified as forest with the help of military and police force.

Although ordinary science is composed primarily of denotative statements, scientific knowledge steps outside of these statements in at least two important ways. First, scientific statements must be made according to a set of rules on which kinds of statements and problems are admissible (Lyotard 1984, 43). That is, scientists must accept a set of rules that (like government policy) are not denotative but prescriptive statements. Because these are prescriptive statements, they are not verifiable, and acceptance depends instead on consensus or enforcement. Similarly, the acceptability of denotative statements depends less on their accurate representation of an empirical reality than on their acceptance by a relevant community (Latour 1987). Acceptance is achieved by alliances, negotiation, and enforcement as much as by empirical verification.

Second, the distinction between a preexisting reality and its neutral representation is slippery. Scientists and administrators themselves in fact often make the reality they represent through denotative statements. This is made easier by science's dependence on community acceptance and enforcement: "denotative" statement that achieves acceptance among the relevant audience can inspire practices that make the reality it represents.

These characteristics of science also extend to national administration, where the acceptance of external and internal boundaries depends less on the accurate representation of a preexisting reality than on building alliances, negotiations, and enforcement. Important examples for national states and national economies include administrative boundaries such as those around provinces, districts, and villages, and boundaries on property in land. The making of maps to represent these boundaries is, in itself, an act of the powerful to construct these boundaries. In this way maps are more than simply denotative. Maps of national territory often precede border posts, while mapping the space inside national territory often precedes the introduction of policies by which state officials attempt to make the reality conform to the map. Nevertheless, unless the state is able to achieve acceptance of these boundaries through negotiation and enforcement, these boundaries will be ignored and undermined.

One often encounters people who claim knowledge that cannot be verified. Such statements are arguably in the domain of narrative knowledge—a second form of knowledge important to nationalism. The clearest modern examples of narrative knowledge are novels and stories. Narrative knowledge, unlike scientific knowledge, is not based on empirical verifiability and can also be situated in a time and space that is not abstract and homogeneous—consider the novels of Gabriel García Márquez. Lyotard (1984, 22) writes that collectivities that rely primarily on narrative knowledge have no need to remember their past: "The narratives' reference may seem to belong to the past, but in reality it is always contemporaneous in the act of reciting them."

Although most national states have been constructed relatively recently—Anderson (1991) traces modern nations to the late eighteenth century—once nationalism emerges as an ideology, the national unit tends to be "naturalized." This is achieved by invoking the idea of a particular nation as if it had existed for a long time: nation-makers must invent national histories and national traditions, because there are no national histories to be remembered. The contradiction between history and the presumed primordial status of the nation has sometimes been resolved by presenting the nation as somehow awakening from a sleep, becoming aware of itself for the first time (Anderson 1991, 195). These histories are not pure inventions in the sense of "fiction," but they are invented in the sense that they re-construct the past to fit the mold of a distinctive national culture (Smith 1986, 178).

The search for national identity often takes the form of narratives that speak of a pure or original nation that existed some time in the past—a nation that was contaminated by invasion and foreign impositions and that therefore needs to be recovered (Smith 1986, 147–48). Thus anticolonial nationalisms are often presented in terms of "the Fall" from some idealized past; accordingly, decolonization requires the recovery of a precolonial golden age. Because the narrative does not rely on an empirical past, nationalists use narratives to invent signs of continuity through time. Symbols that typically provide this continuity can include language, religion, the modern monarchy, and the village, each of which can be portrayed as continuous through many centuries (Hobsbawm 1990). The nation thus defined can, in fact, exist primarily as symbols, or as text, and for this reason, narratives of national history put a great deal of emphasis on culture.[5]

Because the national culture and history is invented, different nationalists may not agree on what constitutes the core national culture. There are often important differences between groups of intellectuals and their selection and interpretation of traditions that they feel exemplify national culture. One of the most important differences occurs between those who favor urban or court culture and those who look to the countryside for national culture. Some intellectuals look to a history of urban institutions such as monarchies, purportedly democratic political institutions (for example, the Magna Carta), national liberators (Washington), a national language, and perhaps the relics of glorious cities that flourished in the distant past. Other intellectuals look to a natural history based in the countryside and in tribal or rural cultures, as typified by the Romantic movement in Europe, and more recently by opposition movements in Asia. In Europe, the Romantic search for an authentic national past was understood as a search for natural "roots," the discovery of which could lead to national renewal (Smith 1986, 181–82). Oppositional movements in Thailand also look to an organic countryside as a potential source of national renewal, while in Malaysia the state has given the nation an explicit organic referent by means of the designation "sons of the soil," conferred on Malays and Dayaks but not on Chinese.

In summary, there are at least two ways of thinking about the nation: one in terms of the national form of the state and its administrative institutions, and another one in terms of nationalism and identity. I call these the nation administered and the nation recovered. The nation administered is based primarily on the claims of scientific knowledge, while the nation recovered is based primarily on the claims of narrative knowledge. This distinction draws on more general contrasts identified by theorists of modernity and postmodernity, and on other chapters in this volume.[6] The verifiable knowledge of science belongs to modernity and control of nature, while the mythical knowledge of the narrative belongs to tradition and control by nature.

These two forms of the nation can be separated conceptually, but in practice they intersect in complex and often contradictory ways. Later we see some examples of how the knowledge of the nation administered can take on narrative characteristics, while the narratives of the nation recovered employ scientific claims. We also see how these two narratives are associated with different and often opposing types of development practices.

Administrative Villages and the Modernization Narrative

National administrations have been set up by mapping and dividing the national territory into nonoverlapping administrative units (villages, townships, provinces, cities, forest, parks). This enables the state to collect taxes, to efficiently regulate people's lives, and to claim territorial sovereignty against the possible claims of other national states.

These administrative relations were developed in Europe and in the Americas, and were extended to Africa and Asia by the colonial regimes. The territorialization of administration in Asia also occurred in areas not directly colonized: Japan, Thailand, Turkey, and Nepal are the outcomes of revolution and "reforms" that drew on colonial and European models.

In Siam/Thailand the administrative village was created at the turn of the century. There is little evidence that villages or communities were defined as territorial groups prior to this (Kemp 1988). Rural administration consisted of personal relations between masters and their serfs and slaves, who were identified not by their residence in a bounded territory but by their common dependency on a master. To "territorialize" state administration in Siam, the rulers in Bangkok broke down personal relations—between serf and master, noble and lord, lord and monarch. The key period was the turn of the last century, when local lords and nobility were replaced with a bureaucratic administration, and the direct masters of serfs were replaced with village heads and subdistrict (*tambon*) chiefs (*kamnan*). The territory of Thailand was divided into provinces, which were divided in turn into districts, then subdistricts, and finally villages. Each of these units was mapped as a homogeneous space, defined by its borders. The villages of each subdistrict were numbered: Village 1, 2, 3, and so on.

Official instructions sent out from the new Ministry of Interior about the turn of the century instructed local officials to create villages and tambons by ordering the "heads of approximately ten households" whose houses were located near each other to elect a village head. Villages were in turn clumped into tambons; the number of villages and radius of a tambon was supposed to be determined by stipulating that no more than three hours' walk should separate the central village from the outer villages in the tambon (Bunnag 1977, 111). Officials were instructed to ask the village heads to elect one of themselves as the subdistrict head. Peasants who had been serfs attached to a master were transformed into villagers under the jurisdiction of village heads. One of the local nobility became the district officer.

The initial criteria by which villages were defined included "natural" features (the location of houses, the time it took to walk from one place another), but with time, the village began to be defined spatially, so that all people living within the borders of a village space were registered as inhabitants of that village. Bangkok rulers territorialized sovereignty in order to facilitate taxation, and to map and assert control over territory before the intruding colonial powers could do so.

Today, the people living in these administrative units are carefully registered and counted. Each village inhabitant must have a village address; that is, each person is assigned to a small area on the grid. The location "house number 14, village 1, subdistrict Klong Ri, District Satingpra, Province Songkla, in Thailand" is a small area of land, basically a cell occupied by a group identified as a "household." The government office at the district center has a card for each such cell, which lists the inhabitants of the cell, categorized by gender, age, and martial status. For example, the card corresponding to a "household" cell (located at 37 village 1...) might be headed by a male, year of birth 1950; a female, year of birth 1953; three children, each born fairly recently; and an old woman, born in the Year of the Goat. A similar pattern is repeated at the level of the village. The village is in effect a larger cell encompassing the household cells. It might have six hundred people, one hundred households, so many men, women, and children. The relationships between these people are not revealed, with the exception of the parents of each individual. Various cells, and the people they contain, can be easily located by the post office, the police, researchers, census-takers, and development extension agents. Thus occupants of a cell can receive instructions, knowledge can be gathered about them, and they can be the object of development projects.[7]

The type of knowledge claims generated about the administered village take the form of denotative statements. The village is constructed and dissected as an item of scientific knowledge—a knowledge that created the referent that it represents. The national territory, the village, the household, a piece of property in land, and the forest were all created by surveying and map-making.

This item of knowledge can also be the object of administrative action, that is, of rural development, or of modernization as a national project. Modernization is not based solely on scientific knowledge; it also has a corresponding narrative, which I call the modernization narrative. In this narrative, the temporal dimension of the nation (past–present–future) is associated with the urban–rural and state–village continuum. That is, the village has become associated with the past, or tradition, while cities, government officials, and schools are associated with modernity. The village is depicted in terms of a narrative—an object to be modernized by diffusing modernity from the city and the state to rural areas and the village. As with narratives more generally, the focus is on symbols, or the cultures of modern and backward people.

Local government officials and many development workers are therefore certain that very little has ever changed in the villages. Villagers are described as backward, and their traditions are depicted as obstacles to development. Officials, urban people, and some development workers continue to believe this in the face of villagers' stories of dramatic social and economic changes over the past hundred years and the availability of "scientific" studies demonstrating rapid changes in the rural economy and culture. This knowledge about the village is thus a narrative, not verifiable in the scientific sense. Although this story is invented, officials use the language of science, of verifiable truth, in depicting villages in this manner.

In Thailand this national narrative often locates an "original" and pure Thailand in the golden period of the Sukhothai, during the thirteenth century A.D. The centuries of dominance by the kings of Ayuthaya, which lasted through the late eighteenth century, are portrayed as a period of contamination of the original Thai culture by Khmer and Brahman influences. The enlightened Chakri monarchs of the nineteenth and twentieth centuries initiated the recovery of the original Thai culture. Key national symbols having the requisite continuity through time include Buddhism, the national language (Diller 1991), the Thai script, and the monarchy. This narrative accepts many Western practices as compatible with Thai identity, in particular, market production, agricultural cooperatives, science, and "democracy," and the narrative also manages to locate many of these practices within a mythical Thai past.

Examples of this narrative are easy to find. The history taught in schoolbooks is a key example—one that aims to incorporate all children living in the territory of Thailand into the nation. In the schools children are taught the national language, national customs such as respect for elders, religion, and the monarchy, and a history in which the nineteenth and early twentieth centuries are described as a period of emancipation and a return to the freedom of Sukhothai. Below, I elaborate briefly on this narrative by summarizing an essay written by the respected intellectual Seni Pramoj (1990).

Seni Pramoj labels a stone inscription officially ascribed to a king in of the Sukhothai period (which connotes the state of prosperity in the kingdom) as Thailand's first constitution, comparable to England's Magna Carta.[8] The theme of contamination of national purity emerges clearly in his discussion of the language in the inscription—"the pure original Thai, not the bastardized Thai of modern times. . . . The language possessed a grandeur and simplicity with which modern Thai, with its additions compounded from Pali and Sanskrit, cannot compete" (Seni 1990, 22). In some places Seni Pramoj's story expresses the antirationalism characteristic of some narratives. For example, he writes about the stone inscription that "the more that is said, the less sense it makes," and he describes his essay as a "story." Nevertheless, Seni Pramoj uses the language of science to back his claims about Sukhothai, and he claims that the inscription itself is also based on scientific, verifiable knowledge: "the stela of King Ramkamhaeng deals with facts, not legends or tales full of miraculous happenings" (Seni 1990, 26). Thus he retains the primacy of the nation administered, and plays down narrative forms of knowledge. He also works within the framework of modernization: at various points in the essay, Seni Pramoj identifies King Ramkamhaeng with constitutions, contractualism, private property, democracy, and the liberty, equality, fraternity of the French Revolution. According to him, the project to recover these qualities was initiated during the nineteenth century by the reformist King Mongkut.

Village culture, from the point of view of the modernization narrative, is incomplete, not yet authentically Thai. Villagers are backward because they are superstitious, fatalistic, and locally oriented, and village culture must therefore be rationalized and nationalized. The most obvious example of the resulting assimilationist policies took place in the 1930s, when the government attempted to civilize villagers by stamping out superstitious practices and signs of ethnic difference expressed in clothing, hair style, and so on. Villagers were associated with wilderness and animality, which had to be tamed by national culture. This policy also had a gender dimension: national culture was masculine; village nature, which was feminine, had to be made masculine. Women were, and still are, represented in official and academic literature as "further from Buddhism," and women's bodies (clothing, hairstyles, teeth) were a central object of the cultural policies of the 1930s. Until the 1970s national culture was also strongly associated with the culture of state officials (Chai-anan 1991), in their role as a male status symbol group only recently transformed from members of the nobility into bureaucratic officials.

These same policies are reproduced today in a number of more subtle forms: the medical system's disdain for indigenous healing, the schools' repression of local dialects, police repression of brewing liquor and gambling, the agricultural establishment's attempts to change farming practices, and the Community Development Department's attempts to create village cooperative groups such as the village housewives' groups. These policies are facilitated by the idea of the village as a bounded territory composed of cells inhabited by villagers who are registered, categorized, and viewed as objects to be developed.

Nevertheless, these cultural policies have met with considerable resistance.

For example, the identification of the nation with symbols of continuity such as Buddhism, the monarchy, and a newly invented national language has alienated Muslims in the far south and inspired a separatist movement. Elsewhere, resistance is expressed in refusals to register marriage, to transfer land titles, and to vacate areas designated as forest. Because the Thai state is often too weak to enforce policies it borrowed from stronger nations (Vandergeest and Peluso 1995), it is often unable to enforce its boundaries. The result is a continual violation of state-defined boundaries, best illustrated by the millions of cultivators who occupy land classified as forest. The state has responded either by a compromise that recognizes existing practices (land reform programs under which forest is reclassified), or by coercive attempts to make practice conform to policy (evictions).

Authentic Villages and the Counter-Narrative

The authors of a second national narrative oppose the modernization narrative of the nation administered—this I call the counter-narrative. In Thailand variations on this counter-narrative are produced by many urban-based NGOs, by the members of some Buddhist movements, by critics of modernization and capitalism, and even by some government officials and agencies. Although they work with diverse organizations on different types of projects, and do not always agree with each other, they do form a discursive community that agrees on a series of key points.

In the modernization narrative the primary symbols of national continuity (the monarchy, language, and the national religion) emanate from the state and city. In the counter-narrative the primary symbols of national continuity are found in the cultural characteristics of the village. The authors of the counter-narrative generally oppose or ignore territorial definitions of the village and instead define the village as a community with continuity through time. That is, the village is conceptualized as a set of interpersonal relations and cultural practices, not as an inhabited territory defined by its borders. In Thailand as elsewhere, the "village" has become a metaphor for "community," which can be extended to encompass urban communities, the entire nation, even the "global village" of an ostensible world community.

The authors of the counter-narrative agree with the modernization narrative's identification of the village with the past, but also believe that the primordial status of the village allows it to be identified with the nation, that is, with what it is to be Thai. Like the modernization narrative, the counter-narrative is told as a story of contamination; however, the primary source of contamination is usually contemporary urban American capitalism and the Thai state, rather than the colonialism, Brahmanism, or Khmer influences of the past (although these are often accepted as contaminants by Buddhist groups). The village is considered to be a primordial site of the nation, because it is a place removed from the polluting culture of cities.

Chatthip Nartsupha (1991) has summarized the ideas of some of the influential thinkers in what he calls the "community culture school of thought," a school that exemplifies the counter-narrative.[9] According to this school, the core values of the village community include harmony, goodwill, equality, mutual help, self-reliance, and popular and practical knowledge. However, villagers are often no longer aware of their own culture as such; it has become ritualized, or has been overlaid with the values of capitalism and the state. Nevertheless, despite this external contamination, the core culture persists.

Elements of the counter-narrative that is based on these notions of an eternal village culture are seen in both academic and popular media. In the political economy school, for example, writers assume that capitalism and the state are "penetrating" villages that are otherwise primordial and natural. The counter-narrative is also the basis of a burgeoning literature produced by small presses associated with the NGO sector. For example, the Moo Ban ("Village") Press has published books by Prawet Wasi, as well as a reader in English on village life in Northeastern Thailand (*Isan*) by Seri Phongphit and Kevin Hewison (1990), who begin with a beautiful review of the essential elements Isan culture and then introduce many ways the state and market have changed this culture. They find that the great changes in the last thirty years "have not, however, uprooted the fundamental structures. Culturally, villages remain *Isan* and the mode of production has not been totally changed from its subsistence orientation. The villages retain their traditional structure, even it is only a shadow of its former glory" (Seri and Hewison 1990, 117). Another key writer of the counter-narrative is Apichart Thongyou (1988) whose collection of poems entitled *Simplicity Amidst Complexity: Lessons from a Thai Village* questions the modernization narrative's picture of the village:

> in my heart a question:
> this? backward undeveloped land
> this? problem people of the country.

Apichart believes that it is the villagers who can teach city people an eternal truth about a life that is simple, virtuous, and content—such lessons cannot be found in texts on physics, economics, or Marxism. While Seni Pramoj, writing more within a modernization narrative, finds the original simplicity of Thai culture in the language of a thirteenth-century Sukhothai, Apichart finds simplicity in contemporary village life.

As Apichart implies in his poems, the counter-narrative, like the modernization narrative, orients certain rural and national development strategies. The task of the development worker is to identify what remains of the authentic village and to assist in recovering and promoting it. Because villagers may have forgotten why they do what they do, community development should help to recover this self-awareness through consciousness-raising (Chatthip 1991). This is in part a fight against a false consciousness created by outsiders. According to Chatthip, different proponents of the community culture school of thought do not agree completely about how this is to be achieved. For example, Prawet Wasi believes that community culture must be fused with a middle-class Buddhism and that the moral community should be created in the present (Chatthip 1991, 126) by drawing on the past, rather than by simply recovering the past. Seri and Hewison (1990, 137) agree with the importance of a return to self-reliance and local traditions, but they also emphasize that these traditions should not be kept as a static heritage, but should be adapted and changed so that they can be "lived with new meaning in a changing society."

NGOs have initiated a series of development projects based on the counter-narrative. In agriculture they reject market- and export-oriented "agro-industrial monocropping" (Seri and Hewison 1990, 129) and promote self-reliance and traditional agriculture. Some NGOs propose community forests as an alternative to state-protected forests and as an alternative to the removal of cultivators from areas mapped as forest.[10] In the south of Thailand where I carried out research, a local NGO is setting up community conservation areas in Songkla Lake as a way of slowing ecological destruction and increasing the benefits that the lake provides for the community.

A key difference between the type of development carried out by NGOs and the type of development carried out by the state is that the state generally treats villages as spatial cells and villagers as inhabitants of these cells who are objects to be developed through the agency of the state. On the other hand, the NGOs are more likely to treat villages as a set of social relationships and villagers as subjects who need the help of the community worker. When the state does recognize community and kin relations within the village, this recognition is preceded by and oriented by spatial definitions of these units.

Although the counter-narrative has been produced chiefly by NGOs and associated organizations, it has also become very influential in middle-class narratives of Thai identity. Some government agencies have responded to critics by appropriating elements of the counter-narrative for their own purposes. For example, a National Culture Commission was created in 1979 to promote local and ethnic cultural practices as components of a "national" culture and has set up provincial and district offices throughout Thailand to accomplish this task (National Culture Commission 1989). According to its Secretary General, the Commission was set up in response to demands that "grass roots" culture be at the center of the development process (Ekavidya 1989).

In another example, in the past ten years, the faculties of various provincial colleges have taken a new interest in local cultural practices, identifying them as authentically Thai. Thus faculties in colleges in the South of Thailand have become increasingly involved in rural performance traditions such as the Southern shadowplay. Up until the mid-1970s, most people who were apprenticed to become puppeteers had little formal schooling and had developed an interest in puppetry while still children living in rural areas. Nowadays, the majority of new puppeteers begin to learn the shadowplay while attending local colleges.[11] Their interest in the shadowplay stems from their studies of Southern Thai culture and from the identification of the shadowplay as an authentic Southern Thai tradition. However, in promoting the shadowplay and other traditions, there is a tendency for government officials and NGOs to attempt to remake them. Government officials, for example, tend to ignore or repress what they consider superstitious practices, such as spirit mediumship associated with local performance traditions.

I have separated out narratives of the village into a modernization narrative and a counter-narrative, partly for heuristic purposes and partly because they represent two often opposing discursive communities. In fact, these two narratives have many elements in common, and many people use aspects of both of these narratives. For example, the influential social critic Sulak Sivaraksa (1985) understands the Ramkamhaeng inscription as basic to Siamese democracy and praises King Mongkut and King Chulalongkorn for recovering the inscription and looking for the roots of Siamese culture in Sukhothai. Yet unlike the modernization narrative and like the counter-narrative, he argues that the contaminant of authentic Thai culture is Western culture and capitalism.

Real Villages?

Up to this point I have taken a scientific approach to this paper, making a series of denotative statements about the literature and practice of development and nationalism. I have been concerned less with identifying the "true" character of the village than with some of the ways people write and talk about villages. Although I have so far labeled two different approaches to understanding the village "narratives," there are also a number of scientific knowledge claims with respect to the real nature of the village. In this section I briefly assess the scientific claims associated with these two narratives, before returning to the question of assessment more generally in the final section. That is, I discuss what we can say about "real" rural people and how historical evidence on rural life in Thailand fits in with the claims contained within the two narratives.

I have implied that the scientific claims associated with neither of the two narratives of the village are verifiable. Both narratives tend to associate the village with the past, with lack of change, and with simplicity, and make sweeping claims about the role of indigenous community organizations in village life. However, most of these claims are contradicted or undermined by considerable historical evidence.

First of all, many studies have shown how rural life has undergone dramatic cultural and economic change.[12] Economic life has become increasingly oriented by market relations and export-oriented production, master–serf and master–slave relations have been replaced by territorial village relations, and local languages and cultural practices have been strongly influenced by the national language and culture, as well as by commodification. This evidence of dramatic change contradicts the modernization assumption of unchanging rural life and undermines the counter-narrative claim about the continuity of rural culture. Second, rural life is hardly "simple," although it may appear so to an outsider. Rural people are enmeshed in a global economic system, and are divided by complex class, occupational, gender, and factional relations.

Third, there is no clear evidence that there ever was a coherent rural "community" throughout the territory that is now Thailand; rather, the evidence suggests that there was great diversity in how local people were organized. In some areas, such as the North, groups of rural people have for a very long time been organized to manage collective resources such as water for irrigation. But in other areas, groupings based on kin, factions, or class are more important than community groups and often serve to divide rural people from each other. Historically, in most areas, there was no political basis for forming a coherent rural community, since during the nineteenth century groups of serfs and slaves were not organized into discrete communities within bounded territories, but rather dispersed throughout the population at large (Kemp 1988, 26–27).

The different ways in which land rights are allocated and enforced illustrates the diversity in community life in rural Thailand. Anan (1989) shows how property in long-settled areas of the Chiangmai Province was allocated by family elders on the basis of kinship rules, not by a community leadership. My observations in rural Southern Thailand indicate a similar kin basis for land allocation. In recently settled areas (Hirsch 1990; Ananya and Nipon 1991; Prayong and Bantorn 1991; Johnston 1975) with no history of locally recognized kinship claims to land, property rights to land have typically been allocated and enforced either by local influential people who employed various means of coercion such as hired guns or by the state-appointed chief of the tambon.

A large proportion of rural people in Thailand settled in their current villages only recently, and community organizations in these areas are therefore often weak. Ananya and Nipon (1991, 69) describe the settlement process in a forest area during the period 1965 to 1985 as similar to a "gold rush": "Rumors about corn cultivation which yielded hundreds of thousands of baht were spreading everywhere attracting people into this area for land occupation . . . villagers here were not parts of the same community. They had no kinship ties with no kinds of bonds among them . . . with the exception of the original community which was by then the minority in this area."

This is not to say that a sense of community is absent from rural Thailand. In some areas there are strong nonstate community organizations—the small irrigation groups in Northern Thailand, and the community forests of the Karen people are good examples. But many such local organizations are bound up with the administrative village put in place by the state, and they are thus at least in part an outcome of state administrative institutions. The most important local organization is usually the tambon council. It is composed of village heads and the kamnan plus occupants of other state-defined offices.

Other community groups are also frequently state-initiated or partly based on state institutions. In his study of a recently settled area in central Thailand, Hirsch (1990, 165) found eleven state-initiated groups, including a housewives group, a bank-credit group, a farmers association, a young farmers group, and the village scouts. These state-initiated groups were based on the territorial village and the registration and categorization (by age, gender, occupation) of residents. Hirsch found only two "indigenous" groups (a water-users group and a temple committee) and two NGO-initiated groups (a Rice Bank and Buffalo Bank). The Southern NGO that has been setting up conservation zones in Songkla Lake has based its conservation groups on the administrative village, while the boundaries demarcating the conservation zones in the lake are set by extending the boundaries of the administrative village into the lake.

My point is that indigenous nonstate community groups cannot be assumed to be a strong local tradition throughout Thailand. Community organizations are very diverse, and often weak in comparison with kin- or state-based authority. Moreover, the state has strongly influenced group formation even for NGO projects. NGOs situated outside of Bangkok, or composed of people who grew up in villages, are likely to recognize this in practice, but the dominant rhetoric among the NGOs most visible in the national media and international funding organizations is that of the counter-narrative, emphasizing the strength of rural community and playing down division and diversity.

Authors of the counter-narrative make their claims in the form of a series of denotative statements about villages. One problem is that these claims are either based on selective evidence (from few areas or from a few village members) or on no evidence at all. Promoters of both modernization and the counter-narratives have played down evidence of rural differentiation, diversity, and conflict. Although studies highlighting rural differentiation were popular during the 1970s and 1980s, when critics sought to document the negative effects of capitalism, recently few academics seem interested in pursuing the documentation of rural class formation. Those who argue for replacing state management by community management of forests seldom take into account the different interests that the rural rich and the rural poor might have in forest utilization (see Chusak 1994).

Recognition that the kind of community described in the counter-narrative may not exist does not mean that the project of promoting local control must be abandoned. However, the project could be conceptualized in a more "realistic" fashion if we pay more attention to the characteristics of real villages and recognize the differences in points of view between many villagers and urban intellectuals.

Assessing Village Narratives

Evidence from the villages is often ignored because participants in the debate over rural communities in Thailand begin from moral and prescriptive positions (for example, regarding the morality of capitalism) and then project their positions onto rural people. My final argument is that we might avoid the problems described above by more clearly recognizing different kinds of knowledge and by giving narrative knowledge greater legitimacy than it has at present.

The hegemony of science in the literature and practice of rural development has led many proponents of particular policies to couch their arguments in the form of scientific claims, even when the scientific evidence on which it is based is questionable. This allows critics to debunk narrative knowledge on the basis of criteria derived from science. Thus narratives of national recovery and the primordial village can be challenged by research that uncovers dramatic changes in the villages, and narratives of national continuity can be challenged by research that demonstrates the fact that Thailand did not exist as Thailand until the late nineteenth century at the earliest. This is not unimportant—I have done similar research myself (Vandergeest 1993a, 1993b). However—and this is a key point—while we should be skeptical of scientific claims when they derive from narratives central to modernity and nationalism, we should at the same time be careful about dismissing these narratives because they fail to meet the standards of scientific knowledge. We should instead assess them for what they are.

An important feature of narrative knowledge is that it is the primary means by which people imagine alternative futures. But because narratives are not concerned with describing and explaining an existing reality, people are able to imagine or invent alternatives to existing situations through narratives. Narratives are therefore central to policies and projects for change. This is one of the reasons that both types of rural development programs that I have discussed were associated with narratives, although their practitioners claimed scientific status for their knowledge claims.

If it is true that developing projects for change and imagining alternatives to an existing situation are based on narrative knowledge, then in some circumstances it may be appropriate to assess narratives on the basis of the kinds of projects that they propose or imply. This does not mean that we should ignore their feasibility in a given "reality" as far as we are able to know it, but it does mean that standards derived from science are not the only relevant criteria. In assessing narratives for the kinds of projects they imply, we should also consider questions of social justice and the democratic process. If narratives are assessed in this manner, then historical research might in fact find that the basis for differences and changes in the stories produced by different groups lies in a particular group's own projects and politics as well as in the scientific validity of their version of history.

I make this argument partly because I am often sympathetic to the political aims of a narrative although skeptical of its empirical validity. With this in mind I can put aside my skepticism about the empirical validity of Seni Pramoj's story about Sukhothai and King Ramkamhaeng and reassess it in terms of how it contributes to the politics of opposition to military dictatorship in Thailand. This project is essential for the well-being of rural and urban people in Thailand, since it is the military who have initiated some of the most coercive policies for removing people from land designated as forest. Intellectuals like Seni Pramoj and Sulak Sivaraksa tell stories about the Sukhothai inscription to argue that concepts like democracy are not exclusively "Western," but can also be regarded as Thai. In the same vein, the community culture school attempts to promote policies and projects in which rural people are the agents of development. As a political project, members oppose the regulatory power of the nation-state and recognize the customary practices that the nation-state overrides and destroys. It is possible to be skeptical about the empirical validity of claims about the village while supporting the policy goals. This does not obviate the necessity for basing policy prescriptions on a good knowledge of rural life, but it does allow us to support the politics of the counter-narrative while remaining critical of some of its empirical claims and some of the means by which its goals are to be achieved.

My argument also extends to how narratives are written: the authors of narratives should be more careful about the kinds of claim that they make. Although authors in the community culture school appeal to hegemonic standards of scientific knowledge, they would no doubt be impatient with scientific challenges to their claims, because for them, the story is more important for its political value than for its scientific validity. Their stories might be more effective if members of the community culture school did not claim questionable scientific status for what they write, but rather identified their ideas clearly as stories with a political point. Similarly, community activists could recognize that village culture never takes a particular form, but is continually reinvented in diverse ways through the telling of stories at the local level. This kind of diverse and changing culture cannot be accurately represented through scientific statements by urban-based writers.

Lyotard writes that scientific knowledge excludes all claims other than denotative ones. This statement can be extended to the scientific claims made in narratives: a claim to scientific validity is also an act of exclusionary power. If an NGO claims scientific status for its story about the continuity of community culture, it is in effect overriding stories produced by villagers. A community culture imagined by middle-class writers, and preserved by these writers on the behalf of the villagers, does not return power to the community, but rather conceals the new power of the development worker in the language of science and participation.

Chatthip's assessment of the community culture school highlights the degree to which the counter-narrative is told for the most part by people who are not themselves villagers—the audience is primarily urban and middle class. He also shows how some producers of the counter-narrative create an image of the village that fits the narrator's image of the ideal community. Although counter-narratives often present voices from the villages, those villagers who do not agree with the narrator's image are often prevented from telling their stories. Urban-based producers of narratives about the village must recognize that their "ideal" village probably differs from the experience of most villagers.

The weakest element in arguments for more community control is the claim that there exists a strong local community that could take over various functions identified by NGOs and others (community forestry, land use planning, fisheries, and so on). In many cases this community has yet to be invented—when it is devised, it must overcome a number of obstacles stemming from class, gender, and occupational divisions. In some instances, community management may be less feasible and less just than management by selected groups of people in a given area, for example, groups based on occupation, gender, or class (Belsky and Seibert 1994). Even where coherent communities already exist, they may have to be reinvented so that rural people will be able to rely on them to deal with current problems such as threats of eviction. This is a process that draws on the past, not to recover the past, but to use it as a resource for dealing with the problems of the 1990s. This process will not happen autonomously of state institutions such as the village, or of nongovernment organizations such as NGOs, banks, or traders. Rather, examples of successful community resource management projects[13] (or resources managed by occupational groups) indicate that people use all of these institutions as resources.

A different approach to understanding the village would recognize and accept these differences, instead of trying to project urban images onto rural people. Culture and tradition could be understood not as something to be "preserved", but as a set of changing resources that villagers can use to deal with a rapidly changing world in a way that is not predetermined by political formulas such as "self-reliance" or "sustainability." Instead of searching for the real culture of the village, development workers and community organizers could pay more attention to how the histories told by villagers seek to recreate village relations, or gender relations, or class relations, in ways that address the current problems of marginalized peoples. To understand villages and nations as recent creations does not mean that they are any less "real." On the contrary, this approach would more likely be an accurate reflection of the reality of village life in Thailand.

NOTES

Acknowledgments: I am grateful to Melanie DuPuis, Luin Goldring, Michael Bell, Philip McMichael, and a reviewer for Temple University Press, who took time to carefully read drafts of this manuscript. The paper was much improved by their thoughtful suggestions.

1. Chatterjee (1986) is an exception.

2. Following Lyotard (1984), who distinguishes between these forms by the type of statements that comprise them.

3. This is the scientific claim; as Latour (1987) shows, the acceptability of a statement of fact depends less on its empirical truth than on the mobilization of support for the statement within the relevant community.

4. Brubaker (1990, 9) and Sahlins (1989) label this process the territorialization of rule.

5. Anthony Smith (1986, 134–38) identifies the construction of a national culture with the transformation of ethnic ties into national ties. He terms this the ethnic nation, contrasting it with the territorial nation. Thus his typology of ethnic and territorial nationalisms parallels my typology of the nation narrated and the nation administered, although in this analysis I am more interested in how the competing definitions of national culture are based on the transformation of urban and purported rural culture into national culture.

6. Lyotard's (1984) contrast between narrative knowledge and scientific knowledge is a typical example of such a contrast, one that I have used in this essay.

7. These modern techniques of surveillance are described by Foucault (1979) in *Discipline and Punish*. For Foucault this type of spatial segmentation and registration is above all associated with techniques of surveillance, and its most ideal form is the Panopticon as a prison.

8. Other intellectuals share this opinion, for example, Sivaraksa (1985, 300). The authenticity of this inscription has been vigorously questioned in recent years by academics seeking to cast scientific doubt on this national narrative.

9. Chatthip reviews the writings of Niphot Thianwihan, Bamrung Bunpanya, Aphichat Tho'ngyu, and Prawet Wasi.

10. See, for example, Weera Attanatho (1993), Yot Santasombot (1993), Uraiwan Tan-Kim-Yong (n.d.).

11. See Vandergeest and Chalermpow-Koanantakool (1993) for a description of these changes.

12. See, for example the various studies in MIDAS Agronomic Company (1991), Anan (1984), Hirsch (1990), Sharp and Hanks (1978), as well as my own study on the Malay Peninsula (summarized in Vandergeest 1993a, 1993b).

13. For example, Uraiwan (n.d.), Prayong and Bantorn (1991, 108), Somnuk and Chavivan (1991, 186), Chusak (1994), the Songkla Lake project referred to above, the projects described in Hirsch (1988).

REFERENCES

Anan Ganjanapan. 1984. "The Partial Commercialization of Rice Production in Northern Thailand (1900–1981)." Ph.D. diss., Cornell University, Ithaca, N.Y.

———. 1989. *Social Context of the Accelerated Land Titling Project: A Case Study of Chom Thong District, Chiang Mai Province*. Bangkok: Center for Applied Economics Research, Kasetsart University.

Ananya Ungphakorn and Nipon Poapongsakorn. 1991 "The Process of Land Settlement in the Central Region." In *Study of Conservation Forest Area: Demarcation, Protection and Occupancy in Thailand, Volume III,* ed. Chermak Pinthong, 17–57. Bangkok: MIDAS Agronomics Company.

Anderson, Benedict R. 1991. *Imagined Communities: Reflections on the Origin and Spread of Nationalism,* 2d edition. London: Verso.

Apichart Thongyou. 1988. *Simplicity Amidst Complexity: Lessons from a Thai Village*. Bangkok: Moo Ban Press.

Belsky, Jill M., and Stephen F. Siebert. 1994. "Landlessness, Forest Farming and Forest Extraction in Two Indonesian National Parks." Paper presented at the 1994 Annual Meetings of the Association for Asian Studies, Boston, 24–26 March.

Benjamin, Walter. 1969. "Theses on the Philosophy of History." In *Illuminations,* ed. Hannah Arendt. New York: Schocken Books.

Brubaker, William Rogers. 1990. "Immigration, Citizenship, and the Nation-State in France and Germany: A Comparative-Historical Analysis." *International Sociology* 5 (4): 379–407.

Bunnag, Tej. 1977. *The Provincial Administration of Siam 1892–1915*. Kuala Lumpur: Oxford University Press.

Chai-anan Samudavanija. 1991. "State-Identity Creation, State-Building and Civil Society." In *National Identity and Its Defenders: Thailand 1939–1989,* ed. Craig J. Reynolds, 59–86. Monash Papers on Southeast Asia No. 22. Melbourne: Monash University.

Chatterjee, Partha. 1986. *Nationalist Thought and the Colonial World: A Derivative Discourse*. London: Zed Books.

Chatthip Nartsupha. 1991. "The 'Community Culture' School of Thought." In

Thai Constructions of Knowledge, ed. Manas Chitakasem and Andrew Turton, 118–41. London: University of London School of Oriental and African Studies.

Chusak Wittayapak. 1994. "Local Institutions in Common Property Resource." Ph.D. diss., University of Victoria, Canada.

Diller, Anthony. 1991. "What Makes Thai a National Language." In *National Identity and Its Defenders: Thailand 1939–1989,* ed. Craig J. Reynolds, 87–132. Monash Papers on Southeast Asia No. 22. Melbourne: Monash University.

Ekavidya Nathalang. 1989. Foreword to *National Culture Commission.* "Towards a New Dimension of Culture and Development" [in Thai and English]. Bangkok: Ministry of Education.

Foucault, Michel. 1979. *Discipline and Punish.* New York: Vintage.

Hirsch, Philip. 1990. *Development Dilemmas in Rural Thailand.* Singapore: Oxford University Press.

Hobsbawm, E. J. 1990. *Nations and Nationalism Since 1780.* Cambridge, England: Cambridge University Press.

Johnston, David Bruce. 1975. *Rural Society and the Rice Economy in Thailand, 1880–1930.* Ph.D. diss., Yale University, New Haven, Conn.

Kemp, Jeremy. 1988. "*Seductive Mirage: The Search for Village Community in Southeast Asia.*" Comparative Asian Studies Volume 3. Amsterdam: Center for Asian Studies.

Latour, Bruno. 1987. *Science in Action.* Cambridge, Mass.: Harvard University Press.

Lyotard, Jean-François. 1984. *The Postmodern Condition.* Minneapolis: University of Minnesota Press.

MIDAS Agronomics Company. 1991. *Study of Conservation Forest Area: Demarcation, Protection and Occupancy in Thailand, Volume III (Occupancy Study).* Bangkok: MIDAS Agronomics Company. (Published in Thai under the title *Wiwatanaakaan kong kaan bukberk thiidin tham kin,* ed. Chermsak Pinthong. Bangkok: Local Development Institute.

National Culture Commission. 1989. *Towards a New Dimension of Culture and Development.* (In Thai and English.) Bangkok: Ministry of Education.

Prawet Wasi. 1990. *Panha Wikrit Daan Chonabot Suu Tangroat.* Bangkok: Mooban Press.

Prayong Netayarak and Bantorn Ondam. 1991. "The History of Forest Land Occupation for Cultivation in Northeastern Thailand." In *Study of Conservation Forest Area: Demarcation, Protection and Occupancy in Thailand, Volume III,* ed. Chermsak Pinthong, 73–111. Bankok: MIDAS Agronomics Company.

Reynolds, Craig J., ed. 1991. *National Identity and Its Defenders: Thailand, 1939–1989.* Monash Papers on Southeast Asia No. 22. Melbourne: Monash University.

Sahlins, Peter. 1989. *Boundaries: The Making of France and Spain in the Pyrenees*. Berkeley: University of California Press.

Seni Pramoj. 1990. "Stone Inscription of Father King Ramkamhaeng: First Constitution of Thailand." In *Development, Modernization, and Tradition in Southeast Asia: Lessons from Thailand,* ed. Pinit Ratanakul and U. Kyaw Than, 17–48. Bangkok: Mahidol University.

Seri Phongphit and Kevin Hewison. 1990. *Thai Village Life: Culture and Transition in the Northeast*. Bangkok: Mooban Press.

Sharp, Lauriston, and Lucien M. Hanks. 1978. *Bang Chan: A Social History of a Rural Community in Thailand*. Ithaca, N.Y.: Cornell University Press.

Sivaraksa, Sulak. 1985. *Siamese Resurgence: A Thai Buddhist Voice on Asia and a World of Change*. Bangkok: Asian Cultural Forum on Development.

Smith, Anthony D. 1986. *The Ethnic Origins of Nations*. Oxford: Blackwell.

Somnuk Tuppun and Chavivan Prachuabmoh. 1991. "The History of Human Settlement in the Forest Areas in South Thailand." In *Study of Conservation Forest Area: Demarcation, Protection and Occupancy in Thailand, Volume III,* ed. Chermsak Pinthong, 150–88. Bangkok: MIDAS Agronomics Company.

Tuan, Yi-Fu. 1990. *Topophilia*. New York: Columbia University Press.

Uraiwan Tan-Kim-Yong. n.d. *Participatory Land-Use Planning as a Sociological Methodology for Natural Resource Management*. Chiang Mai, Thailand: Resource Management and Development Program, Faculty of Social Sciences, Chiang Mai University.

Vandergeest, Peter. 1993a. "Hierarchy and Power in Pre-national Buddhist States." *Modern Asian Studies* 27 (4): 843–70.

———. 1993b. "Constructing Thailand." *Comparative Studies in Society and History* 35 (1): 133–58.

Vandergeest, Peter, and Paritta Chalermpow-Koanantakool. 1993. "The Southern Thai Shadowplay in Historical Context." *Journal of Southeast Asian Studies* 24 (2): 307–30.

Weber, Eugen. 1976. *Peasants into Frenchmen*. Stanford: Stanford University Press.

Weera Attanatho. 1993. "Drafting a New Community Forest Act in Thailand." In *Legal Frameworks for Forest Management in Asia,* Occasional Paper No. 16, ed. Jefferson Fox 97–104. Honolulu, Hawaii: East-West Center Program on Environment.

Winichakul, Tongchai. 1988. "Siam Mapped: A History of the Geo-Body of Siam." Ph.D. diss., University of Sydney, Australia.

Yot Santasombat. 1993. "Community Forestry Legislation in Thailand: An NGO Perspective." In *Legal Frameworks for Forest Management in Asia,* Occasional Paper No. 16, ed. Jefferson Fox, 105–14. Honolulu, Hawaii: East-West Center Program on Environment.

11

Gendered Memory: Constructions of Rurality Among Mexican Transnational Migrants

Luin Goldring

In this chapter I explore the gendering of rurality through a discussion of how transnational migrant women and men from Mexico remember and describe their village of origin. Leaving a rural area for an urban setting provides people with the personal experience of living in two contrasting worlds. When the urban destination is also in another country, the move is likely to involve other contextual changes, for example, in the dominant national and civic cultures, language, racial ideologies, and gender ideologies. Migrants' memories and portrayals of their place of origin offer another perspective on conceptions of rurality. I argue that contrary to many conceptions that tend to homogenize and/or romanticize rurality, rural spaces are differentiated, complex, and ambiguous terrains for women and men who live or have lived in them. I also suggest that gender is an important dimension of this differentiation. This can be seen in migrants' descriptions and memories of their place of origin, ideas concerning return migration, and in examples of community development projects and private spending practices (which involve a reconstruction of the rural landscape).

The discussion is based on fieldwork conducted in Mexico and California, in 1988 and 1989, with people in a transnational migrant circuit[1] that originated in Las Animas, a village in the state of Zacatecas, Mexico (Goldring 1992a; Mines 1981). The transnational community that has developed in this migrant circuit now spans sites in several cities and towns in northern and southern California, as well as the city of Tijuana in Mexico.

When my conversations with people from Las Animas who were in California turned to the subject of how life was different in the United States compared to Mexico, how they felt about these differences, and whether they planned to return to Mexico on a relatively permanent basis, I found there were strong differences between women's and men's responses. In particular, I was struck by the fact that women looked much less favorably on the idea of returning to live in Mexico than men. Women of various ages recalled different kinds of personal histories and projected different futures in comparison to men. They spoke about the differences between doing housework in Mexico and the United States, noted that their children were growing up in the United States and would make their lives *there,* and also touched on the kinds of threats and opportunities that faced their children in the two countries. In contrast, men talked about feeling "freer," like real men, in Mexico, and about not being able to exercise this freedom freely in the United States. In both cases, these comments were intimately bound up with longstanding conceptions of femininity and masculinity and gender ideologies. For both women and men, these gender identities and relations were being affected by transnational migration.[2] Gender roles and identities were changing in different ways for men and women, and this appeared to translate into divergent interests and plans for the future.

Why did women and men have such different responses to my questions about life in Mexico and the possibility of returning there on a more permanent basis? What are the implications of the divergent representations of life in their home village? A response to these questions must recognize that rural areas may be perceived in different ways by different people and that gender (together with other factors such as generation, class, etc.) may play an important role in shaping diverse conceptions of rurality. I suggest that women and men's divergent representations of rurality are rooted in the gendered division of labor and space; gender roles, relations, and identities; and changes in these factors associated with transnational migration.

There is nothing particularly novel about drawing connections between the gender division of labor, the gendered use of space, and gender roles and identities. However, connections are rarely made between the gender division of labor and gendered uses of space, memories of places of origin, and analyses of transnational migration. Linking these areas allows us to recognize that descriptions and representations of rural landscapes are gendered. That is, portrayals of rural places are not gender neutral, but rather, are strongly colored by gender identities and roles, which may be undergoing change. I argue that these representations, as reflected in women and men's memories and descriptions of their home village, may have important implications for migrants themselves, migration scholars, and regional planners. I illustrate this through a discussion of gendered differences in desires and practices of return migration, family politics, and investment in migrants' places of origin.

Rurality and Gender

Rurality as a theme or subject is found in diverse areas of academic writing including literary criticism, cultural studies, migration research, and development studies. In most cases, a sharp contrast is drawn between the rural and the urban. Rather than discussing this contrast, I would like to make two points about constructions of rurality, with special reference to work on the sociology of development, especially rural development, and transnational migration. The first point has to do with the relationship between gender and rural landscapes. While important contributions have been made in the areas of (1) gender and rurality and (2) gender and migration, it is now time to draw connections between these two areas. Adding a discussion of the gender division of labor and gendered use of spaces to this should allow us to see how rural landscapes are gendered, and clarify gendered interests and practices associated with migration. The second point involves the treatment of rural inhabitants' voices. These voices are usually not heard directly, and when they are, men's voices receive privileged attention. Listening to, and analyzing, women and men's voices can contribute to an actor-centered analysis, where social actors are also gendered players.

Rural landscapes have been gendered in at least two ways in writings on rurality, and in related work on rural development. The first way is through the equation drawn between nature and femininity. Images of women, femininity, and the domestic sphere have been used as metaphors of rurality, in opposition to the masculine, public, and anonymous world of the city (Merchant 1983; Mies 1986). Theorists and critics deploy these and other contrasts, including that of modernity versus tradition, to show how these opposing images have been mobilized over time to project the contours of two distinct sociogeographic spaces and ways of life, and to reinforce asymmetrical relations between the sexes and between more or less "advanced" regions or countries. Merchant (1983), for example, shows how the association between femininity, nature, and rurality provided an ideological basis for the scientific exploitation (or taming) of nature and natural resources (Mies 1986).

A second way in which rural landscapes have been gendered is through discussions of the sexual or gendered division of labor in rural areas. Sociologists and anthropologists since Boserup (1970) have examined the ways in which women's work differs from that of men's across societies, classes, and caste and ethnic groups. They have also focused attention on the ways in which gender ideologies and socialization contribute to the maintenance of a gender division of labor with accompanying status and power differences (Nash and Fernández-Kelly 1983; Mies 1986).

These approaches have made important contributions to discussions of the relationship between nature and culture (Merchant 1983; Wilson 1992) and to our understanding of the gender division of labor across cultures. With respect to the latter, for example, we know a great deal about the relationship between women's work, use of technologies, and the social as well as physical spaces they occupy in different strata and societies (Spain 1992). We also have an understanding of the political and economic consequences of gendered divisions of labor, and how together with prevailing gender ideologies they reinforce women's subordination (Mies 1986).

However, these approaches have limitations. The first approach, while offering a critique of the equation of nature with the feminine, also genders rurality in a monolithically feminine fashion. The implications of this equation are explored, but in focusing on male constructions and appropriations of rurality, the ways in which gender shapes women *and* men's constructions of rurality is not addressed. The second approach focuses on structures, but ignores social reproduction and social change. It focuses on the way that men and women work in and use rural spaces but does not address how structural positions are related to social and cultural practices, identities, or interpretations. The subjective and gendered experience of rurality that women and men reflect through their memories and descriptions of rural places rarely emerges in debates on nature and culture or in studies of the gender division of labor. Consequently, it is difficult to know whether and how the gender division of labor translates into gendered differences in plans, desires, and practices connected to rural places.

There has been a gradual gendering of the literature on international migration in the last ten to fifteen years. Having found that "Birds of passage are also women" (Morokvasic 1984), research on international population movements has begun to analyze female migration patterns (Donato 1993). This is important because it fills in more of the empirical picture of migration. Nevertheless, the picture remains fairly abstract and quantitative. The relationship between gender relations and transnational migration has received scant attention (Pedraza 1991).[3] Relatively little has been written about the experiences of women and men who migrate in terms of how they, as actors shaped by dynamics of gender as well as nationality, ethnicity or class, view their places of origin and the places to which they travel. When people's interpretations have received attention, the focus has been primarily on men.[4]

In the literature on Mexico–United States migration, interpretive work has emerged fairly recently.[5] This writing is providing important analyses of the ways in which women and men make sense of their common political-economic settings, and of their distinctively gendered worlds.[6] Studying the process of transnational migration can highlight differences between ways of organizing work in the home and in labor markets, and ways in which gender relations are constituted under prevailing gender ideologies, in different sites of transnational migrant circuits and communities. This follows from the recognition that the process of migration may involve the reconstruction of gender relations in new settings (Hondagneu-Sotelo 1992, 1994; Grasmuck and Pessar 1991). The ways that men and women who migrate recall and describe their places of origin can illuminate how rural areas are gendered through memory and actual practices. This can point to ways in which rural spaces are differentiated, showing us that particular landscapes hold different meanings for different social actors.

Gendered Memories

As noted earlier, my initial interest in the gendered dimension of representations of rurality and the village of origin was sparked by hearing women and men's accounts of life in Mexico and their divergent responses to questions about whether they wanted or planned to return there on a relatively permanent basis. This section describes their responses more fully, but begins with a brief description of Las Animas and the research upon which my material is based. The main part of this section is intended to address the question of what is *meant* by rurality among women and men from a specific locality, and the related issue of how these meanings differ by gender. Only then can we consider the implications of these divergent, gendered, representations.

Las Animas is located in the southern part of the state of Zacatecas, in west-central Mexico. This state, together with Michoacán and Jalisco, is one of the traditional "sending regions" of Mexico in historical and numerical terms (Jones 1984). Animeños (people from Las Animas) began traveling to the United States in the early part of the century. The history of migration from Las Animas follows a pattern common to that of many towns and villages in west-central Mexico. Legal migration during the Bracero period, when workers were contracted to supplement labor shortages created by World War II, provided the social bases for subsequent documented and undocumented migration. By the mid 1960s, Animeños were settling in Los Angeles, Orange County, the San Fernando Valley, and South San Francisco.[7]

I conducted research that focused on migration and employment patterns (Goldring 1992a). In addition to using a survey instrument in Mexico, I contacted relatives of people I had met in Las Animas who were living in California in order to conduct open-ended interviews. I met with women and men living in South San Francisco, Watsonville, Los Angeles, San Fernando Valley, Riverside and Orange Counties, and San Diego. The question of return migration was not originally on my agenda, but I soon noticed that men and women had very different views on this topic, and began to ask more questions about it. I returned to speak with some people on several occasions, and was thus able to raise new questions and return to old ones. During my second visit to Las Animas I had already noticed the different responses of men and women to the issue of return migration, and began to discuss the issue informally with return migrants. The information I present here is thus based on open-ended interviews and informal conversations with Animeños in California and in Las Animas.

Among men born in Las Animas who had spent most of their working lives in the United States, the majority, regardless of age, said that they wanted to return to Mexico to retire. They also spoke enthusiastically about going home to visit during their vacations from work. Men who were in the United States without their wives, and who returned to Mexico regularly and spent more time there, also said that they planned to stop going to the United States at some point in order to spend their later years at home. Men talked about how life in the United States was more constrained than in Mexico. They said that in the United States all they did was work, while in Mexico one was freer (*más libre*) and enjoyed life better.

In Mexico most of these men owned a home, were building one, or were saving to build one; some had land and cattle. Several men owned homes in the United States as well. They maintained economic as well as social ties in the village. In general, their economic status was higher in Mexico than in the United States because their resources went further. Whether they had been in the United States a few years or a few decades, and whether they had good jobs and material resources or poorly paid jobs, the same theme came up repeatedly: Mexico was a good place to spend time, relax, and return to, whereas the United States was good for working and making money but not for spending the rest of one's life.

Working in the United States allowed these men to fulfill the male role of breadwinner, but only at certain costs, which they recognized. Their patriarchal authority could come under attack when their children went to school in the United States or their wives entered the labor market. Several men noted that in the United States "the government can come into your home and tell you what to do," whereas in Mexico, the men laid down the rules at home without such interference.[8] Other aspects of their lives did not find appropriate expression. They could not drink or gather in public in the same way as in Mexico. They could not engage in the kinds of leisure activities to which they were accustomed. Perhaps most significantly, the production/work dimension of their lives had been transformed. Men who had grown up working land and who had later owned land, horses, and cattle talked about missing this aspect of their lives while they were in the United States. A number of landless men who had worked as sharecroppers in Mexico also spoke well about working the land in Mexico, without the U.S. routine of the clock and the boss.

These comments can be interpreted in several ways. They certainly reflected the multiple class positions that people experienced in the course of transnational migration. In the United States, most of these men were wage workers, while in Mexico many had been petty-producers or subsistence sharecroppers rather than proletarians (Goldring 1992a).[9] Also underlying these statements was the implication that in Mexico they were able to be *real* Mexican men, but in the United States part of this identity had to be repressed. Stating that they wanted to return to Mexico was thus an expression of nostalgia for a particular way of life, gender identity, and gender ideology.[10]

For these men, the memory and description of life in the home village and comparisons to life in the United States can also be understood in the context of the social construction of a transnational community and not simply as an expression of nostalgia. The construction of community in this and other transnational contexts involves a process in which social space is increasingly differentiated: Mexico increasingly becomes the privileged site of leisure and relaxation while the United States is defined as the work site (Rouse 1988; Goldring 1992a, 1992b). As migrant men become transnational proletarians who "commute" to work in the United States, Mexico becomes their vacation and retirement spot, where earnings can be translated into particular social statuses (Goldring 1992a,b).

When I asked both married and single women from Las Animas about returning there, their responses were quite different from the men's. Most women said that they enjoyed going back for visits, particularly to see their relatives, but that they did not want to return there to live. After hearing her husband say he wanted to retire to Mexico, one woman said to me, "He can go back there to live; I'll stay here and we can visit each other." She said it in a joking manner, but it was clear that this would become a source of contention if her husband made concrete plans to return to Mexico.

In response to further questions about why they would not want to return to Las Animas on an extended basis, women consistently emphasized differences between their lives in the United States and Mexico, focusing on housework, infrastructure, and work outside the home. Women said housework was easier in the United States. One woman said: "here I go to the laundromat and use a washing machine, there I washed clothes by hand in the creek." Others pointed out that running water was just being introduced in the village—before, they had to carry water unless they had a well. With the new running water, the plan was to have at least one faucet in each house, but even that would not compare to plumbing in the United States. In the United States the women had many faucets, plus toilets, gas or electric hot-water tanks, and sewers. In Las Animas they had to heat water for bathing, most houses did not have indoor plumbing, and those that did emptied the contents into the creek. In the United States things were more convenient and more sanitary for their families.

Working outside the home was another theme that came up in our conversations. Most of the women I spoke to who had experience working outside the home in the United States did not want to give it up, regardless of age or marital status. They recognized that they were working a double day at their jobs and at home, but they also said that the advantages outweighed the disadvantages. "I noticed that when I started working [outside the home] my husband began to help me with the house a little," said one woman. Others said that they would not want to give up the extra control they felt they had, now that they contributed to the household expenses. Most of the younger married women who had not worked outside the home said they planned to do so once their children were older, and they appeared to look forward to this. Some of these women were not "allowed" to work by their husbands, but they said that this would change as the children grew. In Mexico, virtually none of the women had worked outside their homes, although many had done embroidery to make money, and most had experience growing corn and raising farm animals.

Some of the women brought up another concern about returning to Las Animas. They complained that in the village, "you do something and everyone knows about it right away." The social constraints of life in a small village were something they did not want to return to. In the village, surveillance over women by both male and female relatives and other villagers was pervasive.[11] Being in the United States did not eliminate this problem, since women were still enmeshed in social networks and relationships with family members and fellow villagers; however, their social world had expanded considerably. Women made new friends and contacts through work or in their neighborhoods, and they did not want their social and physical world to be reduced to its original boundaries.

These comments serve as a counterweight to idealized conceptions of life in rural communities, and point instead to the possibility that urban life may allow people to feel less bounded in social terms. One person's urban anomie is another's freedom; one person's rural community with face-to-face interaction is another's constant surveillance system. Uniform representations of rural (or urban) landscapes are not very relevant once we begin to listen to people who inhabit them and gain an appreciation for the complexity of the pictures they present.

Many of the younger women I spoke with enjoyed going back with the new social standing of a migrant, which they expressed by wearing new and fashionable clothing and taking gifts to relatives and friends. But while most women said that they enjoyed returning to Las Animas for visits, some women said they felt pressure to spend money on gifts and on clothes for themselves before making a trip back there, and they talked about feeling a growing gulf between themselves and their nonmigrating friends. Some of these women also complained that townspeople gossiped and spoke badly of the way they dressed and behaved if they did anything that deviated from the current norm.[12]

In further conversations, I learned that it was not that women thought the United States was all good and their village was all bad. The distinctions were not clear-cut, which pointed to the complexity of their lives on both sides of the border. Women pointed to crime and drug use in their U.S. neighborhoods to illustrate the dangers to which they and their children might be susceptible in the United States. While most of the women thought their children would have better opportunities going to school in the United States, they were afraid their children could be influenced "by bad people" and did not want them to forget where they came from. Most of the women thought the United States posed more dangers for women in general than for themselves in particular. They said this was especially true for women who did not have documents. Crossing the border would be dangerous for them, and after crossing they ran the risk of apprehension. But women said the more time they spent in the United States, the less fear they had for their personal safety. After all, said one woman, "bad things happen to women in Mexico too."

Recalling their village, most women described it as being in a beautiful setting. Although they talked about the lack of infrastructure, they remembered the landscape fondly. The village was not seen in static terms: women noted apologetically that people in Las Animas were poorer and less educated and didn't have the amenities that people in the United States were used to, but they implied that the situation was not irreparable. With better education, and new jobs, and infrastructure, Las Animas could be improved. Discussions of desired improvements in Las Animas focused on making household chores and daily life more convenient at the individual level, but women also commented on the importance of improving drainage, potable water, and roads in order to improve community-level health and access to services.

Women's recollections and representations of rurality involved a pragmatic comparison of their lives in Mexico and the United States. This comparison was based on an assessment of the kinds of paid and unpaid activities they performed in both contexts, the conditions under which they carried them out, and the environment each place represented. Women saw advantages and drawbacks to life in Las Animas and in the United States, but in the end, most expressed a preference for remaining in the United States and returning to Mexico to visit.

For women, migrating to the United States did not involve compromising their gender identities. They continued to carry out their domestic roles in new settings but often under what they considered to be improved conditions; they acquired broader experience outside the home and sometimes gained relative control and status within their households. They continued to be wives, mothers, sisters, and daughters without feeling that being in the United States diminished these roles and identities. These women engaged in new activities in new settings and experienced and contributed to changes in gender relations, but migration did not challenge their general roles and identities in the way that it did for men.

Men and women who had migrated described life in Las Animas in different ways and expressed differences in their desire to return. Their representations of life in their rural place of origin varied by gender, reflecting the ways in which gender shaped experiences and interests in Las Animas and in the United States and the ways in which migration affected gendered activities, identities and interests (Hondagneu-Sotelo 1992). However, the specific mechanisms that contribute to creating and reinforcing these differences deserve further analysis.

Gendered Visions of Place Among Migrants

There are several related explanations for the divergent representations of rurality and opinions about returning to Mexico offered by women and men from Las Animas. These are based on an appreciation of elements of continuity and change in gendered roles, practices and relations. For women who migrate, there is continuity in at least two important elements of their feminine roles. First, women do not retire from housework. Whether they are in the United States or in Mexico, their role as unpaid household workers is unlikely to end until they die or become incapacitated. Most of the women I spoke with expressed a preference for carrying out housework in the United States. As indicated, this reflected their assessment of doing housework in both settings and their feeling that being in the United States allowed them to renegotiate gender relations in ways that improved their situation, however minimally. Second, being a mother in the United States tends to strengthen ties to the country—women who migrate are likely to bring their children to the United States or have children there. As children grow up and go to school in the United States, they too will most likely remain, marrying and raising their own families there.[13] Women said that it was very important to them to be near their children and grandchildren. Older women with children and grandchildren on both sides of the border often spent part of the year in Las Animas and part of the year in the United States.

Thus, women's memories of their rural place of origin, together with their experience of paid and unpaid work and family life in the United States, translated into specific ideas about returning to Mexico. In the United States they continued to be wives and mothers, but in ways that increased their relative power within the home. They were happy to return to Las Animas to visit but wanted to remain in the United States, where they saw greater opportunities for their children and themselves, despite the dangers.

For men, the situation is different. Most Animeños who migrate either become or continue to be wage workers,[14] and their masculine gender identity and breadwinning role is increasingly focused on this activity. After wage work comes retirement: as men grow older, they can legitimately leave the world of work to enter retirement. Retiring in proper fashion implies being waited on by wives, daughters, or sisters. In retirement, men continue to be fathers, but the very process of migration may have attenuated their patriarchal authority. Retired, they are no longer constrained by the discipline of wage work, but many long to (re)create a petty-production way of life and accompanying social status and gender identity. During their working years, these men may have invested in a house, land, and cattle in Las Animas and may have spent time there managing these resources. Returning to Las Animas to retire represents an attempt to renew ties to the rural landscape and way of life and to reclaim the gender relations that accompanied that life.

In the remainder of this section, I develop the argument that the gender division of labor and gendered uses of space underlie migrants' gendered representations of rurality and divergent desires of return. This requires describing what women and men do, as well as how and where they do it, in the Mexican and U.S. sites of the migrant circuit.[15]

The concept of the transnational migrant circuit suggests that through the process of migration, over time, migrants come to consider their place of origin *and* the U.S. sites where people from their place of origin are concentrated as constituting a single field of social action (Rouse 1988; Goldring 1992a,c). When Animeños are in the United States, they remain in touch with relatives and friends on the Mexican side of the border. People may be asked to participate in and attend weddings and other celebrations taking place across the border or in another site on the same side of the border. An individual from a community like Las Animas who has not spent very much time in the United States is likely to have friends and relatives who have, and these people can help the Animeño/a to find work and learn the ropes if he or she migrates. Transnational migration has become a way of life, transnationalizing many aspects of daily life, from job-hunting to celebrations.

However, as I have indicated, the field of social action of the migrant circuit is not unitary or necessarily coherent. On the contrary, it will contain geographic and social spaces that are differentiated in terms of class identities and positions, cultural identities, use of social space, and social and economic practices. For example, a man may define himself as a landowner and *norteño* (U.S. migrant) in Las Animas but recognize himself as a poorly paid wage worker in Los Angeles. He may work his own land or hire people in Mexico, and he may have a two-story house, television, and truck there, but his social and economic standing in the United States is likely to be quite different. Similarly, a woman in Las Animas is likely to live in a home that she and her husband own and to work at home without necessarily earning a wage. In the United States, she may work at home and also be a wage earner in the labor market. In the United States, Animeños are considered Mexican immigrants, but they are also members of their family and village social network on both sides of the border. In Las Animas people may invoke regional and class identities, identifying as Animeños, as small producers or sharecroppers, while in the United States they will most likely be seen as Mexicans and Latinos and may identify themselves variously as Mexicans, Zacatecanos, workers, members of a Latino minority, and so on. Mexico–United States migration multiplies the identities, statuses, and socioeconomic positions through which people carry out their lives; the social and geographic spaces of the migrant circuit reflect these changes.

The distinctions that people draw between their place of origin in Mexico and the U.S. sites of the migrant circuit are underscored by the fact that when they go to the United States they are usually involved in working and making money under conditions different from those in Mexico. Over time, this has increasingly meant that when they return to Mexico it is generally to relax, make improvements on a house, take presents to relatives, and spend money in a fashion fitting a U.S. migrant who has done well. Thus there are structural and experience-based dimensions to the distinction between the rural place of origin and U.S. sites of settlement.

Rouse (1991, 1993) argues that migration involves differential uses of social space on both sides of the border. His work focuses on migration from the municipality of Aguililla, in Mexico, to Silicone Valley in California, from the mid 1960s through the mid 1980s. When men from Aguililla went to the United States, they found that their movements were limited to traveling to work and returning home and that the absence of street life or the equivalent of a village square limited their possibilities of acting according to traditional male norms. In the United States, Aguilillans experienced pressures to conform to a proletarianizing routine of going to work and returning home and engaging in approved forms of leisure activity, namely as consumers.

This use of space contrasted sharply with men's use of space in Mexico, where they worked outside the home and congregated in public spaces, while women remained within the boundary of the home, the private and domestic sphere. Whereas space in Mexico could be conceptually divided into public and private space so as to reflect men and women's arenas of action, social space in the United States became more complicated. Men still went to work, but they no longer enjoyed privileged access to public spaces. Furthermore, the social landscape in the United States included additional realms—"the street" and the "pleasure palaces of corporate capitalism" (Rouse 1993, 13–14): malls, movie theaters, and theme parks. The street became a potentially dangerous place for those whose principal aim was supposed to be getting from one place to another, since the police could bother people who congregated and did not use the street appropriately (within the U.S. context). In addition to becoming a space with a different use than in Mexico, the street in the United States could not be claimed primarily by men. Malls, movie theaters, and theme parks became the approved places of congregation and consumption, without being the sole domain of men.

Rouse uses his comparison of the social landscape in Aguililla and the Bay Area to argue that the landscape in the United States was inscribed with disciplinary processes that made Aguilillans into good proletarians. This happened through direct means, such as the threat of legal punishment for violating norms of public space use (that is, walking around and drinking on the street), and indirect means, including the effects of marketing and new consumer behavior, which translated into Aguilillans changing their views of space and regulating how they use it (Rouse, 1993, 17).

The gender division of space in the Las Animas migrant circuit is similar to that described by Rouse for Aguilillans. In Mexico, men occupy public spaces while women remain in domestic spaces. Men work in agricultural occupations, as owner-operators, sharecroppers or wage workers. Few women are engaged in wage work; most of them work at home in domestic and reproductive activities. Some women also sew and make embroidery to make money, but this work is very poorly paid. Women go out in public, but not in the same ways as men. Married women leave their homes far less frequently than unmarried women; when they do, it is generally to buy something or visit someone nearby. Unmarried women run errands for married women (for example, daughters are sent out to buy things or to take food to men working in fields). If there are no male siblings, then women may also work in the fields, although they may not admit this right away. As women grow older, marry, and have children, their use of public spaces diminishes. Young unmarried women join the local volleyball games, but they usually stop once they marry. Stores and the church are virtually the only enclosed public spaces where women spend time outside of their homes.

The gender division of space in Las Animas thus reflects the gender division of labor in the village. A gender ideology is reproduced as people in Las Animas socialize their children according to dominant ideas about correct behavior for males and females. In the United States, the gender division of social space echoes emerging patterns of work and consumption associated with that country. Women increasingly become wage workers outside the home, and they become consumers of goods and services in an environment that often requires them to expand their geographic mobility and deal with a broader range of people, objects, practices, and relationships than they did in Mexico. Through the process of migration, the sexual division of labor and uses of social space change, and gender relations may be negotiated (Hondagneu-Sotelo 1992, 1994). This will hold true regardless of marital status, the presence or absence of children, and even employment status.

A woman who works outside the home for the first time in the United States is bound to experience a different set of power relations in her work place. She may come into contact with unions, bosses, slower or faster coworkers, or any number of situations that may challenge her to think of herself in her new roles as worker and immigrant, in addition to her gender role as a woman and mother, wife, sister, or daughter. For women who worked outside the home before going to the United States, being a wage worker would not be a new role. However, being in a U.S. setting places these women in a vastly different work context; they will have new experiences, roles, and identities.

Women with children, whether they work outside the home or not, will find themselves in a new environment in terms of their roles as mothers. They may give birth in the United States and have to deal with the record-keeping aspect of the process—talking with health workers who may or may not speak Spanish. Similarly, they may be asked to talk with teachers if they have children in school, or they may have to take their children to a clinic or hospital. A woman in this situation may have to learn to take public transportation, even if relatives or friends accompany her at first. The terrain of the physical and social places she will traverse in the United States will be quite different from that of her place of origin in Mexico. Unmarried women from Las Animas, who generally live with their families or other relatives, will also expand the nature of their activities in the United States, whether they go to school, work as babysitters or domestics, or work in non-domestic occupations. Even if their movements are restricted by relatives, they will still have new experiences.

Most of these women will also be pressed to buy things in grocery stores and malls, both as family shoppers and female consumers. If women have a job, they will be likely to make some purchases independently of their husbands, fathers, or other male relatives. Whether or not they have a job, women will continue to have primary responsibility in the household arena, although the technology they use will be different from that used for these tasks in Mexico. Appliances and gadgets, icons of domestic consumer culture, are likely to make household chores less burdensome in the United States than in Mexico. Having these goods becomes a constitutive part of the definitions of domestic work, the gender division of labor and social status in the United States.

In summary, the process of migration from rural Mexico to urban locations in the United States sets into motion a series of interrelated changes. For women, this may or may not involve working in the labor market, but it generally means gaining experience in a wider range of geographic and social spaces. Whether or not the gender division of labor is altered within a particular household, it is shifting at a broader (supra-household) level, and gendered divisions and uses of social space also change. Women can reassess their place of origin and recall and represent it in a different light, based on these changes.

Because men occupy different social and occupational spaces in Mexico, compared to women, and because the nature of the change involved in going to the United States differs for men, their representations of their rural places of origin will be different from those of women. Rural Mexico increasingly represents a place where tradition is adhered to and men can be men through either work or leisure activities, while the United States remains the place of work, proletarian and spatial discipline, and diminished male authority.

Implications

What are the implications of identifying gendered differences in representations of rurality and urbanity in Mexico and the United States, among migrants from Las Animas? Four points outline how paying attention to gendered representation of rurality can shed practical and theoretical light that may be relevant to scholars and planners concerned with migrants and migration.

The first point is that descriptions and memories of rurality are gendered; rural landscapes are not genderless spaces. In drawing connections between the gender division of labor and the gendered use of social space, I have suggested that there is a link between these material, institutional, and social aspects of everyday life and the ways in which migrating women and men represent the rural place they come from.

Others have worked on unpacking received notions of the category "village" (Pigg 1992; Vandergeest, in this volume), and on giving a history and context to representations of the rural countryside. This chapter has a related purpose, but I have focused on showing that women and men who come from and return to rural places may have very different conceptions and representations of those places. In addition to considering how representations of rurality change over time or according to class, we must examine how gender, work experience, and spatial/geographic history shape these memories and representations. This also underscores the importance of listening to the representations of actual women and men who come from and return to rural spaces.

The second point to emphasize is that differences between women's and men's representations of rurality can translate into struggles over practices of return migration. If women and men have divergent conceptions of their rural place of origin and of their social and economic role in that place, then it makes sense that they may differ in their desire to return there on a fairly permanent basis or not. This illustrates an important dimension of cleavage in migrant family politics and suggests that the long-term likelihood of return migration is no simple matter. Rather, this decision rests on a potentially molten bed of opposing views between women and men concerning the nature and quality of life in their, in this case, rural place of origin.

The issue of return migration, and the related problem of categorizing migrants according to whether they are circular migrants or settlers or something in between, has vexed migration researchers (Goldring 1992a). My own analysis suggests that some of the fluidity or variation in migrants' actual movements and in their expressed desires concerning moving back and forth across borders is based on gendered differences in the experience of life in rural Mexico versus the United States.[16] Tensions between what one marriage partner wants and what the other wants, especially when women may feel increased confidence in expressing their views, can introduce a great deal of uncertainty and contingency into patterns of migration.

The third point has to do with the micropolitics of the family and possibilities of broader social change. The experiences migrant women have in the United States can build up and slowly develop into a basis from which to resist or criticize established patterns of male authority over female activities and movement (Hondagneu-Sotelo 1992, 1994). Where such social change may lead is not entirely clear, and it does not necessarily follow that it will be "empowering." A woman from Las Animas told me she overheard her husband and some other men talking about how to deal with their wives' increasing "independence" in the United States. "Just beat her and show her who wears the pants in the house," advised one of the men. Thus, challenging patriarchal gender relations may have negative consequences. My research does not permit me to determine whether cases of domestic violence among Animeños are higher in the United States than Mexico. However, one of the things women learn in the United States is that there are women's shelters, laws against battery, and some social services available to immigrant women, even women without documents.

In addition to traversing a wider geographic and social terrain in the course of their daily lives in the United States, Mexican women acquire certain elements of substantive or practical citizenship that were previously unavailable or difficult to act upon. Exercising rights, claiming entitlements, and seeking services may undermine patriarchal and other forms of domination. While it is more difficult for undocumented women to draw legal attention to themselves in the United States, most women's experiences at work, in medical offices, schools, talking with friends, and in other settings give them a basis for beginning to resist forms of patriarchal authority.[17]

The fourth point regards the way gendered representations of rurality may be associated with different views and practices of investment by migrants, at the private and community level, in villages of origin. Private investment of remittances in Las Animas, and other migrant communities, takes the form of home improvements, buying household consumer items including televisions, blenders, washing machines, and vehicles (Alarcón 1988; Reichert 1981; Goldring 1992c). These forms of spending reflect a range of interests, as they can be grouped as "women's" household items (appliances), "men's" things (trucks), and "shared" objects (furniture, radios). While there is a gendered dimension to private or household spending of remittances, I concentrate here on collective projects. My argument is that the major share of collectively mobilized funds is spent on things that are defined rhetorically as benefiting the community as a whole, but that the decisions behind what to fund are dominated by men and their gendered representations and reconstructions of their rural space.

In Las Animas, migrants have pooled their money for several projects. The most expensive projects have been the construction of a rodeo run, a community hall, and, more recently, paying the "community share" of the government's bill for introducing piped water and paving the road to the municipal seat (Goldring 1992a, c). Elsewhere (Goldring 1992a, c) I suggest that community projects may have a measure of success if they are considered to be for the "benefit of the community." Projects seen as serving the interests of one group would not gain the financial support necessary to get off the ground.

Upon closer examination, I propose that these community projects primarily reflect men's representations of rurality—of their place of origin—and that they provide an avenue for the expression of a regional or rural and ranchero Mexican masculinity.[18] It is not that women do not support or take an interest in these things. But if women played a significant role in deciding how to spend money on community projects, it would most likely be spent somewhat differently.

The rodeo run is used for the annual fiesta held in Las Animas. The fiesta involves two days of the *coleadera,* punctuated with a dance the night of the first day. The coleadera is a form of rodeo in which a young bull is let loose, to be chased, grabbed by the tail, and overturned by a man on horseback who follows on the heels of the bull. Men pay considerable sums of money to chase after the bull. The first day of the fiesta is a widely publicized event, attended by people from the entire region. License plates from Texas, California, Illinois, and other U.S. states far outnumber local plates. This has clearly turned into an occasion for migrant and nonmigrant celebration, but particularly for migrant men to display their wealth by spending money on the coleadera and migrant women and the wives and daughters of migrants to dress up at the evening dance.

Money made from the coleadera and admission to the evening dance has been used over the last few years to make successive improvements on the structures that house these events. Periodic collections among migrants provided the money to begin the projects, and to finance major construction phases. The idea is that once the structures are completed, revenue from the fiesta and coleadera can be used for other community projects.

The fiesta has become the epitome of men's representations and reconstructions of their rural place of origin. It is an occasion when they can express their masculinity in a regionally specific context and culturally sanctioned manner that has been difficult to reproduce in the United States.[19] Women can also enjoy the event, but as spectators and displayers of consumer goods. They do not ride in the coleadera.

In conversations about the expense involved in attending the coleadera and the dance, I heard several women in Las Animas talk about how they would like to see money spent on other things as well. "Why don't they install a sewage system?" said one woman. "It would be more useful than this whole production." Her husband was an agricultural worker in the state of Washington. She had not been to the United States, but instead stayed home with her three young children. She said she thought it was a waste for her husband to spend money going to the coleadera when she could use it to buy clothes for the children or something for the house.

As men have come to define Las Animas increasingly as a place for relaxing after working hard in the United States, they have also shaped community projects to fit the emerging image of their village as vacation spot. To the extent that an indoor toilet, washing machine, or other household items fit the image of an improved place for relaxing, men may pay for them. They are improving their homes and village by adding amenities, but more fundamentally, they are reconstructing Las Animas as a place for R & R (rest and relaxation). Their spending is motivated by a representation of rurality as a landscape associated with a particular way of life, social status, and gender ideology. At the same time, these ways of spending money earned in the United States in turn redefine the rural landscape of Las Animas. It is less and less a rural landscape of production, one in which people work, and more and more a landscape in which they play, relax, and enjoy life—always contrasting this to the way life is lived in the United States. Las Animas becomes a site of renewal, where a sense of identification with the local landscape, history, family ties, and way of life can be renewed and reconstructed.

This discussion points to the importance of drawing connections between gender, representations of rurality, and development planning. Outside interventions that are consistent with dominant (male) local representations and reconstructions of rural spaces are more likely to succeed than interventions that are at odds with these representations. The particular representation and reconstruction of rurality projected by Animeños may or may not apply to other migrant circuits. That is an issue that has to be addressed through research. However, I suggest that agricultural development projects in Mexican regions of high United States-bound migration are not likely to be very successful if local men are reconstructing their place of origin as a place of relaxation, rather than agricultural production.

Conclusion

I have argued that gender shapes divergent representations of rurality depending on the nature of women and men's work and use of social space. Women do not retire from housework, whether they are in the United States or in Mexico, in the city or the country. For women, the Mexican countryside does not hold the same allure it holds for migrant men who can retire there, assuming they will be taken care of by their wives or daughters. Women's housework in the Mexican countryside generally involves more drudgery than it does in U.S. towns and cities. In the United States, migrant women usually expand their use of space by working outside the home, and becoming consumers of commodities and services. These changes often translate into gains in relative power within the family. Raising children in the United States also makes women more likely to want to stay there. In comparison, men prefer to retire to a rural landscape that holds memories of a way of life and pattern of gender relations that they are eager to renew.

Differences between the gender division of labor and gendered uses of space in the United States and Mexico are the material and social bases of women and men's divergent experiences and representations of rurality. This shows the importance for rural sociologists, planners, and others to recognize that rural spaces are not homogeneous and that gender differences may underlie divergent memories of rurality and plans about the future use of rural places. Examining changes in the gender divisions of labor and social space in the context of migration from rural to urban settings can increase our understanding of how particular landscapes are viewed by women and men who have lived in them.

By the same token, we should not underestimate the complexity of rural (and urban) spaces. The romanticization of rural places is belied by women's experiences there and should be guarded against to the extent that it privileges some voices and plans for the future while ignoring others. Similarly, the city, or the United States, and its modern ways, is not all bad. It may offer some people a context in which social citizenship can be exercised more fully and where patriarchal authority is attenuated while family ties are retained. Attention to complexity should also allow for a certain measure of ambiguity: I have focused on the difference between women's and men's memories and assessments of a rural locality, but I have also noted that migrant women identified advantages and disadvantages in their places of origin *and* destination.

Women and men's different experiences and representations of rurality have important practical implications as well. For example, they are linked to different interests in returning to the home village. Divergent gendered memories may translate into family-level struggles over return migration, which may account for a certain amount of contingency and uncertainty in migration patterns.

Gendered representations of rurality influence how migrants spend money in their villages. Men's social power in decisions about collective investment projects will influence the nature of such investment, although the form of particular projects may vary from one setting to another. Leisure-oriented projects may reflect men's representations of rurality in one setting, while production-oriented projects may fit their conceptions of rurality in another. The recommendations of outsiders, whether they are development scholars or extension agents, are likely to stand at odds with local initiatives as long as these recommendations rest on yet another set of representations of the rural landscape. The point is not that planners and scholars have to conform to local gender ideologies. Rather, that they should investigate the relationship between gendered representations of rural places, prevailing gender ideologies, and existing local projects in assessing the possibilities of new interventions.

I have argued that gender crosscuts distinctions between the country and the city and shapes migrants' representations of the places they come from and travel to. This calls for using gender as a category of analysis at the level of everyday practice, where concrete actors, women and men, are the representers and potential reconstructors of rural and urban spaces. The argument is based on an analysis of the way that migration affects divisions of labor and uses of social space for women compared with men. It also involves listening to the voices of women and men, paying attention to the ways that they remember and represent their lived spaces.

NOTES

Acknowledgments: I am grateful to Melanie DuPuis, Peter Vandergeest, Pierrette Hondagneu-Sotelo, Anna Garcia, Shawn Kanaiaupuni, and Gail Mummert for comments. The usual disclaimers apply. Field research was funded by a Rural Policy Fellowship from the Aspen Institute, and through a project of the Center for U.S.–Mexican Studies, University of California-San Diego.

1. Rouse (1988) uses the phrase "transnational migrant circuit" to refer to settlements of migrants from a particular place of origin living on both sides of the Mexico-U.S. border. He suggests that "through the continuous circulation of people, money, goods and information . . . [these] settlements are probably better understood as forming a single community spread across a variety of sites" (Rouse 1988, 9). See Glick Schiller, Basch, and Blanc-Szanton (1992) and Basch, Glick Schiller, and Szanton Blanc (1994) on transnational migration. Elsewhere (Goldring 1992a, b) I analyze the development of transnational *community* in a transnational migrant circuit.

2. Gender roles and identities undergo change in the process of internal migration, and without migration. However, transnational migration brings these changes

into sharp relief because broad comparisons can easily be drawn between women's legal and de facto rights and statuses, and prevailing gender ideologies in the two national settings.

3. See Simon and Brettell (1986) for an early collection on women in international migration, DuBois and Ruiz (1990) for a multicultural approach to U.S. women's history, Gabaccia's (1992) collection on immigrant women's experiences in the United States, and Grasmuck and Pessar (1991) for an excellent analysis of gender and migration among Dominican migrants.

4. Part of the explanation for this in the area of Mexico–United States migration may have to do with the predominance of male migrants during this century. *Men* were contracted to work in the United States through the bilateral agreements on contract labor from 1942 to 1964 that are known as the Bracero Program. Until recently, major field studies of migration between the two countries were conducted by men (Mines 1981; Reichert 1981; Wiest 1979; López 1986; Massey et al. 1987). Male researchers who collected qualitative data tended to do so by interviewing men, thus presenting predominantly male representations of migration, whether their own or their informants'. The entrance of women researchers into the field of Mexico–United States migration did not necessarily mean that the experience of female migrants was given explicit attention, as many issues remained to be explored (Dinerman 1982).

5. For background on Mexico–United States migration see Massey et al. (1987) and Massey, Goldring, and Durand (1994).

6. In a case study of a migrant community in Michoacán, Cárdenas (1988) focuses on how the process of migration affects women's lives—from mate selection to the exertion of social control over women whose husbands are in the United States. Hondagneu-Sotelo (1990, 1992) has studied family and gender politics in the context of Mexico–United States migration. Rouse (1993) discusses the differential use of social space by men in Mexico and the United States. Smith (1992) notes that public space in New York—the street—is seen as dangerous for women by both Mexican men and women. His analysis offers an explanation of why women may be willing to run risks associated with working as flower vendors in the street, despite the acknowledged danger.

7. For information on migration from Las Animas see Mines (1981) and Goldring (1992a); for background on migration from west-central Mexico see Massey et al. (1987).

8. These comments echo those reported by other researchers for men from Mexico (Rouse 1987, 1992; Hondagneu-Sotelo 1990; Smith 1992) and the Dominican Republic (Grasmuck and Pessar 1991).

9. Some men had begun small businesses in the United States. While these men were clearly in a better economic position in the United States, they also expressed the desire to retire in Mexico.

10. The men's representation of this life sometimes involved selective recollection in that the difficulties of living in Mexico and growing rain-fed corn and cattle were often glossed over.

11. In most homes, unmarried daughters needed permission to go beyond their house, even on routine errands. Stories of women being "stolen" (*robadas*) and forced into marriage were sometimes told to illustrate how things had changed in the last twenty years, but there was an underlying tone of warning, that young women who were not careful were subject to danger even in the village.

12. This discussion went both ways. Nonmigrating women, particularly younger single women, complained that when migrant women returned, they acted stuck-up (*presumidas*) and showed off by wearing new clothes and speaking English in an exclusionary manner.

13. Parents' employment and migration patterns can play a key role in shaping children's educational and U.S. settlement trajectories (Goldring 1992a). Children whose parents migrate back and forth, or spend substantial periods in Mexico, may be less likely to raise their families in the United States compared with those whose parents return to Mexico less frequently or for shorter periods of time.

14. Several Animeños became business owners in California, but these were a minority (Goldring 1992a).

15. I do not claim that all women and men conform to these patterns, but rather, that the patterns hold at a general level.

16. See Hondagneu-Sotelo (1992) for an analysis of gender politics associated with women's migration from Mexico to the United States, and Grasmuck and Pessar (1991) regarding Dominican migration to the United States.

17. Whether ensuing reconfigurations of gender relations empower women by significantly altering power asymmetries is an issue that strongly warrants further research.

18. By referring to "ranchero" masculinity, I draw attention to a construction of masculinity associated with cattle ownership. See Barragán (1990) on ranchero culture.

19. I know of one place in southern California where Mexican-style rodeos or *charreadas* are held, but these events are performed by professional equestrian teams. They are not events in which average workers participate.

REFERENCES

Alarcón, Rafael. 1988. "El proceso de "norteñización": Impacto de la migración internacional en Chavinda, Michoacán." In *Movimientos de población en el occidente de México,* ed. Thomas Calvo and Gustavo López, 337–57. Zamora, Mexico: El Colegio de Michoacán.

Barragán, Esteban. 1990. *Más allá de los Caminos*. Zamora, Mexico: Colegio de Michoacán.

Basch, Linda, Nina Glick Schiller, and Cristina Szanton Blanc. 1994. *Nations Unbound: Transnational Projects, Postcolonial Predicaments and Deterritorialized Nation States*. Amsterdam: Gordon and Breach.

Boserup, Esther. 1970. *Woman's Role in Economic Development*. New York: St. Martin's Press.

Cárdenas, Macrina. 1988. "La Mujer y la migración a los Estados Unidos en Chavinda, Michoacán." *Revista de la Universidad del Valle de Atemajac* 2, no. 4 (January–April) 17–21.

Dinerman, Ina R. 1982. *Migrants and Stay-at-Homes: A Comparative Study of Rural Migration from Michoacán, Mexico*. Monographs in U.S.–Mexican Studies No. 5. La Jolla: Program in U.S.–Mexican Studies, University of California, San Diego.

Donato, Katharine. 1993. "Current Trends and Patterns of Female Migration: Evidence from Mexico." *International Migration Review* 27 (4): 748–71.

DuBois, Ellen, and Vicki Ruiz. 1990. *Unequal Sisters: A Multicultural Reader in U.S. Women's History*. New York and London: Routledge.

Gabaccia, Donna. 1992. *Seeking Common Ground: Multidisciplinary Studies of Immigrant Women in the United States*. Westport, Conn.: Greenwood Press.

Glick Schiller, Nina, Linda Basch, and Cristina Blanc-Szanton, eds. 1992. "Towards a Transnational Perspective on Migration." *Annals of the New York Academy of Sciences*, Volume 645. New York: New York Academy of Sciences.

Goldring, Luin. 1992a. "Diversity and Community in Transnational Migration: A Comparative Study of two Mexico–U.S. Migrant Circuits." Ph.D diss., Cornell University, Ithaca, N.Y.

———. 1992b. "Blurring Borders: Community and Social Transformation in Mexico–U.S. Transnational Migration." Paper presented at the Conference on New Perspectives on Mexico–U.S. Migration, University of Chicago, 23–24 October.

———. 1992c. "La migración Mexico–EEUU y la transnacionalización del espacio político y social: Perspectivas desde México rural." *Estudios Sociológicos* 10 (29): 315–40.

Grasmuck, Sherri, and Patricia R. Pessar. 1991. *Between Two Islands: Dominican International Migration*. Berkeley: University of California Press.

———. 1992. "Overcoming Patriarchal Constraints: The Reconstruction of Gender Relations among Mexican Immigrant Women and Men." *Gender and Society* 6(3): 393–415.

———. 1994. *Gendered Transitions: Mexican Experiences of Immigration*. Berkeley: University of Caliornia Press.

Jones, Richard C. 1984. "Macro-Patterns of Undocumented Migration between Mexico and the U.S." In *Patterns of Undocumented Migration: Mexico and the United States,* ed. Richard C. Jones, 33–57. Totowa, N.J.: Rowman and Allanheld.

López Castro, Gustavo. 1986. *La Casa Dividida.* Zamora, Mexico: El Colegio de Michoacán.

Massey, Douglas S., Rafael Alarcón, Jorge Durand, and Humberto González. 1987. *Return to Aztlán: The Social Process of International Migration from Western Mexico.* Berkeley: University of California Press.

Massey, Douglas S., Luin Goldring, and Jorge Durand. 1994. "Continuities in Transnational Migration: An Analysis of 19 Mexican Communities." *American Journal of Sociology* 99 (6): 1492–533.

Merchant, Carolyn. 1983. *The Death of Nature: Women, Ecology and the Scientific Revolution.* San Francisco: Harper & Row.

Mies, Maria. 1986. *Patriarchy and Accumulation on a World Scale: Women in the International Division of Labour.* London and Atlantic Highlands, N.J.: Zed Books.

Mines, Richard. 1981. *Developing a Community Tradition of Migration: A Field Study in Rural Zacatecas, Mexico, and California Settlement Areas.* Monographs in U.S.–Mexican Studies No. 3. La Jolla: Program in U.S.–Mexican Studies, University of California, San Diego.

Morokvasic, Mirjana. 1984. "Birds of Passage Are Also Women." *International Migration Review* 18 (4): 886–907.

Nash, June, and María Patricia Fernández-Kelly, eds. 1983. *Women, Men and the International Division of Labor.* Albany: State Univerity of New York Press.

Pedraza, Silvia. 1991. "Women and Migration." In *Annual Review of Sociology,* Volume 17, ed. W. Richard Scott, 303–25. Palo Alto, Calif.: Annual Reviews.

Pigg, Stacy. 1992. "Inventing Social Categories through Place: Social Representations and Development in Nepal." *Comparative Studies in Society and History* 34:491–513.

Reichert, Joshua S. 1981. "The Migrant Syndrome: Seasonal U.S. Wage Labor and Rural Development in Mexico." *Human Organization* 40 (1): 56–66.

Rouse, Roger. 1991. "Mexican Migration and the Social Space of Postmodernism." *Diaspora* 1 (1): 8–23.

———. 1993. "Men in Space: The Politics of Urban Form among Mexican Migrants in the United States." Manuscript. Ann Arbor: Department of Anthropology, University of Michigan.

Simon, Rita J., and Caroline Brettell. 1986. *International Migration: The Female Experience.* Totowa, N.J.: Rowman and Allanheld.

Smith, Robert. 1992. "Mexican Immigrant Women in New York City's Informal

Economy." Conference Paper No. 69. National Resource Center for Latin American and Caribbean Studies. Columbia University and New York University Consortium.

Spain, Daphne. 1992. *Gendered Spaces.* Chapel Hill: University of North Carolina Press.

Wiest, Raymond E. 1979. "Implications of International Labor Migration for Mexican Rural Development." In *Migration Across Frontiers: Mexico and the United States,* ed. F. Camara and Robert V. Kemper, 85–97. Contributions of the Latin American Anthropology Group, Volume 3. Albany: Institute for Mesoamerican Studies, State University of New York Press.

Wilson, Alexander. 1992. *The Culture of Nature: North American Landscapes from Disney to the Exxon Valdez.* London: Blackwell.

About the Contributors

and

Index

About the Contributors

Amita Baviskar is a lecturer in the Department of Sociology at Delhi University. She is the author of the book *In the Belly of the River: Adivasi Battles over Nature in the Narmada Valley* (1995) and is currently working on a project regarding tribal rights to land and forests.

Michael M. Bell teaches environmental sociology at Iowa State University, where he is an assistant professor. He is the author of two books, *Childerley: Nature and Morality in a Country Village* (1994) and *The Face of Connecticut: People, Geology, and the Land* (1985). He is also an avid organic gardener, environmental and community activist, and banjo player.

E. Melanie DuPuis is a policy analyst in the Environment Unit at the New York State Department of Economic Development. Her research has focused on the relationship between economic development and environmental regulation. She is currently involved in a joint project with the New York State Department of Environmental Conservation to set up a workable emissions reduction credit trading system for the state.

William H. Fisher is an assistant professor of anthropology at the College of William and Mary and was a post-doctoral fellow at the Smithsonian Institute. He has done fieldwork in Brazil, Jordan, and the eastern United States. He is currently engaged in ethnographic and comparative work on the history and anthropology of the Kayapó and culturally related peoples of the Gê language family in central Brazil.

Luin Goldring is an assistant professor of sociology at York University, Canada. Her current research interests include Mexico–U.S. transnational migration and property rights and agrarian change in Mexico.

C. Clare Hinrichs is a research associate in the Center for the Environment and Waste Management Institute at Cornell University. Her research interests include the social and economic restructuring of rural areas, land use planning, and environmental justice.

Barbara Deutsch Lynch is an environmental sociologist and visiting fellow in the Latin American Studies Program at Cornell University. She recently completed an assignment as program officer for the Ford Foundation, managing the foundation's environment and development program for the Caribbean, and is an editor of *Right to Know: An Opportunity to Learn* (1989).

Nancy Lee Peluso is associate professor of resource policy at the Yale School of Forestry and Environmental Studies in New Haven, Connecticut. She has conducted research in Indonesia on forest-related issues for the past fifteen years. She is the author of numerous journal articles and the book *Rich Forests, Poor People: Resource Control and Resistance in Java* (1992) and coeditor (with Christine Padoch) of *Borneo in Transition: People, Forests, Conservation, and Development* (1995).

Peter Leigh Taylor is an assistant professor of sociology at Colorado State University, Fort Collins. He has published research on rhetorical practice, organizational culture, and change. He is currently working on a book entitled *Cultures of Argument: Economic Restructuring and Economic Democracy in Spain.*

Peter Vandergeest is an assistant professor at the University of Victoria and a senior fellow at the Faculty of Environmental Studies at York University, Canada. His research is on resource tenure and customary property rights in Southeast Asia.

Index

Italicized page numbers indicate an illustration or table.